Jocelynne A. Sc

Even in the Best of Homes

Violence in the Family

McCulloch Publishing

Published 1990 by McCulloch Publishing Pty Ltd
292 Rathdowne Street, North Carlton, Vic., 3054

Copyright © Jocelynne A. Scutt, 1983, 1990

Cover illustration and design by Julia Church
Typeset by Optima Typesetters, Brunswick, Vic.,
Printed by Griffin Press Limited, Netley, South Australia

Cataloguing-in-publication information

Scutt, Jocelynne, 1947–
  Even in the best of homes : violence in the family.

  Bibliography.
  Includes index.
  ISBN 0 949646 35 0
  1. Family violence — Australia. I. Title
306.87

This book has been printed entirely on 100% APM Re-Right recycled stock.

Even in the Best of Homes

After graduating LL.B. from the University of Western Australia, Jocelynne A. Scutt studied at the Universities of Sydney, Michigan and Cambridge, where she obtained LL.M. degrees, a Diploma of Jurisprudence, Diploma of Legal Studies and S.J.D. In 1984 she graduated M.A. from the University of New South Wales.

Jocelynne Scutt spent some time at the Southern Methodist University in Texas, and at the Max-Planck-Institut in Freiburg im Breisgau, West Germany. She has been Senior Law Reform Officer with the Australian Law Reform Commission, Research Criminologist with the Australian Institute of Criminology, Associate to a High Court Judge, Director of Research with the Victorian Parliamentary Legal and Constitutional Committee, and Commissioner and Deputy Chairperson of the Law Reform Commission, Victoria.

She has long been active in writing and lobbying on feminist politics and problems confronting women in the legal system, particularly in criminal justice. She has published widely on these topics, both in Australia and abroad. In 1980 she edited *Rape Law Reform* and *Violence in the Family*, and in 1981 co-edited *Women and Crime*. Other books include *For Richer, For Poorer — Money, Marriage and Property Rights* (with Di Graham); *Growing up Feminist — The New Generation of Australian Women; Poor Nation of the Pacific — Australia's Future? Different Lives — Reflections on the Women's Movement and Visions of its Future; Lionel Murphy — A Radical Judge; The Baby Machine — The Commercialisation of Motherhood;* and *Women and the Law — Cases, Materials and Commentary.*

Currently Jocelynne Scutt is in private practice in Melbourne, Victoria. She is at present compiling books on the diversity of women's lives, and on women, work and careers.

Three hundred and twelve families make up this case study. In the interests of protecting the privacy of those women, men and children who were courageous and concerned enough to write to me, all names, geographical locations, and in some cases, sex of children in the family have been changed. Apart from those cases appearing in official law reports, every name of victims and their families is fictitious.

Acknowledgements

In the writing of this book, I am pleased to acknowledge the assistance of the Women's Electoral Lobby, for enabling me to make contact through W.E.L. newsletters and conferences with many victims of violence; the New South Wales Premier for appointing me to the New South Wales Women's Advisory Council from 1978 to 1981, where on country and city visits held all over the state I was able to inform women of my study and gather vital data; and the Australian Institute of Criminology, in particular David Biles, Assistant Director (Research) and Dr Eric Cunningham-Dax, member of the Board, where I officially began researching crime in the family.

For her enthusiastic encouragement and support from the beginning of this project, and her professional editorial expertise, I thank Carla Taines of Penguin; for her reading and re-reading of the chapters, and important suggestions as to style and content, I thank Robin Joyce; and for her editorial assistance in producing the finished product and going through the last throes with me so expertly, I thank Meryl Potter.

Many women, through their enthusiasm, responsiveness, ability to listen, gave me more help than they could possibly know in working toward completion of this project. My thanks particularly to Carla Taines, Meryl Potter, Robin Joyce, Lesley Norris, Di Graham, Kerry Heubel, Yvonne Carnahan, Jennifer Aldred, Felicity Beth, Virginia Blomer Nordby, Elaine Thibou, Barbara Jubb, Anna Davie, Peggy Walsh and Ulla Svennson. I am grateful also to those women present at the Canberra and Melbourne National Women's Refuge Conferences in 1980 and 1982 for their appreciation of ideas developed in conference papers, and to the Louisa Women's Refuge Collective Queanbeyan.

To all those women and children, and the few men, who wrote to me, filled out long questionnaires, and courageously confronted the abuse in their lives in the interests of promoting a climate in which effective measures can be taken to stop crime in the family, my sincere thanks. Without you, this book could not have been written.

Jocelynne A. Scutt
Canberra 1982

In the reprinting of *Even in the Best of Homes*, I reiterate my thanks to the foregoing. I also appreciate the continuing debate within the Women's Movement on violence against women, a debate which has spread to the wider community, and efforts undertaken to eradicate that violence. Thanks also to Carolyn Cartwright for word processing and to my publisher Susan McCulloch.

Jocelynne A. Scutt
Melbourne 1990

Contents

A man's home is his castle.
Seymanes's case (1604)

A woman's place is in the home.
Old English proverb

CHAPTER 1   INTRODUCTION

The public life of a people is a very small thing compared to its private life.

G. d'Avenal, *Les Français de mon Temps*, Paris, 1904, p.1.

There can be no doubt that, in Australia in the 1980s, marriage is alive, well, and here to stay. Demographic analyses show a decline in the rate of teenage marriage, but the overwhelming majority of Australians still intend to marry legally, though later than in the past. In 1980, in the largest survey conducted throughout the country, a substantial majority of women over the age of 15 stated that they believed in the future of marriage: 89 per cent of 30 000 respondents. The single most important reason put forward by these women was that they 'are convinced they have found the right partner':

Four out of five married women believe they found Mr Right. Even 50 per cent of those permanently separated still believe they did find him. And, after divorce, Mr Right can actually regain some of his lost lustre, with 64 per cent of women continuing to accept that he was the correct choice.[1]

As for men, research shows that marriage substantially satisfies male needs: married men, as opposed to married women, rate most highly on satisfaction scales; unmarried men rate lowest, after married women, married men and unmarried women.

Yet despite a seeming contentment with marriage and the status quo, the ugly side of marriage has shown itself through the ages and today is exposed on a wider scale than ever before. In England, from the mid nineteenth century, voices were raised against brutality in the home — so much so that on the Continent Frenchmen called it 'the English disease'. (History does not record by what name French-women called it.) John Stuart Mill spoke out strongly in the British Parliament against husbands beating their wives. In the 1870s Frances Power Cobb waged a campaign against 'wife torture' that led to the passing of the 1878 United Kingdom *Matrimonial Causes Act*, which enabled a wife to bring a complaint before justices, on grounds of cruelty by her husband, so that she could legally be released from the duty to live with him. Parallel debates lie in the records of Australian Parliaments of the day.

Today, wife beating cannot be ignored. It takes its place on the agenda of the socially concerned, along with child abuse, rape in marriage, marital murder, and incest. At last, crimes occurring within the hallowed grounds of the family are being talked about by governments, by church groups and, most importantly, by the victims themselves. In the past, despite cyclical recognition of brut-ality within the home, that recognition limited itself to particular socio-economic groups. Those in the upper echelons who were rela-tively socially aware spoke with horror and concern about the crimes occurring in working class families. High-born ladies took to themselves charitable works, serving out soups and sympathy to local women beaten by their rough miner husbands. Researchers recorded with horror nineteenth century households where children of all ages slept in beds together with their parents, for want of room. 'Incest' was whispered around the earnest tables of busybodies train-ing themselves in the art of scientific social analysis. The incest, beating, bashing and rape that occurred in higher society was not a subject of socially scientific concern. When Freud uncovered a high proportion of forced incestuous encounters between middle class men in Vienna and their daughters, he preferred to label it 'hysteria', the fantasy of highly emotional female minds. The bashings that led to actions for divorce on grounds of cruelty were always depicted as aberrations. Indeed, those reaching the divorce courts *were* aber-rations: the standard of cruelty was set so high that those women who availed themselves of the divorce route had suffered severely for years.

In the final quarter of the twentieth century, the women's libera-tion movement has swept aside the hypocrisy that previously enveloped the family unit and covered up the crimes within. The movement began with a reanalysis of the crime of rape, initially looking at the paradigm case, rape between strangers. Women began to talk about their experiences with men. Slowly they realised, one by one, that the rapes they were talking about did not occur most frequently when some strange psychotic creature leapt from a dark alley. Each woman telling her story of rape recognised that she had known her attacker. Women began to talk about their relationships with men: with men of their acquaintance who had raped them; with boyfriends who had forced them to open their legs in the backs of cars; with fiancés who had pressed them, with tragic looks in their eyes, with whimpered words of 'I can't bear it any longer', to submit when they had not wanted to submit. They began to relate tales of husbands, refusing rejection, forcing themselves upon them at night. They remembered the angry fights, the tussles ending in black eyes and aching pelvic muscles. They recalled the kicks and the punches; the demands in the middle of the night that the floor be scrubbed; the refrigerator be cleaned out; the dinner, cold from the night before, be reheated or recooked so that he, after a night spent where, she did not know, could eat what he should have eaten when she had made it on time for his return from work. They regained their childhood days, the nights when daddy had begged them 'just to touch it'; when father had demanded they do 'it' 'just this once'; when mummy's new uncle had threatened he would make mummy go away if they told her he made them lie down with him, naked, in mummy's bed while he 'did things' to them. The shame and the guilt, repressed for so long, surfaced, was grappled with, and was replaced with anger.

Women around Australia have begun to stop blaming themselves for the damage done to them within the confines of the home. They have begun to analyse the family unit to determine why that unit should be set up to promote violence against those members not holding the position of power, who are not the authority figure, the father/husband. They have begun to ask why this structure is promoted as the only way for Australians to live. They question the validity of theories asserting that children *must* be brought up by two parents rather than one, by heterosexual couples rather than lesbians, by men and women who have mothered and fathered them, or adopted them, rather than by collectives of adults, interested in and loving towards children. Why is one structure 'right' and all others wrong?

Yet for every woman who questions the traditional, there may be ten who have not yet begun to look back into their own lives as children. There may be ten who have not yet acknowledged that 'Mr Right' is 'right' because they have been brought up on a diet of pulp romantic novels. And for every ten women who have challenged the family as being uncaring, exploitative, and inimical to the full development of women and children, there are ten thousand men who have never questioned the stability of their lives surrounded by dutiful wife and daughters, and sons who grow up to embrace the same standards as their fathers.

Crimes in Australian families occur because social mores demand that women and men fulfil 'appropriate' roles: women are there to serve in the family, men are there to be served. Family members are beaten and abused because we believe, as a society, that the wife/ mother, husband/father couple is the most appropriate combination for training children in social skills. That combination reinforces 'appropriate' roles for children as they grow to be adults. The crimes of child beating, and sexual molestation of infants, young children, and teenagers in the home could not take place if children were not seen as being owned by their parents, if their most suitable place of living were not seen as the family. Spouse assault, marital rape and marital murder would not happen without the tacit agreement of society that women are owned by men; that men have a right to push women around, to use them sexually as they choose, and finally to kill them out of 'passion' if a wife decides to leave — with another man, a woman, or simply alone — because she has had enough. When this is the reality, the position of the family in society must be reanalysed. If women continue to believe, after marital breakdown, that their once-chosen partner was the 'right' partner, then marriage itself must be 'wrong' for many. Why else would a partnership between Ms and Mr Right go wrong? Women (and men) are reared with romantic notions of marriage that do not accord with marriage, as research shows. Indeed, some women and men throughout their lives acknowledge that marriage is not to their taste and do not marry, thereby avoiding marital breakdown, or the even more significantly anti-marriage phenomenon of domestic violence. That the numbers of the never-married are not greater can be attributed to social attitudes that force upon women and men the ideal life-style: marriage and family in a suburban home, bordered by pocket hand-kerchief lawns, encumbered by a mortgage. What the community, family, and friends demand, the law supports. Men and women seeking to live their lives differently find that they are not only fighting social mores: they are also in direct conflict with legal attitudes and laws built up over centuries. Together, mores and laws push women and men into the age old pattern of marriage and family establishment. And in support of each other, mores and laws promote violence in the home.

The case histories making up this study of crime in the family were gathered over five years, from all over Australia. I first became concerned about sexism in criminal law when my research showed women who kill were treated more harshly than men by the legal system.[2] After researching rape in marriage in Australia, the United States, England and West Germany I was convinced that domestic violence in all its forms happened in more homes than is ever ac-knowledged. In 1978 I formally began looking into all aspects of family violence. Word went out to Australian women, men and children that an Australia-wide study was in train, and anyone who had suffered violence at home should, if they cared to, write to me documenting their experience. After initial publicity, questionnaires were sent out to all persons asking to be included. The return rate of questionnaires, despite their length, was about 80 per cent. Finally, 312 participants were included in the study. Some questionnaires were not included because there was insufficient information about parents or family status to obtain a good indication of family back-ground, or they were not sufficiently explicit about the violence suffered. However, none was culled because of bad grammar, poor writing, or initial difficulty in deciphering.

Researching crime in the family is not easy. It is impossible to con-duct a telephone survey, or land on anyone's doorstep, questionnaire and pencil in hand to conduct an interview along the lines of 'when did you last beat your wife?' or 'when did your husband/father/mother last beat you?' Some assert that self-selection studies are inherently suspect. Yet the nature of the crime necessitates a self-selection approach. I have no doubt that the stories written to me are true. Nor do I doubt that the 'other side' would have some light to shed on each story as it was told by one party. Whatever the other side might have said, however, it could not deny the experiences of the women, men and children who outlined in stark terms the crimes they had suffered.

Today, research is conducted according to the major principle that the researcher maintains his or her objectivity — that he or she takes a neutral stance. This objectivity or neutrality is predicated, in reality, upon the type of society in which research is being conducted, and the type of people doing the research. Neutrality and objectivity are defined according to the dictates of the establishment or accepted values. In Australia, they accord with a middle-class demeanour, university education, and comfortable background. It is within this context that research in the field of domestic violence is analysed, and most often, persons of this type do the research. I have no hesitation in acknowledging that had a white, Anglo-Saxon, middle-class male done this study his results could well have been different from mine. My femaleness was fundamental to my receiving the stories of many victims of crime in the family. A male researcher would not have been privileged as I was to become a confidant of many strong women who decided that now was the time to reveal the damage they had suffered in their own homes. He would not have become a member of the Women's Refuge Evaluation Committee in New South Wales, or attended the National Women's Refuge Conferences held in Canberra in 1980 and Melbourne in 1982, where I could talk with refuge workers about the demands of their job, about the philosophy of the women's liberation movement, and the women's refuge movement. Nor would he have attended the numerous women's liberation conferences where I talked with women's movement women. No male researcher could emulate the work undertaken in this study: no male researcher can ever be a part of the women's liberation movement, and no male researcher can experience the political resurgence women feel in being a part of that movement. My advantage lies in my women's liberationism.

It is not 'neutral', nor is it 'objective', to be sceptical of the value of victim's stories of their victimisation. To be cynical about victims of family violence recounting the damage done to them and the traumas they have suffered is to adhere to a non-neutral, subjective philosophy. It is to adhere to a philosophy that has been dominant in our society for as long as history has been recorded. It is to enforce the view of the patriarchy. My analysis of the questionnaires completed by women and men participants is coloured by my view of the world. It is coloured by my belief that women's opinions and experiences are of equal value to those of men. It is biased by my political stand that what women say happened to them is the truth as they see it — and probably is the truth as any reasonable person would see it. The truth women experience is no doubt different from that experienced by men. The men who did the beating, the battering, the bashing and the raping in this study are men who sit in offices pushing pens; they are executives who pontificate around board tables; some work on building sites; some work down mines; some live in Melbourne, some in Wollongong, some in Alice Springs; some of the bashers and rapists go on regular holidays overseas; some travel interstate or abroad on business, some do both; they are men who may sit on Supreme and County Court and magisterial benches in Australia; they are men who may sit in our Houses of Parliament. These men are part of a powerful regime that rules Australian society with an iron fist and beats its women and children with a flesh fist that is no less powerful. These men make up the society in which we live today, a society that denounces the women's liberation movement as a force designed to put an end to Australian family life.

The women's liberation movement *is* designed to put an end to Australian family life where it oppresses women and children. The movement is premised on the belief that women and children are not property to be torn and mangled at male whim. For me, no family life that destroys women and maims children can be tolerated; it cannot be supported when it grants men the right to destroy and maim. If crime happens in the family — and the evidence proves it does — then the family promoting it must be ended. No one desiring peace, order and good government, love, tenderness and care can tolerate any abuse meted out on women, children — or, for that matter, men. Governments promoting the 'family life' revealed in analyses of the family in law and society today are deliberately promoting crime. And they are promoting crime against members of the very unit they allegedly hold so dear: the Australian family.

Governments and people who care about human beings must begin to reassess their view of the world. No one who has read the stories of women and children in this book can continue to live complacently in the belief that all's right with the world and the family. Rather than becoming angry at me for writing a book telling the truth of many Australian lives, as no doubt some will do, it would be more useful to reorganise society so that women and children needing help can get it. What is chillingly obvious in reading of the lives of victims of crime in the family is that it matters not whether neighbours and friends are sympathetic or unsympathetic; it matters not whether they are willing to recognise the problem, or not to recognise it: concrete help is not forthcoming, whatever the attitude. A participant in the study, June Meister, wrote: 'It's hard to say whether anyone believed me or didn't — either agencies, friends or relatives — because they all remained really impassive when I talked to them. They couldn't help, so they didn't want to see.' Pamela Friar found 'Everyone believed me, but most said sorry there isn't anything we can do. Police wouldn't. Friends didn't want to get involved. I didn't see there was any point in waiting then.'

As long as those on the outside refuse to see, don't want to get involved, or fail to acknowledge we can help, crime in the family will continue. We can begin to help in so simple a way: by sitting down and saying firmly to ourselves: 'violence in the family is a reality; the anger that I want to direct at those pointing it out to me should be directed into anger at a political system promoting crime in the family as a way of life. The anger I feel should be redirected into altering power structures and the economic system so that the inequalities that exist at present, between women and men, adults and children, are eliminated, and no one has a right to exert power over others, simply by reason of parenthood or marriage.' It is only then that crime in the family has any chance of being eliminated. This book is designed to display the horrors of family violence and to ask people to direct their anger at the system that promotes crime in the family.

CHAPTER 2   THE FAMILY IN LAW

Until comparatively recent times . . . the doctrine obtained that the husband and wife were but one person possessing but one will, and that that will resided in the mind of the husband as the person 'fittest and ablest to provide for and govern the family'. It was a doctrine of elegant simplicity and one capable of remarkable results. It was a doctrine that removed, in theory, the burdens of responsibility and the sanctions of morality from any woman that entered the holy state of matrimony. Logically considered, all her crimes and all her sins emanated from the duplicated brain of her husband and her lord. Not only did she convey to him her person and her worldly goods, but she added the entire responsibility of her personality to the weight of his own. The creator took from Adam a rib and made it Eve; the common law of England endeavoured to reverse the process, to replace the rib and to remerge the personalities.

J. E. G. de Montmorency, 'The changing status of the married woman',
Law Quarterly Review, 13, 187, 1897, p.192.

Historically, the family is seen as the mainstay of civilisation. In Roman slave society, the family provided the overseer, or 'lord', with his social position and identity. 'Family' referred to the total number of slaves belonging to any one man: the more members of the family, the more important the man. Women and children, like slaves, were defined not as persons, but as things: 'The term [family] was invented by the Romans to denote a new social organism, whose head ruled over wife and children and a number of slaves, and was invested under Roman paternal power with rights of life and death over them.'[1] The power to punish wife and children, and the punishments inflicted upon them, were akin to those imposed on slaves owned by the head of household. Slaves were required to wear short hair; one of the punishments a husband was entitled to inflict upon his wife, particularly where she engaged in sexual activity not to his liking, was cutting off her hair. A common form of punishment used against slaves was flogging; a husband had a right to strip his wife naked and 'flog her through the village in the presence of kinsmen'. The head of household possessed the power of controlling his slaves by whatever punishment he chose. Of children it was said: 'The justice of a master or a father is a different thing from that of a citizen, for a son or a slave is property, and there can be no injustice to one's own property.'[2] Wives were also subject to control and punishment by their husbands. Freemen, on the other hand, were disciplined at the hands of the state.

The control a head of household exercised over members of *his* family was replicated in other civilisations. In the United States women not only lived under a marriage bond like the slave bond, but they were also sold into slavery to provide men with wives. Women were transported to America after 1629 'in considerable numbers by ruses and devices which will forever remain obscure'. Young women were 'persuaded' to sail to the colonies by methods 'approaching kidnapping'.[3]

In the United States the slave status of women predated that of slaves brought from Africa: 'In the earlier common law, women and children were placed under the jurisdiction of the paternal power. When a legal status had to be found for the imported Negro servants in the seventeenth century, the nearest and most natural analogy was the status of women and children.'[4] Laws governing slaves ran parallel with those concerning wives and children.[5]

In Australia, too, women were sold into bondage. No evidence exists of the American shanghai method being used to provide men with wives; nonetheless, the English government treated women as a commodity. To decrease the imbalance between the sexes, all women convicted of crimes, however petty, risked transportation. Only those men convicted of the most serious offences were transported. The authorities believed that if the southern colonies were to be established, men had to be provided with women, as servants and as spouses. Some women were taken by overt force from their natural habitat to become slaves and concubines. British women were treated like chattels, but the treatment of Aboriginal women was worse.[6] Not only were Aboriginal women a commodity to be bartered, sold, or used to repay debts, they were also forced into slave labour. George Augustus Robinson recorded in his *Journal* in 1829 that sealers at the Straits between Van Diemen's Land and the mainland carried on a system of slavery:

they barter in exchange for women flour and potatoes; ... the aboriginal female Mary ... was bought off the black men for a bag of flour and potatoes; ... they took her away by force, tied her hands and feet, and put her in the boat; ... [the] white men beat black women with a rope ... The aboriginal Fanny states that this slave traffic is very common in the straits, and that women so bartered or sold are subjected to every hardship which their merciless tyrants can think of and that from the time their slavery commences they are habituated to all the fatiging [*sic*] drudgery which their profitable trade imposes ... This information is further confirmed by the man Baker, who was himself a sealer in Bass's Straits and has for a considerable length of time cohabited with the female Fanny. He was transported from Launceston to Hobart Town on a charge of having forcibly taken away three native women from Brune Island; but the charges not having been proved he was dismissed, although there was little doubt as to his guilt.[7]

That woman's position was akin to slavery (and many black women were legally acknowledged as slaves) in both the United States and Australia is due to British tradition. The family in Britain held much the same position as under Roman law: the husband/father was head of household and thus in control; women and children were chattels to be used and abused by the paterfamilias as he chose. It is said that slavery exists only in societies based on private ownership of property. When land is owned communally, slavery does not exist; where land is owned by some members of the community and not by others, the landless become slaves to land owners. Property ownership may be the central issue when head of household and his subjects, wife and children, are under legal scrutiny.

Women, Children and Property

At common law a single woman had rights, upon reaching the age of 21, to own property. She was obliged to pay taxes, although she did not have the commensurate power to vote for members of Parliament. Her rights were, however, subsidiary to those of any brothers she had, whatever their age. Fathers had the power to leave all family property to sons or strangers. If a man died intestate, a daughter took

equal share with her brothers and sisters of any personal property —
goods, chattels, moveables — but her first-born brother was entitled
in full to ownership of the real property — land and the like — as
heir-at-law.

Where a woman married, her rights to her own property were at
risk even before the marriage ceremony. Upon betrothal, a woman
lost any right to dispose of or give away her property. Any disposition she made without the knowledge of her husband, whether or not
he knew she owned property, was void. Upon marriage, her personal
property — money in hand or in a bank, jewels, household goods,
clothes — belonged absolutely to the husband. He had the power of
assigning or disposing of that property without reference to her.
This power remained in the husband whether or not the parties were
living together. Real property became the property of the husband:
he held the freehold estate, with absolute possession of the land as
long as both he and his wife lived. Any money earned by a married
women, including rents, wages and the like, became the absolute
property of the husband. A husband could will all his property —
including his wife's — away from his wife and children to anyone,
but his wife could only make a will with his permission and he could
revoke it.

Upon marriage, women were thus entirely stripped of property
rights, although the courts of equity made minor attempts to
mitigate this. Through the sixteenth and seventeenth centuries, a
complicated system was established so that profligate husbands were
unable to make off with their wives' property. But this depended on
the wife's father taking action, gaining legal advice, and setting up
trusts. Equity was not concerned to protect the interests of the
woman, the aim was to protect family inheritance.

Women, Children and Maintenance

The courts took a stringent view of the needs of women during
marriage. On marriage a wife was subsumed in the person of her
husband. Her personhood was suspended during marriage, 'or at
least was incorporated or consolidated into that of her husband,
under whose wing, protection and care she performed everything'.[8]
She and her husband became one. This was not favourable to the
woman. It did not mean she owned all property of the marriage

equally with her husband. It did not mean she had an equal right, or any right at all, to his money or her own. The most she had was a right to pledge his credit for 'necessaries' — meaning only sufficient food, clothing and shelter to enable herself and any children to survive. The most the law required of a man was that his wife and children not starve; beyond this, the law refused to intervene. Although a man could with impunity act in a profligate manner, spending not only his own fortune but also his wife's, a wife had no power to spend her own money (which in law was his), much less any money her husband brought into the 'partnership'. Neither at common law nor in equity was there any real power to oblige a man to support his wife.

Power rested in the ecclesiastical courts and in the magistrates' courts of the local parish to enforce a man's duty to pay toward upkeep of his wife and children. Where the parish intruded, however, it was often to the detriment of the wife. The parish was not interested in her wellbeing. Its interest lay in its own responsibility for keeping the wife if her husband would not. Under the English Poor Laws, parishes had to fund workhouses and almshouses for those unable to find work or unable to keep themselves. During debates on the Married Women's Property Acts in England, numerous cases, including that of one Ann Stokes, showed a lack of concern for the woman herself. Ann Stokes's husband, a labourer, was found poaching and left home and parish to escape lawful punishment. Ann Stokes remained behind to care for their three children. Many years later she was granted parish relief, being by this time elderly and crippled from rheumatism from a lifetime's toiling as washerwoman. After some years, the Board of Guardians discovered Ann Stokes's husband was not dead, as presumed; he was alive, well, and prospering in a neighbouring parish, with a flourishing farm and public-house, as well as another wife. As was their right under the law, the Board of Guardians demanded of John Stokes that he provide for his wife Ann. John Stokes refused, and was threatened with seizure of some of his property. No fool, he had allowed the farm, public house and licence to stand in the name of his *de facto* wife, so the parish could claim nothing from him. After much argument John Stokes compromised, allowing Ann Stokes two shillings and sixpence a week. Soon he grew tired of paying and stopped. She again applied to the Board of Guardians for upkeep.

The Board again approached Stokes. Finally he agreed to maintain Ann Stokes on certain conditions. These included leaving her village home and going to live in a dirty, rundown hovel on his own property, and receiving food from his kitchen: 'in other words the wife was to be a pauper at his gate, receiving such scraps as would be doled out to her'.[9]

In Australia, women did not even have the doubtful advantage of care from the parish or of pressure from the parish being placed upon recalcitrant husbands. The Poor Laws did not apply, and women were forced to rely upon husbands for upkeep, or on their own efforts in the paid workforce. Frequently women were obliged to take up domestic service, subjecting themselves to brutality, exploitation and rape, or 'go on the game' to survive. So too children: reports are numerous of youngsters begging alms, or following the paths of women into prostitution. The system reflected the power of the head of family, for he was entitled to the society of his wife and children, and originally at common law some authorities held he was empowered to take out a writ of habeas corpus to have them delivered up to him, if they deserted and he wanted them back. Where he chose to desert or simply refused any responsibility for their upkeep, there was no way dependants could oblige him to take the responsibility.

The irony was that, according to social dictates, a woman was required to marry. Economics also forced her into marriage, for social propriety meant women in the upper echelons could not take on paid employment, and those in the lower orders struggled on pay far less than men earned. Paid work was regarded as temporary for some women and, in any event, deplorable work conditions made women long for escape. Yet marriage was no escape. For women and children of all classes, family life was dependent upon the benevolence of the father and husband. He took the lord and master position in *his* household. Women were disadvantaged by lack of adequate laws for maintenance operating in conjunction with discriminatory property laws.[10]

Why, it was asked by women rebelling against their oppression, should marriage so profoundly affect the legal standing of every woman, whilst it affected not at all the legal standing of men? If it were true that women and men became 'one' on marriage, women should by rights enjoy all powers and privileges of their husbands.

As they did not, the least the law could do was place married women, *vis-à-vis* property, in the same position as single women. Wives would thus gain access to the means of maintaining themselves. Agitation began for the passage of Married Women's Property Acts in England, the United States, and Australia.

Women, Children and Custody

At common law, a father had total control of the children of the marriage. Legal custody of children belonged to the father alone. His wife had no rights. The father might at any time remove the children from care of their mother and dispose of them as he saw fit. Upon divorce, the father had the right to custody, however incompetent he was as a parent. If the parties separated but did not divorce, the father's legal position remained unassailable. The father not only had sole custody, but he also had an exclusive right to determine how the children should be educated, what religion they should follow, and how they ought generally to be reared. Only in cases of his 'gravest misconduct' might children be removed from his custody. At common law, a mother did not even have a right of access to visit her children, or a right to have them visit her, if the parties lived apart. If a child were under guardianship, the guardian stood in the position of the father and the mother's rights were equally non-existent. That children might have rights of access to their mother was never considered; nor were the rights of children, regarding a choice of the party to hold custody rights or with whom they wished to live. Thus in *Ewing and Ewing*, Chief Justice Lilley said: 'There is no question as to the legal right of the father to the custody of his children. The law makes the father the absolute lord of both wife and children — under certain conditions with respect to nurture — he could take the children from his wife so long as he did not commit a breach of the peace.'[11]

As with property, equity tempered the law a little, by looking at the welfare of the child. If it was clearly for the benefit of the child, equity could waive the legal right of a father to custody, but this occurred only in the most extreme cases. Still the mother had no more rights than a stranger. When a court determined the father's legal right should be overborne, the children did not automatically

pass to the care of the mother, but the court might consider her request if the father had been held, according to standards undeniably
favourable to him, as unworthy of custody. The issue was not what
expertise, care, consideration and love the mother might possess, but
what the court considered to be 'best' for the child.

The welfare of the children was, in equity, a concept based on
a background of property law. That meant that what was 'best'
was tempered strongly by the existing legal standard that granted
supreme rights to the father. Thus in *Agar-Ellis*, a land-mark decision, Justice Bowen said: 'Then we must regard the benefit of the
infant; . . . It is not the benefit of the infant as conceived by the court,
but it must be the benefit of the infant having regard to the natural
law which points out that the father knows far better as a rule what is
good for his children than a court of justice can.'[12] The law saw
children as unworthy of having rights. Rather, the rights lay in the
father: the purpose of having children was to perpetuate the male
line, and thus it was imperative that the party controlling the family
fortunes should be the party in control of those carrying the line into
posterity.

Women, Children and Divorce

The law of divorce and separation makes it quite clear that children
had no rights but were, on the one hand, chattels to be dealt with at
will and, on the other, significant in law only as carriers of the family
name (and fortune, if there be one). If a woman wished to divorce her
husband and had grounds for doing so, unless he agreed that the
children should go with her, they were obliged to remain in his
custody, whatever their wishes. Despite the Maintenance Acts eventually passed by various jurisdictions in Australia, acknowledging a
responsibility in the father for payment of upkeep, if a woman
deserted her husband and took the children with her against his
wishes, the children lost any statutory entitlement to be maintained
by him. The father could decide whether or not he would support
the children. His right not to support them rested not upon anything
the children did, but upon the actions of his wife.

The law of divorce and legal separation locked women into the
legal limbo into which marriage transported them. At common
law there was no right of divorce. The ecclesiastical courts dealt

with matrimonial breakdown by granting parties a judicial separation, within narrow grounds of adultery. A wife could not appear as plaintiff, defendant, or witness in the proceedings; a third party represented her. When judicially separated, the parties were no longer obligated to cohabit, but they could not remarry. The woman remained a wife in every respect apart from cohabitation. Without a special settlement, the husband retained her property. He could return at will and take from her any property she built up in his absence; she was unable to contract, to sue, or to be a plaintiff where her goods were stolen. Marriage could be dissolved only by an act of Parliament applied for after a judicial separation was granted. In the two centuries prior to 1858 (when legislation providing grounds for divorce was passed and divorce became relatively more accessible) in England there were only 250 divorce acts. Of these, relief was granted on the petition of a woman in only nine instances; four of the nine acts were for divorce, the remainder being for separation only, or for nullity of marriage. The proceedings were costly, 'which makes the possibility of release from the matrimonial bond a privilege of the rich.'[13] The privilege, then, extended in the main to rich *men*, for as they owned no property, women were hard placed to find the money; only those with sympathetic male relatives could go to Parliament for relief. Thus once a woman was married, she not only lost control of her person and property for the duration, but also lost any means of legal escape. Apart from the practical issue of cash, if a woman chose to leave by separation, divorce, or simple desertion, she had to find somewhere to live and the means to live, and she lost the company of her children. Each disabling factor was referred to during debate in England on divorce reform in the mid nineteenth century:

It is said that if equal facilities of divorce were given to women, the courts would very soon be choked up with their applications. *But I know woman's character better than that.* I know that in none but extreme cases would she resort to this remedy . . . [for as has been said] . . .

'A man who has lapsed in his observance of the marriage vow may nevertheless be a kindly husband and father, with whom reconcilement would be a safe and blessed generosity. If we add to these admissions, woman's natural lingering love for the companion — love undeniable, indisputable — love evidenced every day, even among the poor creatures who come bruised and bleeding before the police courts; refusing to give evidence, in a calmer hour, against the man such evidence would condemn to punishment; if we add the love of children; the dread of breaking the bond which shall perhaps help a step-mother into the mother's vacated place; if we add the obvious interest, in almost every instance, which the woman has to remain in her home; and the horror most women must feel at the idea of the public exposure and discussion of such wrongs — it is evident that they would not be so very eager to avail themselves, in usual cases, of the extreme remedy.'[14]

Women were bound into marriage, practically and legally, and sentenced to a lack of personhood for life, and where they had means to divorce, their rights were less than those of men. Under ecclesiastical law, a wife or husband could obtain a legal separation on grounds of adultery committed by the other, and a wife on grounds of personal cruelty causing reasonable apprehension of injury to life, limb, or health. Parliament would exercise its powers of divorce '*invariably*... in favour of a husband of irreproachable character, whose wife has been guilty of adultery', as long as he could pay the heavy expense. But an act of Parliament would *never* be passed on the petition of a wife, unless the adultery her husband committed was incestuous or had been further confirmed by his bigamously marrying his partner in adultery.[15] The property concept of women was thus maintained: if a wife engaged in a single act of sexual intercourse outside marriage, a man was entitled to dispose of his wife because she was tainted, spoiled. Her infidelity might also bring children into the family, with legal entitlements to inherit, who were not truly 'of the blood'. Men, however, had the right to conduct themselves freely in marriage and outside it, unless in doing so they offended against some other law, namely, the law against bigamy or laws against consanguinity of sexual or marital relations.

Nineteenth Century Reforms

During the nineteenth century, women's groups tried to improve the position of married women and children by reforming marriage laws in four areas of concern: married women's property rights; maintenance of wives and children; custody of children; and rights to divorce. Each battle in Australia duplicated those in the United Kingdom and United States. The motivation of feminists was to gain some identity for women within the family context.

Parliamentary debates during the passage of Married Women's

Property Acts in the colonies have a familiar ring. Those arguing against granting women limited rights over their property appealed to the need of husbands to control their property, their wives, their wives' property and their lives. Thus in the Legislative Council debate in New South Wales, William Foster, M.L.C. argued on the basis that women should not be independent in any way:

> in the present state of things it was scarcely fair that the law should be altered in this respect in such a wholesale manner. It would tend to a total separation of interest between husband and wife, and an unhealthy state of married life. He admitted that there had been cases of hardship where a husband had spent the money of the wife, but such cases were the exception, not the rule ... He thought it would be better to leave the matter in the hands of the man who was trained in business matters, rather than put it in the hands of the wife who had never had any such experience ... It was quite an unusual thing for ladies to have control of large sums of money; it was generally vested in trustees for them, because of their not being able to deal with it.[16]

Similarly in the lower house, J. Leary, M.L.A. thought the legislation 'might have the effect, in a large number of instances, of severing the ties of affection between husband and wife by giving to the wife a position of independence apart from her husband'. To these gentlemen, the very existence of marriage and the preservation of family life depended upon the oppression of women. To grant to women a right to own property would be to 'unhinge the great framework of society'; it would serve to 'unhinge the greatest institution of civilization'; the 'sanctity of married life' would be torn apart. Yet despite the outcry, the first proposals for married women's property rights were modest indeed. They provided only that earnings, savings bank accounts, shares, debentures and stock in joint stock companies and funds in building societies and similar organisations should be classed as the married woman's own, where she brought them into the marriage or earned them during the marriage. Despite the objections, limited rights were afforded to married women, and finally, towards the end of the century in each jurisdiction, married women gained legal rights to property akin to those of single women. But it did not follow that marriage thus became a non-oppressive state for women. Few women brought large sums of money into marriage, or any money at all. Where women were in paid employment, they were hardly likely to build up reserves of property, because women's work was usually broken with pregnancy and maternity responsibilities; they could not save over long periods, and they could not move up the ranks to high paying jobs. Women's work was also far less well paid than men's, so a married man and a married woman stood on unequal ground despite legal changes. And women tended to use their funds for family upkeep, clothes for the children, and the like, which would not constitute 'property' and, therefore, could not make up accumulated funds for women. Women continued to play the role of unpaid worker in the home, help meet, and recipient of housekeeping money from a husband. The prevailing philosophy was that women should remain in the home as objects of prestige for their husbands rather than take on paid work outside. Thus social attitudes preserved the slave role of the married woman.

From the 1840s, magistrates' courts could order a husband to support his wife and children if he left them without means of support and if his leaving was 'without just cause or excuse'. Theoretically the legislation was important for wives, mothers and children: many Australian men deserted their families to go to the goldfields, and many simply left when they chose — Australia was notorious for its large number of fatherless homes. Even in theory, however, there were drawbacks. The onus lay upon the woman to show she was without means of support. One of the greatest difficulties was that if she had managed to survive between the time her husband left and the time the matter came before the magistrate, there was a strong suggestion she could survive without payment from the errant husband. This assessment of 'need' made by the magistrate was influenced by social attitudes toward women and marriage. The assumption was that women's needs were few and that subsistence level maintenance was her due. This arose from the nature of marriage, wherein women 'made do' with home-made clothes for themselves and the children, whilst the husband purchased his clothes; where women cut down on their own bodily needs, believing that men required a 'proper diet'; where women required no money for entertainment, business lunches or regular Friday night pub drinking. The proposition that an ex-wife should be maintained according to the standard to which she was accustomed helped few women. A wife had to establish that her husband left 'without just cause or excuse', which meant a wide ranging enquiry into the circumstances of the marriage, and whether indeed the husband had deserted, or whether he had been driven from home by a shrew of a wife. And there was the practical problem of the law being put into effect: women had to have some money to bring the action — yet if they were deserted without means, where would they get the money? If the case were brought and won, the husband had to be found to be forced to pay maintenance. Many men went interstate and could not be brought back. In some jurisdictions Fugitive Offenders Acts provided machinery for bringing home the non-paying husband, but without success.[17] In the enforcement of maintenance for children, difficulties were almost insurmountable.

Thus laws that could be interpreted as giving women and children some rights when husband and father broke the master tradition in fact did not. Rather, the laws confirmed that the man was in charge of the unit, by placing upon him a legal obligation to support it, when in reality many men did not adequately support their wives and children and the law did not make them do so. By paying lip service in legislation to that obligation, the law gave further ground for the proposition that a man had unassailable rights to deal with wife and children as he wished. They also created strong pressures on women to conform to the 'acceptable' wife and mother role, so that the husband would not desert, or if he did, the woman would be able to claim successfully he left without just cause or excuse and that her wifely duties were religiously fulfilled, entitling her to maintenance. They perpetuated the only 'proper' family model as that of husband, wife and children, requiring coercive legislation for survival, and the single-parent family — particularly where headed by a female — as abnormal. Finally, maintenance laws often succeeded in placing the wife and children back under active control of the family head. Because women feared giving evidence against their deserting husbands, which might result in a prison sentence, no maintenance during the passage of the sentence, and an abusive partner when release date came, the laws brought husband and wife together again.

Statutes passed in Australian jurisdictions in the late nineteenth century created the right of a mother to seek custody of the children of the marriage. In 1899, New South Wales passed the *Infants Act*, which contained basic provisions following British legislation of sixty years earlier. On application by a mother to the courts of equity, the court could grant to the mother a right of access to an infant under the age of 16 years, or order that the infant be delivered up to the mother, to remain in her custody and control. If the child were already with the mother, the court could order that the child remain until it reached an age, not exceeding 16 years, directed by the court. Even then, interpreting a similar Queensland law, Chief Justice Griffith said: 'A father cannot be deprived of the custody of his infant child unless it appears that he is unfit to be the custodian of it, or that his so remaining would be an injury to the child. Where the wife is innocent, the Court, on an application for an order for the custody of children must exercise a wider discretion, bearing in mind first of all the parental right, secondly the marital duty, and thirdly the interests of the children.'[18]

That courts continued to enshrine the position of head of family as one to be occupied by a dominant male person, with wife and children submissive adjuncts to his authority, is clear from the New South Wales case of Emelie Polini, decided under the nineteenth century legislation in 1924. Emelie Polini, a successful actress who regularly sent money to and visited her daughter (who was in the care of the paternal grandparents), sought custody of the child. She intended going abroad to England and the United States, resting and touring alternately. Her care of the child would be supplemented by a nanny, whose wages she would pay. The court held custody should remain with the grandparents. On the basis of parental right, being mother and not father, Emelie Polini's application failed. As for marital duty, a wife should remain with her husband, a mother with her children. Marital duty, according to the court, did not encompass any woman playing the part of family breadwinner, or being sufficiently independent to run her own (successful) career; neither did it include going off, unaccompanied by a husband, overseas. And the court found it impossible to believe any child's interests could be well served by being with a mother who was independent, living apart from her husband, and conducting herself very nicely thank you — indeed brilliantly — as an independent woman. This type of determination confirmed children in their submissive position, for there was no suggestion that a child might profit from a strong role model in the person of her mother, or that the child's interests might best be served by leading an unconventional life with an actress mother.

As for attempts at divorce law reform, women in Australia remained unequally served by the law. Before the late 1850s, there was no means of divorce in the colonies, because the ecclesiastical courts did not operate. Only one petition for an act of Parliament was ever lodged, and that in New South Wales, where a girl of 14 years and 6 months had been inveigled into marriage without the knowledge of her parents. The husband and his associates were convicted and imprisoned. The act of divorce was passed by Parliament but never given assent. The rationale of those protesting even at the passage of the bill was that 'encouragement would be given to those who favoured the dissolution of the marriage tie', and the bondage constituting marriage ought to be maintained. Those supporting the divorce bill did so because of the parents' objections to the marriage — their daughter was a wealthy heiress — rather than being mindful of the girl's views.[19] Divorce laws were framed and passed in South Australia in 1858, in Tasmania in 1860, in Victoria in 1861, Western Australia and Queensland in 1863 and 1864, and in New South Wales in 1873. Divorce on the petition of the husband alone was permitted, solely on the ground of his wife's adultery. The colonial legislatures adhered to the chattel standard for women: that women's bodies were sullied by engaging in sexual intercourse with any person other than a husband, that the husband's property rights in his wife were thereby damaged, and that he was thus entitled to rid himself at once of the damaged goods. Reforms to the law later gave women a right to divorce their husbands, but on more restricted grounds: a wife had to prove not only adultery of her husband, but also cruelty, drunkenness, or other aggravating circumstances, such as rape, incest, sodomy, bestiality. Cruelty alone would not grant a woman a right to divorce. Women could be used and abused at will. Thus Charlotte Elizabeth M'Neilly failed to gain a divorce, despite having a witness to cruelty and adultery; her husband threatened to take her life, chased her around the room threatening her with a meat fork, and cried out his intention to murder her.[20]

Children were equally ill-treated. They could not escape alone and, like their mothers, were caught by usage and abuse. While Charlotte M'Neilly was being tortured by her husband her youngest child cried, and the husband 'violently pushed a stick down the child's throat, tearing lumps of flesh off and nearly choking the child'. He made broth which he forced down the child's throat, and the child died. Wife and children ate some of the broth and were treated for poisoning. That the bodies of wives and children remained husbands' and fathers' property was endorsed by those called to enforce the law. In the M'Neilly case one James Rush, sub-inspector of police, told the court that Mrs M'Neilly 'often complained of her husband's ill-treatment, but she came so often that no one took any notice of her . . . He looked on them both as mad characters.'

Even the reforms granting a woman a right to divorce for extreme cruelty combined with adultery were deplored by parliamentarians and churchmen on grounds that 'family ties' would be damaged. Their remarks show they were concerned with the ties binding women, for men were to be allowed to retain, unimpaired, their rights to divorce where a wife 'misbehaved'.

I cannot but think that the proposed changes would be in the highest degree injurious to society. Whatever tends to weaken the permanence of [t]he marriage tie . . . is, I believe, most loudly to be deprecated. I feel keenly for the misery entailed on . . . the wife . . . by such forms of wickedness as those referred to in the new Bill . . . But I cannot see that these considerations are adequate to justify any tampering with a sacred institution, on which, as much at least as on any other, the welfare of society depends, and which needs to be strengthened rather than weakened against the corrupting influences of modern days. The practical adoption of the Christian idea of marriage . . . has been, I believe, one of the most exalting and purifying influences of modern society. Ill will it be for that society if it relinquishes or even impairs what has been hitherto its safety and its strength.[21]

No doubt the views of Mrs M'Neilly and those of the thousands of women like her differed as to the meaning of 'safety', though they tasted too well the 'strength' of the strong arm tactics used against them in the oppressive relationship they served in with the master of the house.

At the close of the nineteenth century New South Wales had altered laws of divorce, after twenty years of debate on the matter, so that women, like men, could sever marriage ties on the simple grounds of the spouse's adultery. Nonetheless, women in that jurisdiction, as elsewhere in Australia, did not enjoy equal rights with men to divorce. Women faced, still, problems of inadequate wages, if they were in paid employment, and thus difficulty in gaining legal advice; they faced the social stigma of divorce: scandal touched the wife, whoever petitioned for divorce, rarely the husband.

Thus the editorial of 5 November 1880 in the *Dawn*, the feminist newspaper, drew an analogy between woman's position in the home and that of lackey to a despot.

Working-men strike for higher wages, shorter hours, 'smoke-ohs', or in defence of one of their number unjustly or despotically treated, but though sensitive as to their own rights does it ever occur to them to think of the women? . . . Never! The social constitution may be turned upside down and stood on its head so to speak, when men's demands require hearing, but no one thinks of the women . . . not a soul asks 'Have the women any claims?'
  Does a man concede to his employee-wife, defined hours of rest, fair pay, just and considerate treatment? The wife's hours of work have no limit. All day the house and at night the children . . . A wife has no time to think of her own life and development, she has no money to spend, it is 'her husband's money', the complete right to her own children is not yet legally hers, and she is not even in independent possession of her own body . . . What is a wife's pay? It is certainly what no Union would allow any member to accept from an employer. She did not marry for pay, you may urge. True, but her work is worth as much as the man's . . . What of the treatment. Some are happy. Yes, and others bear a petty despotism, rough handling, rough language, selfish indifference, overwork. There are many of these. They endure far more than any man would tolerate from any master.
  . . . if you have ever seen a beaten woman, if you have ever seen a woman exhausted by housework, if you have ever seen one broken down by perpetual suppression . . . you may understand in what manner the great Strike Question presents itself to a woman.[22]

Twentieth Century Protest

One of the major tenets of the twentieth century women's movement has been that until women's oppression in the family is eradicated, women's equality will remain unwon. Thus reforms have been fought for in a replay of nineteenth century agitation for equal rights to divorce. In 1959 the *Matrimonial Causes Act* was passed by the federal government to consolidate the law relating to divorce and make the law uniform throughout Australia. The act included four-teen grounds for divorce, including adultery by husband or wife, on the petition of the 'injured' party; drunkenness, cruelty, insanity; desertion for three years and separation for five years. The separation ground was nicknamed the 'consent decree', because fault did not have to be shown on the part of either party. The party petitioning had to prove only that both had been living separately and apart for the required length of time and that no reconciliation was foreshadowed. The act was applauded by lawyers as achieving 'in its completeness, its internal consistency, its logical approach and its liberal attitudes, a peak of legislative excellence so far unequalled in countries which have inherited the English tradition as to marriage and divorce'.[23] Probably women's views were different.

The act did nothing to improve women's position as to domicile. On marriage, a woman acquired her husband's domicile. His domicile was hers for determining certain legal rights and duties. Thus if a woman did not know where her husband was living, she could not bring certain legal actions. If her husband was living in a foreign country, she could not bring a divorce action in Australia. If a woman permanently resided in New South Wales or Tasmania or Victoria, but her husband lived in Queensland, the law treated her as if she were permanently resident in Queensland. If he lived in South Australia, the law said she did too. It ignored her reality. A husband's right to sue for damages for enticement of his wife by another man remained in the law, as did his right to sue for damages for adultery. The *Matrimonial Causes Act* extended to wives the right to sue where the husband had committed adultery. Yet it was 'very difficult to turn a very male privilege into a female right':[24] the law in practice could not turn the proprietary interest a man had in his wife into a proprietary interest held by a woman in her husband. And historically, adultery by a husband was acceptable; in Victoria it took the 1959 act to change the law so that simple adultery of a husband became actionable in a wife's divorce petition.

Under the *Matrimonial Causes Act* 'fault' and 'guilt' remained the major basis of divorce. This was particularly relevant to women, for the double standard continued to operate, making it more difficult for women than men to prove grounds. Cruelty, a ground under which many women could have brought actions, had to be established to the same high degree as in years past; yet if a woman left her husband because of his cruelty, she could easily be sued as being in desertion. She had to prove extreme cruelty to justify her leaving. It was not unknown for husbands to have their wives committed to mental institutions to use the divorce ground of insanity. Women are seen as intrinsically neurotic, so this was an avenue open to men; as men are seen as the norm, women could not make similar use of the ground.[25] Because drunkenness is more acceptable in a man than in a woman, drunk men are perceived as generally 'normal'; drunk women are debased, so a divorce sought by a wife would be less easily obtained than one sought by a man on the same ground. The stigma attaching to divorce remained, and women were its victims.

'Fault' was also used against women in seeking maintenance and against children in relation to custody. A wife had a right to permanent maintenance from her husband, without regard to whether she was capable of earning her own living, as long as her conduct during the marriage and through the divorce was 'innocent'. As long as she was not a deserter, a drunkard, an adulteress, or simply 'guilty' in the court's eyes, she would gain a formal right to maintenance. This confirmed that women must preserve their standing as devoted hand-maidens and mothers, otherwise they would have to fend for themselves. It also continued to promote the idea that women need not earn in their own right but should be rewarded by 'marrying well'. The maintenance law thus reinforced socio-political attitudes toward discrimination in the paid workforce: women did not need paid employment, and so there was no need to secure them equal opportunities; marriage was a woman's career. Meanwhile ex-husbands adeptly escaped their obligations, travelling interstate, changing jobs frequently, ignoring orders, engaging skilful lawyers to downgrade their incomes — so wives did not benefit from the law. Women still suffered the problem of lack of access to funds to bring divorce suits and continue with proceedings for maintenance enforcement if, although ordered by the court, maintenance ceased.

Children's rights were secondary to the aim of the law in keeping women in their place and asserting the authority of husbands by endorsing a man's right to govern his wife's sexuality. Although the interests of the child were said to be paramount, they were secondary to the reinforcement of sexist standards. If a woman committed adultery, she lost custody of the children. If her husband deserted her and she then took up a relationship with another man, she lost custody of the children. In interpreting similar English legislation, Lord Hailsham went so far as to say that the welfare of the child might be impinged upon where a parent was not only culpable or callously indifferent, but also engaged to excess in 'sentimentality, romanticism, bigotry, wild prejudice, caprice, fatuousness or excessive lack of commonsense'.[26] In a world where women are commonly called sentimental and capricious, where their arguments are dismissed as fatuous or romantic, and where they are charged with being illogical, unreasonable and lacking in commonsense, their chances of being chosen, in accordance with this formula, as the parent appropriate to serve best the welfare of their children would be remote. Custody of children thus continued to depend, not upon what the children might want, but upon the conduct of the wife and mother, according to courts steeped in prejudicial mythology about 'woman's place'.

The early 1970s brought moves for further reforms in divorce law. Women's organisations exerted pressure. Divorce became available on one ground only under the *Family Law Act* of 1975, that of 'irretrievable breakdown' of marriage. So long as parties had lived separately and apart for twelve months and there was no hope of reconciliation, divorce was assured. Ancillary matters such as custody, property settlement and maintenance became the focus of litigation. One women's organisation favoured the legislation:

Under the present law there is still some difficulty in showing exactly what property a married woman has in matrimonial assets, especially the matrimonial home. Where the title to the house is held in the joint names of the spouses effect will normally be given to this. If the house is in the husband's name only, the wife usually has to show that she has made some direct financial contribution to the acquisition of the property. If the wife has special needs, for example small children to rear, it may be that she will be granted sole proprietorship of the home until the children have grown up ... Under the new Act women's contribution to marriage in the capacity of homemaker and parent will be regarded as having economic value. This is a tremendous breakthrough. It means a woman will be automatically entitled to a fair share of the property and income she has helped her husband to acquire. A woman's full time and unpaid career as enforced child minder and dinner producer at last has its rewards![27]

The court should look at financial and other contributions to property, the effects of any proposed order on the earning capacity of either party, any other orders affecting a party under the act, and issues relevant to award of maintenance, including age and state of health of the parties; income, property and financial resources of each; financial obligations and needs of each. But property remains the property of the person making the financial contribution (rarely the woman), and it is at the discretion of the court only that such interests may be 'altered'. Nineteenth century social standards still influence Family Court property settlements, and women continue to be cemented into a dependent position, for although efforts in the traditional role of women are now given some recognition, that recognition comes through the 'glorious benevolence' of the judge in the particular case. In court, women are met with an inquisition as to their homemaking and parenting efforts, and a sceptic's view of their needs. In practice their rights to participate equally in the marital assets are not within contemplation. The court has a broad discretion to award or not to award any of the property to a woman. Until the 'natural biases' against women are eradicated from society outside, judicial discretion within will always disadvantage women.

Often . . . male bias shows up at one stage or another of the legal process in the exercise of 'discretion'. That built-in flexibility which allows a judge . . . to use 'better judgment' is essential, experts agree, to a legal system that tries to deal fairly with individual cases. But since discretion usually is exercised *by* men (or by women trained to the male standard), it is usually exercised *for* men, for the male standard. Judicial discretion, repeatedly exercised to protect the same male interests, becomes a mask for the law's underlying systematic discrimination against women.[28]

The thrust behind the *Family Law Act* was that women should no longer be regarded as dependent, or as deserving lifetime maintenance because they were 'innocent' of matrimonial fault. Spouses should receive maintenance only when stipulated factors are taken into account: age and state of health of the parties; income, property and financial resources of each and their physical and mental capacity for employment; responsibilities of either party to support any other person; eligibility to receive a pension; duration of the marriage and the way it has affected the earning capacity of the party seeking maintenance; financial needs and obligations of each of the parties and the like. But the act betrays a conventional belief that the proper role for a woman *is* as a dependant at home, caring for the children. The section on maintenance contemplates that after separation or divorce a woman might 'wish only to continue her role as a wife'. How could a woman do this without a husband? The act also looks at the woman who wishes to 'continue her role as a . . . mother', yet not at a man who might want to continue his role as a father. Parliament obviously did not seek to go too far in its ideal of equality: there was no recognition that, if men and women are to become equal and be treated equally, fathers should participate equally in child care and the responsibilities concomitant with having children.

Attitudes prevalent in society are also given full rein in the interpretation of the act. Women lose out thereby. Thus when looking at 'financial needs and obligations' of both parties, the conventional view that men need more than women prevails. Since time began, women have 'made do', and those on the bench have grown up with the self-effacing attitude of women impressed upon them. The 1930s story of a Victorian woman no doubt recurs today:

I helped in all kinds of manual work milking cows 26 at one stage for just the two of us to manage, rabbiting to get a few shillings to get clothing for self and children and . . . bed linen or necessities for house apart from food . . . One day I helped to hold fencing wire which touched a vital spot and before I knew where I was my husband threw me down by catching hold of my throat with his muddy hands. A gentleman called and the first thing — 'oh get a cup of tea' — I wonder did he think of his cruel marks which were left when I gave out the cups of tea.[29]

Many women would empathise with the wife whose husband earned a low wage who said: 'I looked after my husband and children well, but I often went short of food myself'. Many men would think that is the proper state of affairs — after all, men *need* more food than women.

Women are at present less well-trained for the world of paid work than men. The act on its face attempts to overcome this in a small way by providing that maintenance might be awarded to enable a wife to 'undertake a course of education or training'. But women wishing to do this are sometimes confronted by a court seeing their aspirations as unworthy of consideration. One ex-wife was allegedly told by a magistrate that 'a woman of 50 should not be studying. It is frivolous of her to hope to get a job after finishing her studies; a woman of 50 should know better'. Yet a woman of 70 was allegedly required to show evidence that it was impossible for her to obtain any paid employment, as the solicitor for her husband contended that instead of receiving maintenance or any property settlement after a marriage of nearly fifty years, the ex-wife should take the initiative and get herself a paying job instead of being dependent upon her ex-husband's largesse. In one case a man told his former wife he was deliberately delaying an appearance at the Family Court for property and maintenance settlement because he was trying to find another woman to marry, so he could claim his second wife was dependent upon him and his resources, and that he was, therefore, unable to contribute to his former wife's upkeep. This, despite the more than thirty years his former wife had been married to him and supporting him by bolstering his ego, fetching and carrying, cooking, and looking after the children they both decided to have.[30]

As for custody, the act contemplates either mother or father or both may retain custody of the children of the marriage. The court is to 'regard the welfare of the child as the paramount consideration' and where a child has attained the age of fourteen years 'the court shall not make an order . . . contrary to the wishes of the child unless the court is satisfied that, by reason of special circumstances, it is necessary to do so' (s. 64). Each case is decided on an individual basis. What constitutes the 'welfare of the child' accords with the opinion of the judge in the case. General rules are laid down that neither father nor mother has inalienable rights to custody, so the law on its face does away with the earlier idea that children were property to be awarded to one or the other parent — in earlier times, to the father. Although it might seem a giant leap forward that children's wishes are to be taken into account, one of the difficulties for children is that it is often said that they are unable to say what they want, or know what they want, or that their choice of parent is a result of duress by the parent. Others say that children, wishing to please one or other or both parents, will make a determination contrary to their real desires. Using these arguments, the wishes of the child may be dispensed with in practice, and the court will apply its own idea of what is best for the child.

If parental affection and care are seen as equal for mother and father, property holdings and income become highly relevant. It is likely that courts will, in such cases, look to the party who is best equipped financially, because our society is materialistic. Children will, probably, receive a better education in formal terms when living with a parent with access to a 'good' school, who can supply the requisite books, sports equipment, and the like. Children will, of course, be better cared for where the weekly wage packet can cover food expenses adequately. A child's welfare will be better served if the child has access to after-school playgrounds, organised entertainment, clubs and sporting facilities, rather than being thrust, owing to residential area and lack of pocket money or parental finances, into the pin-ball-palour scene, or playing in the street. Who, then, will become increasingly likely to gain custody, if the parent chooses to request it? Not the mother, who has no access to highly paid jobs which would enable her to provide all those things. It might be to the benefit of the child that the parent with greater material benefits is chosen for custody, but as long as children are unable to have society and the courts take their views and rights seriously, the issue will remain clouded. 'Father right' is also bolstered by conventional views of the single parent family and the alleged need for children to live in the 'typical' nuclear family. Fathers (frequently remarried) are, therefore, in a position where, should they wish it, custody will be likely to be awarded them.

That conventional views of what women should do and how they should live dictate custody decisions, rather than the wishes of the child or the child's welfare, is illustrated in the alleged remark of one judge who said to researchers that he 'would never award custody of a child to a career woman'. He would thus be obliged to award it to a 'career man', for no doubt the woman's former husband would be such — most men are! He had no thought for the woman's abilities as a mother and no thought for the right of the child to have his or her wishes taken into account. Research shows that children admire mothers with business and paid-work interests, but we are back at the stage reached in 1924 with Emelie Polini and her daughter. To the particular judge, such issues were irrelevant.

Finally, the rights of children not to be abused are given short shrift by the legal system generally. Courts are reluctant to remove children from abusive parents. With sexual abuse at least, fathers are more likely to be at fault. But there is scepticism about the extent of abuse: 'the law [has] presumed that children in the home receive love and affection and that child abuse and emotional deprivation [are] rare'.[31] Although child abuse and neglect are well recognised as occurring, in the court room during custody cases, allegations that a father has interfered sexually with his children are, at least sometimes, ignored. In some cases fathers receive custody or gain access to children despite the mother's very real concern about his exploitation of them.[32] Thus although the law pays verbal regard to the child's welfare as paramount and lawyers deny that children remain commodities, social reality asserts otherwise.

Men, Women and Marriage

In 1898 Elizabeth Cady Stanton, debating the need for changes in divorce laws in the United States, said: 'Before we can decide the just grounds for divorce, we must get a clear idea of what constitutes marriage.'[33] In her view, the contract of marriage was never equal. In entering into marriage, the man need give up nothing he possessed. A woman's existence was nothing in marriage, she being 'nameless, purseless, childless — though a woman, an heiress, . . . a mother.' Stanton concluded:

Marriage has ever been a one-sided matter, resting most unequally upon the sexes. By it man gains all; woman loses all; tyrant law and lust reign supreme with him; meek submission and ready obedience alone befit her. Woman has never been consulted. Her wish has never been taken into consideration as regards the terms of the marriage compact. By law, public sentiment, and religion, — from the time of Moses down to the present day, — woman has never been thought of other than as a piece of property, to be disposed of at will and pleasure of man. And at this very hour, by our statute books, by our (so-called) enlightened Christian civilization, she has no voice whatever in saying what shall be the basis of the relation. She must accept marriage as man proffers it, or not at all.[34]

The irony is that despite Stanton's apposite summing up of the situation — that 'what constitutes marriage' should precede any review of grounds for ending the relation — law reformers in the twentieth century have focused upon divorce rather than upon marriage. By rendering it seemingly easier for women to escape from marriage, the reforms of today have not ended the fundamental position of servitude created for women through marriage. Rather, attention has been drawn away from what is basic to the relation and oppresses women and, in consequence, children.

At common law, the only concerns about marriage relate to the nature of the service creating it, and the capacity of the parties. Notably, the church, synagogue, or chapel service did not speak of the parties becoming 'man and woman', or 'husband and wife', nor of 'woman and husband'. On marriage, a couple became 'man and wife', connoting the true nature of the relationship: that it involves an *individual* man contracting with a *woman in service*. The law was also concerned that parties not be within prohibited degrees of consanguinity. The law also dealt with the age at which parties could contract marriage and always set the male's age higher than the female's. Thus the law ensured as far as possible that a habit would be established, or promoted, of younger women marrying older men. This supported men in their dominant role and promoted dependence in women, for where a younger person contracts with an older, particularly where the latter is male and the former female, the relationship will almost inevitably be one of inequality. This inequality was further promoted by a lack of any attention to the terms of the relationship during the course of the marriage.

In Australia today the law relating to marriage itself has rarely been reviewed. Regarding the law in England, Diana Leonard Barker comments:

The usual reasons advanced to justify legal regulation of, support for, and intervention into marriage and the family are: the protection of women and children (assuring support obligations and assigning responsibility for child care), ensuring family stability (for the psychic good of all its members, and hence the stability and well-being of the polity), and the promotion of public morality . . . The law is presented as supporting the weaker party in the marital relationship . . . Women are seen as benefitting from marriage as a state-supported institution, and it is they who are more likely to feel a vested interest in the maintenance of their 'rights' i.e. in the *status quo*. Thus state support for marriage acts . . . to stabilise a potentially disruptive (class) struggle. It helps to mute or silence women's demands for equality of treatment in the labour market; to ensure that they continue to accept the assignment to them of the care of the young, sick, and the elderly, and that they are prepared to drop out of paid employment to provide such care; and to encourage them to put their energy, and occasionally even the money for their own food or clothing, into the maintenance of their husband (their current provider) and the children.[35]

During the course of the marriage, women and the children they bear are no better regarded than during divorce. There is no effective means of ensuring adequate provision is made by a man for a woman during marriage, nor for their children. If the man is the major or sole financial contributor, he is the owner of the marital assets; a woman might own some assets, such as gifts from her parents, items purchased with her own salary, or gifts from a benevolent husband. Yet the parents' gifts might be joint gifts and, therefore, owned equally by the husband. The items from her own salary will be less valuable than those bought by her husband, as he generally has a higher income. Her money has frequently gone on items disappearing through use. Married women experience a lack of self-esteem, a failing of independence, and feelings of servitude when they become pregnant, leave paid employment, and take on the full-time housewife role. Many women would understand the position of a married woman who accumulated money in her own business before marrying, then gave up the business at her husband's request to look after him and *his* home. The money saved, she used to keep herself during marriage. She prepared him three hot meals each day on top of housework, looking after the children, renovating the house, but he now says she has done nothing as 'she had the pleasure of waiting upon him'. She is reluctant to break up the marriage. She would have nowhere to live. He did not allow her sufficient housekeeping money to cover her own food and other needs, so her money has gone. At 62 years she realises that the only chance she has of accommodation for old age is to begin divorce proceedings and hope for a fair distribution of property. Yet she believes the husband will conceal as many of the assets as possible and is unsure that a fair distribution is possible at the Family Court. She concludes:

I feel I am denigrating myself in doing so, but will probably have to play along with the existing relationship and hope I die before he does. It is a disgrace that the laws are such that I have to live a lie just to keep a roof over my head in my old age. Yet my husband is in comparative affluence, and considers the affluence to be his entitlement alone. I am seen as a sucker and hanger on, a beggar on his doorstep that he need only throw a few scraps when he wants to.[36]

Throughout the marriage, until they grew up and left home, the children were similarly dealt with, having no rights in their father's eyes, simply being recipients of his bounty should he deign to oblige them.

Thus despite changes to the legal position of women and the granting of formal though tentative rights to children in restricted areas, women and children remain chained as dependants upon a property owner — the man. Property ownership remains with the major financial contributor. The other party must gain a divorce in order to seek benevolence. They have no *rights* to property. They have only the hope that the benevolence not granted them by husband and father will be directed toward them by the state, through the court system. Women remain dependent on men through unequal work opportunities, inadequate child care facilities, and the prevailing ideology, which demands that women live in marriage or at least be attached to a man. Children remain minors in law, subject to parental control — and mainly to control of the father. If there is no father, the child is often removed to the care of the state, which steps into the paterfamilias role. Children of single-parent families — that is, mostly, families with a mother, not a father — run the risk of a delinquent label. Those living in the 'acceptable' way, with mother and father, however unhappy that relationship, are less often brought before children's courts as juvenile offenders or in need of care, and thereby under control of the state-as-father.[37] Although the law on its face has changed, in interpretation and execution women and children are bound by the family ruler: father is in control, and if he fails, the state rules. Historically, the legal system thus sets women and children up for exploitation: they are bound to live in a unit supported by law and society as being rightly unequal in powers of the members. If they remain, they are subjected to the rule of the head. If they remove, or the head departs, they become 'abnormal' in the eyes of society, the law and the body politic. They frequently become 'burdens' on the state. Within the family unit, women and children are subject to the rights of individual men, with obligations to those men. Outside the family unit, women and children become displaced persons, subject to the rights of the state, that is, to collective man. The law represents the interests of individual man and collective man; woman's interests are not represented. Those of children are even less so, although male children, eventually, gain representation simply by growing up. For female children, like women, there is no escape.

CHAPTER 3   CHILD ABUSE: VIOLENCE AND NEGLECT

'The history of childhood is a nightmare from which we have just begun to awaken'. The further back in history, the more likely children were to have been killed, abandoned, whipped or sexually abused by their caretakers.

Children were sacrificed in religious rituals, sold into slavery, beaten to exorcise the devil, maimed to exploit them as beggars or performing freaks.

The way children are treated in our society relates to the way we value children and the way we define their rights. It relates to the degree of submission and conformity we expect from children and the extent to which we sanction physical force as a means of getting children to obey.

The fact that our society is now concerned with the problem of child abuse does not mean that parents have suddenly taken to beating their children, but that our tolerance to child maltreatment has declined, and we are now appalled by acts to which our ancestors would have been indifferent. It is part of a growing awareness that the human rights, dignity and integrity of every man, woman and child should be protected.

> Royal Commission on Human Relationships *Final Report*,
> A.G.P.S., 1977, Canberra, volume 4, p.159.

Our world paints conflicting visions of childhood. Firmly entrenched in the common mind is the view of gurgling, jolly babies, rattle waving, snuggly booted and blanketted, responding lovingly to baby talk with smiling dimpled chins and cheeks. The reality is often a grumpy, squalling bundle, a damp and smelly nappy, a small face stubbornly bunched into a recalcitrant grimace, spitting half-chewed lumps of inedible mess onto the table cloth, high chair, and floor. Stage two sees the young child off to school, Mummy waving good-bye from the gate, with a welcome later in the day, excellent report cards rewarded with thick slices of bread, butter and jam, and large glasses of milk. The other side? Neighbours tut-tutting as loud screams emerge from the house next door: 'He's at it again, beating that poor child black and blue. There'll be a death in that house yet.' Teachers talking in the staffroom about the Stantons: 'Those three children don't want to go home in the afternoon. Their mother doesn't make them a proper lunch, mustard sandwiches they had yesterday, and saying they liked them. That Susan put them up to it, too proud to let anyone know it's the mother's doing. And the red marks on their thighs you can see under their sports tunics. Not much of a life for a child'.

Although childhood is depicted as a golden age of laughter and happiness without responsibilities, the truth is somewhat different. Maltreatment of children has been recorded throughout history, sometimes simply as a factual account of cultural and social mores, sometimes with moral overtones, when reformers called for the introduction of humane standards into factories, mines and shops. Every text on child abuse records the late nineteenth century scandal when it was recognised that, although society had agitated against cruelty towards animals, setting up societies for their protection, no associations existed to protect children from cruelty. Today, child beating has a modern title, 'the child abuse syndrome'. Deliberate injuring of infants has passed into present language as 'non-accidental injury' to children.

Two major social attitudes interfere with assistance for children. First, society clings deeply to the notion of parents having a right to control *their* children, which includes the right to physically chastise in the name of discipline. Second, despite romanticisation of childhood, society sees children as 'provocative' or 'troublesome' and so condones in advance the parent (who, we fear, might be any one of us) going over the edge and lashing out in anger. Society absolves the parent who hits: bad children must be brought into line; parents have a right (even a duty) to socialise their children into being good, even if it takes hitting to do so.

Asking 'when does hitting become abuse' highlights the central problem: as a society we accept a need for disciplining children by corporal punishment. In condoning child abuse in some of its forms, sometimes even requiring it, society faces insurmountable problems of definition: when does punishment become abuse? when does a parent overstep the boundaries of obedience training and become criminal in intent? how much abuse justifies removal of a child from a parent, or requires society to remove the parent from the child, by imprisonment? The irony is that society never asks the victims of child abuse *their* opinion of 'how much abuse is too much abuse'; their opinion of corporal punishment is not officially sought; their view of a world outlawing assaults against adults but legalising those against children by parents, teachers and guardians is irrelevant to courts, legislatures and governments. When those suffering abuse have the opportunity to speak, they echo the words of Michael Terry, victim of his father's devotion to obedience and the 'value' of a strict upbringing, exemplified by his adherence to the notion that children must be hit to be brought into line: 'I don't feel well disposed towards my father, or to bullying tactics, etc. Definitely it affects my attitude toward women and makes me care about how all people treat each other. Don't think anyone should have to put up with the same sort of treatment my father doled out. And nor should a child/teenager/anyone.'

Incidence of Abuse

The Royal Commission on Human Relationships estimated a nation-wide figure of 37 juveniles injured daily, or 13 500 cases of child abuse annually. Even this is probably an under-estimate. Many cases never come to the attention of anyone apart from participants and other family members. Estimates are influenced by the definition of 'child abuse' or 'non-accidental physical injury': the more stringent the definition, the less likely child beating will be included as 'abuse'. In the United States a 1968 Harris poll found that 93 per cent of the 1500 respondents were spanked as children. If spanking is child abuse or assault, estimates in Australia, as in the United States, would reach astronomical proportions.

The extent of child abuse in Australia cannot be determined. In five states legislation requires the reporting of child abuse; other jurisdictions have informal reporting systems. In New South Wales, medical practitioners are liable to a penalty on failing to report an incidence of child abuse. In South Australia, Queensland and Tasmania medical practitioners must report child abuse. Yet in all states abuse is seriously under-reported.[1] New South Wales boasts high numbers of reports: 889 cases reported in the first year of

reporting legislation (1979), whereas in the decade before the legislation came into operation, only 645 cases were reported to welfare
authorities.

A major failing of child abuse reporting schemes is that victims are
unlikely to seek redress through the system. In a survey of reporting
figures for two periods during the 1960s and 1970s in Western
Australia, the majority of reports were made by hospitals, relatives,
neighbours and friends; police reports were proportionately far
lower, corresponding with reports from parents. No victims reported
abuse during either period. Under the statutes, the tendency is to
enlarge groups mandated to report abuse to authorities. No statute
requires victims to report; they refer to medical practitioners,
dentists, social workers, teachers, police and nurses.

Victims may indirectly signify victimisation by running away.
Many children have escaped abusive homes in which parents or
masters beat them or imposed onerous tasks on them. How many
still run from physical violence and neglect? There are few youth
refuges. Young people are often reluctant to go to them, anyway,
afraid their parents will be told of their address. Social security
statistics do not help: children under school-leaving age do not
qualify for employment or unemployment benefits; family allowances, granted on numbers of children in a family, are not paid to the
children. No records exist of children for whom family allowances
are payable but who have left home because of abuse. Similarly,
handicapped children's benefits and orphan's allowances are not
paid to the child, but to a guardian or other person having care and
control, although that care and control may be neglectful or abusive.

Extent of the Violence

Child abuse reporting laws in Australia cover only physical abuse or
neglect. However, a definition of abuse or maltreatment including
emotional or psychological violence is accepted by state welfare
administrators:

A non-accidentally injured or maltreated child is one who is less than eighteen years of age whose parents or other persons inflict or allow to be inflicted
on the child physical injury by other than accidental means, or gross deprivation which causes or creates or allows to be created a substantial risk of such
injury other than by accidental means.[2]

In the present study, psychological abuse appeared almost as often as physical abuse. Of seventy-seven child abuse cases, fifty-one victims suffered both physical and psychological abuse; nine, only psychological abuse, and seventeen, only physical abuse.

Hitting hard with only a hand occurred in five cases. The majority involved more extensive violence. Slightly more than half the cases involved hitting hard with a hand and other abuse. One-third of victims were hit with a strap; one-third were battered with a stick or piece of wood; one-third were punched, particularly in the stomach, head and back. Slightly fewer were belted with a leather strap. Ten were hit with 'anything that happened to be handy at the time', including a child's school case, a bar of iron, a feather duster, a steel ruler, the pipe of the vacuum cleaner. Two were hit with chairs. Four were threatened and chased with knives; one was threatened with a gun and hit about the head with the butt. Four children were scalded with boiling water from the stove. Five were shaken bodily. Three children in one family had their heads bashed against the table. Two children were kicked, two had various items thrown at them, including ashtrays, rolled newspapers, plates, and beer cans. Three were burnt with cigarettes. One child's head was held under a running tap in the garden; she was then locked, soaking wet, in the toolshed. One had a pillow held over his head; one was thrown into a basinette and baby carrier. One mother clamped her young baby's wrists so hard the bruises lasted for two weeks. One mother bit her child. Another squashed her toddler so firmly into the car seat, pulling the seat-belt so tight the child could hardly breathe and was bruised about the body for almost a month. One child was stabbed with a table fork. One was struck with a broken bottle. Margaret Tanner and her brother Bobby were abused by their father from early infancy until their teens: 'He would hit us both with anything handy, like a torch or spanner, etc. He punched us both and one time threw hot water all over me from the stove. He had to take me to hospital and threatened me with being thrown over a cliff if I told them the truth. He told them I had tipped the water over myself and I think he believed it by the time he said it a few times to them.'

Abuse often included deprivation of attention and affection. In some cases, the abusive parent constantly ignored the children, sulked, or refused to talk. Locking the child in a bedroom or bathroom, or in a cupboard, sometimes for hours, was common, and

children were locked out of the house or in an outside shed. Some
children were forced to eat or to drink; others were often refused
meals. Ruth Sanderson's mother began living with a *de facto* husband when Ruth was 7 and her twin brothers 4 years old:

He was a very cruel man, and we were subject to terrible cruelty and were
punched in the stomach and hit around the head, belted with jug cords, more
so my twin brothers were treated the worst. We were all got out of bed on
cold winter nights and made to stand on cold concrete floor for hours at a
time, when we did close our eyes we were pulled up by the ears or hit around
the head, we were treated worse than dogs. One of the twins was born with a
hare-lip and was tormented for hours about his poor little mouth. Then
when the little boys were older and had to go to school, he was afraid they
would tell someone of our treatment so we all had to miss a lot of school, and
mum stayed all that time knowing what terrible heartbreak us children were
going through but said she was helpless and to help us. She got away from
him and we went back to dad and grandma, but then she went back and we
had to go back too. Dad kept telling us he was trying to get custody but
nothing seemed to happen.

Those mentioning psychological abuse wrote of deliberate taunting,
fierce tempers and raging at minor things, such as untidiness in
the lounge room or bad manners at the table. Michael Terry began
suffering abuse from his father during his early teen years. He was
raged at, his life 'made a misery':

Stringent obedience was required at all times. He taunted me for my
'weakness' (of course I was not as strong as a grown man). He was a bully as
long as I was younger and only growing up. I stayed for as long as I could to
protect my mother from his yelling and taunting too, although if I hadn't
stayed he would maybe have calmed down. He didn't want another man
around.

Mary Smith and her sister Jean were very young when the abuse
began. They recalled often being hit hard by their father and his
constant changes of mind about their upbringing:

When practising the piano he would tell us to stop. Then when we were not
playing the piano, we were hit and abused for not doing so. We were stopped
from going out — for no apparent reason, except that he wanted us to stay
home. At times he locked us out. When he was asleep, our mother would let
us in. (The locking out consisted of nailing up the doors and windows.)

Inconsistency of treatment was a recurring theme. Marion Henderson's father was patient for some time, then he would lose his temper without warning. There was never any continuity of discipline. Constant domestic arguments and violence by her father towards her mother made Marion and her brother Steven jumpy, nervous and confused.

In other instances, children were expected to live up to almost super-human standards. Of the psychological violence directed at her son Morris by his father, Barbara Stephens wrote: 'Morris was not allowed to play in normal ways. His father was a strict Catholic and very narrow — a very religious person. No friends allowed to the boy in kindergarten or play group; not allowed books, T.V., radio or music. The child was under constant restraint, restrictions.'

Unpleasantness often revolved around outings or the prospect of outings. Abusive parents tormented their children by promising outdoor activities, then denying them. Until they were 15 and 17 years respectively, Margaret and Bobby Tanner were physically abused by their father and not allowed out of the house, other than to go to school. On occasion they were told to get ready for the pictures, were taken to look at posters outside, then taken home. Out fishing, they were made to sit and watch. If they moved, their father became abusive and violent, shouting at them that they were upsetting the fish and deserved to be drowned. They prepared for outings, only to be told the outing was off, because they were unfit to be seen with. Pet birds were deliberately let out of cages; pet cats, dogs and goats were deliberately killed. Mr Tanner made no secret of his role in their deaths.

In some cases, the abuser told the children they were adopted or said he was not their father, because their mother had 'slept around' with other men. For some, the abuse was accompanied by denigrating remarks about the other parent. Donald Collins, father of Trevor and Ian did this:

He was always saying he was not our 'real' father. He kept on saying he would leave our mother because she didn't want him. He kept saying she was selfish, mad, fit to be put in an asylum. He spent his time not speaking to us for long periods at other times, ignoring us when we tried to talk to him. Even today although mum keeps saying he was our real father, I sometimes think he wasn't. I know sometimes I even wish what he said was true. It's upsetting to really have a father like that.

Reasons for the Violence

Our society is reluctant to accept violence between adult strangers as
justified. Retaliation and revenge are not lawful. The onus rests on
the party using force or violence to show that provocation, self-
defence, necessity or coercion occurred as 'excuses' or mitigating factors in courts of law. Even with domestic violence involving adult
victims and aggressors, the law on its face outlaws the assault, and
courts and legislatures are slowly recognising that sexual abuse by a
married partner is unlawful. With children, attitudes are different.
The law distinguishes between assaults against children by a parent
or guardian, and assaults against adults, and social attitudes endorse
this.[3]

What justification for violence exists, particularly where the
assailant is patently better equipped than the victim? Of the seventy-
seven cases in this study, although violence runs the gamut from
verbal abuse and withdrawal of affection to strangling, choking
and threats with knives and guns, often combined with verbal and
psychological abuse, justification is elusive. In twenty cases fierce
tempers, hitting hard with a strap, belt, or hand, and raging were
triggered off by minor things: untidiness at home, untidy dress, bad
manners at the table, talking during meals, or no obvious reason.
'My father used to belt us for the silliest things', wrote Therese
Sullivan. 'This included talking in bed, not running when we were
told to do something. I don't mean just a smack but really belted
with a jug cord, anything my father could lay his hands on. He used
to end up kicking us and really bashing us he used to be so mad. I
don't think he could stop himself.'

'Discipline' was an oft stated reason for shouting at children, hitting them, kicking, belting, or throwing things at them. Although
discipline may be positive for social reasons, the extent of discipline
adopted by parents was hardly reasonable. Katherine James and her
two sisters were sent from the table if they spoke out of turn, being
banished to their bedrooms, without dinner, for long periods. The
rule was not to dance in front of the television set during teenage programmes and if 'caught', they were locked in the cupboard under the
stairs. They were never allowed to go to the pictures, to hamburger
shops, or to ice cream shops. Once Sandra James was found eating
chips, obviously bought at the local hamburger store, and was hit

about the legs with a steel ruler. Red welts lasted for two weeks, preventing her attendance at school.

Often the violence was entirely unconnected with the actions of its victims. Laurel Trevor, her brother and her sister were belted and kicked by their mother's *de facto* husband over fifteen years:

If we were watching something on T.V., he'd come in and annoy us until we would just stop watching it. Then in bed we might be sound asleep and two o'clock in the morning he'd come and wake us up, because he wanted to talk (in his drunken stupor) and if we said no or told him to get out, he'd start belting, kicking or throwing things at us. Believe me trying to go to school after no sleep and bruises all over you is not easy.

In one particularly violent example, a father deliberately provoked his children into doing something he could use as an excuse for abuse.

My mother had eight children the eldest my sister of 25 years and the youngest is 13 years. I feel terrible about writing all this and ashamed, but I just feel that you might understand. My father was always being very strict with us and mum. He has a very bad temper which leads to violence. He almost killed me when I was 16 years old I don't know for what reason really. He just gets that he could not stand the sight of me around the house, he would pick on me for about anything. Till one day he really got me scarred for life and we never told the police or the doctors at the hospital what actually happened. We were frightened that if we told it would be worse because of him. In the past six years he almost murdered my older sister for leaving home at the age of 21 years. He took her back home by force. But she soon left for Perth. She was so scared of him she did not let anyone know when she left. We are a decent family — all the children — we are good kids I think. We were brought up in Belgium before migrating here eleven years ago. He threatened to kill my second brother. He swore he was picking on him, deliberately waiting for him to answer back so he could really put his hands on him. That's how he does to all of us.

Sometimes verbal abuse and violence raged where a parent wanted children to achieve scholastically beyond their capabilities. Two fathers 'put enormous pressure' on their sons to be competitive with other children in the classroom. For one, failure led to fierce belting with a strap; for the other, the father withdrew and sulked for days, with an occasional rising out of the mood to snap at the child that he was 'hopeless, a moron'.

Chris Denton's parents demanded she live up to standards of 'femininity' and traditional female achievement. Covert and overt violence and verbal aggression were sparked off by clothes she wore, her hairstyle, teenage puppy fat and pimples. If she left her hair untrimmed, her parents told her she was, 'in their opinion, revolting in appearance and temperament, that she was an ungrateful burden with a life long debt to them'. When she ventured to the hairdresser, they received her changed appearance with charges that she 'was wholly bad and without any redeeming features whatsoever, that she was incapable of love and kindness and she should be "put away" and deserved to be confined to a mental institution as she was a "raving nut case" to get around looking like that'. They accused her of deliberately getting fat to humiliate them and said she made herself unattractive to men so she could live off her parents for the rest of her life. They constantly told her they were ashamed of their daughter and believed there must have been a mistake at the hospital 'because your mother and I could never produce such a revolting specimen'.

Alcohol and Drugs as Factors

With little reason behind the physical, psychological and neglectful abuse suffered by children, is demon drink the root cause? Although Australians — at least, Australian men — are amongst the world's greatest beer drinkers, no studies support the suggestion that child abuse is related only to drunkenness, or related mainly to drunkenness. An Australian survey of child abuse studies and incidence of alcohol use concluded that heavy drinking 'undoubtedly contributes to family violence, although it is difficult to know whether alcohol features as a cause of the violence or as a result of the frustration which produced it'.[4] Even this cautious conclusion is not supported by the evidence cited. A figure of one in five child abuse cases 'having a connection with alcohol' is based on a study of forty-one abused children at a Melbourne hospital. In 'at least eight' families, 'alcoholism was present'.[5] There is no necessary connection between the abuse and the alcoholism. Were both parents alcoholic and both implicated in the abuse? Was only one parent 'alcoholic', and he or she the abuser? Was the parent drunk when abuse took place? Is violence meted out only during a drunken bout, or does it occur both during times of drunkenness and times of sobriety?

In the present study, thirty-six respondents said abuse did not occur when the assailant was drunk. Ann Gregg was beaten regularly 'from as early as I can remember until I was 16 and left permanently'. Her father, an economist, never beat her when drunk: 'My father hardly ever drank and only did so when he was away on business trips'. Renata Transom's father was 'just overstrict and wouldn't tolerate drink in any way not even in the house'.

Of the remaining forty-one cases, for eight victims violence sometimes occurred when the assailant was drunk, but more often when he or she was sober. In eleven cases, abuse was equally likely when the aggressor was drunk as when sober. 'He drank beer a lot', wrote Rhonda O'Keefe. 'He hit me with a strap and with a belt when he was drunk, but he locked me outside for hours when he was sober, and sometimes he hit me then too. It was about equal, drunk or sober.' In four cases, abuse occurred during drunkenness and during sobriety, but with greater emphasis during heavy drinking bouts. In eighteen of the seventy-seven cases, child abuse occurred always when the assailant was drunk or drinking. Diane Browne's father 'took to drinking all day and nearly all night at the pub'. When he arrived home he frequently attacked the three children. The entire family suffered psychological abuse, lying terrified in their beds, waiting for his footsteps on the verandah and dreading his angry mutterings, even if it did not always come to blows.

In five cases drugs were present when child abuse occurred. Each time the assailant was male, and the drugs were on prescription. In two cases antidepressants were used; in two others Mogodon and Serepax were mentioned. These drugs are relaxants, used to induce sleep. They could not 'cause' child abuse. In three cases drugs were 'sometimes' involved, whilst in one drugs were never involved, although the father sometimes took them. None of the respondents said abuse happened only when drugs were used.

Why the concentration on drunkenness when child abuse is mentioned? It is convenient to label abuse an anomaly in our society. If abuse happens only when the assailant is drunk, the problem is whittled down to comprehensible dimensions: not all children, indeed a minority, suffer abuse; aggressors are 'sick' and can be sent off to Alcoholics Anonymous courses for cure; people who are untreatable as alcoholics could have their children removed from their care without any real disruption; society as a whole is immune from blame — the culprit is alcohol. Yet on the results in this study, drunkenness and child abuse are not closely related. Alcohol does not 'cause' child abuse. Cases of child abuse occurring without any alcohol far outnumbered those where alcohol was always present. To find 'causes' of child abuse, it is necessary to look beyond alcohol.

Economic Factors

Folklore has it that child abuse, like wife bashing, occurs only in the working classes. Yet children are abused in professional families, families from the lower socio-economic bracket, families with high incomes, families of Anglo-Saxon origins, families of ethnic minority background, those following known religions, those without any religious beliefs. The abuser may be unemployed, or employed in the top income bracket; may be a skilled worker or a professional. Single parents may abuse; members of the traditional two-parent, two-children family may abuse. *Reported* cases of child abuse mostly involve families in the lower socio-economic category, but whether this is because poverty is more likely to lead to child abuse than is relative affluence, or because the poor are more likely to be scrutinised by welfare agencies and police remains open to debate.

In the present study there was no preponderance of assailants in the unskilled category. Of seventy-seven families, only nine male assailants were unskilled. Of the remainder, one-third were professionals; about one-fifth were 'managerial'; one-third were engaged in small business ventures; less than a third were skilled. One was at all times an invalid pensioner. As for the role of unemployment, a factor contributing to poverty, seven male assailants were on unemployment benefits at times during the infliction of abuse on the children: four were unskilled workers, two were skilled, and one was professional.

Relative incomes of child abusers could not be determined, for most respondents were unable to gauge an amount. But there is no support for the conventional proposition that child abuse arises only out of frustration and aggressions intertwined with poverty and lower socio-economic status. Where the father was unskilled, low income was indicated in a number of cases. In some, finances were depleted regularly by alcohol, cigarettes and gambling. But the skilled had no monopoly on spending money this way. Tom Sandry, an accountant, belted his four children, forced them to eat, and banished them to their bedrooms for long periods. Consistent with the 'me always first' ideology, his income was frequently spent on alcohol, even during unemployment. Don Thompson's father, a school teacher and later inspector of schools, inflicted psychological abuse on three sons by constant sulking, withdrawal of affection, and verbal violence. He made no monetary provision for family needs 'beyond the bare minimum of food, clothing and a roof over our heads'. His 'good' salary went on gambling and drink. The children felt unwanted — they were an unloved financial burden borne with little grace.

In canvassing occupational and economic factors, one Australian review contended:

The fact that some parents neglect and even harm their children often stems directly from environmental conditions which may be hard to change. Poor people have fewer alternatives and fewer escapes from dealing with their aggressive impulses than those who are not poor. Moreover, violence tends to be part of the culture of the poor. Feelings of powerlessness and frustration may arouse aggression which is taken out on the child.[6]

But in the present study, violence was no more a part of the culture of the poor than of the wealthy. Danielle Anderson and her brother Sam were victims of an abusive father with large land holdings in Western Australian cattle country. Harry Anderson chased his son Sam with a knife, belted both children severely, and often when drunk taunted them with threats of abandoning them in the scrub or 'leaving them with the Abos'.

The rich have greater resources to ameliorate the pressures of everyday life: if the children are rowdy and intrusive, the middle-class man may depart to the club — even to spend the night. At home, the rich have dens of their own, or a large back garden, to the end of which they can send the children until the noise has died down or the youngsters have 'forgotten' they wanted dad to participate in their games. One of the problems may be that pressures on the higher income father to keep up with his peers means he carries such a large mortgage, the fees for the club cannot be paid. Or school fees for the children, who *must* 'go private', are an intolerable burden that prevents a man from spending *his* money as he wants. Thus the children, reason for his lack of control over spending, are natural targets. Why should he absent himself from his own home to the club to escape his children's gleeful shouting? If he's paying for their schooling, their clothing, their every wish, shouldn't they conform to his wishes, rather than his putting himself out for them?

That a large number of professional and managerial fathers are represented in the present study denies the theory that feelings of powerlessness and frustration solely underlie child abuse, or that these are experienced mainly by lower socio-economic strata men. Perhaps *powerfulness* lies at the bottom of child abuse. Our society applauds the exercise of power: witness the glorification of magnates regularly involved in takeover bids, amassing fortunes on the stock exchange, buying, selling and manipulating governments. On a smaller scale, see the reverence in which a teacher is held: 'Sir said I *can* do it'; 'Teacher said you don't concentrate in maths, Donald. Pay attention to him'; 'One hundred lines for chewing in class, boy'. Similarly, power is glorified in the parent–child relationship: parents have a *right* to tell *their* children what to do; father is head of household, and don't you forget it; as long as you're living here, you won't treat it like an hotel, Missy; while you are in *my* house, I make the rules, sonny Jim. As long as husbands and fathers are indoctrinated by a society telling them they are powerful on the home ground, they will put that perceived power into practice. While society dictates that the use of power is a good thing, glorifying whoever exercises it, fathers will continue to utilise power in the course of 'their' children's upbringing. Higher socio-economic strata fathers no less than lower socio-economic strata fathers internalise the dominant message: fathers are rulers in their households; he who rules is powerful.

Role Conditioning

If fathers hold the power, what of mothers who abuse their children? Are economic and occupational factors relevant? In the present study, there were seven reports of abuse by mothers, five written by the mothers themselves. In five of the seven cases, the mother was a full-time housewife at the time of the abuse. One was a housewife and part-time secretary and student; one worked full-time as a nurse, combined with household duties and care of the children. The seven were married to men in employment categories from skilled to professional, and income levels also varied: two classified themselves in the high income range; three classed income as average; two said income was low.

In two instances, the husband wrote of his wife's abuse. In both, she began abusing the children in early infancy, continuing over a period of some six years. One mother smacked the children hard with an open hand and banished them to the bedroom for long periods. Finally: 'Their mother left them when they were six years and three months respectively. She rejected them. She denied them the maternal care they needed.' The other had three children, one son and two daughters. One daughter was the sole victim of abuse, being hit with hand and stick, banished for long periods to the bedroom, stabbed with a table fork, and 'ridiculed because of occasions of nocturnal enuresis'.

With the other five abusive mothers, abuse began at birth or shortly after, and continued only during infancy. Violence was directly related to child care. The mothers who wrote of their own aggression remarked on forcing the child or children to eat and drink, 'possible psychological abuse through constant conflicts showing my hateful disposition towards Suzanne, screaming abuse at her', and placing the child outside when she refused to eat. Ellen Fitzjames-Simon commented: 'I would say I inflicted psychological damage on her. It was a continuing series of acts. I would *scream* at her to eat, stay clean, etc. At this time she wasn't even 3 years of age.'

In three cases, although the mother had other children, she abused one child only. Trisha Maine graphically explains a new mother's experience:

In 1973 I gave birth to my first child four weeks prematurely. He weighed only 2½ lb and was in a humidicrib for five weeks and in the hospital a further one week after that. He was planned and wanted.

When he finally came home I found it very difficult to cope with him when he cried and I bashed him. He was so small because of a condition known as placental insufficiency, but nobody could tell me how or why it happened to me. At birth, the doctor told me he didn't think he would live and the next day he was baptised in the humidicrib. My own doctor, who was on holiday when the baby was born, came to see me a few days later and as he was about to leave, just happened to mention that although the baby was holding his own, we wouldn't know about brain damage or mental retardation for some time! The hospital staff were fairly insensitive about the situation. (After I went home from the hospital and then came to visit the baby, one young nurse shouted to me: 'We've all had a nurse of the baby and you haven't.') I was well drugged in hospital but sent home for five weeks with nothing. There was no counselling. Before picking the baby up from hospital I had my six weeks check up with my doctor and I went with loads of questions about the whole situation. The doctor was extremely hostile, didn't give me any information and to my query about what would happen if I wanted another child and the same thing was happening, he replied, 'What would you want us to do, kill it off inside you?' He shouted at me to stop being so pessimistic then grabbed me by the shoulders and pushed me out of his surgery. This doctor is now employed by the Department of Infant and Maternal Welfare, where he advises parents who are having difficulties!

A couple of months after he came out of hospital we moved to a country town for a few months. I knew nobody there and my husband worked long hours. I was still in an extremely agitated state over the baby's size: I tried to make him eat a lot to catch up and the more I tried, the more he baulked at eating, then I would fly into a rage and end up hurting him. I smacked him a lot, a couple of times I bit him, a couple of times I bruised him.

With my husband I went to a new G.P. who referred me to a psychiatrist, who prescribed valium, and who told me I did it because I wasn't loved as a child and therefore couldn't give love to the baby. Thank goodness we then moved to South Australia and I was unable to attend the psychiatrist any more. In South Australia I made friends with many other women, who all had babies and I fell pregnant with my second child. I never once bashed her, and I didn't have any more trouble with the first one.

Since this time I believe hospitals have completely revised their handling of premature babies and their parents. I did report this to the Royal Commission on Human Relationships.

Both mothers and fathers gain a problem and a potential joy in a new baby. Our society encourages the view that every woman magically manifests caring and all-encompassing competence immediately upon giving birth. Fathers, if thought about, are supposed to 'fit in' with the new situation and, in this modern age, even to give a hand in baby care by changing the occasional nappy, rocking the crib at odd times. Yet an ability to care for children is not sex-linked and is not instinctive. The mother with a new baby may take months to relate to it: studies show many women feel unconnected to the child until the stage of smiling and responding is reached. Very young babies are sometimes seen as 'biological systems with orifices' by their parents, the first months often being almost entirely spent in serving these orifices, with little let up.[7]

Given current social structures and expectations, the mother's role initially has greater potential for difficulty than does the father's, at least with child abuse. First, society expects women to perform their functions as 'real mothers' with little training and little or no outside help. Mothercraft classes at school, pre-natal and post-natal classes at hospital, regular visits to an overworked baby-health clinic sister, with mothers and their newly born scheduled sausage-machine-style, are patently insufficient to assist mothers in learning about child care; they are inadequate for teaching fathers about child care — even where the father takes over the traditional female role.[8] Second, society has a distorted picture of women as mothers. Women are expected to assume every major responsibility for the care and upbringing of children, apart from the financial aspect, almost entirely without support. (And today even the financial aspect is fulfilled frequently by mothers.) Chris Sims, mother of two daughters, whom she neglected and abused from early infancy, saw the traditional mothering role as too great for any human being to handle without stress.

I used to lose my temper, shout and scream at them and generally abuse them with threats of spankings. Some times I spanked, too hard, then the screaming would start, I would scream back and the house would be in an uproar. Then I would shove them into their room and lock the door. I even went out sometimes to the shops, just leaving them screaming, locked in. I would be muttering under my breath 'Serve you little buggers right. Next time you wait, I'll throttle you.' I was half just saying it to calm myself and half the time I was scared I was serious.

Martin was no help whatsoever. He would come home late after working back at University and the kids would be in bed, after screaming their way through dinner and baths, but he missed it all. He couldn't understand what they were like when they were with me in the day when they had all the energy in the world. He only saw them asleep and could get all the pleasure out of seeing them clean, with cherubic faces in the cot. The whole time I was breast feeding, changing nappies, cleaning up, getting him breakfast and dinner, doing the housework and getting round like a zombie after being up all night feeding or worrying about teething and their crying keeping him awake at night; I think he might have changed enough nappies that you could count on the fingers of one hand. One hand!

The times I just wished I could walk out the door and forget. Leave the screaming and the nappies and the feeding behind and forget about it all. I was having problems with Martin, too, because he couldn't understand how tired I was and started on at me about sex, saying if I didn't want him I must be getting it from somewhere else. He couldn't understand I was too exhausted to even think about sex.

When women are fully involved in caring for young children, men are generally equally involved in clambering their way up the corporate ladder, expanding from a small business into a large one, venturing out from a position as electrician–employee to electrician–employer, writing that doctoral thesis, finishing off the book that will get that professorship, struggling to stay in the employment stakes without any skills. It is ironic that, in a society structured to direct women into the mothering role and men into the career role, at a time when both sexes in those clearly enunciated roles require the greatest support from their partner, each partner is fully engaged in looking after his or her own socially programmed destiny. If it were truly natural for women to play out the one role and men to play out the other, surely nature would have organised matters more efficiently: with women giving birth late in life, when men have finally reached the peak of the corporate ladder or its equivalent; or with men leaving their run for the top until all the child bearing is over and the kids well and truly capable of arranging their own lives.

What is evident from the lives of the seven women engaging in child abuse is that all were responsible for the children, with little help from their husbands. Only one had her own full-time income. The pre-marriage training and employment of the others did not enable them to take lucrative jobs to provide for the best child care available, or perhaps any child care at all. Two were secretaries before marriage, one a shop assistant, one an office clerk, and one a secretary and freelance journalist. Even with money, would child care be available? In late 1980 Adele Horin reported:

Finding someone to look after the children is the continuing crisis faced by all mothers who work. The child care situation in Australia is still grim. Only in 1972 was Federal Government money put into childcare, but this year funds have effectively been cut. Places are hard to find . . . One centre's director said . . . 'I already have 150 children on the waiting list. I'll give you a list of all the other centres in the municipality and suggest you see them . . .'

This year the Federal Government cut by 10 per cent real spending on child care services. No existing programs will be cut, but none will expand, and proposals for new child care services are unlikely to get approval this year . . . Waiting lists for care are long, especially in New South Wales. These are an inexact measure of need because people put their names on more than one list. But the picture emerges: most women have no choice about child care. They take anything they can get.[9]

Without adequate child care, a woman's opportunities are severely curtailed. She is housebound, a 24 hour a day carer of the children she and her husband agreed to have.[10] Even where she chooses not to enter the workforce, as with three of the five women respondents, this does not mean assistance, or equal sharing, in caring for the children is unwanted. Cheryl English abused her son from early infancy until he was 6 months old. She shook him, shouted at him, put a pillow over his head and shook the crib roughly. 'Sometimes all I wanted was to get away. John could always get away. He was always off on a job and wouldn't believe me when I said I was scared I would do something terrible to the baby. He said I was making a fuss about nothing.'

Not only can she not escape her role as full-time carer, a woman with small children is dependent: finance coming into the home is (often) supplied by the husband/father, or by the state, and society traditionally sees the money earner as the money owner. The five women writing of their child bashing commented on their financial dependence. 'I would try to talk to Martin about my need for something I could call my own', wrote Chris Sims:

He couldn't understand how I felt everything was his. I had contributed more than half the deposit of the house, but he seemed to forget that and I felt mean if I kept harping on it, or as if he didn't listen to me half the time. Because I couldn't get through to him how important it was to me to have some income I earned, I took it out on the children. I felt they were tying me down and making him disregard me as a person. He just thought of me as a burden, and it wasn't fair.

Each of the five also mentioned her isolation. There were two threads: isolation of physical location, the family home being away from cities, shops and social gathering places, and psychological isolation stemming from lack of interaction with adults.

Effects of Child Abuse

Australian studies show the effects of child abuse, ranging from death or permanent neurological damage including spasticity, paraplegia and blindness, to fear persisting through youth and old age, 'personality disorders' and lack of self-esteem.[11] Immediate effects in the present study included a boy with a broken nose, a girl with a broken leg, welts on legs and buttocks, bruising, scalding, aching limbs from twisted arms, malnutrition, black eyes. Apart from direct physical damage, children suffered psychologically. Depression, nervous tension, 'nerves', repression of feelings, hysteria, constant fear, confusion and hostility were mentioned. Children became 'withdrawn and nervy', 'depressed, grumpy and withdrawn', 'upset and frightened', 'withdrawn and antisocial'. Some children avoided making friends because the abuser frightened friends away, embarrassed the children, refused to allow the children to make friends, or refused to allow them out to visit. Sometimes children were afraid to make friends because the home situation would be discovered, something they wished fervently to avoid. Some respondents were 'given no chance to be a real child'. Bed wetting occurred in several cases, drawing more abuse. Several victims mentioned difficulties in concentrating at school and missing out on school work as injuries forced them to stay home. Frances Timms remarked on abuse meted out by her father, involving herself, a sister, and brother from early infancy until she was about 12 years old: 'The constant fighting took its toll at school. Our school work all suffered. My brother became very aggressive towards us and towards mum, too. We got withdrawn, particularly my youngest sister. She started bed wetting, too.'

Some victims suffered-long term physical effects. Kathy Peters and her four sisters and brothers 'all suffered except for the youngest. She is eighteen . . . Dad bashed us all the time for nothing. He kicked us in the back and threw knives at us. In the end he left mum so it stopped. But we all suffered malnutrition because we were neglected. I have had an infection from being bashed because the wounds didn't heal properly.'

Psychological problems continued for some after departure of the abusive parent. One mother wrote: 'My son is happier without all the psychological pressure from his father to achieve. But he seems to feel guilty and a bit of a failure because he couldn't live up to his father's expectations.' In other instances, children began to recover their equilibrium after the source of their terror departed. Of her sons Norman and Ivan, subjected to black moods, violent tempers, long silences, temper tantrums, invitations to outings later reneged on or taken up with bad grace, Doris Watkins commented: 'Now we've left the boys are beginning to recover their bearings. They are happy for the first time now we have left him. They were depressed and withdrawn when he was there, but are coming out of it as the days go by and we begin to make our way.' In some cases, although the ending of the violence was welcomed, negative aspects of a different type were mentioned. Diana French found that when her mother left the father who beat Diana and her brother, she felt guilty about her mother's financial situation:

The beatings didn't make me and my brother happy and we were glad when we got away from him, but mum had to struggle along on next to nothing. She used to laugh about it with us and say that the finances went from poverty to not enough, depending on whether any maintenance came through from dad, which was not often. It was good not to be hit and psychologically tortured, but it was deprivation of a different sort, and feeling guilty about mum having to go through it alone. We had to go without some things at school, too, like school excursions and sports uniforms.

Overall, three female respondents said the abuse during childhood had made them hate men; five trusted no-one; six had an increased fear of males. Twelve men and women thought back to the past with hatred and fear. Together with her two sisters and three brothers, Therese Sullivan endured beatings and bashings until the late teens and made numerous efforts to escape by running away. When she was 27, following the death of her father, she wrote: 'But what can anyone do now? I mean it was a long time ago when it happened. But my brothers and sisters have terrible chips on their shoulders and probably always will. One dear brother committed suicide. One wonders why, because he had a terrible hatred for his father. Many things I haven't time to write about, but one thing I can say is I will hate my father until the day I die.' Three women mentioned unhappy marriages, attributing them in part to an abusive childhood. One had a sister who had also been abused, but whose marriage was reasonably happy. Another said that despite her childhood, she was happily married, but her brother and sister, both also suffering abuse, were, respectively, constantly in trouble with the law, and scared of men and marriage. One woman thought the abuse had no effect on her. Beryl Harris, victim of being locked in the bedroom, hit with hand, stick, belt and electric cord until her mid teens, commented: 'I don't think it affected me, apart from an awareness of what can and does happen in the best of homes, behind closed doors.'

Cycle of Violence?

The United Kingdom Select Committee on Violence in the Family, reporting in 1975, said that there are 'at risk' groups with a potential for domestic violence. According to the Committee, 'those women who marry (and become pregnant) very young and after a short or non-existent courtship, are particularly at risk [of being battered] . . . and children living in an environment of domestic violence may be predisposed to violence in their own adult lives'.[12] Erin Pizzey expands the argument, contending child victims of abuse are the batterers of tomorrow:

You've only to watch the boys in the [refuge] to see that they are the next generation's potential batterers. Many of them are extremely violent by the age of three. By eleven they are potential criminals. Where ordinary children would have a tussle or just shout in annoyance, they fight to kill. It's just as the Jesuits said, 'Give us a boy until he is seven, and we will give you the man'.

Violence goes on from generation to generation. All the men who persistently batter come from homes where they watched violence or experienced it themselves. They saw their fathers beating their mothers or were themselves beaten as children. Violence is part of their normal behaviour. They learned, as all children do, from copying what they saw, and what they experienced.[13]

What is astonishing about statements like this is the paucity of evidence on which they are based. J. J. Gayford's study of a hundred battered women, constantly cited as backing the proposition that battered children in turn become the batterers, found that although some wife bashers were abused as children, many were over-indulged by their parents.[14] As Vivien Johnson points out, it is little wonder that children of mothers escaping battering husbands are noisy, rough and perceived as 'monsters of destruction':

In the initial fervour of our concern with the women [in refuges] and their needs, it was for a long time overlooked that more than half the refuge residents were children — except, that is, when they were being singled out as the main factor in producing the chaos of the physical environment. Child care at the refuges consisted originally in getting this noisy nuisance factor out of the way of the women and the workers. Treated as appendages to their mothers, their separate needs ignored just as their mothers' had been ignored in the family situation, it is hardly surprising that as an expression of the upheaval in their lives, in an attempt to attract adult attention, or out of sheer boredom, they often became violent and destructive.[15]

To explain child abuse and other forms of family violence, it is necessary to go beyond the simplistic notion that those who are beaten as children turn into adult bashers. In the present study, of respondents indicating whether the abuse had any effect upon their parental treatment of children, or on the way they hoped they would treat children when they bore them, only three said their victimisation made them believe that child abuse was 'pretty normal' or that aggression and violent acts against children were tolerable. In stark contrast to some psychological research on conditioning and experience, seventeen respondents said the violence made them realise how vulnerable children were, and how damaging child abuse could be. Ann Gregg eventually ran away from home, married four years later and began a family of her own.

After being beaten by Dad like that and putting up with tempers and a generally unsettled childhood I could never put our children through that. David and me have talked about children and discipline a lot and we agree not to hit the girls. We are treating them like people and don't believe anything gives anyone, parents included, a right to hit and yell at children. I could never use violence on anyone at any time except maybe in self defence, but especially not anyone younger and weaker.

Sometimes I think of Dad as a bully and a bossboy. Other times I think he was just a misguided type at the mercy of this competitive and basically violent world. I have never made contact with my parents (it's ten years ago now) and never want to see them again. Luckily David's parents are good to the girls so they have a granny and granddad.

Chris Denton recognised feelings of pent up anger and a potential for hurting others. Although her parents' abuse and ridicule affected her deeply emotionally, a desire to hurt others began to pass as she grew older.

As a teenager, spending my time at home after leaving school at 16, I was aware of feeling extremely angry when my dogs (I was showing pedigree dogs then and had several) didn't do what I wanted, exactly when I wanted it. I realised at the time I'd feel like that with children. (I feel uncomfortable with children anyway and was teased and ridiculed by other kids at school all my life. I was lucky to always have a few friends, sometimes neighbours who attended other schools.) It used to get so as I'd shut the dog away and not go near it until I felt better. I would have been quite capable of belting hell out of anything which annoyed me, anything which didn't have authority over my actions, and felt like I just wanted to murder whatever stood in the way. I find I feel differently now and much more loving towards people outside the family and all animals and growing things. I haven't yet been able to achieve love for my family. I am unable to cry in anyone's presence and find it almost impossible to show affection towards people.

I feel very uncomfortable when anyone touches me — if it's a warm, caring person I feel rigid, can't move or hardly breathe, and feel severe emotional pain. If they persist, I panic and can't stand it, feeling I've got to escape, and become extremely frightened. I have a great deal of difficulty coping with dependent feelings which I can't express to anyone.

I care very much about other people. It hurts me severely to see people feeling neglected, unhappy, alone, angry (and therefore hurting inside), and I always want to help. Sometimes other people don't notice how people feel and add to someone's unhappiness without even knowing and I find that very difficult to bear also. I am now 30 years of age.

With respondents who inflicted abuse on their children, one had been a victim of abuse in childhood. Cheryl English found emotional scars from her victimisation led to abusive treatment of her own child.

My sister cannot bear children but says the abuse hasn't affected her nerves. I will not stand for any abuse from my husband, but I abused my own child for six months, then had a nervous breakdown because of what I was doing. I think couples should be taught to bring their children up and not just expected to. After I bashed my child, it made me realise that children aren't there for me to take my anger out on. I don't want my child to think of me as I do of my father. As soon as I realised what was happening I got help.

Cheryl English was told by a psychiatrist, when she went for help, that she became a child basher because she was abused as a child. Trisha Maine's psychiatrist also attributed abuse of her prematurely born son to 'lack of love' in childhood, although her (more apposite) analysis of the situation was that the abuse came from her inability to cope, without guidance or assistance, with a child born weighing only two and a half pounds, with a placental deficiency.

The danger in clasping too readily the cycle of violence proposition is pinpointed by Sarah McCabe:

> We are much addicted to inventing risk groups in all sorts of context, but particularly in those areas where social control is thought to be appropriate. In the context of domestic violence it is particularly offensive to attempt such a categorisation since the evidence for it is minimal and all that is effected is the addition to the bitter consequences of assault of one more social disadvantage, this time the labelling of the victim's children.[16]

To this could be added the social disadvantage of labelling the child victim. Trisha Maine's concern revolved around this: 'The abuse left me with a lot of guilt feelings about the child involved. I worry that he will suffer some long lasting psychological effects even though he seems fine now. I also worry that he might abuse his own children should he decide to become a parent.' Rather than concentrating on child abuse as wrong because it might lead children to beat, batter and bash when they become adults, it is better to concentrate on child abuse as wrong in itself — because it hurts the victims directly, not because it might, according to some, hurt adults or children in the future. Rather than concentrating on identification of future batterers from the infinitesimal ranks of those who are identified as victims today, it would be more profitable to set about altering the structures and attitudes leading to child abuse and supporting its continuance, such as the institutionalisation of violence, not only in blatant battering and bashing as in physical combat, but also in its more subtle forms.

The Institutionalisation of Violence

The most disturbing feature of research directed at unravelling the causes of child abuse is its adherence to the comfortable idea that the use of aggression against children is isolated among the ranks of a few (mostly poor) families. But the evidence that child abuse occurs on a more basic level than previously recognised is undeniable. Any quick survey of mothers elicits the immediate response: 'I understand completely why mothers resort to hitting'; 'I am only lucky I did not become a child basher'; 'I have so often come near to beating my child'; 'I am only surprised it doesn't happen more often'. And if we acknowledge that the use of force in the guise of discipline qualifies also as abuse, we must also acknowledge child abuse as endemic in our society.

Current and past measures taken ostensibly to stop child abuse, or to highlight its existence, fail to encompass the political dimension. The mother who, when criticised for slapping *her* toddler at a busy shopping centre replies: 'But it's mine' expresses in the clearest terms the political nature of child–parent relationships. Our society is based on ownership not only of land, but also of powerless groups of people, most noticeably, ownership of all children by their parents, or by state institutions substituting for dead parents or those declared legally inadequate. The people in power do the owning — of the land, the corporations, the banks, and of oppressed peoples. In earlier times it was important for parents to own children. It gave some viability in a world needing workers: those owning no land, no crops, no sheep, owned children as potential workers. Today, ownership of children by their parents plays an important role in propping up a society in which concentration of high levels of real economic power in the hands of the few is obvious to most citizens. Although few inhabit the highest echelons of power, derived from ownership, many gain some satisfaction from owning their own group of powerless people, their children. Children are not so often needed to keep families above the breadline (although still, today, some families demand children leave school to supplement adult wages in the household), but the tradition of ownership continues despite this.

If we are truly serious about creating a world in which child abuse no longer exists, we must reject the materialistic approach to parenthood — the approach of 'this is *my* child'; 'these are *our* children'. In a materialistic world where the constant cry is one of bigger and better ownership, in a throwaway society where if it doesn't live up to expectations the solution is to chuck it away, it is no wonder that children are dispensable if they fail to live up to expectations, that they are abused if they fail to 'sit straight', 'pass exams properly', or if they 'make messes with food', 'wet the bed', and so on.

The rejection of the ownership approach to offspring must bring with it a recognition of autonomous rights for the child. A proper appraisal of children's rights has been avoided in the past, as being too difficult. Some no doubt recognise that granting children rights would so alter political and power relationships as to radically change present society. Society must recognise the right of a child to exercise some say in her or his fate. Children's refuges must be established so that child victims of abuse have a real alternative to remaining in a place where they are victims of that abuse, or placing themselves in an equally risky position in the world outside where they have no access to legitimate finance. Access to unemployment benefits for the young and the child's right to child endowment must be granted. Where children cannot, by reason of infancy, take full control of their lives, a child advocate system, with adequate funds and appropriate training, must be created to give young children a thoroughly equipped voice that acts in their interests, not in the interests of the adults seeking to control them.

If child abuse is to be ended, parenthood must involve women and men equally in child caring and child rearing. A woman expecting to develop her 'in-built' maternal desires will feel guilt and have difficulty in admitting that her 'instinct' is not all embracing, indeed is downright elusive. If a man is told that it is sissy to show emotion, that boys shouldn't have an interest in babies (it's unnatural ... they're only for girls ...); if a man believes that changing nappies is women's work, or occasional work only for men ('I *help my wife* change the nappies once in a while' ... 'I *babysat for my wife* last week'), no wonder men have difficulty in empathising with helplessness and dependency. If men and boys continue to be socialised into interacting aggressively and dominantly, they will continue to utilise this mode of conduct. It will remain difficult for them to gauge their own overwhelming strength in opposition to the vulnerable, who have fewer skills and less physical equipment. If men are involved regularly in child care, they will be better able to realise how much greater is their strength than that of a small child: no longer will they be able to brush off loud cries and tears with the words 'it was only a tap'. If men are socialised away from a position where domination and aggression are good, proper and masculine into one in which co-operation, caring, tenderness and affection are positive male characteristics, they will be less likely to use their physical strength and authority against those smaller than they.

When women and men are equally involved in child care and rearing, our approach to welfare funding will also change. A government comprised solely of men who have never had any real involvement with caring for children can easily ignore social needs, such as adequately funded, interesting, and caring child care centres. A government comprising women and men equally involved in rearing of children must realise with clarity the pressures placed on those caring for children, the pressures that lead to child abuse.

Child abuse can be solved only by rejecting philosophies that uphold the resort to force as a legitimate means of dealing with disputes and commend the manipulation of power against the powerless. As long as the powerful are applauded in their efforts at controlling the powerless, those who are powerful, however small the realm of their command, will continue to adhere to the philosophy that possession of power means one must exercise it against others. As long as we organise our world thus, many children will choose not to remember the truth of their childhood. When sufficiently brave to recall it, they will echo the words of Dana Richards, victim with one sister and three brothers of more than twenty years of bashing, threats, hitting with belt, strap, hand, electric cord: 'A human being can't go through years and years of violence and abuse without it having an effect. I felt despised and hated as a child. Now I feel bitter that my childhood was marred by such horrors. I won't forget.' How long before fathers, holding the power, acknowledge the extent of the abuse they meted out? How long before mothers recognise the oppression of children that lies in the smacking, the beating, the shaking? How long before fathers demand a revision of roles so that equity and altruism, not inequality and selfishness, determine their actions? How long before mothers rise up in anger at the superhuman task demanded of them in their sole responsibility for childhood development round the clock? How long before parents recognise the profound effect on children in their families, of the shouting, tempers and hitting simply because one has the 'right'?

Any mother runs the risk of having her children echo the thoughts of Jane Daniels: 'She hit me because she was angry at Dad for not helping, but why could I a child see that, but she couldn't see how it was hurting me, so we were both hurting, her and me, and I was angry at her, and sorry for Dad'. How long before mothers determine they will take control over their own lives, and cease making themselves vulnerable to an attack on their own children?

Any father guilty of exercising his 'authority' against the children in the family could be etched on their memories as Ruth Simpkins remembers her father: 'I could write a book on the rottenness because of him. Life for some children can be rotten. He died when I was sixteen. I am 60 years of age now and I've never wished him back and he didn't drink alcohol.' How long before fathers prefer to be recalled with humanity rather than with hatred?

CHAPTER 4   CHILD SEXUAL MOLESTATION

The taboo on incest in our society is so strong not because incest is 'unnatural' but because, given the structure of the family, it is only too natural. Things that are unlikely to occur do not need such powerful efforts at social prevention. Families are supposed to be close, warm, loving and physical. The parents are supposed to have sex with each other and not with anybody else — especially their children. The basic contradiction at the centre of the family is the concurrent social demand for closeness and prohibition on sex. Not only this, the family is the place where sex roles are learned, and in our society, males are supposed to be 'manly', aggressive and in control, whereas females are valued primarily if they are attractive and charming, and prepared to be willing pupils. . . . what researchers describe as the incestuous family, is in fact usually indistinguishable from the normal family, except perhaps that the sex roles of all its members have become somewhat exaggerated . . . the central problem is not incest, but power. Incest is an expression of power in many cases — the power of men to control women, and the power of adults to control children.

Carol O'Donnell and Jan Craney 'Incest and the Reproduction of the Patriarchal Family' in *Family Violence in Australia*, Longman Cheshire, Melbourne, 1982, p.155.

If child abuse by beating, bashing, emotional violence and neglect has continued with little acknowledgement of its existence or a reluctance to take positive steps to avoid it, sexual molestation of children by family members is even more ignored. Although on the one hand incest is reviled by society, with harsh laws remaining on statute books, on the other, society gives tacit approval to it by providing little support to victims. Many studies say victims are responsible for the activity: the little girl was precocious; she

66

led her father on. In legal treatises, comment is made of youthful victims of sexual interference by members of the family exhibiting 'an intensely erotic propensity . . . in wanton facial expression[s], . . . sensuous motions, and manner of speech'. Little girls may, the treatises preach, falsely accuse their fathers and conceal their lies by 'a madonna-like countenance that such a girl can readily assume; . . . [a] convincing upturn of the eye, with which she seeks to strengthen her credibility'. Little girls, the books continue, may fantasise about sexual activities with their fathers, leading them again to make false accusations: 'hysterical girls . . . living through fantastic sex dramas' are cited; so too is the 'erotic imagination of an abnormal child of attractive appearance [who] may send an innocent man to the penitentiary for life'.[1]

Where the truth of the stories is recognised and a father or other family members are acknowledged as sexually molesting a child of the family, authorities are reluctant to intervene. Social workers assume that breaking up the family by removing the aggressor is a false move: the family should be kept together and 'counselled' — after all, it is a 'family problem'. In many cases, rather than the sexually abusive adult being taken away, the child-victim is moved out and labelled as a troublesome problem disrupting family life. The community also prefers not to see untoward happenings in the family circle. Thus it is not surprising that in 1980 a survey of 30 000 Australian women concluded that 3 per cent of women at present over the age of 15 years had at some stage in their lives been sexually molested by a family member, yet each year there are only about thirty prosecutions for incest throughout the country.[2]

Incidence of Incest

Apart from the 1980 survey, few estimates of the incidence of incest involving minors have been made in Australia. From October 1974, when first established, until June 1978, the Sydney Rape Crisis Centre received nearly 1000 child sexual molestation calls. In July 1979 the Centre, in a week long phone-in on child sexual abuse had over 250 calls. Simultaneously, a questionnaire was circulated through the community, at women's health centres, women's community groups, and refuges. Over fifty completed questionnaires were received. After publicity about the results of the phone-in, child sexual molestation calls received daily rose to one-third of all contacts.[3] In September 1978, Western Australian Women Against Rape ran a phone-in: 50 per cent of 100 calls received related to incest against minors. In Adelaide, the Rape Crisis Centre received 312 reports of rape during 1979; 115 were of child rape. Biological fathers constituted 25 per cent of sexual abusers and a minority were strangers or acquaintances, 4 per cent in each category. For the majority, step-fathers, mother's 'boyfriends' or *de factos* molested them. Sexual abuse had continued over a number of years. Twenty-two victims were aged between 7 and 10 years when the abuse occurred.[4]

Some young women molested by family men run from home seeking shelter at women's refuges. Compiling information between 1976 and 1977, Naomi Women's Shelter in South Australia noted a large number of residents were aged around 14 and 15 years. The Shelter reported:

An alarming number had both mother and a father and had been sexually assaulted by the father. Some mothers defended them when they were younger, by taking them away, but later returned to the family home. We are seeing a lot of this with mother bringing her children to the Shelter because father sexually assaulted the 10 to 11 year old.[5]

In Tasmania, the Annie Kenney Refuge was established in 1976 to provide shelter for homeless young women. A large proportion of residents have run from sexually abusive fathers, step-fathers, uncles, and *de facto* fathers.

Difficulties in determining the incidence of sexual molestation against minors by a member of the family closely parallel those encountered in looking at child battering and abuse. Yet the problems are greater. Small children, particularly, may come to attention where they have been severely physically damaged by rape and attempted rape, or after contracting venereal disease. But in many cases sexual abuse is likely to leave less obvious signs than plain physical abuse. Emotional or psychological damage may be both immediate and long-term. As Ellen Longmore recounted, both are less detectable than physical violence:

I'm not sure I understand what you mean by 'psychological abuse' but I think you mean how I feel about things now I know the truth. I'm really scared of men — I know that all men aren't like him but I'm still scared. I used to think that all families were like ours but now I know they're not. I never, ever want to get married or sleep with anyone because I can't imagine it being different to what I already know and I couldn't stand to get married and find myself in the same situation.

Society's belief in the value of the family and its reluctance to intervene may be stronger where abuse is more easily concealed or more easily ignored. Attitudes toward sexual activity and sexuality may interfere with outside intervention where a father has sexually abused his daughter, or where a son has been sexually molested by father or mother. Attitudes commonly observed with victims of rape — the victim being held responsible for the rape and viewed as a pariah — also exist where the victim is related to the attacker. Such attitudes conspire to keep incestuous rape concealed. The victim is just as reluctant as a victim of stranger rape to make her plight known (or perhaps more so); by believing that the victim desired the activity and so needs no help, outsiders absolve themselves from responsibility for action. Estimates of incest are therefore bound to minimise the incidence of the crime.

Relationship and Background of Victim and Aggressor

Of the forty-seven families in the present study in which child sexual molestation occurred, twenty-eight concerned incidents between fathers and daughters. In four of these, the man also later molested his granddaughters. In three cases a grandfather interfered sexually with his granddaughters, but there was no evidence of his having sexually molested his own children. Seven cases involved step-fathers and step-daughters; one involved an adoptive father and daughter; another, a *de facto* husband of the victim's mother. Of the remainder, three incidents involved an uncle and his niece; one, an uncle committing acts on his nephew and niece; one, a man who sexually attacked his younger sister-in-law and his daughter. In one case, a mother sexually molested her son who, as an adult, continued the relationship, despite his marriage, and molested his own daughters. In one family, father-son incest occurred in conjunction with molestation of daughters.

The present study discounts earlier assertions that sexual relations between family members occur only in the lower socio-economic levels, or preponderate there. It confirms that activities cut across class lines and socio-economic standing. Of the total of forty-seven, seven aggressors were professionals, nine were managerial. Nine were in the small business category. In the skilled category there were twelve aggressors. Five were classed unskilled, whilst two father-aggressors were unemployed throughout, apart from occasional odd jobs requiring no skills. Two grandfather-aggressors were pensioners during the molestation. Where incest occurred between mother and son, son later molesting his daughters, the mother-aggressor was a full-time housewife and a widow; on adulthood her son became one of the fourteen aggressors in the skilled category. In the same category was the man molesting his sister-in-law and daughter.

Whether in one or another occupational category, the sexual molestation took no obviously different form. Laura Miller, daughter of an engineer holding a commission in the army, said his interference began when she was about nine years old and ended when she was about eleven. Her breasts and genitals were fondled and her father inserted his finger into her vagina on a number of occasions. He also forced her, with threats before and during the acts, to touch his genitals and later to rub his penis. He offered her kindness and appreciation in exchange, making general comments about future presents and outings. He threatened her about telling anyone, 'especially telling my mother', she wrote. Doreen Carter, whose father worked as a clerk, went into car sales, and became a manager and later director of a large retail firm, was similarly fondled and penetrated by her father's finger. This happened over three years from when she was a toddler until early school age. As for completion or attempts at intercourse, respondents reported variously on a butcher, unskilled labourer, public servant, business executive and unemployed worker in the family — usually the victim's father — raping or attempting to rape. Two public servants, a business executive, a grocer, restaurant owner, and an owner of a cement-mixing and bricklaying business each penetrated the victim's genitals with spoon-handles, pencils, or similar objects. There was no pattern to methods used by members of various occupational categories in gaining a victim's compliance: threats, abuse, promises, pleading were used without regard to socio-economic status.

In twenty-eight cases the victim was in the 11 to 13 age group when the sexual molestation began. The second most vulnerable age was 5 to 7 years, where twelve respondents were imposed on. Six victims were aged 2 to 3 years when sexual abuse began. For three respondents, sexual molestation began when they were about 9 years old.[6] Lynda Messer was 7 when her mother's *de facto* husband began abusing her. At 9 years the abuse ended, but recommenced when she was 15 years old. She wrote:

I have a story which happened in my own family. As a child (I am female) aged 7, my mother left my father with my younger sister, brother and myself to live with her *de facto* husband. He appeared wonderful at the beginning until approximately six months later he started trying sexual relations on me. He soon convinced me it was the right thing to do, but we shouldn't tell anyone. In this time he started belting all three children and my mother (also a bad drinker).

I'm not sure of the reason, but eventually I realised all these things were bad and finally got the courage to visit the police station. I was interviewed and after many hours was placed in a children's home (which all three of us children had previously been in one night when my mother and her *de facto* were put in jail for being drunk and disorderly in a public place).

The matter eventually went to court. He got off scot free. Apparently because my mother helped him by saying I made it all up. Then she had the choice of having me back but not while he was living there. She chose him.

I then went from children's homes to foster families and back and forth. I then went through the cyclone in Darwin, Xmas 1974.

My mother had not made any contact with me or anyone involved with me for over eight years. Then after the cyclone she decided to get motherly and sent telegrams left, right and centre trying to track me down. (I had moved to Perth with my foster family.) We finally made contact. She was living in Melbourne. Her letters were signed Mum and Dad. So I thought it would be nice to go back and see them. They paid my air fare across to them.

Well I got to Melbourne airport and when I saw her with him, her *de facto*, I wanted to turn right back to Perth, but they had seen me. The first few weeks were okay (I was now aged 15). I started school nearby determined to go right through school. Then started the drinking, the bashing, him trying to rape me and the sheer hell, I left school and home under the watchful eye of the children's services.

But my poor sister still stayed. She is treated like a slave, get this, get that. At age 5 she was severely bashed and raped by one of my mother's *de facto's* friends. She nearly died. She hates the *de facto* and I am scared he'll be trying sexual relations with her too but she can't get out. She just wants to leave school and get a job so she can leave.

Also my sister has been told he is her father and must call him dad (I have told her otherwise).

Although it would be no excuse, it has been argued that men who sexually molest their own children do so because they are young, relatively inexperienced in sexual matters, and unable to control their sexual urges. The evidence does not bear this out. The majority of men began molesting their children or other family members when in the mid thirties, continuing until the early forties, that is, in full adulthood. Nor can it be argued that the culprits are mostly men who have grown old, losing control of their ability to discriminate, due to the onset of senility: only three aggressors were in their late sixties when commencing the activity and in the early seventies when ceasing; four were in their early fifties, ending the activity in the mid fifties. Other aggressors covered a broad age range, from mid twenties to early fifties.

Extent of the Abuse

In structuring their phone-in on child sexual molestation, the Sydney Rape Crisis Centre classed a child as a person under 15 years. Acts qualifying as 'child rape' involved sexual abuse of any kind, running the entire range from full exposure of the aggressor's genitals to the child, masturbation, fondling genitals, to oral, anal and vaginal penetration. The Centre concluded that each of these acts should come within the ambit of child rape because victims assessed the acts in this way:

After we spoke to victims during the survey the women said they felt that they were being raped [during the incident]. They often said that they were not raped in the legal sense but that they felt what was happening to them as children amounted to rape. This is why we have decided that the term 'child sexual assault', which we had earlier used to describe the activity, or incest, which seems to imply consent on the part of both parties, do not give the real picture. The acts were felt by the women to be rape. Therefore we call those acts rape.[7]

In the present study abuse covered broadly those acts identified by the Rape Crisis Centre as child rape, as well as other acts in some cases. One man masturbated in front of his daughter, showed pornographic pictures to another, and raped a third. Twenty-eight fondled the victim's breasts outside her clothing; twenty-eight fondled breasts inside clothing. Thirty touched genitals outside clothing, and twenty-five touched genitals inside clothing. Three men held the victim's body close to their genital area; three kissed a victim's body all over; in six cases anus and buttocks were touched; one child had the tops of her legs constantly rubbed. Twenty were forced to touch the genitals of the aggressor; nineteen were forced to rub his penis. Twenty-six men inserted a finger into the victim's vagina. Eight inserted a finger into the victim's anus. Twelve men attempted sexual intercourse. Seven men managed penis-vaginal penetration but full intercourse did not take place. In five cases, full intercourse occurred, and in eight ejaculation occurred during intercourse. One male child was forced by his father to lie still during anal intercourse. Three children, two girls and a boy, were forced to perform fellatio. Seven girl victims were penetrated vaginally or anally by pencil, spoon-handle or unnamed objects. Several girls were forced to engage in other activities, including being ordered to walk around the house without clothes; being observed whilst showering; being threatened frequently by a father, step-father or mother's *de facto* that he would 'show them how' when they were older.

Sometimes more than one child was victim to a father's sexual aggression; all but one involved interference with daughters only. Of her family, where there were four daughters and two sons, three daughters being exploited by their natural father, Shirley Woodhouse wrote:

I have just gone through the Family Law Court having attained a Separation and Sole Custody Order on 6th May 1979. The Sole Custody wasn't contested by my husband with regard to my daughter, because he had previously sexually assaulted my eldest daughter, now 28 years old, when she was at the age of 6 years. Later at the ages of 12 and 14 years debased her sexually by making her expose her Modess pads to reveal that she was indeed menstruating. You might ask why all these facts were hidden in the light of what is to follow, but let me explain here and now that nothing was revealed to me until this girl was 23 years of age; terrified and mix up. Terrified of her father at whose hands she had experienced together with myself and other members of the family some violent assaults.

The second eldest daughter, now 26 years old, only saw her father masturbating in front of her. The third as far as can be ascertained wasn't touched that we know of, but said she was always aware of this with him and kept her distance. The eldest boy was often beaten badly and left home with a dislocated hip, body bruised black and blue and two black eyes. He is now 30 years, married with three children (an alcoholic and neurotic).

The youngest girl, now 13 years of age when I have Sole Custody, was shown pictures by her father of men's penises (12 years then) from — Magazine and worse and when she objected to looking or reading about them was told to get out. Where was I, you may well ask? On my way home from work on the other side of the city. It now appears from this little one that he attempted to touch her a couple of years ago when we were living in Darwin, and too afraid to tell me, she confided in her older sister, the one who hadn't been debased in any way then 16 years old, who said to her the younger one to keep away from her father and take no notice of him.

With Tom Dinslow, father of three sons and two daughters, the sexual abuse involved each of the children. Tom Dinslow attempted several times to rape the older daughter and in an isolated incident molested his younger daughter, attempted rape and failed, but penetrated the girl's vagina with his finger. The three sons, particularly the eldest, were exploited by anal intercourse and forced fellatio. For the eldest son, the acts occurred over about seven years.

For some victims, molestation began in a relatively mild way, progressing to more serious interference, but was interrupted before any attempts at sexual intercourse. Fran Jenkins and her sister Glenys initially had their clothed breasts fondled. Their father then proceeded to fondling their unclothed breasts, making them touch his penis and forcing them to comment upon his erection while he held them close. The acts occurred 'quite often' over seven months until Susan Jenkins discovered her husband's activities.

With some children, 'relatively mild' abuse continued over years. Monica Smart and her brother Donald were molested by an uncle living in an outhouse on their farm. 'It went on for years but happened only occasionally throughout that period', wrote Monica. 'He didn't go any further than touching our genitals. He kept coming in to say good night putting his hands under the bed clothes. Once he tried to put his finger into my genitals but I moved so he couldn't. I don't remember that happening again. It went on for about four years until he left the farm.'

With some, the acts were confined to touching genitals and attempts at intercourse only, because the victim was able to resist sufficiently to deter the aggressor. Often there were multiple female victims, some who fought off rape and others forced to submit, suggesting that the aggressor was prepared to attempt molesting any child available to him through the father-daughter relationship but, not prepared to over-exert himself, was satisfied with 'mild' molestation with the less vulnerable children and more serious activities with those less able to fight back. Carol Bunter commented: 'He started on me with touching my privates, but I wouldn't let him and fought back. He was touching my other sisters and I told them I wouldn't let him do it. A couple of times he said he would "put it into me" like he was doing to them. It never happened but not for want of trying. I held myself very stiffly. He tried about six times then he stopped and went back to them. I just wouldn't let him, but it wasn't easy.' Some who resisted fought over years to be let alone.

A Threat or a Promise?

A recurring theme in discussion of incest is that the child victim colludes in it, is precocious and provocative toward the aggressor, or that the breaking up of the relationship between child and adult would cause severe trauma to the child. It is said:

Many young girls are easily aroused sexually and eagerly seek further stimulation until someone sizes up the situation correctly and informs the authorities. There are frequent reports in the Press of the horror expressed by judges at the debauching of young and innocent girls in sex orgies with youths and older men. The men usually get the blame but, on the other hand, there are judges with a more realistic approach who describe the girls as 'jail bait' and the men as fools, rather than sinners.[8]

That incestuous relationships have in many cases continued for years, or at least have involved a continuing series of acts rather than a single attack, is often used to bolster the idea that the child was a willing, even an initiating, participant. Few acknowledge that even if a single act by an older family member towards a young girl might be classed 'foolish', a continuing pattern shows a more sinister design.

The 'luring abilities' of girl children are not borne out by the present study. Only four respondents were not forced by threats to submit. Even then, simple authority of the aggressor, lack of standing of the victim, and the child-parent relationship as a whole made it difficult for the child to disobey or demur. In five cases the aggressor 'did it without asking'. In half the cases in this survey there were threats on his part, frequently made before, during and after the sexual activity. Threats were of 'harm' or that the victim should tell no one. Other threats involved telling the child 'mummy would go away' or 'mummy will hate you' if she finds out. Four victims were threatened with being sent to a home if they told; one was threatened by her father that he would leave home if she did not comply. Multiple methods were often used: some were generally abused, being beaten, hit and kicked into submission; others had their hair pulled, were thrown against the wall, were shaken bodily, or were simply 'forced' to comply. Three were held down, one with a hand across her throat. One had her hands tied. Victims said the assailant resorted to 'shouting and yelling' to force compliance, or noted 'general aggression'; two were threatened with knives. One girl was shut in a cupboard for long periods after the sexual abuse; her father used this to persuade her not to tell anyone. Tansy Turner, threatened before, during and after her father sexually molested her, often was beaten with his fists:

My ordeal started when I was about 6 years of age (before that I cannot recall anything much) while living with my parents in Sydney and then, one brother two years older. I used to wake up sometimes when my father was touching me in private places on my body and if I made a sound was threatened with violence. During further years the same thing happened time and time again and if I cried I would be thrashed as I was too frightened to tell my mother. It seemed my father hated me and still does to this day.

Eight fathers told their daughters the acts were 'a part of life' or that he was 'teaching them the facts of life'. Ellen Longmore was 11 years old when her mother died, shortly after remarrying. She and her younger sister, Celia, remained in the custody of their step-father:

After my mother died he started doing stuff to me and he said it was alright and that it happens in everyone's family like that and it was just fathers teaching their daughters about life. I didn't like it but I just thought I had to.

It went on for ages and I guess that was my stupid fault for not questioning it earlier. I found out one day at school. We were having science and talking about babies and things, and the teacher was telling us things that could be wrong with babies and she said that people of the same family shouldn't have a baby and I just knew that what he said was wrong and that it didn't happen in everybody's family so I came to my English teacher and asked her and she said no it doesn't happen to everyone and yes, it was wrong. So I told him that I knew it's wrong, and I was going to tell if he did it again but he just laughed at me and said that if I tell anyone they won't believe me anyway, but I don't tell lies. And he said if they did believe me he would find out and then he'd get me with a knife and I reckon he would too. He kept doing it, but I kick and punch him and bite him when he does so he tied my hands together so I can't but I want to hurt him like he hurts me.

In some cases presents were offered; occasionally gifts were forthcoming, though mostly the offers were false. In four cases the man succeeded by 'wheedling and pleading'. Ivy Hudson's father used varying means to force compliance with his fondling of her breasts, genitals and buttocks, and to force her to touch his penis and rub it. He often offered her sweets; threatened her with smacking if she told her mother or grandmother; and often used the 'mummy likes this' or 'daddy likes it but mummy won't do it' approach. Sometimes he forced submission by telling her that 'when she was a big girl she would have to be able to do this' and like exhortations. Marion Smith's father changed his method mid-stream: 'The initial "excuse" for the acts was that it was to teach me "the facts of life". Then the acts were used as punishment against me for being cheeky or uncooperative at home in matters of housework. I was 14 when it began and 17 when it ended.'

Had victims solicited the activity, aggression or bribes would have been superfluous. The majority of adults used explicit force to gain submission, or threats of harm: hitting, belting, 'trouble', and in one case 'showing a knife and placing it against my throat with a warning to keep my mouth shut, leaving me in terror if in any way at all I might slip up and let something drop'. That aggression was used against the victims *to secure compliance in sexual activity* does not reduce the negative nature of the violence. But this is suggested in the belief that the child involved in a sexual relationship with a parent would be traumatised by the breaking up of the family. Our society cannot accept that physical child abuse warrants the keeping of records and reporting to authorities (thus acknowledging the negative effects of such abuse), yet recoil from intervention where that violence leads to sexual exploitation, believing that some how the child would be harshly affected by removal of the abuser and sexual molestor. A child living under these conditions could only be assisted by intervention.

Where adults did not use explicit force, they relied on the natural fear or awe a child has in the face of a person bigger, stronger, and in an authority position, or upon fear attached to specific issues, such as the loss of mother's love, loss of the aggressor's love, being institutionalised, 'mummy being jealous', general regard for the mother or for the abusive father. The need to rely on these factors refutes the assertion that the child was collusive, much less initiated the activity. Two respondents commented directly on this. Tansy Turner, abused by her father over seven years, being raped for the first time at about twelve and a half, after years of fondling and fingering, was sceptical of psychiatrists:

As for psychiatrists saying the children want an incestuous relationship, all I can say to that theory is it is a lot of bloody rubbish. They have never had to endure what I and many others had to suffer at the hands of these monsters we have to call father. No one would encourage such a relationship. Perhaps between brother and sister but never father and daughter. Even now at the age of 43 it is almost more than I can bear to think about, let alone write. Many times I throw up when I think about what happened during those years.

Where children were offered incentives such as sweets, presents, or promises of outings, it is wrong to suggest the child welcomed *sexual* activity, desired the activity, or initiated it. What the children desired were presents, sweets, outings. If the child wanted sexual activity to happen, or was precocious or deliberately 'led the father (or father surrogate) on', why would there be any need for promises of gifts, or threats and bashings? The child could hardly be classed a free and willing participant, or an initiator: the bribery and payoffs (or promises of payoffs) were all going in the wrong direction!

Motherly Collusion

In *Smith* v. *The Queen* the Tasmanian Court of Criminal Appeal on 6 March 1979 held that the trial court had rightly decided that

Smith, mother of the victim of rape, had colluded with her *de facto* husband to commit the crime on her daughter. The prosecution case was that Smith was guilty of rape, as abetting a man who had been her own lover, in raping her 14-year-old daughter while Smith lay in bed without any indication by word or sign that she disagreed with his doing the act, thus encouraging him. The man had previously displayed violence, often when he had been drinking. Man and woman were jointly tried. Smith appealed on grounds of misdirection and inadequacy of direction, particularly where the trial judge's summing up covered her alleged encouragement, intentional encouragement, and wilful encouragement. She also appealed against admission of the evidence of the victim and her 11-year-old sister of previous physical behaviour of the man and conversations with him. The court said the direction on encouragement was adequate; that inadmissible evidence of the 11-year-old sister had been admitted, but that there was no miscarriage of justice. Whether the common law defence of duress was still available where the crime was abetting rape and whether the woman qualified for a defence of compulsion by the *de facto* husband were raised by counsel for defence, but the court did not decide them because the facts would not have supported the defences.

This case would be quickly grasped by those who have little hesitation in concluding that the incest victim's mother is complicit, even encouraging, in the crime. In Australia, this analysis has been made:

Violence is rarely found to accompany the incestuous act, possibly because seduction, passive compliance, or sexual curiosity and exploration promote such relationships. At times it has been seen as a vengeful or competitive challenge to the other spouse by the adolescent. Generally, the onset of incestuous sexual relationships is said to frequently follow frustration in the marital sexual activity by illness, death, absence, or refusal and disgust by the spouse. Occasionally, the rejecting wife will offer the daughter as a compensation to her husband for her own promiscuity . . . By and large, . . . there frequently exists a disturbed and hostile wife, so that [the husband and father] seeks gratification elsewhere.[9]

Despite *Smith* v. *The Queen*, the Women Against Rape findings discount any overall suggestion that mothers collude in the activity, deliberately encourage it, or know about it but refuse to act. Even if some mothers, like Smith, do know of the coercion their daughters suffer, rather than glibly asserting that the women deliberately collude, or push their daughters into the situation because of their own inadequacies, analysts should look at the social, economic and political factors surrounding wife/mother roles and father/daughter, mother/daughter relationships.

During the Western Australian phone-in on child sexual molestation, calls came from elderly or middle-aged women who had only recently been told by their now grown-up daughters of the abusive acts they suffered during childhood. The mothers, who had known nothing of their husband's activities at the time, were distressed that their lack of knowledge had prevented them from helping their daughters when small. Some also suddenly recognised why bad relations existed between themselves and their daughters: although at the time a daughter had not told her mother of the exploitation and her mother had not discovered it, the daughter had felt that her mother *did* some how know what was happening or *should* know and do something about it. Because her mother did nothing, the daughter-victim felt betrayed and more alone.

In the present study, eleven respondents said they were sure their mothers had no inkling the activity was occurring, and they did not look to their mothers for help. Marion Smith wrote simply that she told no one: 'As far as I know mother was not aware of what was happening'. Some respondents had ambivalent attitudes. Pat Parker was abused for four years by her father until, at the age of 16, she ran away from home with a boyfriend. She did not tell her mother of the problem, thinking 'she was horrible too, like dad, and wouldn't of helped me anyhow. I'd say sometimes she knew.' Tansy Turner expressed similar attitudes, although in more detail. She was too frightened to talk to her mother of her father's attacks:

Several times when drunk my father came into my room and layed on top of me and I was so petrified although my mother came in a few times and got him away. There were no relatives to talk to and even if there were someone, I really didn't know what was happening at that age. Any friends I had didn't come around much because they would be made most unwelcome and so therefore I was almost a total wreck, and as my teens came closer the fear grew as I had learned a few facts from school friends. The last time he tried to molest me, I ran to a neighbour's home about half a mile away and collapsed with fear. Not long after that I managed to get away because my mother packed up and left him and I never went back again.

One child's mother died before the sexual abuse began and another's died shortly after it began, but before her daughter could seek her help. In four cases victims tried to tell their mothers, but were too scared to do so; had been diverted from doing so by the mother's embarrassment; or had sensed the mother did not wish to hear. Joan Ramsay's uncle fondled her breasts and genitals once only. She approached her mother and 'tried to tell her but I could tell she didn't want to hear about it so stopped. She really went blank and shut herself off.' Later, thinking about the incident, Joan Ramsay summed up:

I resent that it happened and that my mother didn't want to hear. Now when I think back I can see I suppose that she couldn't do anything. From her point of view in simple terms it was better not to hear about it. It was my father's brother and the whole world would have exploded if she told my father. I guess she was too embarrassed. But I am aware now that this sort of thing happens and wouldn't tolerate anyone doing that to my own daughter if I had one or to anyone.

Six respondents, as children, told their mothers, who did nothing. Some of the six believed the mother colluded in the activity, or at least did not want to help. Carol Bunter's father fondled her breasts and genitals, placed a finger in her vagina, and tried to insert his penis. She matured early, at 10 years, and woke up at night with her father interfering with her: 'I was too scared to do anything so I just took it. My mother was there. At times they took me into their bed — about six times just trying to talk to him to stop him. I shouted at her to help me. But she was scared of him too.'

Two victims said that on learning of the child's exploitation, the mother chose to remain with the aggressor and the child was dismissed from the household. When Lynda Messer's abuse came to attention of the authorities, her mother helped her husband to escape, by saying her daughter had 'made it all up'. Forced to choose between daughter and *de facto*, Lynda Messer's mother chose the *de facto*; Lynda was sent to an institution. Similarly Maureen Hamilton was sent away to a home: 'When my mother caught us she was furious at me as if it was my fault and not my step-father's and I got put away in a girl's home. I was at Parramatta for nearly five years until I got out. Then I got married and my husband kept beating me up after I told him about my step-father. My mother shouldn't have done that to me.'

In twelve cases the victim told her mother what was happening, or the mother discovered the activity, and she finally left the husband. In some instances leaving with the children to seek a divorce was immediate and directly related to the incest; in others she discussed the matter with the child, with the husband, or sometimes with outside confidants before departing with the children. Belinda Boggs's mother was shocked and startled when first told of the abuse by her two daughters, who were in their early teens when it began. She believed them and went to social welfare for counselling; they were no help. She left and sought a divorce. Marilyn Kennedy's mother said at first that her daughter was 'having a bad dream'. Later she helped and went to the police.

Some mothers described their own reactions on learning of a husband or *de facto* husband's sexual exploitation of the children. Rather than revealing a don't care or collusive attitude, they showed concern and difficulty arising out of initial disbelief. The disbelief in most cases was not directed at the child, but at the circumstances being described. Because it is not generally accepted that fathers or men *in loco parentis* should commence sexual activities with their daughters, it is not surprising that women are taken aback when the activity is clearly outlined to them, or when they come upon the man in the act. *Even where they have been exploited themselves, the realisation that their children are suffering the same fate is not immediate.* In remembering her childhood, Julie Ludgate, fondled in the breasts and genitals by her father, as well as being sexually penetrated by spoon-handles, pencils and her father's penis, said:

At the time I didn't know what to do. I had believed my father at first when he said that this was what all fathers did. I then realised something was wrong, especially because of the secrecy and I felt soiled and dirty. But I had nowhere to go. I tried to talk to my mother, but I think she thought I was talking about 'boys' generally, not about him. Our father was always overprotective and we didn't have outside friends, so didn't have anyone to go to for help.

Sometimes I think she knew and should have helped all of us to get away, because it was happening to my two sisters too, but now I know that as a mother I didn't realise he was doing the same thing to *my* daughters and my sister's daughters — and we didn't realise for a long time.

Mothers responding to the study were supportive toward their daughters. One was threatened and abused by her husband, who raped her often. It was the exploitation of her children, however, that prompted her to leave the matrimonial home, although she had been subdued into remaining by the brutality that had been directed at her, and inadequacy of funds: 'One night I came home from the shop and caught him trying to have sex with the eldest daughter, then 5 or 6. I got the children and left. He only laughed and said I would be too scared to tell anyone because he would kill me.' Beverley Martin felt disgusted and upset when she discovered her husband sexually molesting their 16-year-old daughter; the attacks had begun when the child was 12 and continued without her mother knowing. She could not believe it of an adult man and left immediately to gain a divorce.

Some victims wrote warmly of the support given them by their mothers. Sally Campbell's mother had been victimised by her own father. 'I told her', wrote Sally, who was 'very grateful for my mother's support ... I reject theories that say mothers condone or encourage the act. Also reject theories that say children encourage it. I *know* I didn't.' Others, although angry at their mothers for not being supportive, understood. Thus Tansy Turner said:

I tend to blame my mother and wonder why she couldn't of taken me away sooner than she did, she surely must of known. She and I have never been close — even now we don't communicate.

But like my mother, other mothers won't come forward because of reprisals from the husbands they mostly fear, but as well they don't want the neighbours to know and so they keep silent, but what a price to pay for silence and the supposedly good family name.

Reactions of Others

Some victims told their mothers, friends, or other family members years after the events. Many told no one. Generally, telling did not assist them much. Laura Miller told her sister, mother and husband, although 'not for many years'. She then discovered her sister had had a similar experience, despite Laura thinking that, by submitting to her army officer father, she was preventing her sister from being used in the same way. Her husband was disgusted with her father, 'but I don't think it affected his feelings', she wrote. When she and her sister talked with their mother, she went to a minister, also in the army and a friend of their father. He didn't believe the story. The army medical officer to whom their mother spoke suggested the exploits 'had something to do with the war — war wounds. It was easier for my mother to believe this.' Belinda Boggs's mother told a social worker, whose reaction was 'to rehabilitate the poor sick father'. Lola Brandon gained no help from her priest, who thought she 'led her father on'.

Linda Friend told her husband, who was 'livid':

Now I am suspicious of men, even if it happened years ago, and am lucky that my husband is caring and good to the children. He was wild when I told him about my father. He was livid. He says he can never speak to him civilly again. Sometimes I am glad we have sons, not daughters. If they were girls I could never let them visit Mum and Dad alone and would have to keep an eagle eye on them and on him. Also — however paranoid it is — I would sometimes even worry about my husband. As he was very angry that probably means my fears would not be justified.

The abuse she suffered not only blighted Linda Friend's childhood, but also affects her adult married life. When she told her mother, years afterwards, she went to the family priest. He 'backed her up about it being due to "stress" and working too hard'. If Linda Friend's father had worked harder, he might not have been free during the day, in the evenings, and on weekends to force himself on his daughter!

This would really be no solution, for whatever their hours of work, men seemed to find time to fit their incestuous activities into their schedules. As a pensioner, Tony Dempster's grandfather had time to molest his granddaughter. When she complained to her parents, they discovered that earlier, as a father with a full-time profession, he had molested his own daughter. The parents consulted a doctor 'after much doubt'. This was 'not much help', wrote Carol Dempster.

He only told us to accept the situation. He said it was a common occurrence, just don't leave her alone with him. He had a general acceptance that it's been going on for years Australia wide, and who were we to get upset. He had the attitude that we were over-reacting when we even mentioned in passing the possibility of court action. The doctor gave no acknowledgment that it was criminal in any way. His reaction was that we should warn the other parents of females (girls) in the family, which we did. That's when we learnt that he had abused his youngest daughter. I had never known this and if I had would have never left her alone with him. But my youngest sister's fright and guilt stopped her from saying anything. I feel there has been a massive coverup. We have never reacted outwardly to my father, so outwardly there is no change and he doesn't even know we have consulted a doctor. Now I am very unsure of whether we did the right thing. My daughter seems to have hate for him and the feeling that we should have exposed him. It has made her particularly angry with me, but we are able to talk about it like reasonable human beings. I do not think the doctor's advice was right, but it is some years ago now and too late to do anything.

In seeking help, mostly with reluctance, victims were rarely supported. If they were, mothers were the major source of support. Generally, outside agencies didn't want to know, or excused the incest on grounds that the exploiter was 'sick', 'overworked', 'stressed', or 'not himself'. Rarely was any responsibility placed on him. Often parents of victims were told they should be understanding of the exploiter's sexual needs. No one, apart from some mothers, confronted the man with what he had done. The aim was to smooth matters over and ignore victims' needs. The dominant ethic was that the 'problem' should not be shouted from the rooftops, that where some fathers or grandfathers exercised their ancient 'rights' of controlling their daughters' and granddaughters' sexuality by engaging in sexual activity with them, it should not be condemned. The approach harks back to ancient times when elders of the tribe had sexual rights over virgins.

Escaping Exploitation

Some respondents did not escape; some were too young. A few fought back, or stopped their fathers by fighting; one attacked with a bowie knife. Where abuse ceased, it mostly did so because, on discovery, the mother removed the victim and herself and sought a divorce. Carol Bunter 'stuck it out' until she left home at 19 and married. Susy Johnson ran away, was caught, and was institutionalised. Her elder sister ran away overnight several times, but she was always brought back. In two cases, abuse stopped because the man responsible — an uncle in each case — left the area. In five families, children went to other relatives overnight, for holidays, or for shorter or longer periods to keep out of the way. Linda Burrows spent her holidays with her grandparents, escaping for periods during the seven years her father spent fondling her breasts and genitals. At 13 she left home for boarding school and the abuse ceased. Linda Friend often got away to her grandmother to escape. She spent long periods after school at friends' homes, often terrified to go home, dreading being alone with her father. Margaret Hall eventually went to live permanently with her grandmother.

Apart from children sent to institutions as being 'in moral danger' or 'incorrigible' through running away from the abuser, only six victims commented on court action. Although the authorities were told of her father's attempted rapes of his three daughters, Susy Johnson wrote 'nothing was done'. Lynda Messer's father was prosecuted, after she approached the police, realising 'something was wrong'. But 'he got off scot free' because her mother took his part. Meg Barnes's mother complained to the Attorney-General's Department in an attempt to have a prosecution launched 'but nothing happened'. Court action was taken against Carmel Paine's step-father, but the probation officer writing a presentence report emphasised that the problem was Carmel's, not John Fisher's: her twin brother, Daniel, had been run down by a car and at 7 years of age, Carmel Paine had lost her main source of affection — that was the problem, not John Fisher's exploitation of a 9-year-old child. In only two cases was the offending father imprisoned. In both cases, the wife took action after discovering the offence. On the advice of friends, both went to the police and proceedings were begun, resulting in prison sentences of a maximum of six years. One man was released after serving four years of a six year sentence: he had admitted to raping his 5-year-old daughter at least three times over a period of months.

Effect of Sexual Exploitation

When analysing women, Sigmund Freud found that many complained of their father's sexual interference with them. Not caring to believe that respectable Viennese merchants, doctors and lawyers would indulge their sexual appetites by exploiting their own daughters, the convenient explanation for him was to create 'female hysteria' and the 'Electra complex'. According to Freud, his patients were not telling the truth; that was why they were his patients. They had strong sexual feelings for their fathers, and they indulged them by concocting false tales of sexual encounters. Their fathers were innocent. Thus Freud 'discovered' that severe trauma can be caused to women manufacturing fantasies of being raped or importuned by their fathers. In the twentieth century psychologists and psychiatrists have acknowledged that not all tales of incest are untrue: they say girls do engage in sexual activity with their fathers, but often as a result of their own desires. Far from being traumatic, they assert that this is a 'natural' part of growing up. Stopping the activity would cause trauma, by breaking up the relationship. There are thus two contradictory schools: on the one hand, incestuous behaviour is a figment of young girls' imaginations, causing severe trauma resulting in hysteria and other neuroses; on the other, incestuous behaviour is real, is caused by young girls' sexual desires, and causes no trauma at all, unless righteous busybodies swoop down to intrude, villifying the participants. A third approach is that incest is real, and exploitation by fathers severely affects girls' and women's emotions, esteem, and views of the world and of themselves.

This study bears out the last approach. No victim said the activity had a positive effect, although three women said that, despite the trauma of exploitation, they felt better able to cope with the world: it was necessary to 'suffer' in order to understand others, wrote Pauli Crampton. Marilyn Kennedy found 'in ways it's helped. I can pick the no gooders, the ones like my father. There's a lot of them. I have no time for them.' All other victims were in some way traumatised by the events. Three felt 'anger' at the world in general, or at men, or at their fathers, on a rotating basis. Five women hated their fathers or step-fathers for what they had done. Laura Miller said: 'It has definitely affected my outlook. Made me suspicious, cold, to my father and some other men — not affected my relationship with husband. Still makes me ill — same for my sister who can hardly speak to father.' Fortunately for Laura Miller, her father is frequently in a different state, owing to his army commission.

Two women suffered mental breakdowns as young women in their twenties. Although in her case the sexual interference was 'probably pretty trivial', Doreen Carter felt the real damage was 'the rage, guilt, hate and confusion I picked up from my father'. She went on:

I can see his expression as I write and it still frightens me. I don't know how the law fits that, but it should. Until two years ago it was all completely repressed, and was definitely affecting all relationships, particularly with men. Despite growing intellectual feminist convictions, I was trying to work out desperate needs to replace the confused and ambivalent 'daddy' in my head with every man I got close to, and this put far too heavy a load on them and on the relationship. I also had all the common female Western problems with expressing and acknowledging anger and hurt. At that time I had a massive breakdown (aged 28) (Easter 1979) and was amazingly lucky in finding five people who kept me alive, safe and out of hospital, one of whom is a gay man with whom I was able to get rid of my father without the usual complications of a sexual relationship. Future relationships with men — not easy, but at least the load of the past has been shed.

Some women commented upon their fears that their daughters would be similarly abused. Leslie Morrow married and bore three sons. When her daughter arrived, she left her husband:

Because of the way my father treated me I loathe anyone who abuses children. But it led me to the point of putting up with the same from my husband. When my daughter was born, I could see it happening all over again so I removed myself and the children *especially* Penelope before he had a chance to start on her.

Every respondent commented upon the effect her father's sexual exploitation had upon her relationships with men, and particularly on her marriage or her desire to marry. Twelve attributed their divorces, at least in part, to their childhood relations with their fathers. Tansy Turner married and had a family of her own, but the feeling of being dirty never left her. She could not feel worthy of any man; her childhood had greatly affected her self-esteem.

Mothers commented upon the effect incest had upon their daughters, some becoming 'precocious' or 'mad about boys', others becoming 'withdrawn'. Jan Smith's two daughters were afraid to leave her side after they escaped from Brisbane and Jan's *de facto* husband to Canberra. He had forced them to shower in front of him, fondled their breasts, buttocks and genitals, and promised to 'teach them a few things' when the oldest reached 14: 'Now they are scared to talk to men or have anything to do with social gatherings where males attend. I am trying to get them to see a counsellor but they won't even agree to talk to her about him.'

A number mentioned the pall incestuous activity had cast over a once seemingly happy relationship between grandparents and grandchildren. The grandfathers' exploitation of granddaughters 'upset the lovely times we had on holidays' with grandparents and damaged relationships with both grandfather and grandmother, said Tess Breton. 'We cannot let the children go there alone now.' Several women mentioned guilt they felt, although some recognised their fathers rather than themselves should be experiencing guilt and shame: 'It made us both despise our father', wrote Marilyn Kennedy, 'and we fear that good relationships with men are not possible . . . Although I am married, I still think about the past and feel guilty, although he was the one who had the power to force sexual activity and physically abused us both too.'

The evidence, then, runs directly counter to both Freud and to modern day analysts of sexual activity in the family. If no women who were subjected to sexual activity with a member of their family wrote of it with pride, joy, excitement or pleasure, but all commented upon their shame, guilt, mental breakdowns, lingering fears, doubts about their worth, desire not to marry, their horror at consigning a daughter to a like fate, it is hardly satisfactory for psychologists and others to cling to the view that women are not harmed by male sexual exploitation of them. The psychologists, being male and fathers themselves, or being women trained to the male standard, have much to lose if their own analysis is discredited. In asserting that women, as children, desire their fathers to engage in sexual activity with them, and that they are helped rather than hindered by it, the status quo is reinforced. This assists those members of society who hold power positions and retains their primary power base. In providing those men who do not have great power in the outside world with a microcosm wherein they are entitled to wield full power, and in maintaining that structure intact, those at the top of the public hierarchy are able to continue unchallenged. If men did not have their own family members to exploit, they might look outside at power structures that maintain them in a comparatively oppressed position, away from the real centres of power. This structure is primarily exploitative of women, and of their daughters. But in enabling female exploitation to take place on the home ground, political structures are able to continue their exploitation of men and women in the public arena. In perpetuating the myth that women and girls are not harmed by their father's sexually exploitative acts, they promote bondage of woman and blind those men who have no exalted place in class structures to their own oppression.

Ending Incest

Ten respondents specifically touched upon the patriarchal family as the structure promoting incest. 'I feel absolute guilt and tension about my daughter's suffering', said Meg Barnes. 'I don't believe in the so-called ideal family anymore and think it is a system operating only in favour of men and totally against women and children.' Kerrie Senior was terrified at the time her uncle forced himself upon her and because he was her mother's brother, her mother failed to help:

I blocked it out of my mind for many years and have just come to terms with it again recently. It has contributed to my view of the patriarchal nuclear family. I am determined never to live in that situation again, but in an extended family or communal environment. It has affected my political/personal views on the family but not my sexual life or life in general (as far as I can tell).

It is ironic that the family structure places the husband/father in the power position, yet responsibility for incest is most frequently placed upon the least powerful in that structure, the children who are victims of incest, or upon the less powerful adult in the unit, the wife/mother. In placing responsibility for incest upon wives and mothers, analysts take contradictory approaches. Sometimes, they say, a husband is forced to seek sexual comfort with his daughters because his wife is so promiscuous she has no time for him — or because his wife is so cold, uncaring and sexually rejecting that he has no other choice. Apart from absolving men from any responsibility for their own sexuality and abuse of power, these conflicting approaches ignore women's sexuality, women's sexual rights, and the place of the wife/mother in society. Rather than looking at male sexuality and asking why it should be that a wife is turned off her husband, they cast blame on women and demand that in order to fulfil their appropriate role as wives, women should be ever ready and willing to participate in sexual activity with their husbands. Yet recent work on sexuality suggests that men are presently ill-equipped to satisfy women's sexual desires.[10] They demand their own sexual satisfaction as a 'right', ignoring any need to take into consideration women's sexual needs. They use sexual aggression as a means of asserting power and authority. Although they are free to participate sexually outside marriage, and many men do, they demand faithfulness of their wives. If men act in this way, it is no surprise that a number of women withdraw more and more from the marriage bed, feeling relieved if their husband's demands lessen. As this study shows, that relief is shattered when they learn that the husband's demands are lessened because they have taken into their beds their own daughters. Women did not thrust their daughters upon their husbands. The fallacy of the argument is even clearer where, despite engaging in sexual activity with his daughters, men continue to sexually harass their wives. Sandy Lomond was shocked when she discovered her husband interfering with their 10-year-old daughter Cathy. 'He was at me every night in bed and I thought he was getting his sexual satisfaction that way', she wrote. 'That made it all the more unbelievable when I found him with Cathy.'

Some analysts infer or state openly that women are to blame for incest by being away from home 'too much', indulging themselves in the world of paid work when they should be on the home ground. The inference is that women should remain at home to guard their daughters from their daughters' fathers. Enmeshed in the conservative argument for women to return to full-time household chores rather than engage in paid employment, it would be ironic to discover the rationale that if women are not at home 24 hours a day, husbands and fathers will be free to indulge their allegedly insatiable sexual appetites upon their own offspring. Women have a right to work for money, and in many cases they are forced by financial necessity to join the paid workforce. In the case of the two unemployed fathers in this study, the wives and mothers had an insurmountable problem: if they did not work for money, the family would be destroyed financially, and the children could well have been consigned to a welfare institution. When they worked for money, the unemployed husband/father had the freedom of the home and the hours between the end of school and the return of the woman to her family: during that time, he exploited their children. This meant the children ran the risk of institutionalisation through being 'in moral danger'.

The majority of mothers are not engaged in a cover up of their husband's sexual exploits. They know nothing of them or, if they have suspicions, hastily shy away from them. They do not shy away because they wish their daughters to be exploited, but rather because they are realists: they tacitly acknowledge their lack of power within the family unit and in the world outside. If a woman faces up to the sexual indignities to which her daughters are subjected, she will be forced to reassess her entire relationship with her husband — a man whom she married in the belief that he would love and protect her and any children they might have, not debase them all, or use them selfishly for his own private ends. She will be forced to leave her husband, in order to assist her children to escape from a self-indulgent, exploitative personality, and be obliged to go through court proceedings, at least at divorce court level, in order to sever the ties between the family. She has no assurance that the court will recognise fully any efforts she has put into the financial build-up of assets during the marriage. Although it is simple enough to talk of leaving and to demand that a woman do so when she discovers her husband is involved in incestuous activity with his daughters, the reality is that few women will be financially able to leave. Few will have a financially stable future to look forward to, not only for themselves, but also for the children they seek to liberate from a coercive household.

For those women who, rather than turning out their husbands or themselves removing from the family home, turn out their sexually abused daughters, the explanation that 'women are women's worst enemies' is hardly satisfactory. In the present study, the two women who tossed out their daughters by having them committed to institutions, were living with *de facto* or second husbands. Perhaps already having had one husband depart from the matrimonial home with another woman, leaving these wives without a male partner, may create the fear that the *de facto* will set up a permanent liaison with the daughter and toss out his *de facto* wife. Women as a whole have been socialised in a world in which women are admired for their youth, not their maturity; where older women are thrown on the scrap heap at a younger and younger age; where older men become more rather than less attractive; and where men are permitted to set up with women twenty or thirty years their junior without social condemnation. Rather, this positively reinforces a man's desirability, and his opinion of his sexual prowess, always important to him, flourishes. Women have also been conditioned to accept a dependency role: following their release from financial dependence upon a father, their major financial assistance should come from a man/husband/*de facto* husband. Women are not taught that financial independence is a worthy goal to be reached by one's own efforts in the paid workforce, and even if women are taught to see their own income as desirable, men invariably earn more. Women are indoctrinated with the idea that a male income, to which they are attached by marriage or *de facto* marriage (despite their having no control over it in reality), is far more valuable than their own income, gained in an independent, paid job. They are taught to be competitive with other women — even if those other women are their daughters — and to compete for the man. It is no wonder that some women, faced with their husband's sexual exploits taking place within their own homes, with their own daughters, feel sorely threatened, not by the abusiveness of the men they have married or set up with, but by their relatively helpless daughters.

For daughters, it is easier to turn upon mum than upon dad, although it is dad, not mum, who is doing the exploiting. Where daughters express anger at their mother's inability to help, or suggest that, although she acted as if she did not know of the activity, 'really' she did, they too reveal the strength of socialisation women suffer in a patriarchal world, and the way in which the patriarchy is designed to turn women against each other rather than direct their attention at their true oppressors. A daughter may feel angry at her mother for doing nothing. That anger would be better directed at her father *for doing something*. But a daughter, being female, senses the truth of her situation: she is powerless to stop her father indulging his head-of-household role. This is translated into an unrealistic demand: that her mother, who is almost as powerless as she, should stop her husband from indulging his head-of-household role. This is the supreme example of patriarchal fascism. Rather than turning upon the oppressors, young women turn upon older women, beginning their lives by feeling betrayed, not by their fathers, but by their mothers. Because they see their mothers either as helpless or as selling them out, the irony is that they are forced to see males as their only hope of salvation. Effectively, the patriarchal vision of the perfect mother who protects her children from all evil, being entirely unrealistic, makes young women demand help from their mothers. When their mothers fail to live up to the patriarchal ideal and cannot give that protection, daughters may despise them.

For some young women, victims of their father's sexual exploitation, anger and despair are directed towards their mothers, who signify for them their own inability to escape from a powerless position. As daughters, they are powerless against their father's strength, authority, position; their future they see written in their mother's eyes — continuing powerlessness through adult womanhood into old age. Although some young women begin to understand the role played by the real oppressor, others never overcome their antagonism towards their mothers.

I hate my mother even now. It spoiled my chances of a marriage without fear. My husband and I are basically happy. But I told my husband what my father did, and he is probably more upset about it than I am. We rarely see my parents because of it. Jack sometimes gets very angry about my father's treatment of me. It took me a long time to adjust to sexual relations in marriage. I used to lie worrying about why my mother never helped me. Now I still have nightmares about the sex with my father sometimes. Other times I am going along quite happy then it all comes back. That can happen any time, on the street or having tea with a friend, or at a party and sometimes in bed at night.

For other women, being victimised sexually in their own homes has given them a political view of the nuclear family and its role in perpetuating the subordination of women. Family men who put their patriarchal rights into practice often, unwittingly, give impetus to their daughters' total rejection of masculine domination. As Ruth Simpkins, just turned 13 when molested by her father, found:

If that hadn't happened, I might be a good little wife sitting in a suburban matchbox with three kids by now. As it is, I despise the nuclear family and am working actively to eliminate it. That family structure meant I had a father in a position to interfere with me at his choosing. For every family that exists, there is a father living in that position with his daughter. I am working to stop any woman ever being in that position with any man.

Although their childhood experiences have a profound effect upon them, some victims of sexual molestation by their fathers manage to maintain their humour, however. Ruth Simpkins concluded: 'It didn't put me off sex, though, just off men!'

CHAPTER 5   SPOUSE ASSAULT

The effect of the house upon women is as important as might be expected of one continuous environment upon any living creature. The house varies with the varying power and preference of the owner; but to a house of some sort the woman has been confined for a period as long as history. This confinement is not to be considered as an arbitrary imprisonment under personal cruelty, but as a position demanded by public opinion, sanctioned by religion, and enforced by law.

. . . the human mother has been for endless centuries a possession of the father. In his pride and joy of possession, and in his fear lest some other man annex his treasure, he has boxed up his women as he did his jewels, and any attempt at personal freedom on their part he considered a revolt from marital allegiance . . .

The extent and depth of this feeling is well shown by a mass of popular proverbs, often quoted in this connection, such as 'A woman should leave her house three times — when she is christened, when she is married, and when she is buried' (even then she only leaves it to go to church), or again, 'The woman, the cat, and the chimney should never leave the house.'

Charlotte Perkins Gilman The Home — Its Work and Influence,
McClure Phillips & Co., U.S.A., 1903, pp.207–9.

Society is faced with two diametrically opposed pictures of marriage. The one comprises ideal man, ideal woman, perennial roses, smiles, blessed matrimony, wedded souls, bliss, made-in-heaven, happily-ever-after. The other is painted dark: stormy rows, long brooding silences, violent tempers, bashing, lashing, wounding, broken bones, and endless years of hell. To explain away the contradiction between the two, analyses of domestic violence have leant toward the belief that spouse assault is caused not by the institution of marriage, but by personal failings of one or other or both parties to the marriage. The cause is personal inadequacy of the wife or husband; it is psychological failing of victim or aggressor. Wives 'provoke' husbands into beating them; some women are 'predisposed' to being beaten: they deliberately set out to marry an abuser and, when they do, delight in the beatings. The cause of domestic violence is sometimes seen as external: alcohol, drugs, unemployment, poverty; it may relate to position in the socio-economic hierarchy or ethnic background. In a new twist on the 'blame the victim' syndrome, the 'cycle of violence' thesis is thrust to the fore: victims of domestic abuse in childhood become spouse beaters of the future. How far are these 'causes' related to reality?

Incidence of Spouse Assault

Although no overall assessment of wife abuse in Australia has been made, a random sample study in Canberra in 1979 estimated that about 15 per cent of married women — 6679 of 44 523 — living in the Australian Capital Territory at that time had suffered physical abuse from their husbands. This count excluded divorced women abused by former spouses and women in violent *de facto* relationships.[1] Thousands of women every year run from violence to women's refuges. From the early 1970s the refuge movement has burgeoned, and although the number of refuges has risen from twenty-five in 1975 to almost a hundred in 1982, women and children continue to be turned away owing to lack of space. Despite assisting thousands of women, the refuge movement serves only the minority. Some women seek help from other sources; others seek no outside help but eventually extricate themselves from violent marriages. Some women remain in abusive relationships. Most of the women accommodated in refuges in Australia have lived with unskilled workers and in rented homes. Victims of violence living in their own homes in middle income suburban areas and married to skilled or white collar workers rarely appear in refuge counts. Whatever the estimate based on refuge counts is, therefore, it minimises the extent of violence in Australian homes.

Male victims of marital violence are rarely noted, except where the violence results in death. A review of available statistics from the

United States and Canada concluded 'husband-beating constitutes a sizeable proportion of marital violence'.[2] A study of divorce actions in the United States found that over 3 per cent of 600 husbands in mandatory conciliation interviews said physical abuse by the wife led to the action: almost 37 per cent of wives said physical abuse by the husband was the reason.[3] Steinmetz's estimate of police records and a random sample of families found 7 per cent of wives and 6 per cent of husbands were victims of severe physical spouse abuse. In Gelles's 1974 study, 47 per cent of husbands used physical violence on their wives; 33 per cent of wives used physical violence on their husbands.[4] That research, like the present study, thus supports the view that wives more often than husbands are victims of abuse. Nonetheless that other side exists, which may show husbands as victims along lines similar to wife-victims; it may reveal retaliation by victims against husbands who are abusing them; it may uncover mutual abuse in some families; or it may support each diagnosis.

Extent of the Violence

Victims of domestic violence suffer both physical and psychological abuse, of varying intensity. In 1974 a New South Wales study showed a majority of attacks were perpetrated by punching, pulling hair, slapping, kicking, twisting arms, and throwing against walls and furniture. More than 75 per cent of 184 victims were punched repeatedly, mostly about the upper parts of the body and head. Punching in the eyes and mouth was usual. In 10 per cent of 177 cases weapons were used:

In most cases where the weapons were actually applied the attacker appeared to have seized the nearest available object in the heat of the moment. Household objects such as an ashtray, a hair-brush, a chair leg, a wooden stool, a saucepan, a shoe, a burning match, a garden hose, a leather dog leash and even the kitchen sink figured in assaults involving blunt instruments . . . One woman had a knife held to her throat and another was poked in the stomach with a chef's knife.[5]

The Royal Commission on Human Relationships reported similar patterns of injury to women contacting them during a phone-in: 'He'd knock me over, slap me, try to strangle me and his eyes would stand right out and he'd lay an open razor on the bed and threaten me and black my eyes.'[6]

Punching was the most popular form of abuse of the 119 female victims in the present study: 85 victims were punched, often in stomach, breasts and head, by a husband saying 'that way the marks won't show'. Slapping with an open hand and hitting with hands were next in frequency: seventy-four victims were slapped and sixty hit, fifty-five women were victims of kicking — in the shins, the stomach, buttocks; one was pushed to the ground and kicked in the face; another was kicked in the stomach and breasts after being flung to the floor. Jack Moss forced his wife Betty to scrub the kitchen and bathroom floors, kicking her while she was on hands and knees and shouting 'that's all you're good for'. Thirty-six respondents were threatened with gun or knife; one was threatened with an axe, another with an iron waved at her menacingly by her *de facto* husband; a third was threatened with broken bottles on numerous occasions. In only ten cases involving guns did the wife know the husband had a licence. Guns were sometimes war weapons a husband had kept. Thirty-six women were hit with an object, ranging from steel rule and hockey stick, through frying pan, chairs, small dustpan, chunks of wood, sticks, an ironing board, brooms, an electric cord, a belt and a strap, and cushions. Contrasting with the cartoon depiction of wife as wielding a rolling-pin to attack her errant husband, two female victims were attacked by husbands with rolling-pins, but no male victim was. One woman had the kitchen table up-ended on her when she was drinking a cup of coffee (the coffee spilled onto her lap, scalding her). Twenty-nine had various items thrown at them — including a garden fork, a spade, hammers, brooms, ashtrays, magazines, beer cans empty and full, cups of hot coffee, empty cups and plates, plates full of food, books, bottles both full and empty, a spanner, and glasses. Six women had drinks or food thrown over them. Dan Loftus frequently came home demanding dinner late at night, with threats of beatings if his wife Evelyn did not comply; when she had the dinner ready on his arrival home (when he came on time), he often threw the plate and food at her. Once when Sally Purvis was lying on floor after a beating, her husband Tony poured a can of beer all over her. When they were at the dinner table, Hans Meister was in the habit of throwing cups and plates at his wife June; he threw glasses when she was looking at television in the lounge room.

Susan Davey's husband Jack hit and punched her, often grabbing her head, banging it on the table and attempting to crush her skull because 'this will leave no bruises'. Others had their heads banged on tables, walls and wooden bed ends; some had their hair pulled. Some were intimidated by immobilisation, pushed up against tables or walls and held there, unable to move; or pushed into chairs and held, unable to rise. Another was fastened into a seat belt in the car, which her husband knew to be faulty. He looked on unmoving whilst she struggled to free herself. Margaret True's husband Tom stood over her so she couldn't move; if she did, she was punched or kicked.

Pushing took on several forms. Thirteen women were simply 'pushed'. Sixteen were shoved down stairs or down front steps to the house. Fifteen were pushed out of the car. Once Sally Purvis was shoved, together with her young baby, out of the car. Janet Coney wrote of her *de facto* husband Len:

One day we were driving along and Len started speeding and driving dangerously. When we stopped at the lights he kicked me with his heavy work boots. He kicked me out of the car and onto the road and threw my belongings after me, onto the footpath. I was screaming and crying but he didn't care. I got back into the car somehow, but he drove off leaving my things behind and wouldn't go back so I could pick them up. I lost some things I really cared about, besides the grazes and the sprained ankle.

Two women were chased, one by a husband wielding an axe. Cars also figured: there were threats of running down, or terrifying rides, the husband 'driving like a mad man' or 'driving furiously', threatening to run the family car off the road. Helen Trent said: 'Often he had me on the floor, bashing my head. He bashed me against the wall. Once he held a pillow over my head, I bit him, escaped from the house and hid under a bush. I watched him driving around and around and sat under a bush physically shaking, hoping he wouldn't find me.'

One woman's face was thrust into a hot plate of stew. One husband often burned his wife with cigarettes and the iron; another stuck to cigarettes only. Women were kicked out of bed, often late at night, with demands that dinner be cooked, the kitchen be cleaned, the laundry be done.

Simple threats of 'you wait' or 'look out for yourself' were frequent; others involved custody of the children, divorce, deprivation of various belongings. Two women were threatened with death; one feared she was being poisoned. Others remarked upon shouting, rages and abusive language; bursts of bad temper, bossiness and bullying. Faith McDonald's experience was typical.

Duncan suffered from temper and lack of control, lack of self discipline. The beatings took a permanent form on and off. There was shouting for long periods about nothing. Also door slamming — door kicking — architraves cracked around doors; holes in doors often. There was punching with his fists; kicking with shoes on; fingers bent back too far. He scratched my face with his finger nail from lip to chin — hands pressed against wall above head to prevent me being able to protect myself. Arm bruising. Often aggressively chased and sent flying across the room; threatened by holding chair above his head, but did not use it directly as a weapon. Sugar bowl thrown — smashed on wall beside me. Also large heavy alarm clock thrown while in bed. Caught my shoulder and could have broken my teeth. Arms bruised often. Hands pinned against wall above head and pressed there by his other hand to prevent me defending myself. 'A life of bruises.' The abuse made me feel hurt and depressed. Often told 'drop dead you useless flop of a thing', 'no one cares if you live or die' — I'm anti-social according to him, he's a people addict, women especially, so I am told 'get back in the human race'.

Thirty-nine women noted psychological abuse; four suffered it without accompanying physical violence. Husbands sometimes involved the children. Trudy Smart's husband accused her of immorality, deliberately calling the children in to hear the arguments. He then attacked her physically, making the children hysterical with fear. The immorality charges were untrue. Sam Kennedy's conduct was similar:

It is six months ago before I left my husband that my daughter saw him beat me on several occasions. To me this has left a scar on her. But what to do about it? . . . He used to come home drunk. Calling Susan (daughter) get up I am going to belt your mother, and get great satisfaction of seeing us both upset. What I am worried about now is that he lives in Western Australia and he is coming across at Xmas to see the children. But what effect this has on them also — there is nothing I can do about it and I have seen solicitors police etc. and personally think he is deranged. But he makes life very difficult for us by ringing up friends. He always did that and drove them all away. So the children and me end up with no friends. I am not one to talk about the hell I went through with him. Most people think you are lying but I assure you it is a real problem. Also no-one wants to help — when it really gets down to it my nerves aren't the best. After all I have been through.

Some husbands engaged in long brooding silences. Frieda Thomsen endured six months of moods, bad temper, lies about debts and money, periods of moroseness, long sulking sessions and a refusal to communicate. Ultimately *she* visited a doctor for depression! Some husbands flaunted their sexual activities. Joan Trevor's husband Thomas suddenly came home with another woman (after seventeen years of marriage), wanting her to move into the family home. She did. After three weeks Joan Trevor moved out and began making divorce arrangements. Jean Garton-Smith had a similar experience: 'How about adding to the psychological damage with this: my husband brought a young woman home from a party one night and, after putting me in the bedroom (a *thin* wall away) took her to the living room rug and made love to her. "It's okay", he said, "this doesn't count because it's *not on our bed*"!'

Wives were regularly charged with adulterous behaviour or wanting to commit adultery. Some were isolated in one room of the house, forbidden to move about other rooms. Husbands confined wives to the house with threats; they were allowed to shop only upon the husband's say-so. If women took longer than expected or went to the 'wrong' shops, husbands shouted, had temper tantrums, and sometimes beat them. Two women were frequently locked out. One climbed through a window to find her husband 'asleep' on the couch with safety chains in place on the doors: when he 'woke', his bland response was that he had 'overlooked' them.

Wives were constantly insulted, criticised for their housekeeping, isolated from friends, and not allowed to participate in sporting or social activities. One had to live up to stringently enforced notions of religion and morality. Others were criticised daily for lack of sexual ability or attractiveness (according to their husbands). Many were called names: one was called stupid, her friends were called stupid — and soon she had no friends. Eve Sharpe was told she was 'over the hill' and other women 'were better in bed'. Rick Sharpe kept saying she should 'do something' about herself, and 'making stupid jokes like "happiness is a tight fanny", as if mine wasn't'. Receipts for expensive gifts were left around the house, unconcealed, to be found when she cleaned. The gifts were never for her.

Of her seventeen married years, Dorothy Sands wrote:

[David] often slapped me and pushed me up against the wall in a threatening way. There were violent outbursts of rage and jealousy about friends, relatives, outings. He pushed me out of the house on many occasions. He was constantly accusing me of acts of adultery when this was completely untrue. He was jealous always and wouldn't let me have friends. Tried to stop relatives (particularly my parents) from visiting, made to stay at home, then charged with having relationships with neighbours, the milkboy, newsagent who called on rounds, postie — anyone and everyone.

Cheryl Davies's husband played at inviting her out, then not following through. She endured fourteen years of physical and psychological violence:

I put up with punching with his fists, hitting with his hands. Violent tempers. Moodiness. Invitations to functions then refusal to go and blaming me because I didn't look good enough, my hair wasn't right, etc. Dress was wrong, etc. (Never any money to get a better one. Never any gift of a new one.) Constant criticism of house, cleaning, etc. etc. Constant criticism of ironing — e.g. one day shirt not sufficiently pressed (in his view) so he screwed it up, then screwed up my clothes and threw them out the window, more tempers, moods, criticism than actual hitting and punching, but this happened more than enough.

Little research systematically recounts acts of violence against husbands. Frances Lovejoy and Emily Steel surveyed Australian marriage guidance counsellor reports. Of 282 cases, about 27 per cent involved wife beating; 4 per cent, husband beating. On counsellors' impressions of the violence, the researchers concluded:

Men were more likely to use violent techniques compatible with their strength and social conditioning, such as punching or hitting with the hands or a weapon. The women did such things as pouring boiling water from a kettle on the husband or tipping the contents of a frying pan, say (with hot fat), on him; such actions can cause quite severe injury and yet require little physical strength.[7]

Studying causes of separation and divorce in Australia, from a sample of 233 women and 102 men, Ailsa Burns noted 'only two clearly violent wives were described'. The violence used was not indicated.[8]

Of the eight husband victims in the present study, each recounted acts of violence in categories similar to some violence used against women victims. Half or more were slapped with an open hand or hit with hands; beaten with fists; kicked, scratched and bitten; had hair pulled; were hit with objects, including a frypan, saucepans, skillet, brooms, mugs, an ashtray and a squeegee mop. Three were threatened with a kitchen knife; two had crockery thrown at them; one was poked with a peeling knife. One was pushed down stairs and one had a pannikin of hot, soapy water from the washing-machine thrown over him.

No husband victim was punched about the head and shoulders, or in the stomach. Punches were aimed at the-chest. No husband was attacked in the groin. No wife directed punches so injuries would not show; nor did wives say this is what they would do. One husband was frequently attacked from behind: his wife may have been realistic about her lesser ability to damage, due to less physical strength, and a need to come upon her husband by stealth to have any effect. No husband was threatened with a gun or chased with guns, knives, axes, broken bottles, or by car. Husbands were not kicked or stamped on with steel-capped boots or heavy work boots; no husband was 'driven furiously' in the family car, nor was any tossed out at the traffic lights. None was pushed against a wall, or flung across the room; they were not held down in threatening positions, or against the wall unable to move. Strangling and choking were not used. No wife attempted suffocation with a pillow. Husbands were not locked out, confined to particular areas of the house, or isolated from friends, nor were any given ultimatums about time spent away from home shopping.

Although jokes about nagging wives abound, no husband reported psychological abuse. One husband commented on his wife's 'strident shouting'; none wrote of angry silences and brooding, of invitations extended then revoked, or of insulting language. Many beaten wives were criticised about clothing, lack of sex appeal, alleged infidelities, dirtiness of the house, lack of housekeeping abilities, bad ironing, their hair and general appearance, but only one husband made such a complaint: this related solely to aspersions his wife cast upon his build. No husband's capacity as breadwinner was criticised. No husband had arms twisted and fingers bent; none was frogmarched out to the garden to hose, dig or mow the lawn. None was ordered to weed the garden whilst being kicked from the rear. Nor was any husband dragged out of bed at midnight to change the washer on the kitchen tap.

Husband-victims' views of abuse were sometimes based on stereotypical expectations. Maurice Markham said his wife served up burnt dinners and threw shirts in a heap, then refused to wash them. He also cited his wife's refusal to stay at home full-time to take care of the house and children as abuse, although she had taken full responsibility for making child care and pre-school arrangements for their children, as well as taking care of them during the holidays while her husband chose to stay at the office. Ron Longman said his wife's 'confusion' at breakfast times was abuse:

It was upsetting to the children when Tania went off teaching and breakfasts were likely to end up in a brawl. She never thought ahead like making the kids' lunches the night before. She used to take it out on *me*, because *she* couldn't get away early those mornings. Sometimes I'd have to get coffee at the union out of a machine. I took to making it in my office ... It got that bad people sniggered behind my back about me making toast on campus.

Results of the Violence

Australian studies show large percentages of women receive hospital treatment following abuse by husbands, injuries ranging from severe bruising to concussion, fractured skulls, broken teeth, internal injuries and fractures of vertebrae, ribs, arms and nose.[9] In the present study injuries to women victims far exceeded in severity those of men victims. Eighty-four (70.5 per cent) of the one hundred and nineteen women suffered from bruises, as did six (75 per cent) of the eight men. Eighty-three (70 per cent) women and three (37.5 per cent) men had severe or 'very bad' bruises. Small numbers of women and men were scalded by hot water, soup or coffee; had cuts or lacerations; suffered abrasions. No men had broken bones following an attack, but several women did, ranging from broken ribs to a broken pelvis and fractured skull. Others suffered broken teeth, spinal injuries, nerve and eye damage from a smack in the face, and internal injuries; one was kicked repeatedly on a spot where she had had a cancer operation.

Only one man suffered psychological injuries: impotency resulted from Dan Summers's wife's attacks. Five women developed agoraphobia: they were unable to go to the shops or hang washing on the line, or both. Many were 'in fear' or 'terror'. One said 'it was like living on a volcano — but there was never any warning of an eruption'. Victims were constantly upset or suffered emotional problems, and lost self-esteem; some were simply 'unsettled'. One male victim said he suffered no damage, physical or psychological. (He was victim of an isolated attack of hitting and slapping, early in a marriage now in its twenty-second year.) No woman victim said she suffered no damage.

Occupation of the Attacker

Accepted wisdom has had it that marriages 'made in heaven' are the reward of the upper stata of society. Traditionally domestic violence is labelled 'a problem of the lower classes', defining the problem out of existence:

As social workers mostly deal with problem families they have come to accept that violence amongst their clients is the norm. They will produce arguments to prove that an uneducated man who beats his wife is showing an inarticulate form of love for her . . . Too many [social workers] accept that beatings are a part of life and urge women to put up with them.[10]

Today research discounts both the idea that the upper echelons are immune and that romantic ideals of the 'lower classes' are lived out with the parties locked in eternal combat.

In the present study of 127 spouse assault cases, wife-beaters in the professional/managerial and sales/skilled categories far out-numbered those in the unskilled category. Of 119 male aggressors, 26 were professional; 25 managerial; 49 were in sales, small business, clerical, trades and skilled categories; 17 were in the unskilled category and only 2 were unemployed throughout the period of violence.

Occupational status did not affect the type of assault. A medical practitioner's wife, Rose Randell spent twenty-nine years of marriage being roared at with rage, her husband tearing her clothes and throwing meals down the sink: 'One time he gave my eternity ring away to a woman with whom he was having an affair. I verbally attacked him about that — at least he could let me keep my dreams, however unrelated to reality they were. He became physical and struck me in a towering rage.'

Mary Holdsworth's husband qualified as an engineer and began his own business to rise to an entrepreneurial position. Violence continued throughout her married life. Her husband adopted the dual character of many wife-beaters: he was respected in the community and disguised with great facility their home lives of beating, battering and domination.

In my married life, twenty-eight years, I suffered repeated abuse, mostly verbal, but at times physical. Victor told me early in our marriage that his mother had always made life unhappy for his father and that no woman was going to do that for him. Then he proceeded to do it to me. My parents had had a very amiable and affectionate marriage and I was very unprepared for what happened . . .

To get to the point, it was not long before he would scream abuse to me and manhandle me for no apparent reason. Everything had to go his way. I would say he had a personality problem. He was very self conscious with no confidence in himself at all. I tried to boost him, without making too much of his problem, because that he did not appreciate. Soon after we were married he refused to have anyone come to the house and we did not visit either, he did not want anything to do with the neighbours. It wasn't long before we were living a very isolated existence. Apart from our parents we saw practically no one. (He did not like my parents either.) I told no one of his anger.

I hated what it might do to my little son but I was powerless to do anything and he would not listen. He was always demanding sex and I was abused if I didn't comply. We had a second son and then my husband started his own business. Things went from bad to worse then. I know it was difficult for him because he started on a shoestring, but life became unbearable for me. We had practically no income, his business then was engineering, working on his own.

He worked days and nights practically for years and we struggled along, financially. It was years before we had a reasonable income. There were beatings and threats and many more things I could mention of the story of our life together but it followed a pattern right through.

Things improved as my children grew older. Then I had companionship, I made friends of my own and finances improved, but my husband never gave me anything of value (without spoiling it by creating some unpleasantness) to show his appreciation of my contribution to our marriage.

I was threatened with divorce all my married life and then when there were children, that if I left him (I never once in my married life even said I would) he would spend every penny he had just to make sure I didn't get the children. When I finally left, I just left, and that was that.

I have little contact with him since then but each time there has been more abuse and threats. He has carried a loaded shotgun in his car and has told several people that he intends to shoot me. The police say there is nothing they can do.

The strange part is that he is now a big business man, a member of the Rotary Club and a J.P. and respected member of the area in which he lives. The outside man is a bit different from the one I lived with . . .

This is a really long letter and just scrapes the surface. I did not describe his rages which were frightening to see. He would froth at the mouth and his eyes looked maniacal, and afterwards the children and I would feel that it couldn't have been as bad as it seemed, then the next time we would realise that it was.

But not only professional or company men behave in this way. Married to a fitter and turner, Sylvia Palmer endured twenty-four years of abuse. Her husband engaged in protracted bouts of shouting and swearing. She was not allowed out of the house without his permission. There were numerous threats of killing and constantly insulting remarks, such as she was 'an ugly old bag worth nothing to no one'. Trevor Fisher, a self-employed painter-decorator, physically abused Margaret Fisher for twenty-one years until she left him. He accompanied physical attacks with verbal insults, threatening her with a gun and telling her 'a decent man should kick your bloody face in'; he frequently emulated his version of a 'decent man'. He seemed to want to destroy his wife physically and mentally, isolating her from friends she made and from her family. He seemed jealous of her. Fisher also had the facility exhibited by some others, of showing a very different side of his personality to the community at large. When Margaret Fisher approached the family doctor for help he was both inept and disbelieving, commenting in quick succession 'You must be able to get out of this situation' and 'He is a nice man at cricket'.

The small numbers of husband-beaters make it difficult to gener- alise, but it is significant that of the eight, six were in full-time paid employment. Although married women are moving into the paid workforce in greater numbers than previously, 75 per cent of all married women are not in full-time paid employment. None of the women was in the unskilled category; two were professional. Of the two homemakers, one administered her 'husband's' business interests full-time (when she eventually left him, she took a considerable part of the capital with her). One victim of violence attributed his wife's attacks to her occupation:

I was a husband victim. I am not stupid, and did not sit still and wait to be hit. If I saw anything coming I moved out of range. My wife would come up behind me and hit me over the head with stainless steel pans or similar heavy objects . . .

Strange as it may seem my wife's violence increased during times when she had outside interests, that is, a job or full-time training. Perhaps the pressure of a house to look after and a job was too much.

Husbands of full-time housewives attributed the aggression to 'spirit'. Dan Summers thought his wife Maureen would eventually stop slapping, hitting and punching him, as well as threatening him with the kitchen knife, and turn into 'the good wife and mother nature intended'. Andrew Travers, whose wife Christine was a full-time hairdresser as well as a housewife, also attributed the attacks to spiritedness.

My wife Christine was pretty firey. She attacked me with long fingernails and I was scratched everywhere. I told my mates it was the cat. I came home from work one day and she got me on the face, but luckily the scratches didn't last over the weekend. At night in bed she would kick me in the back and shove me out of bed. It wasn't a joke. She was deadly serious about it and diabolical at times.

No husband said his wife was a Jekyll and Hyde personality, able to deal with people outside the matrimonial home whilst concealing the enormity of what was happening within it. Indeed, in three cases where the husband resorted to the medical profession to solve the problem, psychiatric hospitals had no hesitation in classifying the attacking wife as suffering from a psychiatric problem requiring her long-term hospitalisation, a salutary warning to husband bashers.

Income of Attacker

Is income — not necessarily related to occupation — the key: domestic violence may be more likely in poverty-stricken households. Is perceived inadequacy of income a factor: the husband may have a 'good' job but violence could result from an insufficient income to keep afloat in circles aspired to. Michael Hotaling states:

> If in the presence of others, a wife expresses the desire for certain material goods that are beyond her means, a husband who is sensitive about his earning potential may feel threatened by such a statement. While her intent may have been to share her feelings about things she would like to have, the comment may be threatening to the husband because he knows that she knows that he is sensitive about such things, he is likely to feel, she would not have said it unless she meant to comment on his earning capacity. If a nonintimate had expressed the same desire for material goods, there would have been no reason for the husband to perceive such a statement as threatening to his self-identity.[11]

Domestic violence studies indicate that low or inadequate income is not a necessary factor in spouse assault.[12] In the present study, only two wife-beaters were permanently on unemployment benefits throughout the violence. One aggressor, an engineering student, was on a student allowance rating below the poverty line, although his family and hers contributed substantially with rental accommodation and household goods. Of the eighty-two respondents giving a yearly income for the years 1976, 1977, or 1978, none earned below $100 a week: the lowest annual income, applying in one case only, was $8000 ($154 per week); the next lowest was an income between $8000 and $9000. Twenty-nine respondents said income was between $9000 and $14 500; eighteen set it between $15 000 and $20 500; fifteen said between $21 000 and 30 500; eighteen were in the over $31 000 category, some of whom set income at over $80 000 or $90 000.

Despite seeming affluence or adequacy of income, did victims perceive it as insufficient, leading a husband to sense he was an inadequate provider, so 'causing' him to lash out violently? Only sixteen of the one hundred and twenty-seven respondents classed income as 'low' during the abuse. Thirty said income was 'average'; forty-two said it was 'above average'; thirty-nine said family income was 'very good'.

It is often assumed that wife beating is accompanied by profligacy, such as excessive drinking and gambling. Few respondents said income was frittered away on such pursuits. Only four respondents specifically noted that gambling, drinking and smoking depleted family assets, and they were all from different income groups.

Husband-beaters, S. K. Steinmetz suggests, who earn lower incomes than their husbands, may harbour desires for dominance, prompting them to resort to brutality.

Another man, who lived in terror for two years and did not know when his wife would attack him with knives and other objects, an almost daily occurrence, remained because as an orphan, he knew what it was like to be without a father. Also he considered his wife to be attractive, personable, a good housekeeper and mother and, except for her violent attacks, a good wife. *The wife, however, had low self-esteem, and was uncomfortable with her low position as a secretary, and with a paycheck which was smaller than her husband's. She wanted a career and to be the economically dominant partner.*[13]

The eight husband-beaters invariably earned less than their victims. Two wives had incomes approximately equal to the husband's. Greater discrepancies arose in the remaining cases: in two, the wife was a full-time housewife with no direct income. In the third case, a lawyer earning $35 000 annually was victim to a pre-school teacher earning $15 000; in the fourth the aggressor was a relief teacher earning $73.00 a day, her victim, an associate professor on $35 000. Finally Kingsley Samuel, company manager on $30 000 annually, was victim to his wife Carol, a student social worker with no income. Steinmetz's contention cannot on these figures be unquestioningly supported. Almost without exception any wife in paid employment earns less than her husband because of education and work discrimination.[14]

Discrimination on grounds of sex may be heightened for some women when, having married a person of similar background, intellect, training, qualifications and abilities, they see him forging ahead in the same or a similar discipline to one they originally chose. Women are discriminated against in the work world in terms of appointment, promotion, income, and other aspects. Not seeing the political dimension — that structures promoting sex-based discrimination should be fought against and destroyed — the wife may direct her disappointment, frustration and aggression against the husband who has the career. These feelings could be increased when she knows that she has promoted his progress, by looking after the children; coping with day to day running of the household; giving her own intellectual input, without charge or repayment, into *his* writings or business ventures; drawing up indexes of *his* books, or typing the manuscript or both. Yet why don't all women react against husbands, and why is wife beating more prevalent than husband beating? Is there a different explanation for husband beating from that appropriate to wife beating: husbands earn more than their wives; their careers are more advanced in conventional terms; they cannot be beating their wives through a desire to 'have a career and to be the economically dominant partner'.

In every case of husband beating, although six wives were in full-time paid employment or full-time studentship, all eight did housekeeping. No husband did housework. Rather, wives carried out two occupations: housewife and career position. Working two jobs whilst the other adult member of the household works only one could lead to resentment. Kingsley Samuel noted explicitly that his wife's violence 'increased during times when she had outside interests', such as in the paid workforce or as full-time student. Doubtless 'the pressure of a house to look after and a job' *was* too much. In every case the major or only violence occurred in the kitchen, dining room or laundry. Wives attacked husbands with cooking implements, or with brooms, mops, and similar ware, suggesting the wives' resentment at the irresponsibility of husbands in the household sphere.

An interview recorded by Yvonne Carnahan gives an insight into the dual role of women working in the home and in the paid work-force. Rather than supporting the view that the *woman* is necessarily precipitated into violence by her career orientation and 'desire for dominance', the husband may attack where his wife is engaged in work outside the home. Robert Chalmers, a wife-beater whose wife was in part-time work and whom he was 'trying to push' into full-time employment, said:

I'd be pushing her to do something, like I'd want her to go to work or be helping me in the garden, those sorts of things, niggle her and that'd cause an argument, or she'd be running around like a blue-arsed fly, cleaning things or chasing the kids, 'cause she's one of those terribly houseproud girls — that's why I think I'd be really stupid to push her into full-time work 'cause that's when an argument would start say in the morning and if she happens to get full-time work for a day at Myers say when they've got a sale and I'd still expect my breakfast and she'd say 'why don't you bloody help me' and I'd use some excuse like 'I've got to pick up John in five minutes, I'd better go now' (I know I'm guilty) and that'd start an argument. That'd be a real problem; roleplaying and who should do what . . .

I think if she went into full-time work it could be a real problem. That's why I'm really re-thinking whether I should be pushing her into full-time employment because ultimately I could be bringing about my own downfall, the relationship's downfall. Just talking with blokes at work whose marriages have broken up, it's been over things like one bloke his wife went into full-time work and became career-orientated and is a higher status than him and there were arguments like she'd want to go to a booze-up after work or a meeting after work and he'd say 'No, you're going to be home looking after the kid, I'm not a bloody babysitter' and that broke the marriage up because she said 'Like hell, you're as much responsible'. And I thought Christ, if I push my wife to that point she might start to enjoy the environment [at work], and it's a selfish attitude, I'd have to give more to make it work, and I'm starting to think would it be worth it? She could legitimately hold me over a barrel. But I'm a survivor, I wouldn't want to see our relationship go down the drain after all this time because I was too lazy to get off my arse and do the vacuum-cleaning, but it wouldn't mean I wouldn't fight the issue.[15]

Women in paid employment and working two jobs — one in the home, one outside, whilst their husbands work only one — may, as Chalmers thinks, be less likely to accept violence, less inclined to adopt a submissive pose, and sometimes more likely to use violence as a tactic or expression of inarticulate rage at a perceived and real injustice. In cases where the wife retaliated, she was in two roles. Margaret Fisher, clerk and later tax agent and affiliated accountant, earned $9000, equalling her husband's income. She was twice 'provoked into hitting back. He was sitting at the kitchen table while I was doing the dishes. He yelled at me for clattering, then pushed me up against the sink with my face in the hot water. I kicked him in the ankle and butted him away. I never thought I would be a violent person but everyone has their breaking point.' A plant operator, Peter Harris earned between $8000 and $9000, equal to his wife's earnings as a trained nurse. They were married for twelve years before Peter began beating Maxine. During the two years of continuing violence Maxine retaliated about four times.

On occasions I 'cracked' and slapped my husband's face . . . The second time we were at the dinner table. I'd come home tired from work, with a class following it. (I was studying for my second certificate.) He started on complaining about the dinner, the table cloth, the knives, the forks. He said the dinner wasn't hot enough, tasted foul and was too tough even for a goat to chew. He said that the cloth and cutlery weren't fit for a pig to eat off. I 'cracked' and hit his silly red face. He punched me in the stomach.

Unemployment of Attacker

The Royal Commission on Human Relationships listed unemployment among factors present in abusive marital situations:

Unemployment, poverty, inadequate housing, excessive drinking and job pressures are all factors which can lead to marital conflict. Although working class families are more vulnerable to such circumstances, middle class families are also susceptible . . . we have also to look to cultural factors. [It] has long been an accepted part of Australian society . . . that most males are expected to be breadwinners . . . [This] can lead to feelings of failure and frustration when a man loses his job. Someone who feels powerless to control his own life is likely to compensate by trying to control others close at hand, and violence is often the only way that is known.[16]

In the present inquiry, unemployment was relevant to only two throughout the violence. In Norma Collie's case, her husband Tom was perennially unemployed and, throughout the time they were living together, he meted out ferocious attacks upon her, made constant threats on her life, and chased her up the street with a tomahawk and broke down the door of a neighbour's home where she was sheltering. But he was frequently away from home. Unemployed, he was free to 'run around with other women and stay away from home. He would go and live with them and drop in once every few weeks.' He was not permanently underfoot, and only once every few weeks, later months, did he terrorise his wife. This counters the view that unemployment inevitably increases wife beating, as the husband is constantly in contact with his victim, who is unable to escape even for a short time. On the other hand, unemployment made it more difficult for Norma Collie when she left her husband.

He came after me and had a gun in a paper bag. I told him I didn't believe him and he pulled it out and told me he would shoot me where I stood if I didn't come home. I had nowhere to turn so I went with him. At that time I had two small children and had them with me so I would go with him till I got a good chance to go again. So about five years ago he went to jail again, but this time he got three and a half years. My chance to escape at last, so I did. All my children were happy and so was I. It was really great then.

On his release from jail, Tom Collie followed her once more. This occurred frequently during their twenty-three year marriage. Not tied to a job, Tom Collie had no restraints on his movements apart from times in prison. Although many other instances of dogged pursuit of wives by husbands occur, an unemployed husband may be harder to shake off than one having to turn up regularly at work. Lack of a substantial income did not hinder Tom Collie in tracking his wife, athough she went interstate several times to escape.

In sixteen cases the husband was unemployed at times during the marriage. No direct link showed between periods of unemployment and abuse. However, only four of the sixteen victims were full-time homemakers. When his wife regularly brought home the wages necessary to family upkeep, tiding them over periods of male unemployment, the husband's desire to dominate may have been increased.

Alcohol

Another traditional belief is that violence occurs 'only when he's drunk'. Two apparently contradictory premises absolve the aggressor from responsibility. The first is that husbands do not normally beat up their wives, resorting to violence only when their control has been so loosened by alcohol that they do not know what they are doing, or alcohol has so fired them to make them release aggressions in violence. The second premise is that because of womanly nagging, husbands are forced to resort to drink; getting drunk is the natural outcome of the relationship, and beating itself follows naturally.

A direct connection between alcohol and domestic violence is difficult to sustain. In Christine Gibbeson's study 'excessive drinking' was the 'main reason' women gave for their partner's violence. Yet the example given confirms it is lack of drink, not over-indulgence, that led to assault: 'I don't know why [he does it]. He just seems to get the shits with himself when he can't get enough to drink — when he's broke he'll take it out on me.'[17]

The initial issue is vital: does alcohol play a significant role in domestic violence? Of 127 cases, the respondents in 9 said assaults occurred only when the aggressor was drunk. Five of these were isolated instances. Four involved violence of a continuing nature. In those four, the respondent said the husband was 'an alcoholic'. For Marion McNair alcohol affected the entire family:

My husband turned violent when under the influence of alcohol. It is a sheer relief to tell someone after having bottled it up for years. Although I still feel guilty about it as my husband took to alcohol after contracting polio and losing the use of his right arm. This in my mind somehow gave him 'licence' to live a cycle of sober and drunken periods. For some reason this vicious circle was 'covered up', repressed and tolerated by my whole family. We lived in the country and my parents never gave me help and never mentioned it, but they must of known it was going on. By some miracle no 'murder' took place, although my husband over the years continually threatened to shoot me and my son was chased by my husband (with a knife) threatening to kill him. I yearned for a normal life without the fear and emotional 'starvation' alcohol brought. I never knew what to do to get out and no one ever talked about it or told me what to do. The kids got bashed too and we were all glad when he finally died. But we felt guilty about that too. The kids and me used to lie awake at night listening for him coming from the pub even after he was dead and we never had a good night's sleep until it was years afterwards. The kids still think about it sometimes but it is years ago now and they would never touch a drop of drink because of him.

In seventy-one cases the assaults occurred often when the aggressor had been drinking and often when he had not. Ethel Rampling's husband 'drank every day — he mostly attacked me when he was drunk but sometimes he wasn't and sometimes he was even more brutal when he wasn't drunk'. Leonore Connors endured eleven years of assaults, abuse and rape. She was always terrified of what would happen next: 'Most of the time he was drunk. Even when he wasn't drunk he was abusive. Once when he was stone cold sober he threatened to cut my throat with a knife if I went to the police.'

In forty-seven cases alcohol was not related to the violence. In fifteen of these, neither party drank alcohol. In the remainder, either one or both parties were social drinkers, but the violence occurred when the parties has not been drinking. Jackie Trencher's husband John drank in moderation, but whenever he assaulted her, he was sober. His assaults included hitting her with his hand, pulling her around by the hair, kicking to deliberately aggravate her haemorrhoids. Jackie Trencher separated from him to escape his violence. Sober, he came to visit her without warning. She was in her flat, he was in the stairwell. He pulled her leg by the foot, ramming her pelvis against the edge of the door. Although the pelvis was not broken, the lower half of her body was sore for six weeks after. Another victim, Marjorie Christensen, said, 'My ex-husband didn't drink, so one never knew what would trigger off a session of brutality'. Her husband's attacks continued for nineteen years. One of his favourite ways of terrorising was by flaunting firearms from his army days. He would wake her late at night and press a loaded service revolver at her head whilst demanding she confess to being unfaithful. She had nothing to confess. Later, when divorced under the old *Matrimonial Causes Act*, evidence was given of her husband's sexual relationships with twenty-one women during their marriage.

Do husbands conceal their drunkenness, as did Duncan McDonald? Faith McDonald did not discover her husband's drinking until after thirty years of marriage.

I discovered his secret drinking in 1975, but possibly it had been going on behind my back all through. He always had a bad temper, with no control or self-discipline. He often cleared out all night. I believed that often there was no drink involved, until discovery. Other people told me in 1975, and then I discovered all the bottles and where a lot of the money was going. I am a teetotaller. Never touch it.

Perhaps each respondent stating no drink was involved in the violence was the dupe of her husband, but how likely is that? Another explanation of the difference in results of this study and studies purporting to show a link might be that drunken behaviour is more likely to come to the attention of authorities: neighbours are more likely to inform police where they know drunkenness and violence are present in a neighbourhood dispute; police are more likely to intervene where a man is drunk. Women suffering drunkenness and beating are more likely to seek refuge, thus appearing in welfare and women's refuge statistics more often. It is less difficult for women to cover up violence in the home than it is to cover up alcoholism or drunkenness as well. Women suffering domestic abuse may be less motivated to reveal it to researchers than women carrying a double burden of drunkenness and abuse.

Where the aggressor was female, in five cases no drink was involved. In three, violence occurred with or without drink, and in one of these occurred more often when there was no alcohol. No husband suggested his wife was a closet drinker and that this led to the abuse.

Reanalysis of studies alleging a link between domestic violence and alcohol shows the relationship is meaningless. In a comprehensive review of the literature and a survey of agencies dealing with spouse assault in Canada, Joanna Downey and Jane Howell acknowledged that the extent and nature of the association between alcohol use and family violence varies widely amongst studies and agencies. What constitutes abuse of alcohol leading to abuse of a spouse?

Little distinction is made in the findings between pathological drinking (alcoholism) and episodic drinking associated with violence . . . [furthermore] some studies . . . indicate that drunkenness is not always followed by violent behaviour . . . Moreover it was found that in many families drunkenness may occur without precipitating violence, and violence may occur without any alcohol being consumed.[18]

The present study strongly confirms that conclusion.

Childhood Background

The 'cycle of violence' theory is fashionable: boys who see their mothers beaten at home will grow-up as wife-beaters; girls seeing their mothers beaten will be adult victims of domestic violence; children beaten and abused will emerge, in adulthood, as batterers and the battered. Some studies said to support the theory in fact show a large number of assailants not experiencing violence in childhood, and many having 'spoilt' childhoods.[19] Australian research queries 'the common assumption that a violent family background creates the setting for a woman's future violent relationship with men'.[20]

In the present study of the 119 beaten women, 47 were not abused in childhood; 37 said father or mother or both were 'strict discipli-narians', using hitting or belting or a combination of these when the child had 'done wrong'. Thirty-five had had abusive childhoods. For eight of them, abuse involved both physical violence and sexual abuse by a parent. (In every case the sexual molestor was the father; with physical abuse, sometimes the assailant was father, less often mother, sometimes both.) One of the thirty-five respondents suffered sexual abuse from her father without physical abuse. The broad range of comments from respondents reveals nothing special about their backgrounds. Rather, responses like this were commonplace: Olive Smith, who was severely attacked over twenty-five years and made numerous attempts to escape the marital home, said: 'My parents were kind and loving. I don't remember being unhappy as a child.'

Sondra Lemmert was abused by her father, both sexually and physically, in isolated instances throughout her infancy and youth. She 'thought abuse was pretty normal and put up with it' when her husband followed her father. Janet Cantor's background fits the traditional sociologist's view, but hers was only one of many varied accounts of childhood abuse, lack of abuse, or strict discipline:

Mum and Dad both thrashed my sister and me but not my brother who was the pet. He could do anything he liked. My Mum was always saying 'wait until Dad comes home and you'll get a belting'. She belted us anyway for doing nothing and was always saying we'd come to a bad end with boys so we both got pregnant and got thrown out. My sister and me stuck together always and said we'd never forgive Mum and Dad. We hated them both.

Six respondents — covering the range of abused, not abused, and subject to strict discipline — volunteered that there was no relationship between childhood and the violence experience in marriage. One said: 'Dad used to shout at us all and hit and get real violent sometimes. Did it have any effect on me later on? I don't think so. I never used to notice him and his tempers, really.' Ten remarked on seeing their mother severely beaten with some regularity. Two witnessed isolated instances of mothers being slapped and hit. A number said witnessing the violence established a pattern repeated in their own marriages; one said 'I felt subconsciously I should ride out the storm, like Mum did'. Others married specifically to escape the violent atmosphere — only to find themselves in like circumstances. One despised her mother for 'putting up with it', until she found herself in a violent marriage and it was difficult to escape.

Of the male victims, five were not abused in childhood; for three discipline was strict. One mother 'tended to be a bit on the stormy side'; one victim said women in the family were 'kept in their place' during his childhood. None described any acts of abuse between parents, or alluded to violence. One grew up in what he classed as an egalitarian and caring household:

I grew up in a family of great love, mother and father married almost sixty years, women were respected, all did washing-up and floor cleaning, father included. Confrontation situations were treated with care and gentleness. But I now have to accept that women can be as aggressive and as violent as men, no longer the strong voice of the community conscience to reduce cruelty.

Aggressors' backgrounds were less often recorded. One male respondent, filling in the questionnaire with his wife, wrote: 'My mother brought me up. She was gentle and kind and I tried to be that way to my wife and daughter. I feel disturbed that things happen so quickly. All my life I have been quiet and non-violent. I had a settled childhood and adolescence. Then suddenly at age 33 I find myself bashing a woman.' Of the four women victims mentioning the husband-aggressor's childhood, two commented on 'over-indulgence' or 'spoiling' by parents; two said their husbands had had unhappiness during childhood. Of her husband Angus, Iris Fenton wrote:

For me, the violence of marriage began when my husband's mother and father 'had' to get married a few months before he was born. Two such incompatible people were doomed from the start — she, an unloved member of a large extremely poor (and dour) north country family, he, a bad tempered but intellectually brilliant member of a not quite as poor (as his wife's) family. My husband was born in August, 1917, the eldest of five children. As a result of never ending quarrels, violence, and grinding poverty, the home was not a nice one to be in, and certainly difficult in which to study. Because of his high IQ, my husband won a coveted place at — Grammar School. The only way for him to study was to mentally switch off, which he successfully achieved — to this day, one can drop such remarks as 'the whole of Milson's Point was swamped beneath a giant tidal wave today' and he doesn't even look up from his book!

Just as victims covered the spectrum of possible childhoods, even on the small numbers available, aggressors' backgrounds also covered the range: loving and caring, spoilt, or abusive. Neither victims nor aggressors need be emulating violently abusive patterns viewed in infancy and youth on their own hearths. Carol O'Donnell's and

Heather Saville's findings that few women had successive violent relationships were supported by the present study: there was little 'predisposition' in victims to 'seek out violent men' (or women), marry them, then 'provoke' them into violence, leave (or be left) and find another violent spouse.[21] No male victim had a prior violent relationship, or a subsequent abusive relationship. Following divorce, two remarried and were living happily. One remained married to the woman who had meted out an isolated attack on him early in their marriage. As for women victims, three had had good marital relationships before marrying the violent man; one woman was divorced before the violent relationship, but her first marriage broke down through arguments, not through violence. Two had had bad relationships involving violence and ending in divorce before the relationship in the study. Ten women escaped from the violent marriage to remarry without violence. Finally putting paid to the idea that certain women are predisposed toward violence and marry into it, only two women who left the violent relationship said they desired to remarry (apart from those already happily remarried); neither indicated a desire to re-enter any relationship involving abuse. Leonore Connors despaired at ever finding a caring partner:

Now that we're separated, Peter doesn't bother to see any of the children, does not support the children. All I can say is that thank God I left when I did as I do not think we would all be alive today. It gets lonely at times as I do not have much adult company. Many men that I have been out with seem to think that it is too much bother to take on four children. So I stay at home. I have joined a few clubs without success, joined a dating service but haven't met anyone yet. Surely somewhere there are genuine males around.

Loss of trust and an inability to make good, new relationships were a recurring theme in battered women's responses. The majority said: 'I more or less am scared to be with another man'; 'I don't think I would trust another man entirely'. With a divorce pending after twelve years of marriage and two years of intensive violence, Maxine Harris remarked, 'I am very suspicious of personal relationships and of character generally. My husband was such a "nice guy" to the rest of the world, I find myself now looking and waiting for "nasty" aspects of a person's character. I feel very guilty about breaking up our family.'

The women in this study were not engaged in 'picking out violent men to marry'. On the contrary, after experiencing violence they did not expect and finally escaping it, most were reluctant to 'pick out' *any* man to marry.

Menstruation

'The curse' is blamed for numerous ills. Not surprisingly, it is implicated in domestic violence. As early as 1865 Richard von Kraft-Ebbing wrote:

The menstruating woman has a claim to special consideration by the judge because she is at this period 'unwell' and more or less psychologically disturbed. Abnormal irritability, attacks of melancholia, feelings of anxiety are common phenomena. Inability to get along with the husband and domestics, ill treatment of otherwise tenderly cared for children, emotional explosions, libellous acts, breach of peace, resisting authority, scenes of jealousy, craving for alcoholic beverages because of physical pains, neurotic and anxiety conditions are everyday experiences with innumerable individuals.[22]

Over one hundred years later, six of the eight battered husbands in this study said menstruation was a possible or probable cause of the violence. Two said in passing that they had at times thought the violence was probably due to 'the monthlies'. Ron Longman, for four years beaten, scratched, kicked, hit with saucepans, skillet and frypan, and threatened with a kitchen knife, was more expansive:

At first I put it down to 'monthly blues' and thought all women got that way sometimes. (My mother used to shout and carry on a bit the same way at certain times of the month, but never really got violent the way my wife did.) I just thought Tania was a bit worse than most other women, my mother included, at that time. I thought the children needed their mother even if she got a bit tense with the menses so we stayed together. I also thought it would eventually pass and she would go back to being steady again. I kept out of her way a lot, especially during 'that time of the month' and stayed back at university working later and often worked on weekends to get away.

Dan Summers thought his wife Maureen was driven to violence by her female physiology, although the violence, continuing over seven years, sometimes occurred on a weekly basis. Sam Browne felt his spouse 'wasn't fully responsible for her actions... they occurred during what may be described as "premenstrual stress".'

The violence occurred not every month, however, but 'every few months', and irregularly.

The greatest exponent of the theory that antisocial and undisciplined behaviour in women is related to menstruation, Katherine Dalton,[23] attributes 'those cases of assault where in a sudden fit of temper the woman throws a rolling-pin at her neighbour, a typewriter at her boss, or tries to bite off a policeman's ear' to premenstrual tension with 'its irritability and confusion'. Anecdotally, she instances cases of baby-battering, husband-hitting, and family homicide. But this is not sufficient to found a theory of menstrual tension causing antisocial activity, or, specifically, husband abuse. The husbands' attribution of the violence to premenstrual tension could be influenced by cultural and social attitudes: society has said women are ill or peculiar or unclean during menstruation. The currency of this belief is supported by the present study.

Yet not only are women's violent acts attributed to menstruation, Dalton says men's domestic crimes are also linked with premenstrual tension. She attributes the beating of wives and, sometimes, daughters, to the victim's disposition. One woman is cited as saying: 'Some cakes and biscuits disappeared on Sunday. It was all too much for me and I burst into tears. This is turn upset my husband, who went and found Mary in her bedroom and gave her a good thrashing. At midnight we discovered she was missing. She had spent the night with friends. Both Mary and I started menstruating that day.'[24]

In referring to the attendance of husbands at the surgery together with the wife if she is suffering from the premenstrual syndrome, Dalton concludes that this is 'a most valuable opportunity to learn more of the full extent of the wife's problem'. Yet if a woman is being battered by her husband, it is the husband who 'has a problem' in not being capable of empathising with his wife's psychological or physiological distress, or her human reaction to a world at times engendering legitimate discontent. Perhaps at the time he batters her, the husband is himself experiencing a 'low' in his own biological cycle. Estelle Ramey points out there are male cycles which, like the menstrual cycle, 'are essentially lunar and generate periodic episodes of depression and physical incompetence of the kind (sometimes) connected with the female cycle'.[25] Male moods are cycled in a four to six weeks rhythm producing differences in behaviour and are said sometimes to cause a reaction of a psychotic nature.

Some women might attribute aggression towards a husband to premenstrual tension. The real cause may be stress that coincides, in a particular instance, with the individual's menstrual cycle. Paige says:

When a woman feels irritable and has backaches during her period she may attribute these feelings to the fact that she is menstruating, while if she has the same feelings after a hard day's work, she will attribute them to tensions of the job . . . *None* of the symptoms that women report during menstruation is unique to menstruation; most are common reactions both men and women have to psychological stress.[26]

Every month at least 3.5 million women in Australia experience the menstrual cycle and men experience their own monthly cycles. As it has not yet been suggested that wife or husband battering are universal pastimes, explanations for domestic violence lie elsewhere.

Pregnancy

The 'blame the victim' habit is followed through by Jean Renvoize in relation to pregnancy.[27] 'Many women do provoke violence, even though . . . they hate it when they get it', she writes, concluding that much provocation is 'obviously unintentional on the part of the wife'. She alludes to pregnancy as 'provoking' many men to violence. Yet how can any woman be responsible for 'provoking' a man because she was pregnant? According to J. J. Gayford, men with a low tolerance to frustration, losing control under the influence of alcohol, most often develop into wife-beaters; their brutality may increase during the wife's pregnancy.[28] For Gayford, pregnancy alone does not precipitate domestic violence.

Of the eight male victims, none mentioned pregnancy. Of the 119 female victims, most made no mention of pregnancy. In many cases, violence continued over years, extending well beyond the range of pregnancy. In twenty-three cases pregnancy was mentioned. Ten respondents referred to violence in connection with the birth of a first child. Betty Samuels's husband Bob began slapping, pushing and threatening her four years after they were married. He hit her with rolled-up newspapers and threw beer cans and other items at her:

The start of it was when I was having Jamie and Bob started pushing me around and telling me to stop acting all helpless as if anyone never had a baby before. He said I had to look after him first and not forget who was bringing home the money. I had Jamie premature and I'll bet Bob's pushing and shoving had to do with it. Same thing all over again when I got pregnant and had Peter. Bob hit me with a rolled-up newspaper a couple of times and shoved me in the stomach. You get used to the pushing after a while, so it never surprised me much anymore. I just aimed at keeping out of his way.

Betty Samuels was beaten up about six times in four years of remaining together after the beating commenced. It usually happened during one or other of her pregnancies. Similarly, attacks on Rosemary King began when she was about six months pregnant with her first child. She suffered a miscarriage with her second pregnancy.

Miscarriage was a recurring theme in the twenty-three cases. Nine victims miscarried after violent attacks. Kitty Jordan's doctor had an inkling of the problem:

I can't really recall when it all started, but at some stage I started to see it wasn't going to stop. The first few times I guess I thought he was under stress at work because it was all very cut throat in the business in those years. I recall he got very aggressive when I was first pregnant. He kicked me so hard in the third that I lost that child. When I was having Sonia, he nearly managed to make me lose her as well, but the doctor put me into hospital early and saved her. I say he guessed how things were at home. But I never told him about Mark's beatings.

Pregnancy figured highly in violent acts committed by some husbands, but additional factors were present. In nine of the ten cases where violence began during the first pregnancy, and in one where violence commenced during the second, abuse was not limited to that period but continued over years, ranging from four years in one to fifty in another. In one instance only the incident was isolated, but again another factor was relevant:

I was pregnant when it happened. We had an argument about Christmas. I wanted to go my family and he wanted us to go to his. In the end he won and we went Boxing Day to my parents. I never forgot it. We came to Queensland then and we're still here and we can't go home to my Mum and Dad or to his. He says he's got to stay here to get work but I say that isn't true. He's doing it to spite my Mum and me. He's never really liked her much.

Karen Horney believed men suffer from envy of women's ability to reproduce.[29] Where battering coincides with pregnancy, the husband may be suffering from womb envy. R. J. Gelles says the husband may attempt to hurt the foetus through his wife, or that the violence relates to changes in family life:

In many marriages, the pregnancy caused a changed in the family routine. Often the husband did not want to change his routine of work and leisure. This led to conflict, arguments and in some instances violence.

The crucial point in bringing about violence was that the stress of pregnancy was added on to an already high level of structural stress in these families.

Husbands who marry pregnant girls may feel increasing stress as the baby approaches (or as the wife swells). One woman related: 'Our problem was getting married and having the baby so fast . . . that produced a great strain . . . I wasn't ready. I had the baby six months after we were married.[30]

Jealousy and demands for attention may also underlie the violence. Sally Beckett wrote: 'I really love my husband and our baby, but . . . it seems I am constantly being asked to make a choice between the two of them.'

Early marriage has been pinpointed as one of two peak times for domestic violence, due to a combination of attempts by the parties to adjust to marriage, increased responsibilities in starting a family, and large outlays for home purchase.[31] If the wife is pregnant and leaves her paid job, the husband's duty as economic provider is emphasised. Expenses increase whilst income decreases. Conflict may lead to abuse which, rather than being directed at a world creating demands for material satisfactions going beyond simple needs, is directed at those who seem to create the demands — wife and putative offspring.

Masochism of the Victim

Ignoring that *husbands* beat wives, past research questions why women 'allow' themselves to be beaten.[32] Clinical psychologist and marriage counsellor James Kleckner considers the acceptance and institutionalisation of physical abuse by women 'is most deserving of scrutiny, for without it, wife abuse would be impossible':

I have never seen a chronically abused wife who truly objected to being abused. The chronically abused wife is one who permits her husband to beat her, refuses to take punitive action afterward, and remains in the same situation so that she may be beaten again . . . A woman who stays passive and allows herself to be beaten, is accepting the validity of beating as a method of communication, and interaction . . . Frequently women offer only token resistance with the explanation that they are aware that it is their husband, and that they do not want to really hurt him . . .

Abused wives often explain that they have no place to go (not true), that they don't know where to go (anywhere), that they are afraid of losing their financial support (how much per beating?) or that they tolerate beatings for the sake of the children — as if the children really thrive in a violent home. What it all comes down to is that wife beating, like all other crimes against people, must not be tolerated. It can only be stopped through action by the victim or intended victims. It can only occur with the tacit permission of its victims. A wife who has been beaten for the first time may be a victim. A wife who is beaten again is a co-conspirator.[33]

The Freudian concept of feminity, embodying an unconscious need for punishment and neurotic self-injury, is often used to explain domestic violence: why do women remain? Because they love it, it is said.[34]

None of the respondents indicated she loved being beaten. After eight years of violence, Lorna Sanders was 'a nervous wreck'. Iris Fenton and her three children 'lived in constant fear'. Iris had phobias about going outside and of being trapped: 'It is only recently, after nearly forty years, that I am able to freely hop on a train or into a lift.' Renate Warne developed a fear of the outdoors and loss of self-confidence: she would not go out to hang washing on the line.

Even after leaving, women remain fearful:

After ten years I left. I now have economic difficulties and sometimes am desperate. I have moved state. But I can't ask any friends or contact anyone I knew before, as they might give the address or drop it in conversation. I have a silent number. We (my children and I) now live in our own flat. I guess I feel no one should 'ever say die'. Still to this day I am scared [Samuel] will do something.

Helen Trent's fears are well founded, for shortly after she left Samuel and before she travelled interstate, he discovered her whereabouts and abducted one of the children.

Although women remaining may speak of 'love' for the aggressive spouse, in the present study only one could be remotely interpreted as connecting 'love' with the violent side of the abuser. Denise Bourke's relationship with her friend Barry Toms was violent almost from the start. He invited her to a dance, and when she was dancing with another man Barry stormed onto the dance floor, told her she was making a fool of herself, dragged her off, and threw a glass of beer all over her. She persevered with the friendship. After two years, he moved in with her, but after three months she told him to leave. Twice during their time of knowing each other she took out a court order to have him stop harassing her. She thought about ending the relationship completely:

I changed my mind sometimes. He took an overdose once — after the first court order. Then he said he'd be good, etc. etc. (so did the social worker at the hospital). I changed my mind sometimes because I liked (and still like) his good side, but not his bad side. Everyone believed how bad he is — even his mother warned me. Everyone said I should kick him out. God knows what will happen when he gets this court order. Everybody fears for me. Some say he'll come and kill me. In his drama I believe it. I still love the beautiful side of him. Hating/loving the other side. I know it is useless.

Even here, to infer the victim loves the abuse and finds some attraction in the attacker's abusive side is wrong. Denise Bourke cares for the *non-abusive* friend: she is simply expressing a frequently favoured view — not only among abused wives — that no one is all bad.

In twenty-four cases wives said they knew the husband as a 'nice' person when he wasn't abusive. The husbands promised not to repeat the abuse, but did repeat it; each begged the wife to return if she left overnight or for a few days or weeks. On her return the beating began again; then came more promises. One husband wrote of their effect on his wife:

I'm a welfare officer so my wife knew what the welfare position was — not good for a single mother. She was once a health worker in the Health Commission so she knew the system. My wife felt like taking action against me after I had beaten her. She changed her mind because I had never done it before and was so contrite.... She also knew how bad welfare was. She didn't want to have to move again and struggle on alone, particularly with a child, as she had in the past.

Thirteen victims hoped their husbands would change, so stayed. With two, love the children had for their father persuaded the mother to stay.

Twenty victims had no illusions of 'love', recognising the relationship for what it was. The victim stayed at the threat, often backed with guns and knives, of worse treatment if she left. Eleven victims left home only to be taken back, forcibly, by the husband. One victim's father returned her, on the advice of a priest. One victim was incapable of seeking help or escaping: she had been pushed downstairs and her hip broken. Her husband refused to help her until three days later, when he took her to hospital. Rose Randell derived no pleasure from abuse:

We stayed together locked in a cruel and bitter union. He needs someone to iron his shirts — he never learned, poor man! and make his dinner. (He rarely throws it down the sink these days. He is getting fat.) I stayed because it's my home — and I need to be comfortable in my old age — it's more than I had in youth. Though I would gladly give it all up if the violence of the past could be removed.

Spouse assault has been attributed to deep feelings of guilt harboured by women. Guilt was expressed by six victims, but in each case the response was initiated or fuelled by those from whom the victim sought assistance — from medical practitioners, psychiatrists, ministers of religion, and marriage guidance counsellors.

Seven women said 'marriage is for life' and stayed to endure years of bashing. Faith McDonald thought marriage vows are 'for better or worse' and 'till death do us part':

I'm an old soldier type. Never deserted my post even under fire. Always used the quote from the Bible 'Whatsoever things are of good report, dwell thee on these things'. Always decided there are garbage bins and flowers. Always pass the bins and concentrate on flowers. Play down the faults and blow up good points. So I stood my violence thirty years by rising above it.

A common response of family, friends, medical practitioners, ministers of religion, priests, and marriage counsellors was that marriage is made to last forever. If the women expressed a desire to leave, it was quashed.

Many women left or tried to leave the relationship. Some women suffering abuse for years expressed the views of Olive Smith:

I tried really to escape hundreds of times. Tons of times I thought about it. Once the kids and me went to the People's Palace in Adelaide but I never knew no one in Adelaide so I had to go back to him in Naracoorte. I never knew where to get help or find a job. The little kids come with me. I couldn't leave them back there with him. In the end we gave up and come home. I stayed mostly because whenever I tried to get away he followed me or else there weren't no refuges to go to. No pensions to speak of. Not that I knew. Never had nowhere to go and nowhere to live if I went. We always went home to him.

Where women escape, showing they do not wish to put up with abuse, the abuse follows them. In 23 of the 119 cases, the husband's abuse continued after the wife had separated to begin divorce action. In ten, the wife went to another state to escape but the husband followed to continue the violence. Norma Collie remarried, changed residence and place of work from Perth to Brisbane and, by design, lost contact with most of her family and all former friends. She could not evade her former husband. After three years of peace she received a threatening letter from him. The message was that he would soon be coming after her once more with a gun. The gun would not be used as an ornament. Although she went to the police, they said they could do nothing until it came to maiming or death. She now lives in constant fear that Tom Collie will turn up on her doorstep and the violence will be renewed with fatal results.

There is no traditional suggestion that men beat their wives because they are sadists; nor that those following their wives from place to place and even chasing them interstate to indulge the habit are the sadistic counterparts to allegedly masochistic women. Just as the majority of women who are beaten are 'normal women', the majority of wife bashers are 'normal men'. Normal men are less likely to be classed as psychiatrically unstable than women.[35] The equation of the wife-victim as a case for the psychiatrist while the husband-aggressor escapes the diagnosis follows naturally.

Nor are male victims called 'masochistic' when they remain with their abusers: a picture is painted of great fortitude, humane feelings for wife and children. The husband-victim accordingly makes a rational decision 'to cry out in pain during the beating and [have] the wife see the injuries' to 'punish' her by 'raising her levels of guilt'. (Would wives suffering injuries who exhibited them to 'punish their husbands' be 'making a rational decision'? Or would it be self-indulgence or enjoyment of the beating, taking a masochistic pleasure in showing off the cuts and bruises that spurred them on?) Yet a psychological analysis is made of the wife who beats the husband: she is 'insecure', 'dissatisfied with herself', wanting dominance and to play a 'masculine' role.[36] When negative psychological assessments are made of one sex only — whether she is aggressor or victim — with no a similar assessment of the other sex, the analysis falls into disrepute.

Why Victims Stay

Women stay in abusive relationships because they are locked into a living situation militating against escape. In addition to sheer economics, social pressures have a profound effect on victims. Women are socialised to believe the happiness of the family unit depends on their efforts: if the marriage breaks down, this is a personal failure for women, not a mutual failing or a failure of the institution itself. Five women said the marriage should remain intact; thirty-four didn't wish to break up the family. Four women said divorce was impossible for them when the violence was at its height: 'One just didn't leave in those days'; 'divorce was unheard of in Peppermint Grove'. Many women affirmed marriage should be persevered with 'for the sake of the children'.

Two hundred and seventy-seven children were dependent on the one hundred and nineteen women victims during the violence. Ten children were dependent on the eight male victims. Each female respondent said the children affected her reaction to the assaults. It was too difficult for many to take the children and go. Where the victim left, with dependent children, fears of being a single parent were justified. Valerie McKenzie, with three children, endured eight years of violence because she thought her husband Donald might change and realised 'it's hard to go anywhere — that is, if you haven't got any money. Accommodation is difficult with young kids because landlords don't like pensioner tenants.' When she left, the violence had affected her:

Well, I've lost my health. I'm on an invalid pension. I'm living below the poverty line. My children are forced to spend each second weekend with a father they dislike. I can't get legal aid to settle affairs my husband left with me. *Of course* it's affected my outlook. I'm constantly in pain, constantly broke, constantly in fear of being assaulted, because he keeps coming back and abusing me and the children.

From an income of $13 000 annually, Valerie McKenzie and her three children have been reduced to $135.00 a week. Child maintenance, ordered by the Family Court, is never paid by her husband. She cannot obtain legal aid for enforcement.

Forty-one victims stayed, not wanting to leave the children behind. Brenda Cashmore does not like her life, but with no money or home apart from the family home, she can go nowhere: 'I have been degraded and insulted and don't have a life of my own I have to obey his rules and wishes or get out with nothing and have a lonely unhappy life. I love my two children and could never go away from them. But I can't see what to do. There's no choice but to stay.' One abused wife left the children with her husband, but this worked against her:

I finally went to the Family Court for a divorce and property settlement. Left the girls with Geoff because thought he could give them a more secure life financially. Have access and intend keeping it up. Unfortunately he is still angry and abusive to me and tries to poison the girls' minds against me by saying I left them 'motherless'. He calls me an abandoned woman and a 'child deserter' and apart from the fact that it sounds like something out of a Victorian novellette, it hurts.

Five victims remained, like Antonia Grey, who left several times to be ordered back by her husband with threats of fighting custody battles and not allowing her any of the family property. Fears are often borne out. Pat O'toole left a seven year marriage in which slapping, punching, hitting with a chair and threatening with a hunting knife had been standard form since soon after the wedding:

I went to the Family Court. At the Court Justice — was a real pig. He made me feel hysterical, useless, and stupid. He couldn't see further than his nose. The solicitors weren't much better. Mrs — the counsellor wasn't any help — after my husband kicked me in the stomach in her office when she went out — she said I was hysterical. Of course I was hysterical. My drunk, violent husband got custody of the kids. I was tired after being in court all day. I had years of violence and trouble. My stomach hurt. Anyone would be hysterical.

Three women were waiting for children to grow up before leaving. Seventeen said children 'need two parents'. Five said the children loved their father. Sometimes children initiated or reinforced fifteen victims' desire to leave. Trudy Smart initially put up with attacks, then her husband began involving the children: 'He attacked me when they were present and they became hysterical with fear. It was then that I knew I just had to leave.'

Of the six male victims with children, one said the child did not affect his reaction. He stayed for seven years. Dan Summers did not want to break up the family, believed all children need two parents, did not want to leave the children behind, and considered it too difficult to take the children and start a new life. Maurice Markham said:

Patricia didn't want to stay at home when the children were born and had them in care of our inlaws then family day-care and pre-school as soon as possible. I always allowed her to go to work, as long as she made proper arrangements for the children. She seemed to resent my work sometimes but I needed to work long hours to keep everything in hand. She didn't seem to think it was fair that in the holidays I had to work a lot of the time and she was the only one available to look after the children ... I tolerated it for as long as was humanly possible but finally decided she needed treatment. It was upsetting the kids too. Now my second wife Sally is a good wife and mother. She accepts the responsibility of the children. It is ironic that she revels in motherhood when two of the children aren't really hers, whereas their own mother didn't seem to want to be a real mother to them.

Responses of male victims differ from women victims. No abused husband remarked on lack of self-confidence and self-esteem. None commented on fear of a wife's angry reaction if he left; nor did any mention threats about custody battles. No abused husband left the violent home to be persuaded by any means — threatening or promising — to return. In every case, apart from one involving an isolated incident where the parties remained together, no husband left the matrimonial home; the aggressor-wife did! Only one male victim left his paid employment on the marriage break up. Dan Summers was reduced from $18 000 a year to living on the supporting parent's benefit. His mother helped him with child care. In every other case, upon the abuser-wife leaving home, the husband's personal income went up, rather than down, or in one case remained static.

With few exceptions, women expressed fear of financial insecurity in leaving an abusive husband, with or without children. Financial hardship on leaving was real for women victims. The majority went on to a state pension of some kind; some had child maintenance orders, mostly unpaid. (One former victim's child maintenance was outstanding for two years.) Women's finances improved or remained static only on remarriage. Those not remarrying were worse off financially on leaving. Women lost their income if in partnership with the husband: four women had joined the husband's business, one farmed in partnership with him. Full-time housewives were particularly disadvantaged. Some had skills or training prior to marriage, school teaching, physiotherapy, nursing and occupational therapy. Some were trained secretaries or shop assistants, but training had lost its saleability after time away. High costs of child care precluded most women from re-entering paid work; age added to difficulties. The reluctance of women to leave was a facing up to cold reality, not the result of some deep subconscious wish to be abused.

All abused husbands were city dwellers and of Anglo-Saxon origin; none had the problems of Dorothy Sands, from a small Western Australian sheep and wheat town:

There were no refuges, and who would go to one in such a small town set-up if there was. It was impossible to get help from welfare agencies. Everyone knew everyone else's business. Imagine the field day for the gossips! (Although now on reflection they must of all known about the beatings, anyway. They talked about it behind my back, not to my face.)

Nor did they experience life as Leticia Smallwood did:

I am a migrant from the Phillipines. My husband met me there when he was on business. All my family is at home and I don't know what to do. I often think about doing something but with my family not here I do not know if there is anything I can do. I don't want to leave the boys behind with him. I don't know what to do in a foreign country. I feel alone and don't know where I can go for help. I haven't got any training to do a job in Australia.

No abused husband wrote romantically of his marriage as a factor motivating him to remain. With wives, however, living 'happily ever after' was sometimes mentioned:

I stayed because I thought marriage was 'for life'. Tim was my childhood sweetheart and I believed in 'happiness ever after'. I couldn't understand that this wasn't 'happily ever after'. I thought I was doing something wrong and if only I could work out what it was, there would be a miraculous 'cure' for our marriage. I tried to talk to Mummy but didn't want to smash everything. I didn't want to let anyone know things were going wrong. I thought about doing something positive but I kept thinking it was *me* that was the problem and kept making resolutions to change. Because we grew up together and always were going to get married made me change my mind about doing anything for ages.

Nor did any husband state pragmatically, as did Rose Randell: 'The devil you know is better than the devil you don't know.'

Can Abusers be Stopped?

Most domestic violence research concentrates on wives as victims of abuse. Less attention is paid to the abuser. Most research emphasises the role of the victim in stopping the violence: 'why doesn't she leave'; 'if she didn't provoke him, it wouldn't happen'. Yet the majority of women cannot 'just leave'. Women who have left are continuing victims of husbands who follow them. Some husbands remarry to continue the abuse, as with Pamela and Tommy Friar: 'It makes me so sad that my first husband was able to get married again and have a wife to bash again as he did me because he does . . . his mother told me she didn't know what to do as she was frightened of what he might do . . . why are people allowed to do this?'

Similarly with provocation: what can *women* do to stop 'provoking' to stop being battered? Jean Renvoize comments on 'studies' of women 'who being married to jealous men would provoke [their husbands] by flirting at staff dances, by going without their husbands to dances and returning late, or setting up situations with their mothers (who often egged them on) which implied infidelity, even though the wives were in fact perfectly faithful'.[37] Apparently this explains domestic violence. Yet what form the 'flirting' took is not mentioned. Is a wife expected to remain mute at the side of the dance floor, waiting only until her spouse chooses to dance with her? Is a wife expected to remain at home unless she is escorted out by her husband? In the present study, Denise Briggs, whose competition dancing seemed to upset her boyfriend/*de facto* husband, took the advice of a social worker and tried to overcome *his* problem: when he expressed a desire to train as her partner, she acceded to this. However, it did not stop his bashing and beating. If anything, it increased the abuse, as well as his possessiveness towards her.

Donna Moore takes a look at the aggressor:

Most batterers are not psychotics, psychopaths, or the demented few. They are ordinary men who have low levels of self-esteem, who have learned male behavior from their parents, and who continue to play out the violence part of that role when life stresses become intolerable. While some continue to believe that batterers are 'sick', most people today would agree that we are dealing with an average man who is under some unusual stress and/or has learned his masculine role, especially as it relates to socially acceptable aggression, only too well . . . frustration or stress in a man's life is one of the major reasons he will beat his spouse. The woman simply becomes the target of his frustration. Frustration may be a result of differences between the man's expectations of himself and the reality of his life. Thus, if he has high expectations but is not successful (in his own image of himself), this may lead to frustration. If he indeed accepts the cultural image of men as being strong, in control, and unemotional, he may be unable to talk about his frustration with anyone. These stresses may then lead to a violent eruption with his wife as target . . . these men may be insecure, moody, and dependent on their wives in addition to being hostile and aggressive. They are also reported to be severely jealous of their wives . . . women also have frustrations but do not usually beat their husbands or otherwise act out in physical ways. Further, in looking for answers, we need to look at the many men who experience frustration but do not resort to physical violence as a solution to their problems.[38]

Moore's thesis is partly borne out by the present study. Some battering incidents illustrate well the frustration, stresses, and high expectations underlying violent incidents. Barry Cannon came home one night very late after drinking with friends. His wife Suzanne lost her temper, asking why he had to drink in the pub all day instead of selling:

Then it started. He slapped my face and something seemed to snap. He just started hitting into me and punching me in the face and kicking my legs and shins. There was blood everywhere because my nose was bleeding but he kept on until he was exhausted and crying too. He went away and came back after two days saying he was sorry and didn't know what had got into him.

He had lost out on a big land sale and was upset about that. He's never done anything like that again.

Yet other domestic assaults seem to be unrelated to specific problems. Women victims frequently said 'it happened out of the blue'. Helen Trent wrote of her husband Samuel: 'He was constantly raising his hand over silly things — for example, opening a cornflakes packet upside down. I would never know when I was doing the right thing. He was constantly telling me "you're wrong, it's your fault".' Jean Selberg often found the mental abuse 'which goes hand in hand with the physical abuse . . . harder to live with than the punching etc. which is dealt out during the attack . . . Living in fear for your safety day after day never knowing when he will come home abusive, or sitting watching him consume beer like water and not knowing which drink will be the one which will change his mood instantaneously, is often harder to endure than physical pain.'

Moore's proposition that traditional expectations held of women by husbands may result in wife abuse is also supported by the present study. Much of the violence revolved around housekeeping, cooking meals and child care. (Violence by women against husbands also had its roots here.) Violence also related to conventional views of sexual attractiveness and female attributes generally. The masculine ideal of wanting to be in control is also revealed. 'Obeying his ultimatums' and 'having to do things his way' were mentioned. Jackie Trencher said violence occurred only after she began to challenge her husband's assumed position of authority in the marriage. Before this, she 'went along with everything he said to prevent arguments'. A batterer confirmed this. When asked about his statement that subconciously he wanted to dominate his wife, Robert Chalmers said, 'I expect it would come down to whether you're frustrated because you haven't got any power in any other field, because in the work environment I have no authority . . . It comes back to the concept of power.' Chalmers, a dissatisfied public servant saving to buy a farm and 'be his own boss' and get away from 'all the crap of being told what to do, where to go, how to shit', also commented about his wife:

She couldn't care less about getting far, she's quite happy where she is, but she'd go along with it for me, she said. She'd rather be where she is, she likes to be with people more than me, so that's [a ground for argument] . . . our personalities, but not really. She's a person who'll give in to me to a point and then she'll jack right up, so with arguing I'm almost testing her and then there's a point where she'll say 'no' and that'll be the point of a major argument, but otherwise she'll pretty well go along with what I do. Say we're going down the coast, I'll make a decision whether we're going down the coast . . .

[With my parents' marriage as an example] I probably accepted that that's how marriage should be, wives should be submissive and I tried to play that out . . .

Again, I'd do my traditional thing and I almost do it as a stir. She'll be watching a bloody trashy show like *Prisoner*, and I'll just turn it over to *Nationwide*. I wouldn't even ask her. I *know* it's going to cause a stir but I do it. I know that ethically, morally it's wrong, but subconsciously I want to dominate her. I suspect it could come down to whether you're frustrated because you haven't got any power in any other area. A guy's home's his kingdom or something like that. That's why I want to be dominant in that area, although I know it's crap. It should be a shared thing. Another thing I do to stir her — she'll be watching television and I'll say 'How about getting me some supper love?' and it's beautiful the reaction [laughs]. Probably five times out of ten she'll whip up and get me supper, and other times she'll say 'Shit, get your own supper' and laugh and it's really good, us both laughing. But other times, that's where I haven't got her beaten, she'll say 'Get your own bloody supper'. But I never feel threatened that she's trying to dominate me. It's a one way thing, for sure . . .

There's this terrible conflict [in me] to act in the traditional dominating way but also to act with respect for the other person's individuality. This has probably all taken place [the respect for her individuality on one level] in the last four to five years. I'm sure [people] could come to a better understanding without all the crap . . .

I feel I'm a bastard some of the things I've done to her . . . I think it's a traditional Australian relationship, you'd have to be blind not to see it. It's part of the ocker image, the male dominating relationship.[39]

Chalmers found outlets other than beating his wife for establishing his authority over her. Despite her adult status he termed her a 'terribly houseproud *girl*'. The glib relegation of women into the realm of 'girls' occurs at all levels of our society, promoting the idea that adult females have no control of themselves, are to be controlled, and are rightly subjected to male domination. (This parallels the relegation of black adult men to 'boys'.) As men already hold 'power' over women generally, it is revealing that they use other forms of domination, including spouse beating. Teaching men to be masculine by being aggressive, dominant, and powerful does not satisfy them when they hold the reigns of power but renders them greedy and asking for more.

There is no similar analysis for women who beat their husbands. Women are not supported in being masculine, aggressive, dominant or powerful. Rather, women are implicitly and explicitly indoctrinated into a diametrically opposite path: that of 'femininity', requiring submission, passivity, dependence and powerlessness. Steinmetz's theory that women who beat their husbands wish to become dominant cannot be supported. It is more feasible to suggest that women who beat their husbands do so as a result of frustration and a lack of power over themselves, rather than over others. They lash out, not to achieve dominance, but to gain some recognition of their autonomy, their equal right to participate and to perform in ways *they* choose, not in ways chosen for them by men. They seek only to reject the confinement of their restrictive role — in the exclusive area of child caring, housekeeping, and general 'wifely duties'.

Moore suggests women 'simply become targets of a frustrated husband's violent explosion', as if the wife becomes a target only because she happens to be present. But men's aggression in the home is directed at the woman who, because of a marriage certificate, is by social, cultural and economic decree inevitably captive there. When women abuse their husbands, aggression is directed at those who, as 'head of household' are backed in their dominating role by cultural expectations: the woman has to lash out to establish her separate, equal identity. In sanctifying marriage, a relationship which, despite modern protestations of being a partnership, is inherently unequal, society sanctifies the violence within it.

How can equality in relationships and the turnabout in vision, seeing the personal as political, which is necessary to deal effectively with spouse assault, be accomplished? Donna Moore suggests that the woman who is victim bears the ultimate responsibility for her batterer and for the necessary change in perspective: 'The most effective way to get men to seek and accept therapy and change is for the woman to either leave him or threaten to leave him if he does not seek help to change his battering.'[40] Yet how can women take on this responsibility when we are patently lacking control of the situation? As so many women said, 'Every time I tried to go, he'd drag me back and belt me more.' The responsibility for violence lies not with the women victims, but with the men who batter, and the men who allow it. Until men themselves initiate change, spouse assault will continue unabated.

CHAPTER 6   MARITAL RAPE

Forcible rape is a criminal category created to protect females from unwanted sexual intercourse. [Between strangers] it always carries with it a grave risk of very serious physical and mental harm. It is the supreme insult to feminine integrity, and in spite of the persuasion of conscience and intellect to the contrary, it usually damages the reputation of the victim. At least historically, it has had great importance in destroying the acceptibility of an unmarried girl as a bride. Forcible rape has been common enough and dangerous enough in its consequences to require a strong deterrent penalty. Because in its classical form it is the expression of an unprovoked, unpredictable and highly brutal impulse, it calls forth fear and vengeance. Accordingly, forcible rape is usually much more severely punishable than other nonfatal invasions of the person.

In the ordinary marriage relationship the classical form of forcible rape is not probable. Presumably the parties have at times been very intimate, and the possibilities of serious social, physical or mental harm from a familiar, if unwanted, conjugal embrace are rather small. Thus neither the deterrence nor vengeance thought appropriate to the classical crime are appropriate here.

> Comment, 'Rape and Battery Between Husband and Wife',
> *Stanford Law Review*, 719, 1954, pp.723–4.

Origins of rape law are akin to those of robbery and theft. Those crimes involve the taking, without consent, of goods from the lawful owner with the felonious intent to convert them to the taker's own use; in robbery, the taking is done in the presence of the owner, by use of force or putting the owner in fear. As a concept, rape originally involved the ravishment of property of another, that 'other' being the male party in control or having custody of the victim. If a woman was raped, her value was lessened as a virgin, ripe for marrying, the property of her father, or as a wife, ripe for procreating, the property of her husband. At common law, a man could not be guilty of rape of his wife. The law held that on marriage, wife and husband became one: how could one commit a crime upon oneself? Further, the wife and any property of the marriage belonged to the husband. No husband could be guilty of theft from his wife, so no husband could be guilty of 'taking her' against her will.

The law was modified through the centuries. In 1891 the courts said a man had no right to take his wife into custody against her will and hold her in his house. Three years earlier eminent judges criticised the 'rule' that a husband may rape his wife with impunity. In 1976 the Western Australian Supreme Court held a man guilty of indecent assault upon his wife, where the assault culminated in rape.[1] Nonetheless, a strongly prevailing view among some lawyers and members of the public is that a man cannot or should not be prosecuted for rape where his victim is married to him. Various rationales are put forward for refusing criminal law protection to wives. Some say that criminal law has no place in matrimonial relationships; that other forums — such as the divorce court — are appropriate; that it would be pointless to extend the law to cover rape cases, when women would probably act as they do in assault cases, 'changing their minds', the day after the assault, about laying any charges against a brutal husband. Equally strongly put, frequently by the same people, is the conflicting view that the 'flood gates' would be opened to the 'vindictive wife': should wives be extended criminal law protection, numerous innocent and defenceless husbands would be subjected to endless charges brought by vengeful spouses.

Opponents of a law against marital rape sometimes contend no need exists for such a law, as rape does not occur in the marital bed: by its very nature, the marriage contract precludes it. Finally, some believe that to open a husband to charges of rape would lessen the harmony of married relations, placing the husband in an unacceptable position: how could he ever feel free to engage in sexual relations with his wife, with the threat of criminal proceedings ever ready in the wings? A philosophy redolent of the last century is seized upon:

The morning after a certain night on which Soames at last asserted his rights and acted like a man, he breakfasted alone ... The incident was really of no great moment, women made a fuss about it in books, but in the cool judgment of right thinking men, of men of the world, he had but done his best to sustain the sanctity of marriage, to prevent her from abandoning her duty.[2]

How acceptable is any one of these propositions in twentieth century Australia?

Extent of the Crime

The first Australian national victimisation survey showed a rape victimisation rate of 95 women per 100 000. Rape crimes reported to the police rated at a low 5.9 per 100 000.[3] The unreported rate of rape is probably even higher, as women who are raped in marriage often fail to define the act as rape, or are reticent about revealing the crime. Where relationships between rapists and victims are studied, a large percentage of women are raped by relatives or acquaintences. In Paul Wilson's study, six out of seventy women were raped by a spouse or partner.[4] In 1980, a survey of 30 000 women throughout Australia showed 13 per cent of women raped by their husbands.[5] Whilst younger women preponderated in Wilson's sample of women raped by a husband, older women in the 1980 survey were more inclined to disclose they were victims of marital rape, the largest percentage being married women over 55 years.

In the present study, fifty-eight respondents were victims of rape in marriage. Of these, one was a male victim suffering attempted rape. He and forty-four women said that, in addition to marital rape, other acts of spouse assault occurred during the marriage. This figure may under-estimate marital rape in the 312 homes comprising the study. Australian research confirms that women are reluctant to state they have been raped in marriage, frequently fail to acknowledge the acts as rape, or see it as simply a part of a continuing violent relationship — just one of many indignities and physically abusive acts they are forced to undergo; therefore, some women may have been raped but did not say so. Indeed, Mary Holdsworth, a victim of spouse assault, said in passing, 'he always demanded sex and I was abused if I didn't comply'. Similarly, spouse assault victim Leonore Connors mentioned rape amongst other acts of abuse, but did not go on to elaborate on the circumstances or regularity with which the sexual abuse occurred: 'Like many families, myself and children have been put through assaults, abuse, rape . . . We were terrified of what would happen next.' Probably other women victims of spouse assault suffered sexual violence but made no mention of it.

For eleven of the fifty-seven women respondents violence took place immediately before, during or after the rape, or at each stage, additional to the violence of forced intercourse itself. For Joan Hart, all marital violence was directly related to the sexual acts, occurring over a period of eight years, starting early in marriage:

My husband always wanted sex after beating me up. He would bash me up, then demand sex. I used to be so upset after being bashed I couldn't stop him. He got more angry when I just lay there and I had to pretend to like it. When I didn't he got madder and madder until he was wild and maniacal. Then other times he got angry and said I was a faker and would never be a real woman. He blamed me for not being good in bed and said I was like an iceblock so he had to punch me around. He said other women were not like me and he never even knew why he got married.

Rape began 'soon after marriage', 'after the first blush died on the rose' for twenty-five women. Alexis Benedict could not remember exactly, but supposed 'the first time was after six months or so when I became aware that marriage wasn't all it was cracked up to be'. A week after Connie Miller was married, she was forced by shot gun to comply with her husband's sexual demands:

I was at the sink doing the dishes (some honeymoon stuff) and suddenly I saw this shot gun barrel pointed at me. My heart nearly stopped and I couldn't believe he would do such a thing. We already had a few arguments, but nothing bad enough for threats with a gun. He marched me off to the bedroom and forced me to have sex with him. Then when it was over he pushed me out of bed and told me to go and finish doing the dishes. He was raving and calling me names, and kept calling out from the bedroom things like slut and whore.

Two women could not remember when the sexually abusive acts began. Dorry Maguire 'didn't ever really think of it as "rape" at the time, so I can't comment' on when it began. Bernice Summerfield said: 'It was nearly always like that. He didn't recognise me as a human being with sexual and other rights.'

Rape was an isolated attack in five cases; in two cases the wives immediately left home and did not return. In the other cases the wife was persuaded to remain. Gordon Kennedy came home drunk from the pub and 'just started bashing into' his wife Kate:

When it was all over he expected me to make up but I was shaking and crying and too upset. The kids were screaming and crying. I tried to go to them but he just forced himself on me and pushed me into the bedroom. He just bodily threw me around on the bed. The kids were left screaming and crying until it was over and he went to sleep like a big drunken sod. The next morning he begged me not to leave him and said it wouldn't happen again. He said he didn't know what got into him.

After Donald Wilson had beaten her up and broken her pelvis, Megan Wilson was taken off to hospital, where she spent several weeks recuperating. On her return home, Donald Wilson forced her to have sexual intercourse with him. She returned to hospital, torn and bleeding, for stitching and another bout of recuperation.

For most victims, rape occurred 'once or twice a month' or 'every week', 'two or three times a fortnight'. June Graham had sexual intercourse forced on her twice each week on average, sometimes four or five times a week, then perhaps not for two weeks: 'but the "holiday" periods were an exception', she wrote. Sam Trewin endured isolated incidents of sexual aggression throughout four years of a seven year marriage. 'But I had to put up with her tantrums in and out of bed', he commented. 'She would try to hit me with a saucepan after dinner, then expected me to perform in bed at night.'

Other Sexual Assaults

At common law, rape is defined as penetration of the vagina by a penis. Reformers contend it is wrong for the law to hold one form of non-consensual sexual penetration more heinous than another. Whether penetration is by a penis, finger, hand or foreign object, the victim's loss of power, invasion of her sexual privacy, and destruction of self are equal. Although penetration of the vagina without consent is traumatic, penetration of the anus without consent is equally so. Forced cunnilingus or fellatio are just as distressing. During the South Australian parliamentary debates on rape in marriage, however, one politician took a different view of non-consensual sexual intercourse in marriage. He accepted that a spouse should be prosecuted for rape where the offence involved oral or anal intercourse without consent; however, where the offence involved vaginal penetration, a higher legal standard of proof of non-consent should exist. Where non-consensual vaginal intercourse was complained of, a prosecution should be brought only where the offence involved penetration and an assault occasioning actual bodily harm, the threat of actual bodily harm, or the threat of a criminal act against a child or a relative of the wife. In reply to the proposal, Anne Levy, M.L.C. said:

I cannot see any justification whatsoever for distinguishing between the orifices of the human body in this way. I am almost moved to suggest that the mover of the amendment is concerned with his own orifices but that he adopts a different standard in relation to orifices that are common to females. Whatever can be the logic behind this distinction between orifices?[6]

In the present study, eight women referred specifically to forced acts other than vaginal intercourse. Five were penetrated anally without consent. One woman was forced to perform fellatio upon her husband and at other times was penetrated anally. She (like two other victims of anal rape) suffered from haemorrhoids and a husband who deliberately undertook the act to hurt her: 'When he was feeling particularly bitchy he would ram his penis into my anus and say he was doing it on purpose so that it would hurt me. It hurt me more than I let on.' Daphne Weber also spoke of her husband's deliberate objective in choosing anal rape:

I think a man raping his wife is as bad as if a total stranger rapes someone — the object is the same — to degrade and humiliate the woman. In my case, that's what my former husband did. He wanted to show me he had the power to do whatever he wanted to me, and that was by acts of buggery. It often resulted in bruising and injury to my bowel, with clots of blood on my thigh.

Two women were raped vaginally with bottles. One husband forced fingers into his wife's anus, his fist into her vagina, and raped her anally with a spoon handle: 'lots of times it got very nasty', she commented. Two further respondents were not explicit about the abuse apart from non-consensual vagina intercourse, commenting only on being forced to engage in 'degrading sex acts' not involving intercourse.

None of the eight women referring by name to acts apart from vaginal rape considered these any less heinous than forced vaginal penetration: they were a part of a pattern of sexual acts forced upon them without regard to their wishes. Only one respondent, who referred to 'degrading sex acts', believed a distinction could be made. For seven years Rose Manchester 'put up with bashings, black eyes, cut lip, made to do sex acts that now fifteen years later make me feel sick . . . He used to force me into the bedroom all the time and make me have sex. In general I was led to believe that's how men treat women and that it's not rape if you're married. But he made me do other things too that I can't write about even now and it wasn't the actual intercourse I object to, it was the degrading sex acts.' Later, however, when commenting upon whether strangers and husbands should be 'treated alike' by the law where they raped, Rose Manchester wrote simply 'Hang them'.

Lack of Consent

An element of the crime of rape is proof of lack of consent of the victim. It is suggested that marriage is so intimate a relationship, husbands would have difficulty determining whether or not wives were 'really' consenting to intercourse; therefore, no criminal prosecution could ever succeed. On the contrary, by its very intimate nature marriage should enable the parties to develop their perceptive skills more highly: husbands and wives, more than strangers, will be aware of nuances in sexual transactions with one another and thereby will be more aware of consent or lack of consent to sexual intercourse. If married men abuse this privileged position of intimacy, perhaps what is needed is a clear direction from the law that going ahead despite knowing of a wife's lack of consent is wrong. Indeed, during debate in South Australia at the time of passing the 'rape in marriage' clause acknowledging a wife's right to refuse consent to intercourse with her husband in that jurisdiction, the then Attorney-General, Peter Duncan, emphasised this need:

One of the Government's most important aims is that the legislation should act as a deterrent to sexual abuse. It is quite probable that it will work to actually *improve* the quality of a marital relationship by introducing a need for more mutual consideration and sensitivity. The 'rape-in-marriage' clause will, in effect, give the wife legitimate and equal right of 'negotiation' — most importantly, equal status and dignity in discussing the situation with her husband, and establishing co-operation within the marriage.[7]

It is ironic that a law should be necessary to introduce 'a need for more mutual consideration and sensitivity' in marriage. Most women, at least, could not be blamed for believing (at least prior to the wedding) that the essence of marriage is sensitivity, caring, mutual consideration and respect by both parties toward each other. Yet this is not always accepted as the basis of marriage. Following Peter Duncan's remarks, a retired member of the judiciary capped off discussion through the media:

the real reason for rejecting the idea [of a law prohibiting rape in marriage] is that, as well as being unnecessary, [the proposed law] is impracticable. It would face the courts with virtually insoluble problems. Most husbands and wives are habituated to sexual intercourse, and it must be obvious that this will sometimes happen against the protests of the wife. The line between yielding to bad temper or persuasion and being actually forced will almost always be impossible to draw.[8]

Opposition was founded on a belief that married women had no right to determine the when and where of intercourse, once they had determined the whom, by marrying the man. Once wed, no woman had a right to refuse intercourse with her husband. Should she do so, it was assumed he had a right to go ahead despite any protestations.

Such views do not correspond with those of the participants in the present study. Victims were asked what, in their own relationship, constituted rape. Forty-nine women said it involved threats to comply. Sometimes the threats were verbal; sometimes they were bolstered with weapons, including guns and knives. Forty-six women said the husband went ahead despite a clearly expressed 'no' to sexual intercourse at the time; eighteen stated it constituted the husband having sexual intercourse although the wife lay without responding; six said it occurred although the wife had a headache and told the husband. One woman was threatened with death if she cried out for help; one was threatened with death if she told anyone; seven were 'physically forced' to comply; psychological pressure was used in one case; eleven said violence occurred during the act itself;

one was 'used as a convenience rather than being treated like a person'.

The rape of Daphne Weber began less than one year after her wedding. For seven years she endured 'a brutal kind of intercourse used to degrade and establish my husband's greater power by having intercourse forced upon me when I said "no".' Bernice Summerfield's position was affected by her husband's religious background:

For me, 'making love' (as they say) was always like that — short, sharp, brutal and all *his* way. He did not recognise me as a human being with sexual and other rights. He knew I didn't want to have intercourse when I was saying 'no'. He is a strict Lutheran and believes in total obedience from a wife. He would not recognise my right to object.

Ten women said at times the husband might not have been aware of his partner's lack of consent. Fran Gordon said simply 'he knew I wasn't interested but just ignored my feelings, though maybe sometimes he didn't realise my lack of interest'. The rape occurred on odd occasions, unconnected with other violence. Dorry Maguire's response was more forthright: 'Sometimes he could have thought I wasn't objecting. But that would mean he has a pretty silly idea of what making love is all about!'

Forty-nine women had husbands who were in no doubt that the wife was not consenting but went ahead anyway. 'When I struggled and shouted at him to stop, he knew bloody well I wasn't consenting', wrote Jan Turner. Others simply said 'he knew I wasn't consenting'. Roslyn Hall was pregnant when her husband James attacked her in an isolated incident of spouse assault culminating in rape. He was under no illusion as to her state of mind: 'He pushed me onto the bed after beating me up and he raped me. He knew I was hurt. I was crying about the baby because I was in pain and knew he had hurt it by his bashing. He didn't care and just kept on. My stomach kept being pounded and pounded. I was aching, hurt and terrified about it.'

As for male victims, an anonymous correspondent wrote: 'Talking of rape in marriage, perhaps a woman can be just as cruel and inconsiderate — but it's not called rape — nor has it any dramatic impact on the community. I am sick and tired of women peddling the idea that cruelty and violence are found so much in men but not much in women.' Sam Trewin, the lone husband complaining of sexual attacks by his wife, classed 'lack of consent' as where he stated clearly 'no'; where he failed to respond; where he told his wife he had a headache; and when he was threatened by her to comply. 'She knew I wasn't interested,' he commented, 'then got really abusive when I didn't have an erection.'

Attitudes Towards Sexual Activity

Do women complaining of rape in marriage have problems with their own sexuality, rather than being victims of a blameworthy husband? A United Kingdom ruling, that where a wife had 'an aversion' to the sexual act, her husband had a right to rape her, was supported in Australia:

Intercourse . . . is a privilege at least and perhaps a right and duty inherent in the matrimonial state, accepted as such by husband and wife. In the vast majority of cases the enjoyment of this privilege will simply represent the fulfillment of the natural desires of the parties and in these cases there will be no problem of refusal. There will however be some cases where, the adjustment of the parties not being so happy, the wife may consistently repel her husband's advances. If the wife is adamant in her refusal the husband must choose between letting her wife's will prevail, thus wrecking the marriage, and acting without her consent. It would be intolerable if he were to be conditioned in his course of action by the threat of criminal proceedings for rape.[9]

Several bizarre notions underlie this philosophy. That it is intolerable for both marriage and the law to uphold a situation where a women's feelings are of no consequence is not remarked upon. No doubt it is more traumatic to be raped by one's husband, a person who has agreed to 'love and honour' than it is for a man to have to control his allegedly sexual urges until his wife is willing, or seek annulment or divorce and find a ready partner. Nor is it acknowledged that rape is as intolerable to the married victim as to one who is unwed. Neither does it occur to these writers that rape in marriage may be equally likely as no sex in marriage to 'wreck' it — and at least abstinence is not criminal, either inside marriage or outside it. Apart from these evidences of chauvinistic tunnel vision, however, does forced sexual intercourse occur only in marriages where wives lack any 'sexual instinct', or do not enjoy sexual intercourse?

None of the female respondents did not like sexual intercourse in itself, but none enjoyed being raped by her husband. Once in their eighteen year marriage Linda Lane was forced by her husband to participate in sexual intercourse: 'I was made to have intercourse against my wish and it was very painful and I was upset. It was very nasty.' Although Bill Lane's physical assaults involved kicking her in the stomach, hitting her with an open hand, confining her to certain parts of the house, using insulting language and being 'mean' with money, he had not previously attacked her sexually. He did not do so again. As the couple had two children born to the marriage, presumably Linda Lane engaged willingly in sexual intercourse at other times. Over a period of years Alexis Benedict was victim to marital rape, which after six to twelve months of marriage occurred three or four times a month: 'But on occasions other than the rapes, I readily consented in the early years', she wrote. These are not the words of a 'sexually frigid' woman, or a woman who 'has to be raped' to be shown how to 'enjoy' sexual relations with her husband.

Some women blamed themselves for lack of sexual desire, seeing this as leading to rape: 'If a woman's sexual appetite is not as strong as that of her husband, and if he is without scruple, rape is what happens. That is what happened to me.' Others were more aware of the roles women and men play in sexual intercourse and did not see enjoyment as the prerogative of the male. If Jan Paxton's husband Allen had been kinder, she 'would have felt more like it . . . But after he had kicked me and abused me I didn't feel like it. You can't make love under those conditions. I slept in the girls' room sometimes for protection.'

Aged 17½ years and 19½ respectively when they married, Gail Small and her husband Thomas's marriage became violent after six months. Gail Small considered youth and inexperience might have contributed to her husband's unthinking brutality, although her first reaction was to blame herself:

I remained because at first I thought I was frigid and I had to endure the intercourse, because it wasn't fair for him not to have it. I felt there was something missing when he began pushing me around because I wasn't responsive to him — I began to think it was all wrong and unfair. I could have put up with it all if he hadn't expected me to be all over him telling him (lies) about what a good lover he was. He wasn't any good. Perhaps too inexperienced (we both were) and I couldn't get involved with his wham! bham! thank you — and roll over for a cigarette attitude.

Lack of responsiveness, as in the Smalls' marriage, occurred in a number of cases. For Mary Dunbar, 'cool, calculated rape' was bearable — just. Responsiveness was, however, difficult. Demands for a response made the situation more so:

I learned to put up with it when he just came at me expecting (as he put it) a good screw. I couldn't see what was good about the 'get it in, screw it round and get it out' method, but at least I could bear it. It was worse when he expected me to respond. I couldn't because it hurt both physically and mentally. Here was this man, telling you you loved him and that because you were married to him he could do what he wanted. Then telling you you like what he was doing. In those times he got really worked up. Once when he was in that condition rape occurred intensely over a period of three days (a holiday weekend, unluckily for me). I got less and less able to put on any response, and he got angrier as the time went on.

Particularly where the rape was a part of continuing abuse in the marriage, women were unable to respond, although they recognised an obvious lack of enjoyment infuriated their husbands.

Perhaps outmoded ideas about male and female sexuality lie at the base of marital rape. By tradition, men have 'uncontrollable sexual desires' and marriage is designed to control 'masculine passions' by containment. Women have a 'duty' to perform in marriage, and by the marriage ceremony a husband agrees to protect and keep his wife, whilst she returns the favour with sexual favours (and later, off-spring of the union). Women are not supposed to enjoy sex, they must simply put up with it. All women should be pure, submissive and passive — particularly during the sex act. Therefore, they cannot be complaining of rape in marriage, when the only problem is their failure to respond, or the husband's going ahead without their assent to the particular act. This view is supported by religious dogma:

A young woman becoming a wife should think of her new state not as one that is to make her happy, but as one in which she is to make her husband happy . . . A good wife realizes that in becoming a wife she contracts to forget herself and put her husband's happiness above her own wishes and desires . . . [in marriage] she contracted to make a home for her husband in whatever place his work might call him; she does not proclaim any spurious independence in that regard . . . in the marriage contract she handed over the right to her body for the actions of marriage; she does not try to take that back again.[10]

Some respondents in the study held similarly traditional ideas about sex in marriage. Terry Adamson said her husband John was guilty of rape in marriage where he threatened her to comply, went ahead although she stated clearly 'no', and he knew his wife was not desirous of participating. Nonetheless she wrote: 'I think a man has some right to expect sexual intercourse, providing his demands are reasonable and not violent or excessive.'

Surprisingly, although Beryl Trewin was said by her husband Sam to have imposed herself upon him, been inconsiderate of his needs and wishes, ignorant of his feelings, and derogatory when he did not choose to participate in sexual intercourse with her, he saw nothing inconsistent in expecting women to play the traditional role in marriage. According to him, a husband has a right not to participate in sexual activity unless he wishes to do so; a wife does not have that right:

I don't think the law should get involved in the sex life of married people. In fact when you get married the wife consents to irrevocable conjugal rights. A man works and supports the family — a wife has a right to expect that. Therefore in exchange a man has the right to expect her to make sexual intercourse available to him. If a stranger does it — it is a crime against both husband and wife (that is, if a stranger stole a man's pay packet, likewise it would be a crime against both husband and wife).

Sam Trewin was adamant that his wife was an uncaring, selfish and abusive woman, yet could not see the corollary: that a husband who engages in sexual activity without considering the needs and wishes of his wife or her feelings is an uncaring, selfish and abusive man. That a male victim of abuse (and Sam Trewin was victim of 'attempted rape' only, not rape) who is disturbed at his own victimisation can neither empathise nor sympathise with a wife who is victim of rape gives reason for pause. How much (or how little) empathy or sympathy may women victims of rape in marriage expect from husbands who have not been victimised sexually?

That a woman must participate in sexual intercourse with her husband as a duty was not only put forward by Sam Trewin, however. It was reiterated by eleven women in the study. Some said 'I didn't think about it as rape at the time, because I thought it was duty'. Mary Morrison became more aware of her socialisation in terms of 'wifely duties' and recognised late in marrriage that she had been sexually exploited by her husband.

Everything regarding rape in marriage related to the home life at the time. I never questioned that I was or was not being raped. I suppose there were times when I really would have preferred not to indulge. Thinking back over our life together, I know there were times when I disagreed, quite strongly, but he always overcame me. Then there were times I remember when I would be upset and crying in protest, and he went on. Then I used to feel so sorry for him with all that puffing and panting he got quite red in the face. It seemed to mean so much to him, so I just put up with the unpleasantness of it all. I had a duty.

Other times my husband was mostly a kind and considerate person in relation to our sex life, and I suppose I believed, too, as did women of my generation, that the husband did have conjugal rights. However now, with all the information and changes to the law — and subsequent case histories and testimonies — I would say that *no man* has those rights over a woman should she disagree.

However exculpatory some women's views were of their husbands, significantly each considered that, at a particular point in their sex lives, her husband had adopted rapist tactics, subjecting her to his wishes regardless of hers. None had any hesitation, finally, in classifying her husband as a rapist.

Background of Husbands Who Rape

Folklore would have it that the 'sex drive' is competitive, aggressive, and essentially anarchic. Some anthropologists say the male is by nature sexually aggressive, ravishing and subduing the female; females are thus aroused. Yet the law endorses the idea that where there is no consent to sexual intercourse, the act is rape — a crime. Anthropological and legal standards appear to be in conflict, for 'ravishment' and sexual aggression do not convey the giving of consent. Indeed, the law holds that 'submission is no consent'. If all men conduct their sexual relations in this way, it is surprising that more are not penalised for their acts. However, 'social control' allegedly comes into play, men being acculturated generally into pursuing their sexual needs in less aggressive ways. The theory thus holds that only a very few resort to the law of the jungle and rape. What characterises these few, and do these characteristics accord with those of married men who rape their wives?

In Menachim Amir's study of rape in Philadelphia,[11] about 50 per cent of rapists had a previous arrest record relating mostly to crimes against property rather than crimes against the person, or more particularly, rape. The average age of persons arrested for rape was 27 and almost 20 per cent were under 18 years. Commenting on the findings, Donald MacNamara and Edward Sagarin point out[12] that most arrests are of males of low socio-economic status, and 'the fact that such a high percentage of the rapists had also been arrested for property crimes would strongly suggest a ghetto or poverty background and a general orientation of disrespect for the law'. Similarly in Australia, studies show a preponderance of lower socio-economic status persons in prison. Most rape cases coming before the courts fit the paradigm, with the offender coming from a lower socio-economic background. Some studies dispute any suggestion that rape is a crime of the poverty-stricken, despite the prison statistics, or that it has any link with socio-economic status. However, husbands as rapists have not been the subject of study: prior to 1976 in South Australia, as marital rape was not classed as criminal, there were no official research samples.

The present study disputes theories that the aggressor, as in domestic violence, generally fits the picture of the rapist in prison, in terms of youth, class status, income, occupation. Of fifty-seven rapist-husbands, fifteen were from the professional category; eight were managerial; twenty-six were in the small business/trade cat-category; five were unskilled and three were unemployed throughout the entire period of rape and violence. (One did sometimes take odd jobs, 'but not so's you'd notice' commented his wife.) In 1976, 1977, or 1978, the lowest income of any husband in full-time paid employment was $6000, and most husbands earned far more than $15 000 a year; some earned $60 000, $70 000, or $80 000.

If husband-rapists desire to dominate, a relevant factor with rapists generally, perceptions of income may be a factor, as suggested with spouse assault. Did the wives perceive their husbands as poor providers, making this clear to the men and adding to a poor self-image, leading to rape? Twenty-three respondents stated income was 'high' or 'very good'; twenty-six said it was 'average', six said 'low' and two said income varied or was irregular. A suggestion that rape arises because wives are derogatory about husband's earnings is not borne out.

Nor is the frequently painted picture of rape as a crime of youth correct. The age of the lowest offender in this study was 18 when the rape commenced. Most began raping between 20 and 35 years; some were between 36 and 49, and a few were over 50 years. In most cases rape continued through youth, middle age, and in some cases old age. The present study included men capable of committing rape until a ripe old age — and committing it. If older men fail to appear in rape statistics, it is because rape in marriage is not a crime, not because older men do not indulge the habit.

In commenting on the high rate of young men in figures of arrest and conviction for sexual offences, MacNamara and Sagarin suggest the figures 'may be misleading':

What we may be dealing with [in relation to the age factor] is a high percent-age of forcible rapists who are unmarried, a status that increases the likelihood that the individual is spending time wandering the streets alone or with other males; that he will be invited to the homes of females or be in a position to invite women for automobile rides; or that he will be able to entice women into situations conducive to rape.[13]

They may also be misleading because they fail to take into account married men who automatically inhabit a home where a woman resides full-time; that he does not have to 'roam the streets' alone to find a woman upon whom to foist his unwanted attentions; that he is not required to 'kerb crawl' to pick up a woman, when he is married to one. Nor does it take into account that the wife at home is automatically 'in a situation conducive to rape', should the husband wish to exercise his power.

Where victims commented on the frequency of the acts, there was little indication that rape ceased or lessened with the passage of years. In ten cases the abusive acts, including non-consensual sexual intercourse, became more intense towards the end of the relationship. This increasing intensity led to some wives departing. Grant Frost began attacking his wife three years after they were married. At that time he was twenty-seven; Gaye Frost was twenty-five. Throughout the marriage, rape occurred irregularly, but on average about once every three months: 'Then around the time I was seriously thinking about going — but I didn't let on to him — he got even worse. It wasn't every three months then, but about once a week. Maybe he got an inkling that I had had it. About that time he was raping me anally too.' When she left him, her husband was thirty-seven years old.

Only one respondent commented upon a possible cessation of sexual abuse due to ageing. Marion Howarth wrote:

It is my opinion that a man who resorts to rape is sick — sick. A strong sexual appetite is perfectly okay, as long as it is met by an equally strong one. If, on the other hand, it is not, and the domestic situation becomes fraught with anxiety as a result, rape, in that kind of marriage, is inevitable. (Unless, of course, the right kind of advice is sought, but the problem is very seldom seen as one by the offender.) That's how it was with John and I. But he's nearly 60 now and I hope I won't have to put up with it so often. In fact the last time it happened was about three years ago. Probably his gluttony in the past has meant today's lack of appetite.[14]

Apart from wives who remained after an isolated attack, in every instance where the rape ceased, it did so not because of ageing, but because the wife left the matrimonial home to separate permanently or to gain a divorce, or because the attacker died. Thirty-seven women divorced or were awaiting divorce after leaving the rapist; eleven were permanently separated; two escaped on the husband's death. Four stayed to face the rape.

However, where the victim sought to escape marital rape by leaving, in nine instances she failed, the husband discovering the wife's whereabouts and visiting to continue the attacks. After enduring twenty years of sexual abuse and other assaults, commencing after she and husband Robert had been married four years, Danielle Sinclair left, taking with her the only child remaining at home. Her husband pursued her:

Now I am going for a divorce but he still comes around threatening me and Tony. The other two kids have left. He got in the first time, because I didn't think he'd have the hide to do anything now we've left, but he bashed me up again and forced me to have sexual intercourse. He said I was still married to him and he could do what he liked. He says he'll get a gun and kill me one day. He has nearly bashed the door down once. I called the police and luckily they came for once and took him away that time but he keeps ringing up to say it won't stop him. I'm thinking of moving interstate when the divorce comes through.

Rhonda Bracton left her husband when both were in their late twenties, after seven years of 'living hell'. But physical attacks involving sexual assaults continued for three years after separation as Saul Bracton followed her from place to place as she tried to elude him.

Perhaps alcohol was involved. As with other spouse assaults, alcohol is often seen as the 'triggering factor': without alcohol, sexual aggression would not be expressed by violence; or perhaps the husband is simply 'overly romantic' through imbibing too freely, and therefore not to be blamed. This exculpation for rape in marriage was expressed in a recent letter to a popular women's magazine: 'If a couple are living separate lives in the one house, or apart, and the husband forces himself upon the wife, then he should be prosecuted for rape. However, an over-romantic or drunk husband, who has normal sexual relations with his wife, is hardly a rapist and should not be prosecuted.'[15] Such theorising immediately raises the question of what are 'normal sexual relations'. Is it 'normal' if a husband returns home after drinking too much and, wishing to engage in sexual relations, ignores his wife's wishes? One of the victims did not agree. June Graham's husband John, an office manager, began raping her after seven years of marriage. She wrote:

I consider 'rape in marriage' to involve:
  i. being forced to have intercourse when you have a headache;
 ii. having intercourse when you have to be threatened to comply;
iii. having intercourse although you state clearly 'no';
 iv. having intercourse when you lie without responding.
I also think it is having intercourse when you are physically forced to do so by a drunken man. i, iii and iv. each occurred in my marriage occasionally, but I felt mentally and physically abused by having to have intercourse with a drunk. As a result, I feel part of me (my sexuality, ability to relate to men) has been totally destroyed.

As for whether alcohol was connected with the crimes, twenty of the respondents said the sexual assaults occurred when the husband had not been drinking. The husbands of seven did not drink, even socially. Connie Miller expressed a sense of regret that her husband did not drink: 'At least if he'd been a drunkard, I'd have got some warning, or a chance to fend him off. As it was, I never knew when he'd be likely to want to get at me, threatening and carrying on.' For thirty-three victims, rape occurred sometimes when the husband had been drinking and sometimes when he had not; of these, the comment was made in six cases that it happened more often when the husband was drunk; six respondents said rape occurred more often when he was sober. Only four respondents were raped when the husband had been drinking. Laureli Tomsett, raped by force at least once a fortnight, said her husband was 'drunk most of the time' he was at home, and it was the drunken times he chose to force himself upon her.

As for women imposing themselves sexually upon men, even less information is available: few women have been documented in criminological literature concerning sexual imposition. With a sample of one, no theory can be expounded. Beryl and Sam Trewin appear on objective criteria to be a very ordinary couple. (As, indeed, do those couples where the husband was the aggressor.) Beryl Trewin was a full-time housewife, working in her husband's business part-time. His income was $15 000, plus property holdings, in 1978. Beryl Trewin did not take an income from the business. The abuse began three years after marriage, when Sam was twenty-eight and his wife twenty-four. He did not drink; she 'did not drink much'. The attempted acts of sexual intercourse took place sometimes after Beryl Trewin had been drinking beer, 'but didn't happen only when she was drunk'. The acts ceased when the wife, not the husband, left. She was twenty-eight and he was thirty-two. Perhaps the problem arose from both parties holding traditional attitudes about male and female sexuality. As previously noted, Sam Trewin firmly believed a wife's role is to serve her husband sexually, in exchange for financial support. Beryl Trewin expected her husband to perform sexually whenever she wished it, growing abusive when he was unable to comply. Perhaps the problem arose because Sam adhered to traditional views and his wife did not: perhaps he was offended rather than pleased that she saw her role as equally initiating sexual activity.

Traditional beliefs may be firmly intertwined with the husbands' readiness to demand sexual submission. Socio-cultural attitudes have been endorsed by law. Religious thought has propagated the idea that a woman 'belongs' to her husband, that she must 'give up herself in kind' to him.[16] In the present study, a number of husbands believed 'I've got my rights', and sexual intercourse with my wife is one of them. Terry Adamson said of her husband John: 'He thinks it's his "conjugal rights".' Marion Howarth wrote of her husband's refusal to accept that her poor health over thirteen years should be taken into consideration.

The belief that a husband has rights is not confined to any particular age group, socio-economic stratum, occupation or income level. Husbands in professions adhered to it, as did men on unemployment benefits, carpenters, barbers, labourers, small-business owners. Unfortunately, many of their wives believed it too, or felt unable to challenge it. Many remained because they accepted their husband's interpretation of the marital contract; many only realised years after the first act of sexual abuse took place, that indeed they had been victims of rape.

Factors Affecting Victims' Reactions

The traditional belief of husbands having rights over wives was one of the most significant influences on victims' reactions to marital rape. Thirty-one of the fifty-seven women victims remained in the marriage despite the rape, because they did not realise the husband was doing anything wrong. Suzanne Donald said: 'I couldn't see how to get out. I didn't even know I should. That I had a right. I thought he was within his rights doing what he did. When the children had grown I finally left. Now I know what he did was wrong and no woman should have to put up with it. No man has that right.' Mavis Brandon did not see the act as 'wrong' until she removed herself from the matrimonial home: 'I never considered it was rape while I was married. He raped me after separation. I saw that as rape . . . I thought it was his right. It was the other violence that was worse.'

Many women were self-effacing, not believing they had a right to leave because of sexual violence, or to take action against their husbands. 'I didn't want to cause more trouble/more fights/more fuss' wrote twenty-one women. Rather than take action, they took the route of 'peace at any price' owing to a combination of being socialised into passivity and submissiveness as females, and being strongly imbued with ideas of the rights of married parties, most particularly those of their husbands and the lack of rights for themselves.

Apart from socialisation and its debilitating effects on adult women suffering acts defined as criminal when carried out between strangers, practical considerations stood between them and escape. Women remain in marriages where sexual abuse occurs for much the same reasons that women remain in marriages involving spouse assault alone: children, finances, not having anywhere to go, isolation from friends, relatives and others who might give assistance, failure of the law to help.

Of the fifty-seven women respondents, only three were childless during the time of the rape. One respondent had two grown-up children by a previous marriage. Between them, the remainder had 143 dependent children when the violence was running its course. The lone male respondent had two dependent children. Sam Trewin said the children did not affect his staying or going. Twenty-four wives took a different view. They said the children had an effect on their ability to leave and frequently mentioned lack of finance as an additional factor. Rosalie Gibbons was raped occasionally over three years. With one daughter born during the marriage, she said: 'I got married too early so as to have a happy family with happy children and security. (Some chance!) What I ended up with was an unhappy family, unhappy child (only one thank God!) and no security. If I had left with Janine we might have been happy for an instant — but you can't stay happy when you're starving.' Linda Lane, victim of an isolated rape attack during an eighteen year marriage where her husband regularly beat and bashed her, said that she filed for divorce 'but tried marriage again because he begged me to come back also I had no money or home to take the children to'.

A large number of respondents were saving and waiting for the children to grow before leaving, or when the children were young adults they did in fact leave. June Graham, raped twice a week on average, remained. 'Because there was no where else to go — worried about him touching the children. Too embarrassed to ask the scarcely known neighbours for help. Legal action wasn't an option as far as I was concerned. I just made long range plans to leave with enough money for security for myself and the children.' June and her husband John had three children; the sexual attacks were not accompanied by other abuse; after seven years of rape during a fourteen year marriage, June Graham left.

Having children precipitated three women into taking action: as soon after the birth as financially possible, they left. Two mentioned that fear of the husband maltreating the child — in each case a daughter, in each case the feared maltreatment being sexual abuse — led to the resolution of the problem by leaving the matrimonial home and seeking a divorce or permanent separation. With hindsight, three respondents echoed in principle this action: 'I would not tolerate such actions today', said Connie Miller, 'I'd leave after one child if things had not changed. In some cases a child can improve a relationship. If after having one this is not the case then no amount of trying will work out. So I'd leave.'

Do women in abusive marriages resort to pregnancy and child bearing in the hope of restoring or creating a loving relationship? Apart from Connie Miller, no respondent mentioned such possibility, although this 'rationale' is sometimes commented upon. As well, mystification is often expressed as to women continuing with pregnancies where they endure abuse at the hands of husbands.

Lack of sympathy on the part of the community [for abused wives] is a residue from the times when the man was traditionally the master in his own house, owning his wife as 'chattel', sitting in judgment of her, his children and servants, doling out punishment as he saw fit. This does not explain however the puzzling fact of girls marrying a man whom they have reason to suspect of brutality, or of a wife to continue to have children by a man who ill-treats her, thus becoming increasingly and helplessly dependent on him.[17]

Mystification has no place in the field. Nor does ignorance of powerful social and physical factors that *do* explain why victims of abuse frequently bear children, making escape more frustratingly difficult and distant. Connie Miller remained with her husband Graham because she feared pregnancy and could not face the stigma involved if she left her husband, then found herself pregnant. As well, she feared her mother 'finding out' she was being sexually attacked by her husband: 'She would have blamed me and not understood.' Sally Smeeton 'put up with it for peace', needed a home, and 'the outside world seemed harder with a child'. She took birth control precautions so the rape would not end in another child, making her existence more difficult.

His family said I was money hungry and went out and worked and neglected my husband and child, instead of making a proper home. They blamed my refusal to have more children on me, not on my partner's behaviour, but since it began when I was pregnant and continued, I could not see that the addition of more responsibilities would help him, or me. With one child I could cope. He was not coping with one. He was not coping. Full stop. If I could not stop the rape, at least I could stop any more pregnancies. He could treat me like a non-person, but in the end this non-person had more control over her own reproductive organs than he did, in spite of his big man brutality.

It is not mere speculation that of the children born to women in abusive marriages involving rape, a large proportion result directly from rape. Women referred to constant douching and struggles with husbands to escape after the act to carry out this task, 'going without' to pay exorbitant costs for birth control pills, 'sneaking off' to family planning clinics to guard against feared results of marital rape. For Nell Rae, the effects were disastrous:

Remained because there was nowhere else to go. Partly thought that's what marriage is for. Couldn't leave because of the three children, particularly the mentally deficient boy. Tried all sorts of birth control methods but the money was short and had to stoop to douching at all times of day and night when he was on a rampage and wouldn't leave me alone. He would rape, get me pregnant, then beat and bash and that's how Greg ended up mental. Vowed it wouldn't happen again, and it didn't. But it was enough having to go through being raped. I had two abortions. The first time in a horrible way, because nothing could be done in Canberra without money or contacts in the hospitals.

And as with spouse assault, women raped in marriage correctly feared a reduction of their incomes if they left the rapist. Of every woman leaving the marital home, apart from those who remarried, only one increased her income: Lesley Matterson, an occupational therapist by profession, lived in an eight year relationship with a husband who began raping her occasionally soon after they began living together; the rape was more frequent during the final twelve months, three times a week on average. On leaving, her personal income of $7500 rose to $11 000 annually, as she entered full-time paid employment. But in overall terms the family income decreased, as her husband earned $18 000 annually and did not pay main-tenance ordered by the Family Court. But thirty-one women suffered dramatic drops in income, being transferred from an attachment to a wage earner to an attachment to the state via a pension. The sole male victim suffered an income drop from $15 000 annually plus share-income, to the supporting parent's benefit: he left paid employment to care for the two children of the marriage, but had substantial help, financial and supportive, from his mother ... and the shares, which he placed in his mother's name.

Often middle class women are more berated for remaining in abusive relationships, for it is assumed they have no financial problems. This notion is refuted by victims. Women married to men in middle class occupations had more to fear financially in leaving. Without exception, incomes were substantially reduced. When Marion McNair left her husband Jim after six years marriage, in which rape was a continuing pattern, she left behind a lawyer's income of $60 000 a year: with two children to support, her income became $100 a week. In Terry Adamson's case, her husband John retained custody of the two children, but her financial position was severely damaged by her divorce. Both accountants and in business together, she was forced to abandon her interest in their firm, where income had ranged between $27 000 and $42 000 during the latter years of their fourteen year marriage.

Like victims of spouse assault, victims of marital rape are often estranged from society and isolated from those who might help them escape. Isolation often arises from the husband's jealousy and possessiveness. The Royal Commission on Human Relationships mentions 'men treating *their* women as possessions, there to provide food and service' — including sexual services — and comments that jealousy is sometimes at the base.[18] Carol O'Donnell and Heather Saville touched on jealousy and, frequently arising from it, isolation of the woman from friends and family.

Jealousy and possessiveness were common features and were expressed in a variety of ways. A number of respondents reported restrictions placed upon them by their husbands which severely limited their social contacts. These ranged from the experience of one woman who was not even permitted into the garden to hang laundry until her husband came home from work, to a refusal to allow 'any wife of mine' to go out with himself and his friend for a drink in the afternoon.[19]

Of the fifty-seven women respondents in the present study, twenty-four mentioned rudeness of the husband, or jealousy of the wives' friends and other companions, or a combination of these, causing them gradually to withdraw from social activities hoping to halt the violence and sexual abuse. Norma Jones gave up her part-time secretarial work when her husband accused her of liaisons with fellow employees. On outings Nat Jones frequently 'caught' her glancing suggestively at passersby or other cinema or theatre goers.

It got so I had to keep my eyes straight ahead or just stare at him. I dreaded going out because I knew he would accuse me of wanting sex with other men, and when we came home it would be on, with him threatening and me crying, and him really hurting me by forcing me to have sex. I tried to make excuses for not going out but he found any excuse for pushing me round in bed. In the end I had the rape and the loneliness as well.

Her husband's attitude estranged Sally Smeeton from her family. Without their support, she could not make a decision to leave; had she left, the family might not have been ready to come to her aid: 'My family were pushed out early in the piece — he did not marry "them" and let them know it. If I contacted them he made things worse. He sought to isolate me, then torture me. I had no emotional back up. If I had I would have left, but I was ground down and uncertain — always hoping for improvement.'

Becoming reclusive did not stop the sexual abuse. It compounded the problem: women cut themselves off from those who might offer help and advice. And they lost the ability to think outside the restrictive boundaries of the home: the husband, his reactions, requirements and views became pivotal to the woman's existence. She frequently thought she had no right to move outside, either figuratively or literally. As Ellen Metcalfe said:

I stopped any visiting and hardly went to the shops, because I hated the third degree when [Sean] came home. None of my friends or family came to visit because I kept putting them off. The neighbours even ignored me finally. I couldn't ask anyone for help because I didn't have anyone I could trust or talk to. I didn't know they would help. I felt as if he had all the rights and I had none. I felt dirty and as if I was the one to blame.

Shame was significant in militating against women seeking help. Of the fifty-seven women respondents, only twelve complained to anyone about the rape. Of these, six complained 'obliquely': thus, Sonia Emerson said she neither complained to nor told anyone, as she thought 'that was the way marriage was' and she was 'too ashamed'. In a conversation with her minister of religion, however, she 'alluded to it'; his reaction was not supportive and she shrank from being more explicit. Her experience was not unlike others, who spoke with relatives, medical practitioners, outpatients personnel, friends.

Ten women took action over general violence in the marriage but did not reveal that rape was a part of the problem. Pam Langridge was subjected to degrading sex acts by her husband Donald throughout their six year marriage. He also beat her, threw her against the wall and down stairs, and banged her head repeatedly on table and bed ends. When she called the police, she 'told them the truth about the bashing, but never about the sex acts'.

Thirty-five women took no action, not knowing where to seek help and being 'too ashamed' to complain or tell anyone of the rape. Joan Hart commented: 'I was too ashamed and didn't know where to go. I didn't complain and told no one. I thought about the marriage guidance but couldn't talk to anyone about sex and they are no different. It's too personal to go around telling everyone. Anyway, I thought there must be something wrong with me because he kept telling me I was different from other women.'

Applying Steinmetz's theory, that where assault alone is the essence of the attack the stigma wives feel may be doubled for men victims,[20] in rape the stigma for men victims would be even greater. Males are presumed by society to be sexually dominant, with greater sexual appetites than women. The man wishing to complain of his wife's sexual attacks may be reluctant to do so, fearing being labelled 'sissy', a 'poofter', 'less than a man'. Sam Trewin's case does not, however, bear out the assumption. He made no mention of shame or guilt interfering with his reaction. He did not refer to such emotions at all. Far from failing to complain to anyone about his treatment, Sam Trewin complained to his mother, the family doctor, a welfare worker, a magistrate, and personnel at the Family Court. As with many of the women victims of marital rape, however, his reason for remaining was 'not wanting to start more arguments'.

The Vindictive Wife

It is feared that 'vindictive wives' will accuse husbands of rape just to get rid of them if the protection of the law is extended to them. Attempting to refute the need for a clear statement that rape in marriage was a crime, in South Australia it was said:

With blind optimism, some talk of improving the marital relationship, whereas in reality it is more likely to be dealt a crushing blow. A husband who is consistently and unreasonably refused intercourse by a vindictive wife could be pushed into ignoring his wife through fear of reprisal and seek adulterous relationships instead. By weakening the resolve of the partners to repair the crack in their marriage, criminal charges would act like a sledge hammer on a wedge.[21]

The argument has little to recommend it. In the present study, despite the lack of provision for prosecution of rape in marriage,[22] some husbands sought adulterous relationships *and* raped their wives. They were not forced into committing adultery through fear that the wife would seek legal redress against abuse; they entered adulterous relationships for other reasons. In seven cases the wife knew her husband engaged in extra-marital affairs but nonetheless imposed himself upon her. 'He'd come from another woman', wrote Connie Miller, 'then force me to submit.' She elaborated: 'Yes, my husband knew I wasn't consenting but went ahead anyway. Whenever my husband was with another woman — and this was on average of twice a week — he'd force me to have intercourse. It seemed an obsession with him as if I had to be in the act too. I felt this most degrading.' But she was too ashamed to complain or to tell anyone — even her mother. As she did not complain to anyone, it is hard to assert that, had the law included marital rape as an offence, she would have necessarily been off to the police to lodge a complaint against her husband.

However, one South Australian committee recommended that the law should protect rape wives separated from their husbands and living apart from them, whilst wives living with their husbands should be refused such protection: 'To allow a prosecution for rape by a husband upon his wife with whom he is co-habiting might put a dangerous weapon into the hands of the vindictive wife and an additional strain upon a matrimonial relationship.'[23] The assumption that legal protection would 'put a dangerous weapon in the hands of the vindictive wife' was reasserted in newspaper editorials of the day, as well as by the Anglican Archbishop of Adelaide.[24] This proposition is not supported by the present study. Although respondents suffered severe humiliation and discomfort, mostly on a continuing basis for years, and in many instances accompanied by beatings and bashings, there were no indications of vindictiveness against their attackers. Subjected to acts of forced sexual intercourse once or twice a month, beginning after two years of a nine year marriage, Christine Wallace commented: 'I think if maybe I hadn't had the children, I might have made more fuss and tried to stop it or might have left'. However, she also expressed a view common among twenty-two respondents: that it was not rape that was a major issue in the decision to go or to stay: 'I didn't consider rape an important issue at the time, as I thought it was only slightly inconvenient and distasteful. It was the violence that made me want to go and it was this that made it so difficult having the children. I could have put up with the rape, but the violence was another matter.'

Generally, women resolved the abusiveness of marital rape by leaving, or by simply enduring the abuse. They did not react 'vindictively' (and even this begs the question whether reacting to a crime by reporting it to the police is evidence of 'vindictiveness' on the part of the victim). Only one respondent said she fought back, and this did not involve resorting to legal processes. Jane Roberts wrote: 'Over a period of months I feared rape and kept quiet; as soon as I said "no" I was raped frequently over two months (approx.); after the last rape I bit him very hard on the penis, perhaps fear of castration kept him in line after that (in that area anyhow)!' Even where women complained about rape, their complaints were not to the police but were veiled asides to relatives or friends. When women did complain to police, rape was not mentioned. Without exception, complaints were limited to violence other than rape. Invariably it was physical violence that made them go to the police; they commented that the sexual abuse was 'bearable'.

As for the sole respondent advocating hanging for rapists, including rapist-husbands, vindictiveness did not appear in her actions. Enduring seven enforced pregnancies in seven years of marriage, black eyes, punching in the stomach, kicking, bashing and sickening sex acts, Rose Manchester maintained silence. When she called the police and complained to them and to a medical practitioner, the shame and degradation she felt were too great to allow her to tell police or doctor of the sexual abuse. Vindictiveness was not a motivation for her, or the other women: there was no vindictiveness to match the vindictiveness of the men who took to raping their wives.

Breaking up the Family

Two South Australian women's organisations objected to any marital rape law reform in that state, one saying it would 'undermine the family and contribute more to the breakdown of marriage', the other lambasting the proposals as 'divisive, an attack on the family, and a ridiculous piece of legislation'.[25] In response:

the view that the law should remain inoperable where acts are being forced upon one party to a marriage ignores that intrinsic to a marriage relationship is, presumably, the caring of the parties for one another, consideration for one another's feelings, wants and desires. More important than no man fearing the intrusion of the criminal law, is that for the maintenance of good married relations no woman should ever fear being attacked and sexually abused by her husband, much less have to endure, without support, actual abuse. The law cannot advocate that such an important aspect of matrimonial relations is of no moment. No policy is comprehensible which professes to uphold matrimony by refusing to intervene where there is inconsideration on the part of one of the parties to the marriage, such as to lead to the other party being forced to engage in sexual relations without wishing to do so.[26]

What is 'divisive' and 'an attack on the family' is any law upholding the right of a husband to rape his wife. Besides harming the victim, often destroying her emotionally, marital rape causes harm to other members of the family unit, particularly the children.

In the present study, eighteen women said they no longer trusted men; in some instances they trusted no one. Dorothy Jones spent three months of a nine month marriage being raped intermittently by her husband Jim. The rape continues, although they have separated and the divorce is scheduled a month away: 'I believe rape in marriage is a crime and should be treated as such. I am convinced that men *know* they are free to abuse women "by law" so they do. I don't have trust in a man's intentions or manner any more. I keep expecting aggression.' Esme Beverage said shortly: 'I am cynical and mistrust men utterly.' For Frances Naylor it was simply: 'Now I hate all men.'

Seven women were unsure, lacking confidence, depressed, and despairing as a result of rape. Karen Trevor, whose husband Lindsey was 'quite decent sometimes' was raped by him over five years in a pattern of two to three times a month with multiple effects. Now 'I'm in debt; I have no home, which means no real security; emotionally and physically exhausted; really pissed off with the Family Law Act and the Family Court; don't really like men too much.'

Fifteen women experienced generalised negative effects from rape. Two continued to live in fear, following an isolated attack after which they remained in the home. Seven expressed cynicism about marriage and thirteen said they would never or could never marry again or live with a man. Even where a former victim remarries or forms a subsequent relationship, the horror of the past lives on. As Rose Manchester found:

After he (my husband) was gaoled for another crime, I met a beaut bloke who is wonderful to me and the kids and we have three children of our own — 11, 7, 5. Neither of us smacks our children because Terry realises just what I went through and all the children too have grown up to be good kids and we have had no trouble with them. The only thing that shocks our happiness is sex. If we have just plain sex it is wonderful but if anything else is wanted I just shake and cry. I don't mean Terry ever asks me to do perverted things, he doesn't. It's just little things I just couldn't write down but I am lucky because I know Terry loves me and the kids and he would never hurt us physically or mentally.

Clearly, marital rape leads to a breakdown in family life. It does not act positively to reinforce loving relations; it can lead to the inability of the victim to relate to men. Support of marriage as a loving, caring union lies in recognising the rights of both parties, their freedom to choose joint activities and those they will perform alone, and the equal balance of rights and responsibilities towards one another. Marital relationships are destroyed where the law supports one individual indulging his own wishes without reference to his partner. More than the destruction of the relationship, this approach tolerates, even encourages, the destruction of the person who is victim to selfishness and abuse by her spouse.

What of other family members? Eight women wrote extensively of the harm caused to their children by marital rape. Sally Smeeton wrote: 'Saddest part of whole situation is that it has affected daughter who is now nearly 21 and cannot stabilise a relationship. Has marriage proposal but will not accept a very suitable relationship "because of Dad" ... It seems she will pass by a chance of a good relationship because of what she saw of marriage.' In recalling her childhood, Stephanie Durack's daughter Norma wrote of hearing her parents arguing, and her mother being punched and shaken bodily on the bed: 'I believed my mother was being hurt and didn't want it. I would hear Mum objecting and I would have a nightmare so she would have to come to me. When we ran away to Nanna's, lots of times, Nanna only said that's how men treat women, what do you expect. I grew up not thinking much of men, for one thing, and not thinking women were worth much, for another.'

Experience of rape in the marital home led many women to the inevitable conclusion that 'the family' was a hypocritical institution. As Mavis Brandon, victim of rape and other violence, pointed out:

I feel disgusted with men. I feel guilty about the way my daughter suffered. Of course the rape and violence affected me. I cannot even think of living with a man in an intimate situation again. I think the police are corrupt. I think society needs to be built again with clear ground rules for human relationships. I think they should stop promoting the family as the ideal situation.

Why Marital Rape?

Several threads underlie the commission of marital rape in the present study. In some cases at least husbands and wives had differing notions of sexual needs and satisfactions. Some respondents said their sexual appetite was less than their husband's, making them sexually incompatible. Sexual inexperience of both themselves and their husbands, or their husbands alone, made for sexual difficulties from the start of some marriages. Noting the work of William Masters and Virginia Johnson on heterosexual relationships and the need for mutual appreciation of male and female sexuality,[27] it is not surprising that couples experience some difficulties early in relationships. However, none of the respondents said rape occurred from the first day of marriage: although with a large number, sexual abuse occurred early in the marriage, husbands and wives must have experienced some non-rape situations prior to the rape or rapes. Was there some fault in adjustment after a period of sexual compatibility? Were husbands gentle and considerate for the first few weeks or months of the relationship, then impatient and self-indulgent, seeking only their own satisfaction and failing to recognise their wives' needs? Whatever the case, clearly greater opportunities for sex education and perfection of sexual techniques for both women and men are essential early in marriage, if not before.

However, even if the onset of rape is attributable to lack of perception, by the husband, the wife, or both, of individual and mutual sexual needs, a deeper and more disturbing element is present. If the wife (or husband) signifies a lack of desire, why does a partner who has agreed to love and care for the other simply ignore her (or his) wishes? The clear message from a large number of cases was the ideology of sex as husband-right: 'it was my duty'; 'it was his right'. Wives expressed this philosophy and husbands were adherents of the same dogma. Because the husband believed in his rights, he felt under no obligation to ensure that his wife was acquiescing and had intercourse despite her objections, and the need for threats and even bashings. Nor did he feel any obligation to ensure she enjoyed sex. This again shows a need for sex education and for inculcation of such ideals as mutual respect and consideration. Engaging in sexual intercourse with a person who is objecting, struggling, crying or lying mute cannot be as enjoyable as sexual intercourse with a joyous partner: men educated thus will increase their own sexual satisfaction. Visions of marriage encompassing caring and love require this.

Yet it would be wrong to rest on the easy assertion that sexual problems in marriage arise only from lack of sex education. The origins of rape as a general phenomenon are no different from those of rape in marriage. Rape is the ultimate act of sexism. It is the objectification of the female person, the end being the use of the female body for an act of sexual violence. Rape is an act of domination rather than an act involving sexual gratification. That ethic is clear in Jane Roberts's case. She was acquiescent for the first two years of marriage, agreeing with her husband's every word and complying with his sexual wishes — then when she began to assert her own views generally, and in particular in bed, he forced oral, anal and vaginal intercourse on her.

The desire to dominate in the home shows not only in husbands' acts of abusive sexual intercourse, but also in the deliberate isolation of women from friends, relatives, neighbours; charges that wives were engaging in sex with delivery persons, office colleagues, or neighbours, so invading their partners' lives as to prevent communication with the outside world; in beating and bashing of wives, then forcing them to be responsive to sex.

Writing of rape generally, Larry Tifft and Dennis Sullivan conclude:

Inextricably woven from the dirty fibre of sexism is the crime, the social harm of rape. Rape . . . is a crime, a social harm of power, a channel for the expression of superiority perhaps undertaken by persons who are frustrated in their attempts to dominate and invade the dignity and freedoms of others in other life contexts. Are these persons unsuccessful in dominating others at home or in the economic sphere, spheres wherein they themselves are dominated?[28]

The rhetorical end question simply misses the point. When research into rape uncovers numerous acts of abusive, non-consensual sexual intercourse within the home and between persons who are known to each other, such as *de facto* spouses, it is more to the point to see rape as an extension of domination of others at home, rather than its opposite. As Bernice Summerfield, complaining to no one, victim of two years of repression, religious fanaticism, slapping, punching, pulling hair and rape, said: 'I remained with him because I was locked into this situation of total powerlessness. I owned nothing, not my own name, income, roof over my head, and as he was so often determined to prove to me, not even my own body.'

CHAPTER 7 MARITAL MURDER

The institution of marriage is either the greatest curse or the greatest blessing known to society. It brings two people into the closest of all possible relations; it puts them into the same house; it seats them at the same table; it thrusts them into the same sleeping apartment; in short, it forces upon them an intimate and constant companionship from which there is no escape. More than this, it makes any attempt at escape disreputable: the man or woman who seeks to loosen or break the tie which he or she finds intolerable, is frowned upon by society. The fracture of the galling chain must be made at the expense of the reputation of one or both of the parties bound together. There is no hope for two people shackled in the manacles of an unhappy marriage, but a release by death; and no wonder that each desires deliverance, and longs for the death of the other.

Yet what can be more horrible or more degrading to human nature than such a situation. Can anything be more demoralising than this position of two people living under the same roof, forced into daily and almost hourly companionship, each of whom secretly desires the death of the other?

That the number of people who find marriage intolerable is not small, the annals of crime prove. Wife murders are so common that one can scarcely take up a newspaper without finding one or more instances of this worst of all sins; and none but God can know how many men and women are murderers at heart.

The Revolution (National Women's Suffrage Association Journal) 1868.

A casual scanning of daily newspapers in New South Wales in 1979 showed that, after little more than a century, nothing has changed. Wife killings — and husband killings — are comparatively commonplace:

A woman, 48, and her four daughters had been subjected to an increasing number of beatings for several years until the alleged murder of her husband, Burwood Court of Petty Sessions was told yesterday.

Sydney Morning Herald, 31.1.79, p.30.

A woman stabbed her husband to death as he lay in bed shouting abuse at her, it was alleged in the City Court of Petty Sessions.

Sydney Morning Herald, 23.2.79, p.9.

A man who shot dead his adulterous wife in a caravan park had made himself prosecutor, judge, jury and executioner, a Supreme Court judge said yesterday.

Daily Telegraph, 15.3.79, p.13.

A woman who was stabbed and beaten by her husband died from an extensive compound fracture of the skull with cerebral haemorrhage, a coroner found yesterday.

Daily Telegraph, 7.4.79, p.6.

A 47-year-old seaman drove his car on to a footpath to run down his wife, the Supreme Court at Paramatta was told . . . Earlier the same day, the man had been served with a court order to get out of the family home.

Sydney Morning Herald, 20.6.79, p.16.

Despite celebrated cases and public uproar against convictions for marital murder in 1981, there is little evidence that events of the past two years herald any change. Wife killings and husband killings are a fact of Australian life. And if victims of domestic violence are to be believed, official statistics are a poor indicator of the number of marital murders that would take place had victims the courage to carry their wishes into action, or wife-beaters the cowardice to bring their threats and plans to fruition. In only three cases in the present study did a killing actually take place; in many more cases, threats and attempted murder were daily fare.

Attempting to Kill: Women Victims

Thirty-three of the one hundred and nineteen women victims of spouse assault were threatened with death, lunged at with knives, endured brandishing of guns or deliberate attempts at murder. Six child abuse victims commented on fathers' threats on their lives and their mothers' lives, as well as lives of other siblings, during bouts of beating. Three women were threatened with death when a husband was discovered sexually molesting a daughter and they decided to report to the police. Threats of killing were often made when victims said they would seek outside help, whether from police, family, friends or medical practitioners. Eunice Georgevic's husband Antonio 'always threatened to kill me, both to myself and to my daughter, when the least thing upset him he wanted to kill whoever did it. All his sports were related to killing.' Unlike some other husbands, all his weapons were licensed.

Attempts at murder were most commonly by strangulation, suffocation, drowning, running the car off the road with the victim in it, or running the victim down. Antonia Grey's husband drove 'like a maniac' with her in the car, threatening to run off the road and kill them both. Other times he held pillows over her head, forcing her to struggle to regain her breath and free herself with reserves of strength she did not know she had. Of her mother, Lesley Minchin wrote: 'My mother is continually bashed in front of my sister. I once saw him pick up and throw a kitchen table at her. He has knocked her downstairs, pushed her into the shower and tried to drown her in the bath, but she stays with him and can't get away.' Trevor Fisher attacked his wife after returning from her father's funeral. He knocked her down, choking her and kicking her in the stomach shouting, 'when my mother dies I'll kill you too'. Lars Christensen made attempts on his wife Marjorie's life on several occasions during their nineteen year marriage. Once, he attempted murder by welding the passenger door on their truck and tipping it into an embankment, with her inside. He also attempted to run her down by car.

When after a very serious attempt on my life I saw a doctor who told me I must leave. I was terrorised every place I went, and my friends were also. I asked for help from the police; they patrolled a street each night, but not the one I'd given them! Stayed at an hotel over weekend ready to attend court on the Tuesday, visit a solicitor on the Monday. Went to see a bed-ridden old friend on the Sunday. Returning to the hotel I ran into a shop doorway to save myself from being run down by him in his car. He jumped out and threw me on the ground before I could reach the other side of the road even.
    When a car stopped he held his hand over my mouth and told the couple he was only subduing me to return me to the mental hospital. They took off.

Two young chaps then pulled up and I was able to get them to drive me to the police station, where they said 'sorry, we don't want to get involved' and took off.

My eye was black, lip cut and swollen, legs abrased and clothes torn. Police drove me around town for two hours but we didn't find him. Then they took me back to the hotel where the owner's wife attended to me. Next day my 16-year-old daughter arrived to go to court also. We were walking from the doctor's towards the solicitor's office when my daughter pushed me into a shop doorway as there he was again trying to run us both down.

Faith McDonald's husband Duncan made repeated attempts on her life from 1943 to 1977, when they finally separated. She noted:

Seven attempts on my life at various intervals, usually after a comment or reproach about his girlfriends or when under the spell of another woman (he had many close women friends always).

1. Attempted pushing from fourteenth floor window in Kenya hotel. After attempt failed threw himself on floor on back, arms and legs spread-eagle. Did latter twice.
2. Attempted accident engineered with car on left, not noticing (deliberately) to give way on right after a work colleague of mine was killed this way earlier.
3. Given his brakeless car to drive (his suggestion and he took mine).
4. Previous to this (3), given his car to drive down the Clyde when brakes going.
5. Attempt to get me on deck in enormous seas, ship listing badly (Noumea).
6. Chain held above head with threat to kill (Wisconsin, Maddison Campus).
7. Brake hose off my car. (After judgment, may have come off by own accord. Not sure.)

Where women sought outsiders' help on being threatened with death or where threats took on a concrete reality as deliberate attempts at murder, they were immediately at a disadvantage. A tripartite problem faces women who are sufficiently angry or concerned for their own safety or that of their children to go to the police when their lives are at risk. First, both police and the community believe that what happens within the family circle is a matter for those within it, even where deliberate attempts on a woman's life are in question. Second, the pervasive idea that because she is his wife, 'he can do what he likes with her' extends even to attempted murder. Third, women are seen as exaggerating, that 'she's imagining it', or that 'it's not really serious'. When Norma Collie received threatening letters from her former husband Tom and reported them to the police, together with the long history of marital violence, including threats with guns and knives, the police said they could do nothing until 'something serious happened'. When Marjorie Christensen sought police help after her husband ran her down, the extent of their concern was to 'drive around looking for him for two hours'. Even had they not been convinced of Lars Christensen's intention to end his wife's life, evidence of the assault and battery was sufficient to have them take the matter seriously. It is ironic that women complaining about their husband's attempts upon their lives should be treated as harbouring fantasies. Three-quarters of marital murders committed in New South Wales in 1958–1967 and 1976–1978 (175 and 77 cases respectively) were committed by men. In over one-third of wife murders, a history of assault was recorded.[1] Taking into account the number of women who do not call the police when they are subjected to vicious attacks by their husbands, this figure is remarkable. Statistics for other jurisdictions are similar. Women — and the police — should take attempted wife-murder complaints seriously.

Attempting to Kill: Men Victims

Husbands are the most likely victims of women killers. Tess Rod's study[2] of police records in New South Wales found a history of assault by the man upon the woman was present in 'nearly half' the husband murders in 1958–1967 and 1976–1978. Eight women victims of spouse assault in the present study made mention of murderous thoughts, although none went so far as planning the killing. Pamela Friar and Pat Renshaw wondered whether, had they stayed longer, each 'would have one day murdered him myself'. Rhonda Hudson and Joan Treggary harboured fantasies about killing their husbands. Joan Treggary wrote: 'I don't think there is really any "excuse" for murder, but I can understand that any woman might feel tempted. After seventeen years of marriage I was placed in this situation and admit to fantasies of "murder on the Bourke express".' Of her husband David, Mary Dunn said 'I nearly killed him often. He nearly killed me often. Lots of *husbands* deserve to get murdered because of the way they treat women and kids.'

Beverley Martin contemplated killing when she discovered her spouse interfering sexually with the children; so did Meg Barnes. Beverley Martin commented, however, 'what good would killing do?' and decided against it. Meg Barnes wrote: 'Many times after I found out about the incest, I was shocked and upset. I can really understand that a woman would kill her husband if he had been abusing her and the kids — sexually and violently. I think that's a good enough excuse. People who sexually abuse their children should be severely punished for it.'

Not only wives thought that killing the abuser would be a way out of an abusive family life. Cheryl James, her sister, four brothers and mother were beaten by Carl James from the time the children were small. Cheryl believed if she 'hadn't been strong, I would have killed my father years ago, and then where would I have been? At least my brothers and sisters would have been able to sleep a lot better at night. Life might have been a lot happier for us all.' Naomi Donaldson went further. After almost four years of being sexually molested by her mother's *de facto* spouse, she finally brought it to an end: 'It ended one day when I grabbed up a bowie knife he had and nearly killed him with it. He was drunk and couldn't protect himself or get away. He knew I was serious and called me a bitch but at least stopped doing it. Soon after Mum left. But I hate to think about it. It made *me* be the violent one. I *hate* him.'

An equal number of women victims thought about killing themselves rather than their husbands. Four of those who found their husbands indecently assaulting or raping their daughters contemplated suicide and killing the children as well. Four women were so distraught after attacks upon themselves and physical violence towards the children, that they too thought of self-destruction and killing the children to get them away from the violence. None of the eight male victims of wives' assaults contemplated suicide or mentioned child killing as a possible way of escaping the abuse. They had no need for such a 'solution': they had real and effective alternatives.

Murder

Of the three spouse murders, only one was a wife killing. The dead woman's sister related the facts. Georgio Vasseliu pursued his wife and children back to Australia from Uruguay, his country, where they had been living for four years. His wife had left him, intending to divorce him, gain custody of the child, and stay in Australia. 'After arriving back here and advising him she would not be coming back', wrote Monica Jones, 'he kept writing . . . I have read parts of his letters to her and in them he had told her he would kill her or both her and their only child, a boy, and later other members of the family if she did not go back to Uruguay. Finally he came out to Australia where for several months arguments, and abuse etc. raged.' Later, arguments centred mainly around the child. He said he would kill his wife if he couldn't have the child. The police were called as the arguments stormed. After a number of visits they advised they would come only if severe violence started. When it did, they were there within ten minutes. But it was ten minutes too late.

They argued each access day over their son. He spoke very little English therefore couldn't or wouldn't converse with other members of the family. She didn't seem to care after a while and also had a female friend staying there at our parents' home whom he did not like and whom he also stabbed approximately nine times and was charged with attempting to kill her which was reduced to grievous bodily harm. She also spoke Spanish fluently with the result none of us could understand their arguments. In some ways she ridiculed him.

It ended in manslaughter. There were a lot of threats from him and like usual Vivienne was very quiet. The day she was killed her husband also burnt our parents' home down and set alight to her caravan and also attempted to kill another woman who was visiting. At the trial there was hardly a mention of the fires he started, and why not?

As I write this I am still trying to soothe a severe nerve rash on my hands and to say anything of upsets in general to other sisters and brother and their families would take me days to try and describe and put in writing to you.

Apart from the parties being from different countries and the accompanying arson, this picture of marital murder is typical of at least 20 per cent of wife killings in Australia today. When women are threatened by their husbands with death if they leave, many are terrified that the threat will be carried out, often rightly so. Almost all women who kill their husbands are living with them at the time, but 20 per cent of male spouse killers stab, shoot, strangle or run down by car women who have left them.[3] Husbands are unable to deal with the affront to their ego implicit in a wife or *de facto* wife separating herself from their lives, or even seeking divorce on her own initiative. Georgio Vasseliu's case has an added ownership theme: that of child ownership. Not only did Vivienne Jones escape from his possession, but she also took with her *his* child. That his pursuit and attempts to regain Vivienne and the child were not founded in real concern for the welfare of the child is evident in his 'solution' to the problem, which was to kill the child's mother, and end in gaol himself.

Yet not all analysts see wife killings of this sort in the same light. In December, 1981 under the banner headline of 'Man who Killed the Wife he Loved' the 'tragic court story' was related of a Sydney man 'who loved his wife so much he killed her'.

The judge who sentenced him yesterday to three years jail, but with a six-month non-parole period, said: 'My sympathy is clearly in your favor.'

John Clarke, 37, of Penrith, stabbed his wife in the heart when she said she was leaving him . . . The court was told he drove his wife to hospital after he stabbed her and then surrendered to the police. His wife's threat to leave him had been the ultimate blow, and he had struck out in despair and frustration.[4]

The judge went on to say that gaol was likely to punish not only the offender, 'but also his three children who had lost their mother'. It is this sort of muddled thinking that could encourage men to kill their wives, should their wives wish to leave them, and locks women into unsatisfactory relationships of no benefit to themselves, to their children, or ultimately to the men murdering them. Men believe they have a right to retain a wife's company and person, simply because, once, she agreed to marry them and did so, and courts support men in that view. Little wonder women despair that, once married, there is no way to leave. If she does leave, a woman lives with constant fear of her ex-husband forcing his way back into her life, to kill her — for if he cannot have her, no one else will.

Husband killings are different. Linda Anderson was married to Jimmy Anderson for twelve years. Once or twice a week, always in a continuing pattern over those years, Jimmy Anderson slapped, punched, kicked, and pulled Linda Anderson's hair. Weekly, he threatened her with a rifle. She suffered very bad bruises, lasting for weeks. She told no one, keeping it to herself. Could she leave? 'No, never. Could not. Was not able. Would have left, but could not.' She had six children, four sons, two daughters. Sometimes she obliquely sought help from outside. 'I did not confide in anyone. I had my own pride. But sometimes I tried to talk with the minister in a roundabout way, but he believed when you're married, you stay married till death do us part. I went to the doctor, but never told the doctor the reason. I always kept things to myself.' Finally, Linda Anderson retaliated to protect herself against the beatings. She could take no more: 'Did not threaten murder, it just happened on the spur of the moment.' Jimmy Anderson was shot with the gun he had so often used to bully and threaten his wife.

Vinnie Bodley's victimisation began four months before her marriage to Danny Bodley. Violence continued throughout twenty-three years of marriage and was meted out on the children, particularly upon one son, who suffered broken ribs and other severe injuries from the time he was five months old. She and the children were slapped, hit, punched, hit with chairs, brooms, a rolling pin, and any other implement available at the time; her hair was pulled; she was scratched, bitten and kicked; threatened with a kitchen knife and shot gun; thrown down stairs and pushed out of the car; threatened and attacked with broken bottles. Over the years she suffered cuts, bruises, a broken arm and a broken collar bone. The police were called often. Sometimes they came, sometimes they didn't. They advised Vinnie Bodley to take action, to leave her husband, to get a divorce, to take out an injunction. Sometimes they simply refused to come. Vinnie Bodley left her husband Danny and divorced him. She married another man. When he died, her family and those she had thought of as friends persuaded her to take Danny back. 'He's drinking himself to death', they said. 'Without you, he'll be dead in a year.' It took a few more years, but finally, Danny Bodley died. Vinnie and her son Roger, like Linda Anderson, used the weapon that had been used against them. It was frightening to be on the trigger end of the gun — but not as frightening, this time, as it would have been had Danny Bodley held the rifle. Vinnie was forty-seven, her son fifteen, her husband forty-nine.

Linda Anderson was 'fortunate' in being convicted of manslaughter only. Vinnie and Roger were charged with murder and convicted. They spent six years in prison before political agitation had them released — not free, but on licence. If they break the terms of the licence, they will be gaoled once more, Vinnie to serve out the remainder of her life imprisonment term, Roger to complete his sentence of fifteen years.

There is a spectacular difference between a case where a woman, constantly beaten and abused, turns upon the abuser in desperation and kills him, and one in which a man, never having been bashed by his wife — perhaps having bashed her himself — suddenly, upon learning she is leaving him, strangles her, stabs her, shoots her with his own gun (a gun for which he often has no licence). The ordinary person regarding these dissimilar circumstances might think the law would react less harshly toward the battered woman, lashing back in desperation, and more harshly toward the pampered man, angrily playing dog-in-the-manger with the woman he married. The ordinary person would be wrong. The law, structured to deal with a male concept, 'justice', treats such cases disparately — in the man's favour.

Marital Murder and the Law

At common law, a man had a right to beat his wife. If he killed her, he could be prosecuted for murder, but his act of unlawful killing was far less serious than that of a wife who killed her husband. The law styled every husband a 'lord', a wife merely 'his woman'. A woman who killed her 'lord' offended against the very nature of civil government; she was guilty of petty treason, with punishment greater for her crime than for any other species of petty treason:

Husband and wife, in the language of the law, are styled *baron* and *feme*. The word baron, or lord, attributes to the husband not a very courteous superiority. But we might be inclined to think this merely an unmeaning technical phrase, if we did not recollect that if the baron kills his feme it is the same as if he had killed a stranger, or any other person; but if the feme kills her baron, it is regarded by the laws as a much more atrocious crime, as she not only breaks through the restraints of humanity and conjugal affection, but throws off all subjection to the authority of her husband. And therefore the law denominates her crime a species of treason, and condemns her to the same punishment as if she had killed the king. And for every species of treason . . . the sentence of women was to be drawn and burnt alive.[5]

In time, equality for women and men who murdered a spouse was outwardly accepted by the law. No statute and no accepted common law precedent any longer distinguished explicitly between husband killing and wife killing. The law is not, however, relevant only in terms of what appears on the statute books. The interpretation of the law is significant and must be seen in context. Judges interpret the laws. Lawyers fight the cases for judicial decision. Judges and lawyers, until the early twentieth century, have all been men, and even now proportionately few women practice as solicitors or barristers. Men dominate the profession, so laws are interpreted with men, not women, in mind. This is nowhere more clear than in cases of murder.

To convict a man or woman of murder, the prosecution must prove, beyond a reasonable doubt, that the accused intended to kill or inflict grievous bodily harm, or did the act causing death with reckless indifference to human life. Other punishable homicides are classed as manslaughter. In Australia, where a person is convicted of murder, life imprisonment is the mandatory sentence; a judge has no choice.[6] Where the conviction is for manslaughter, the judge has a discretion as to what sentence to impose: it may be for a term of years; it may be release on a bond or on probation. A person charged with murder may plead self-defence or provocation. If the accused acted in self-defence, that is a complete answer to the charge: the accused will go free. If the accused acted in self-defence, but used force disproportionate to the threat or attack made by the person killed, the accused will not be freed or convicted of murder, but will stand convicted of manslaughter. If the accused was provoked into doing the act causing death, that mitigates the penalty: the accused will be guilty of manslaughter, not murder. These rules ostensibly apply to both women and men. When analysed, however, they are designed for men, not for women, so that women are hard-pressed to come within them. Women are less likely to escape a conviction on grounds of self-defence than are men. Women are less likely to be convicted of manslaughter, on grounds of disproportionate self-defence, where charged with murder, than are men. Women are less likely to be convicted of manslaughter, on grounds of provocation, than are men.

Self-defence

To establish self-defence, counsel must show that the accused was attacked with deadly force and was in danger of death or serious bodily harm. The retaliation by the accused on the attacker must be commensurate with the nature of the attack: fists must be met with fists, blows with blows. To combat a fist-attack with a knife or a gun suggests immediately that disproportionate force was used. How can a woman 'meet blow with blow, fists with fists'? Most women are physically less well equipped than men to fight. Most women are socialised into passivity and submission; they are not taught to use their fists, or to retaliate against a fist onslaught. The self-defence defence presupposes that both parties fighting are roughly equal in physical stature, in fighting abilities, and in socialisation. When a woman is attacked by a man, to fight back with fists would be unrealistic. Her fists would not do the damage to him that his will do to her, nor will her fighting skills be akin to his. Women, unlike men, are reluctant to fight and this reluctance inhibits their ability to retaliate in kind. Even if the woman is larger than her husband, the demands of her socialisation into submissiveness preclude her from fighting back. Thus Jean Rouse, 12 stone and beaten by her husband Ralph Rouse, 11 stone, was unable to fight back for twenty years. When she left him, she packed up because the children were grown and no longer a worry. She did not kill her husband, but had she wished to defend herself, viewing her own fighting skills as less than those of her husband despite their difference in weight, she would have had to pick up a weapon, putting herself outside any defence of self-defence despite his attacks. Being unable to fight back, fists with fists, the defensive woman picks up the nearest implement she has to protect herself, the kitchen knife, and places herself outside the self-defence rules. (Significantly, most women kill in the kitchen.) Sometimes, the woman picks up the rifle her husband has kept on hand to shoot rabbits, or more often to terrorise her. In pulling the trigger, again she places herself outside self-defence rules.

On the afternoon of 19 December 1979 Georgia Marie Hill discharged from a .22 rifle three rounds, one of which struck her *de facto* husband in the head. He died shortly thereafter. She was charged with murder and convicted, and the mandatory sentence of life imprisonment was passed upon her. The Crown case was that she had obtained the rifle from another part of the house in which the deceased was living with her, that she had shot three rounds from it with intent to take his life, and that her conduct amounted to murder. The charge was defended by Georgia Hill on the ground that emotional tensions had escalated over the two years she had lived with the man and her acts resulted from the state of fear built up. The defence claimed that the deceased was a man who, when affected by alcohol, was given to violence. Georgia Hill was said by the court 'to be frail and slight in her physical structure'. Photos tendered in court showed her *de facto* husband as a 'big, strong man'. There was 'a significant volume of evidence' before the court establishing that the deceased savagely attacked Georgia Hill on numerous occasions. The first witness for the Crown, a nursing sister living not far from the scene of the crime, gave evidence of this:

Q. Did the deceased at some stage, or at any stage, admit to you assaulting Mrs Hill?

A. Yes, yes.

Q. Can you tell us what he admitted to doing?

A. Well, he dragged her around the room by the hair . . .

Q. When was this? Can you remember when it was in relation to the shooting?

A. Oh, six months before, something like that I should imagine.

Q. Now what did the deceased admit to you that he had done to Mrs Hill?

A. Well I spoke to him about it and he admitted that he had dragged her around. He said 'I shouldn't have done it but, you know, I just got mad', and this was a common occurrence. I had witnessed things like this myself.

Q. He said he dragged her around.

A. Well, I confronted him with it and he said 'Yes, I shouldn't have done it, but she made me mad', or something like that. I can't remember exactly.

Q. Did he say how he dragged her?

A. I confronted him and I said, 'You mustn't pull her around by her hair, it's wrong'.

Q. By her hair?

A. Yes.

Q. As you say, he admitted to you that he had, in fact, done it?

A. Yes.[7]

Another neighbour, Ms Longuet, described the deceased's demeanour after he had been drinking as 'absolutely shocking'. 'Well, he was like a maniac really', she said. A police constable gave evidence of having several times been called to the house during domestic disputes. He had asked the deceased to leave the house about six months prior to the shooting. The deceased's criminal record revealed his addiction to alcohol and his propensity for violence. In 1958 he was fined twice for drunkenness; later he was fined for offensive behaviour and fighting in a park. In 1959 he was fined for offensive behaviour and street fighting. In 1962 he was fined for offensive behaviour and twice for drunkenness. In 1964 the fine was for wilful damage, and later in 1964 a conviction for robbery with violence brought him two years imprisonment. After release, in 1966 he received a bond for wilful damage; later in 1966 he was convicted of larceny from the person and drunkenness. A fine for disorderly behaviour was imposed in 1967 and a fine for assaulting a female in 1969. Malicious injury to a window brought another fine in 1971; later that year he was fined for an assault, with a follow up fine for a conviction of drink-driving. In 1977 a similar charge led to another fine. The appeal court summed it up:

This is a record, with one exception, not of major crime but nevertheless it is characteristic of a man with a constitutional weakness for drink and a propensity for unpleasant violent conduct when drunk. It is not difficult to envisage the atmosphere which must have existed in this household in which the appellant [Georgia Hill] found herself living with the deceased over the two years running up to the fatal shooting.

Neither the court of the first instance, nor the appeal court, considered Georgia Hill should qualify as a person killing in defence of her own life; the question was not raised. Yet the killing occurred late in the afternoon, when the deceased returned from drinking after leaving Georgia Hill's home at 2.30 pm that day, saying to her: 'I'm going to bash you, you black bastard. It's a good job I haven't been drinking now or I would throw you straight through that window.' Evidence showed she had called the police many times previously to defend her against his attacks. Neighbours were aware of the daily damage she suffered at his hands. She had no help against his attacks. In these circumstances, Georgia Hill alone could not defend herself. She could not do it by fighting back with fists, or pulling her *de facto* husband around the room by the hair after he grabbed and pulled her by hers; she could not do it by grappling with him and throwing him out the window when he grappled with her, trying to cast her out. To defend herself against him her only realistic method was to pick up the most readily available weapon in the house — his rifle. There are few, if any, women in our society capable of self-defence against an abusive husband according to the legal boundaries of that defence. Nor was any argument put that Georgia Hill had over-stepped the boundaries of the self-defence defence and, there-fore, should be convicted of manslaughter, not murder. According to the evidence, she had deliberately picked up a gun and shot a man. She was not defending herself; she was attacking.

It was even less likely in the South Australian *cause célèbre*, *R*. v. *R*. that self-defence would ever be raised, much less accepted, in legal argument.[8] R. was found guilty of murder, having attacked her husband with an axe while he was asleep. The man had abused, sexually, physically and psychologically, his family for twenty-seven years. His wife had been raped and beaten by him regularly. His daughters were forced, sometimes at gunpoint, to participate with him in sexual acts. On the night of the killing, R. sat on the bed smoking cigarettes whilst her husband slept. She went out to the laundry, fetched the axe, and dealt him repeated blows on the back of the head and the neck. She and her daughters had sought help from police on numerous occasions. No help was forthcoming. She and her daughters were left to endure her husband's rages, although neighbours, school friends and teachers knew or had strong suspi-cions of the torture the family was forced to face daily. Under the law as interpreted, there can be no defence of self-defence if the person killed is asleep. The essence of the defence is that the person who kills is in a situation of immediate danger; this is interpreted to mean that the party being killed is in a state of attack at the time of his death. R.'s husband was not in an active state of attack. Ostensibly, he was defenceless when killed. Seen in the context of domestic violence, however, R. was helpless; her husband was the more powerful of the two. That he was in the marital bed meant that R. was in the presence of a man holding significant power over her and her daughters; at any moment he could have woken and attacked; most certainly he would have attacked had he woken next morning. This was the pattern of life in R.'s household for twenty-seven years.

She had no reason to believe it would change. The law does not accommodate the situation as one of self-defence.

Provocation

To plead provocation, there must be evidence that the accused killed in the heat of passion, lashing out at provocative words or gestures by the deceased. The classic textbook case of provocation is that of the husband returning home to find his wife in bed, committing adultery. He lashes out in anger, provoked beyond endurance, killing her or the other man, or both. He will be convicted not of murder, but of manslaughter. (In some United States and European jurisdictions, the killing is no crime at all.) Little or no time is given to the woman who comes home to find her husband in bed with another woman, committing adultery. It may be that no husband commits adultery — at least within the home precincts. It may also be that for a wife, it is not so natural as it is for a husband to respond immediately with fists or hands to strangle the pair. If she could retaliate thus, her hands would hardly strangle a man and woman together. A woman is less well equipped to drag up a shot gun or rifle from the wardrobe, or a knife from its pouch behind the bedroom door. Unlike her husband, she would hardly be likely to possess a rifle, a gun, or a hunting knife. Had her husband foolishly left these instruments within easy reach, she would usually not be trained to their use. Although some women may find these weapons in the heat of passion and use them to effect, most would be more likely to shout, scream, cry or go quietly away to the kitchen to wash the dishes, make the tea, and think about how to cope with her husband's unfaithfulness. If over the tea her mind dwelt on death, in accordance with the traditional application of provocation rules she would not qualify for the defence of provocation if she later served her husband up arsenic in the dinner. Rather, she would be guilty of deliberately planning murder.

In *R*. v. *R*. the defence argued the accused was provoked into killing, in that before she killed her husband he told her of the acts of incest he had forced upon their daughters. He also abused her and her daughters on the night he was killed. The trial judge refused to allow provocation to go to the jury, telling them wrongly they had no option but to convict R. of murder. The appeal court held that provocation should have been left as a matter for the jury to decide. However, the appeal itself was an anomaly: had there not been an outcry throughout Australia, and particularly in South Australia, R. would have remained imprisoned for life when she should at least have been given the chance of having a jury determine she was not guilty of murder, but of manslaughter on grounds of provocation, or even exercising their inherent right to acquit her entirely of the offence. Had present laws been applied and had the police adhered to their duty by enforcing those laws, R. would never have been in a position where, provoked or otherwise, she could do nothing to assist herself and her family to escape the criminal acts of her husband, except to kill him. Laws exist in every jurisdiction outlawing rape, unlawful carnal knowledge, incest, assault, endangering the morals of minors, and in South Australia at the time, marital rape — all were crimes of which R.'s husband was, on her evidence and that of her daughters, and other observers, guilty. Yet he had never been arrested, much less convicted and punished, for these crimes.

In Georgia Hill's case, too, an appeal against her conviction for murder was lodged — after agitation from women; the time for appeal had elapsed and special leave had to be sought. As in South Australia, had a public outcry not been sparked off by women's organisations, it is doubtful that Georgia Hill's case would have been reviewed.

This starkly contrasts with *Johnson* v. *The Queen*, in which two brothers were convicted of the murder of their father, after a history of domestic disputes and one particular bout ending in the death of the father.[9] An appeal was automatically lodged and the case went from the trial court to the Court of Criminal Appeal of the New South Wales' Supreme Court, and thence to the High Court of Australia. At the trial, both self-defence and provocation were argued on behalf of the accused. Peter and Phillip Johnson lived in a household wracked by spouse assault and child abuse. At the time of his death, their father was 46 years of age and weighed 14 stone. He was a heavy drinker and 'prone to be violent at least when in liquor'. One judgment noted:

[The deceased] had treated his wife over a considerable period of time to frequent and serious assaults: he had been violent in his handling of all his children through their childhood and teenage. He was dominant in his household and seemingly brooked no challenge to his authority as its head. As a result, each of the children in turn . . . left the household at some time and for substantial periods . . . The deceased's wife, forty-three years of age, was an epileptic and an asthmatic: in the week preceding her husband's death she had entered Sydney Hospital for some tests, presumably connected with these disabilities.[10]

Perhaps it was fortunate that Mrs Johnson was in hospital and did not cause her husband's death; taking other cases involving women, she would not have been fortunate to be represented by trial counsel able to put strongly the case for the accused, for the facts of *Johnson* v. *The Queen* closely resemble those in *Hill* and *R.* v. *R.*:

Early on the morning of 5th February, the deceased had accused the appellants of being 'hooligans' and the cause of their mother's illness: he had said that he intended to throw them out of the house; it may be that he exhibited some violence towards them on this occasion. Later that same morning, the deceased told the appellants that they had to leave the house. He said that he intended to throw all their stuff out on the street. There was an argument . . . When told to leave the house, each of the appellants said that they had nowhere to go: the deceased repeated that he intended to throw all their stuff out on the street.[11]

Later that night upon returning home the deceased again said the pair should leave, presenting the elder brother with an eviction notice. An altercation broke out; fists were used; Peter and Phillip armed themselves with knives after the deceased shouted that he would kill Phillip. The deceased grabbed one of the knives:

Phillip and the deceased exchanged blows, including stabs with knives. Phillip reached a point where he claimed 'something seemed to snap'; he 'chucked a big mental' and punched and kicked the deceased in the head whilst he was down on the floor and jumped upon the deceased's head and body many times; he also made a number of cuts upon him with the knife. Peter . . . said that Phillip was 'raging and kept stabbing' the deceased, 'he was pretty wild'. Peter had not seen him lose his temper to the same extent.

Both appellants claim that the deceased was fairly heavily in liquor at the time. Both claimed that because of their earlier experience with the deceased, they believed he would carry out his threat to kill them. Phillip then weighed only nine and a half stone.[12]

Although the similarities between this case and those of the women convicted of murdering their spouses are apparent, there are some striking differences. Wives are more locked into family life; sons aged nineteen and sixteen or more are better able to leave an abusive home life. In Georgia Hill's case she, like Phillip and Peter, was beaten. She, like Phillip and Peter, was threatened verbally and physically. Her life too was in danger. She, however, shot only three rounds from the rifle; Phillip 'kept stabbing and stabbing, jumping on the head and body of his father many times'. Because of her earlier experience with her *de facto* husband, Georgia Hill believed he would carry out his threats to kill her. She was alone; Phillip and Peter were together. Phillip was 'only nine and a half stone'; she, frail and slight in her physical structure, was nowhere near nine and a half stone.

On appeal, the accused in *Johnson* had their convictions for murder set aside. Verdicts of guilty of manslaughter were entered. Georgia Hill eventually had her conviction for murder replaced by a verdict of manslaughter. Violet Roberts, however, was merely released on licence, her conviction for murder remaining, ready to become operative again as a life imprisonment sentence should she break the conditions of her licence. Violet Roberts endured twenty-three years of brutality from a husband who beat her and their six children. She left him many times, returning when he promised to change. Eric Roberts was shot while he was sleeping, after he had returned in a drunken state (from what was a normal bout of drinking) threatening abuse, beating and rampaging. She was charged and convicted of murder.[13] There was no appeal for her and no setting aside of the conviction to be replaced by a conviction for manslaughter. Being asleep at the time of his death, despite the fear he had stuck into the hearts and minds of Violet Roberts and her son Bruce, the courts would not interpret the law of provocation or of self-defence to encompass the killing.

That the courts take a more understanding view of a male accused than a female accused shows again in *Parker* v. *The Queen*. There, the accused man was not a victim of domestic violence. Rather, he was a victim of his own jealousy. There, a defence of provocation was open to the accused. Six weeks before 16 October 1960, he and his wife Joan and their six children went to live at an out-station property at Jerilderie, in the Southern Riverina. During their sojourn in the Riverina, they met Dan Kelly, who began a liaison with Joan

Parker. Dan Kelly and Joan Parker decided to run away together. They told her husband:

There was evidence that the appellant [Parker] was in a state of great emotional shock at the prospect of his wife's leaving him and their children. At one moment Craig [a witness] saw the appellant take a broken rod from an old Ford car and after cutting the end of it off proceed to file it. Craig wrenched it from the appellant and told him to pull himself together and think of the children. The appellant replied 'I won't be here to look after the kids — Joan will — and that other bastard will not be either'. The appellant went down to a place near some trees where he sobbed and cried. In the meantime the appellant's wife had gone away. She went in the direction of a road to which [Dan Kelly] had already gone and where he had left his bicycle. She joined [him] and together they set off . . . she sat on the main frame of the . . . bicycle.[14]

Following the death of Kelly and severe injury to his wife Joan, Parker made a statement to police outlining his part in the injuries causing death:

I started the car up and drove up the road getting up the road I saw Kelly doubling my wife on his pushbike and as I got up closer to them they both got off the bike then stood alongside the road, he was standing on the gravel and the wife was standing on the grass. I aimed the front left hand mud-guard at him and the bike after I hit him I swerved and put my foot down on to the accelerator as I was going off the road and I went through the greasy boggy patch and then swerved up over the wrong side of the road with the nose of my car facing towards the table drain. I got out of the car and I looked for the wife and at first I couldn't see her and when I first seen her she was laying in the table drain face down and I thought that I had killed her. I done my block, lost my temper, and walked to where Kelly was and started hitting him, then I heard the wife moan and struggling in the water. I left Kelly and pulled the wife out of the table drain and she was in agony then. It flashed through my mind that if it had not been for Kelly I wouldn't have injured the wife, I pulled out my knife that I had in my belt and went back and stabbed him in the throat.[15]

Kelly had wounds on the face, throat and chest, some consistent with bashing by a knuckle-duster, some by a knife. Both legs were broken below the knee. It was held that there was evidence of provocation that should have been left to the jury.

This contrasts boldly with Violet Roberts's case and the South Australian case of R. Because the deceased was asleep at the time, and because some time had elapsed between the acts that might have amounted to provocation and the killing, in both trials the approach was that the act was not done 'in the heat of passion'. The decision was not left to the jury. In South Australia, R. sat on the bed, smoking cigarettes, thinking. Although this might signify she was calming down, and that passion was passing and in fact had passed when she took up the axe, it is equally likely that she did not calm down but dwelt more and more passionately on her husband's confession that he had sexually abused their daughters and his abusiveness towards her — and that the killing was done in the heat of that passion. Similarly with Violet Roberts, although the husband had passed into oblivion on the couch, her emotions, her fear and horror at her husband's abuse and continuing attacks, need not have calmed. The attack may well have been 'in the heat of passion', triggered off by her horror at the abuse her husband had heaped upon her and her children over the years and the attack he had made upon her and Bruce Roberts some hours before. In *Parker* it was said that the jury should decide whether the accused attacked whilst in a passion. The jury in Violet Roberts's case and in R.'s case should have been given the same latitude. Parker's case, decided in 1963 and well before *R.* and *Roberts*, should have been applied automatically to those later cases involving women defendants. It was not.

Prosecutorial Discretion

The empathy the criminal justice system has for males who are accused shows up in the Crown Prosecutor's Office. When a crime is committed and an arrest made, the Crown Prosecutor determines the type of offence for which the accused will be prosecuted. With unlawful killing, prosecutorial discretion is exercised differently for women than for men. Georgia Hill was prosecuted for murder. R. in South Australia was prosecuted for murder. Violet Roberts was prosecuted for murder. John Clarke was prosecuted for murder, but the prosecution accepted his plea of guilty to manslaughter on grounds that he had not intended to kill his wife. John Clarke 'struck out in despair and frustration' because his wife said she was leaving him: he stabbed her to death. George Johnson was prosecuted for murder, but the prosecution accepted his plea of guilty to manslaughter 'because he did not intend to kill' his wife. George Johnson punched and kicked his wife because she had been raped.

One evening in an inner Sydney suburb early in 1981, George Johnson and his wife went to the home of friends after a dance. Both, together with their friends, had been drinking and continued drinking after arriving at their friends' home. Later, George collapsed on a couch and slept. His wife slept on the floor nearby. Some time during the night George Johnson was woken by his friend and told his wife was in an upstairs bedroom, where she had been raped by a lodger. George ran upstairs and attacked his wife, kicking and punching her. He dragged her downstairs and out on to the footpath, where she collapsed, and he began kicking her again. He bundled her into their car and drove home where, after beating her again, he put her to bed. She lay unconscious for two days, until on the advice of friends he admitted her to the local hospital. He was charged with causing grievous bodily harm. Later, she died, and the charge was changed to murder. Could a plea of not guilty of murder but guilty of manslaughter be accepted on the evidence? To prove murder, the prosecution had to show George Johnson intended to kill his wife or inflict grievous bodily harm, or beat her with reckless indifference to whether or not she died. On the facts, would this have been difficult to prove beyond a reasonable doubt? It could not be said George Johnson was 'provoked' into inflicting grievous bodily harm on his wife so causing her death. Did his wife 'provoke' him by lying, clothes awry, in an upstairs bedroom? Did she 'provoke' him because she was set upon by another man and sexually abused? George Johnson's attack was so severe that his wife lay unconscious for two days. During that time he did nothing to preserve her life, simply washing her with a face-flannel once during that period. Yet the Crown Prosecutor's office seemed to empathise with his situation, apparently accepting that a man could be swept up unintentionally to inflict harm on his wife under the circumstances. Did any Crown Prosecutor empathise with Violet Roberts or R. to accept that neither had the intention to kill or inflict grievous bodily harm upon the man who had not lain supine after being attacked by someone else, but had a short time before engaged in a deliberate pattern of systematic abuse against them? Did any Crown Prosecutor empathise with Georgia Hill, accepting she had no intention to kill or inflict grievous bodily harm, or did so under provocation, where she was in the midst of being attacked by a man who had severely attacked her over years?

Conclusion

In New South Wales and in South Australia following *R.* v. *R.*, Georgia Hill's case and Violet Roberts's case, there were persistent calls for 'law reform' to assist women, constantly attacked by brutal husbands, who finally take the law into their own hands by fighting back. What laws can be reformed? Laws against the violence R., Georgia Hill, Violet Roberts and every victim in the present study suffered and, in many cases, continues to suffer, already exist. Laws are supposedly designed to protect everyone from violent attacks. These laws need no reforming; they simply need to be applied.

Laws relating to self-defence and provocation in cases of killing are neutral until they are interpreted by the courts to the disadvantage of women. There would be no difficulty in reinterpreting the operation of self-defence and provocation rules, not by wasting time in drawing up new legislation and having it pass through parliaments, but by courts realising the error of past ways, or incorporating into past rulings an analysis of the woman victim of attack or provocation. Courts have recently begun to do this, for *men* victims who are of ethnic origin, black, handicapped or in some way a member of another minority group.[16] Women have not yet been so advantaged — because women come less often before the courts and less often sit on the courts. Until women are viewed as a legitimate part of our society, whether as victims of violence, as accused persons in domestic killings and other crimes, or as prosecutors, barristers and solicitors and ultimately Queen's Counsel and judges, there will be little hope that the courts will reinterpret laws to accommodate women. Law reform can never be expected to do the job — for the so-called reformers are all men; women hold no positions of power in the law-making process; women do not legislate or even do the relatively lowly (though in some ways powerful) task of legislative drafting. Until women and men are equally represented at all levels of the law-making system — in the parliaments, the law courts, the legislative drafting offices, the Law Reform Commissions, law reform committees and in policy advisory positions — laws relating to marital murder, like laws relating to other domestic crimes, will continue to be policed unequally to the detriment of women — or not policed at all. What use a 'law reform' when it is engineered by men, and when it goes into the male-dominated court system to be interpreted in the same old male-oriented way that has held sway in this country since 1788? Until women and men are equally represented in the system, women will have to find more subtle ways to kill.

CHAPTER 8   FAMILY, FRIENDS AND OTHERS

The intent of matrimony is not for man and his wife to be always taken up with each other, but jointly to discharge the duties of civil society, to govern their families with prudence, and educate their children with discretion.

The Lady's Magazine, Vol. 5, 1774, p.240.

In eighteenth-century Scotland the attachment of relatives to one another was warmer, and the duties founded on consanguinity were extended to a wider circle. Even distant relationship was considered as constituting an obligation to reciprocity of love and good offices.

T. Somerville, *My Own Life and Times 1741–1814,*
Edinburgh, 1861, p.368.

Our family-oriented society expects a beaten woman or bashed child to look to family members for help. Where immediate family members do the beating and bashing, parents or grandparents outside the immediate family circle could be called upon. Children beaten by fathers should look to mothers, grandmothers, grandfathers, aunts, brothers and sisters; wives should think of their parents, their childhood home, brothers and sisters and family friends. If the immediate family is not the 'haven from harm' folk tales portray, the extended family should provide that resting place. That, at least, is the theory.

Because society approves of the family structure as appropriate for women, men and children, services are built to support the unit. If anyone within a family suffers harm, those supports should come into action, assisting the victim and holding the family together. With the help of other family members, friends and neighbours, and family support services, the victim will be restored to health and happiness; the family will be saved. Beaten wives should visit counsellors or see marriage guidance officers; abusive husbands should see the error of their ways by attending counselling sessions. Women and men involved in marital disputes should go to their local priest or minister. Some might find help at Alcoholics Anonymous, through welfare services, from community aid. Children will be helped by welfare officers or the community nurse coming into the home and 'making things right'. This is the theory; the reality may well be different.

Women Victims: Seeking Family Support

Sixty-five per cent of all women victims of spouse assault refused to seek help from their families. Three said there was no value in doing so, for their parents were in another state, so could be of no use. Rose Randell was too ashamed to tell anyone, particularly her own family, and did not see how they could help her if she had the courage to speak to them. Rhonda Prince chose not to go to anyone for help, including her parents, because she believed the beatings were her fault: 'I haven't gone to anyone for help, because I don't know how to change him and can't stop him. My parents think we're happy and I don't want to let them down.' Rosemary King was 'too scared to come right out and tell anyone, even mum and dad, because I was scared of what he might do if I did tell. I wouldn't be able to get away and if I told anyone, even mum and dad, he might find out and that wouldn't help. It would just make it worse for us all.'

Women raped by their husbands showed an even greater reluctance to seek family sympathy and assistance. Of fifty-seven victims of marital rape, only seven spoke of the brutality to any family member. The major motivation for remaining silent was shame. Beverley Toms was angry at the abuse she suffered during her thirty-two year marriage; Janey Rivers was threatened and raped throughout the span of a twenty year marriage. Both refused to seek help from anyone, including parents, because they were 'too ashamed'. Other victims combined shame with further reasons for not seeking family assistance. Robyn Iffland's parents lived in another state.

That's not the sort of thing you get on the phone to your parents about. I went off in tulle and lace, with wedding bells ringing in my ears. My parents spent a fortune and didn't stop talking about it (in muted tones of course). I had eight bridesmaids and a matron of honour, and over a hundred at my (!) wedding. After all that mum would've had a fit if she'd known her darling daughter was being raped out of her mind every night in Brisbane. Down in Toorak that sort of thing would go down like a lead balloon. (I mean *talking* about it wouldn't go down well. *Doing it* is a different matter and probably the same in Melbourne, especially in Toorak, if they can still get it up, as in Lamington, Brisbane, if we knew the truth.)

Jane Roberts's wish not to involve her parents was equally strong.

I already had one child; being Catholic at the time, I faced the prospect of living alone the rest of my life; my parents had not approved of him and it was hard to admit to them I was wrong; my father can't stand children so I knew I couldn't move back with my parents; I didn't then know about the widows/supporting parents pension and had lost the confidence to go back to work. I couldn't say anything to my parents. My religion made me feel ashamed of the mess I had made of my life, and they were the last ones I'd look to for help.

Some women had suffered abuse during childhood or teenage, when a mother, more often a father, had beaten or bashed them, or sexually assaulted them. Understandably, they saw no value in seeking help from a person who had previously abused them. But not all women forebearing to call on their parents had suffered abuse in youth. Delys Johnson and Denise Briggs found their home life during childhood 'basically loving'. Evelyn Loftus 'never considered' going to her mother or father for help. Yet of her childhood she wrote: 'My father was a strict disciplinarian and belted the boys, but treated us girls gently. I never expected my husband to do what he did to me. My father would never raise a hand to my mother.' Although she told a doctor, minister, psychiatrist, lawyer, marriage guidance counsellor and a nurse at the outpatients clinic of her husband's abuse, she could not bring herself to tell her parents. That some women were reluctant to 'go home' for assistance, or refused to ask parents for advice whether the family was 'loving' during childhood or abusive, shows the home unit is not the well of care and compassion of the myths. Nor, for many women, is it a repository of wisdom. Many who declined to make use of their family ties when in distress and dire need of assistance sought help from other sources: friends, neighbours, doctors, marriage counsellors, welfare officers, lawyers, magistrates, priests, police, courts.

Women Victims: Gaining Family Support?

Of those victims choosing family members as confidants, few received help from parents. Marjorie Christensen's father, friends and brother believed her when she told them of her husband's threats with weapons, bashings, beatings and general reign of terror. Her mother and sister-in-law, however, had more in common with the police: none of them believed her story. She could not go to her mother for help, because 'she never liked me or approved of me'. Ursula Cranitch went to her mother in New Zealand after a final bout of violence persuaded her to leave her husband. She was more concerned for her mother than for herself. At a time when some comforting and support would have benefited her, she felt she should help her parents.

Everyone I told believed the assault had occurred, but I had difficulty in convincing my friends and relatives of the ongoing danger I was in at the time. My husband was a very convincing liar and seemed to others who didn't know him well (except his sister and myself) to be totally sane. I went to my mother in New Zealand more to ease her mind than to get any comfort for me, and so I could be out of the country for a while. I had long ago given up any idea of getting adult support from my mother, and long before that had given up on my father for anything. But because I had written and telephoned during the worst time and told them some of what was happening to me, I felt an obligation to put both their minds at rest.

Like a number of parents, Janet Coney's mother and father tried not to hear when she told them by phone of Len Coney's biting, scratching, kicking and punching; they were also reluctant to listen when she said he had thrown her down stairs and pushed her out of the car. They did not want to know she was bruised and bloody nosed as a result. Other mothers or fathers said 'that's your bed, you lie on it'. Joyce Reynolds's father 'probably believed me when I told him, but was rather ambivalent as regards the magnitude of the crime. He just stayed being friendly towards my husband, which made me start thinking I was exaggerating something I knew I wasn't.'

Sometimes the beaten wife went back on a semi-regular basis to live with her mother after she had suffered severe bouts of abuse. She invariably returned to the family home and her husband, who recommenced the beatings and drove her away once more. Others tried to return to their parents' homes, without success. Lyn Stanford's parents offered her a temporary home when she was almost strangled by her husband Cecil. 'This', she wrote, 'was unacceptable. I had four children, and mum and dad didn't realise I was an adult. They wanted to treat me like a naughty girl who comes home from boarding school after being sent down. I had to go back to my own home and try to get my husband to be more reasonable, or to get out.'

Eight women sought help from in-laws. Only Rosa Machin found sympathy. Her mother-in-law warned her of her son's temper before Rosa married him. When Rosa turned up on the doorstep, three children in tow, blackened eye and bruised body, she took her in. For Margaret Fisher, the story was different: 'I went to get help from his parents, but the in-laws didn't believe me. I didn't know how else to get him to stop because I had little family support from my own people and felt more secure with the neighbours, because I knew them. The in-laws were protective towards him and scoffing towards me. My father-in-law also assaulted me when I sought help. Like father, like son.'

Victims who approached other family members sometimes said there was more sympathy and careful advice, but no concrete help in living accommodation, employment opportunities, or child care. Sometimes brothers said they would 'bash him up', but rarely did so — and wives more rarely wanted this as a 'solution'. Joyce Reynolds's sister 'gave sympathy and encouragement to change my situation':

I was unable to believe I could escape from it. I thought that was what the rest of my life was going to be. My sister helped me to see that I was an intelligent person who could get out and take on a job and become economically independent again, even with a daughter to look after with a real possibility that maintenance would never arrive from Malcolm. Because of this I am now willing to see that many people may be trapped like I was by their own inadequacies or lack of real choice to do otherwise. I think that such people need to know that they have friends who accept their situation as one that may not be changed immediately but will helpfully encourage and offer a wider choice. Because my sister had that attitude I was able to eventually see my own way out and escape.

Sisters advised on helpful lawyers, welfare agencies to provide financial assistance for the victims to leave, on counselling agencies, or simply provided a 'good listening ear'. Even here, friends more often provided such services. For victims, the mysticism built up around family relationships is clearly misplaced. When women are suffering beatings and batterings in their own homes, ties established between parents and children, between siblings, between grandparents and children are rarely adequate to assist them. Experience after leaving the family home directs victims toward other possible sources of help in their efforts to escape.

Women Victims: Neighbours, Friends, and Family Support Services

Some women gained support from neighbours and depended upon their help in calling police, looking after the children, or providing them with a place to run during severe attacks by husbands. Jennifer Brown's neighbours were obliging at first, but eventually became reluctant to help. 'They probably thought I should have got out and stayed away', she wrote. Marjorie Christensen's neighbours 'were astounded (we appeared to be such a happy family unit) when by chance one came to the door and overheard the abuse going on. In this case the police came over the firing of the revolver when the neighbours rang. They tried to help me after that but it was difficult for them to do anything.' Others found neighbours were unable to give even minimal help. Leticia Smallwood wrote: 'The neighbours ignore me, I think they know my husband bashes me and get angry at the noise. Once they called out to quit the racket. It is bad to have to worry about what he is going to do next.'

Women talked with friends who sympathetically advised on agencies and other sources of possible help; yet like neighbours, friends were reluctant to get involved, or were actively aggressive toward the victim of abuse. Jan Robson's friends believed the extent of the violence and sexual assaults and tried to help by encouraging her to leave. 'But', she commented, 'the myth of a woman's acceptance of the situation (that is, she likes/chooses the situation because she stays) was of importance in their attitudes'. When she did not leave immediately they advised it, friends began dropping off: they could not understand the economic and psychological realities of the situation.

Their urging was important for me and important in my final decision to leave. But it was not possible for me to up and go at the first remark, because it is necessary to get together sufficiently to leave. Friends, etc. are very important in supporting women in the belief that they have strength and in giving some means of knowing how they can get some economic independence, etc. Without that there is no point in just saying, leave, when there is no way a woman can and no way she can see that she can leave.

Raped by her husband, Alexis Benedict talked with a friend about it 'in a general nag session, and we agreed that's part of married life. It helped to know other women had to put up with what I put up with for those years'. Nora Simpson recognised that 'just talking' was not enough. Friends and neighbours advised her to go to an agency for help, but gave no practical assistance:

Most of them acknowledged there was a problem. One person advised leaving. Another couple thought I should stay and order my husband away. They couldn't understand my fear of being in the same town. They only thought I should stay in the house which I wanted to do but couldn't after having Tony charged. They were always ready to talk and advise me to leave home but when it came to the practical issue they were no real practical help. Of course talk is cheap and they could talk all they wanted but it didn't help me get away from him or stop him belting me up when he was drunk or sober. When I did have to leave I had to arrange everything myself. I don't know how I would have managed if I hadn't had $500 of my own to move with and live on until receiving state aid.

Family support services tried to help in their own terms, not knowing or not wanting to know that their 'help' was often the antithesis of what victims required. Too often it consisted of telling the victim she should learn to cope with the violence, or implying she was exaggerating and that she had the problem, or telling her the abuse was 'part of married life'. June Graham went to a marriage guidance counsellor who believed 'what little I told her' about the sexual assaults. 'Marriage guidance didn't help', she wrote. 'The counsellor suggested I had great sexual power over my husband and should use it to my own advantage. She told me to change my attitude to sex or the marriage was on the rocks.' Frequently counsellors told victims that marriages 'go through rough patches' to be weathered.[1] For ten years Sylvia Ernest was beaten with a stick by her husband, suffering bruises and cuts. She went to a marriage counsellor, after receiving no help from relatives or friends. 'After trying to persuade me all marriages have "rough patches" and we must persevere and "ride out the storm" the counsellor finally told me how I could leave the marriage, so I was able to go to welfare services and get finance for a tiding over period until social security was available.' Sylvia Ernest was comparatively fortunate in her counsellor. Many women were less so. Antonia Grey was advised to drop her law studies, or at least go part-time; otherwise her marriage 'would break down completely'. Rather than her law studies causing a marital breakdown, Antonia Grey's husband was an integral part of the disintegration: soon after their marriage, he began a continuing monthly series of punching, pushing against the wall and against furniture, driving furiously when she was in the car, holding pillows over her face in bed. Antonia Grey had described these activities to the marriage counsellor, as well as showing her bruises, cuts to the head and abrasions caused by the attacks.

Ministers of religion and priests held views similar to marriage guidance councellors.[2] Seeking help from her minister after Geoff James had slapped and kicked her severely, Susan James was told 'all marriages go through a rocky patch' and that:

I should learn to love and care for my husband more during such times. He said I should calm my husband's fears about my friendships by doing more together with him and more together as a family (though I was hardly out of my husband's sight except for when I was at work). He advised me to go on relief teaching or give up altogether. He seemed to think I was in it for material things and should learn the joys of being 'poor but content' in the home. Being in a job was the only way I escaped from Geoff's violence, for at least part of the time.

Some women had dual problems with ministers and marriage counsellors. Sally Beckett went to both, receiving help from neither. The marriage counsellor advised 'it happens in a lot of marriages' and partners have to work through it. Sally was asked to have her husband come in with her to guidance sessions; he refused. She persevered with guidance for another hour, then went to her local minister:

The marriage counsellor understands my husband is angry sometimes, but maybe thinks I am exaggerating. The minister wouldn't really understand that I end up with black eyes and bruises. He thinks (at least this is an obvious impression) that I must be at fault in some way and so I am working on improving myself and my cooking etc. to make my husband happy. I think the problem is that I already think I am in the wrong and this is a problem in seeking help because the people I talk to believe me when I say I am at fault but they don't seem to believe me when I tell them how violent my husband is.

Ann Marshall was told by her priest and her marriage counsellor that she was probably paying too much attention to the new baby, and this was making her husband feel unnecessary and unwanted. 'The priest said I must mother my husband too', she wrote. Her husband was raping her regularly.

Some women visited family doctors for help and advice. Some were helped and well advised. Some doctors wrote reports for presentation in court. One doctor rang the police and stayed with his patient during an interview at the police station. On his evidence of broken ribs and extensive bodily bruising, Randall Champion was ordered to stay away from his wife and children, although he was not convicted of any crime. Helen Bridges went to the local community health centre 'thinking they would know who to go to for assistance'. The doctor interviewing her explained the available alternatives and the entitlements from various state and federal departments, as well as giving her 'the fors and againsts in what I was going to do'.

Other medical practitioners were less helpful.[3] Of all women attending doctors' surgeries, only three did not confirm they were offered valium as a palliative. Margaret Fisher's family doctor gave her tranquillisers 'for nerves': no doubt they made it easier for her to endure her husband's brutal bashings. Marjorie Christensen was on drugs 'for nerves, migraine and ulcer treatment'. She was taking prescribed drugs only 'as my health was in a shocking state'. Her husband's attacks precipitated her decline. The drugs made her resistance to the decline less noisy. Brenda Cashmore's doctor was unsympathetic and thought she was 'making it all up'. He prescribed valium. Cheryl Davies suffered bruises, depression, loss of self-esteem. Afraid to go out, she thought no one would like her, lost all contact with friends, and began to cut herself off from relatives. She visited the local doctor after one of a series of attacks by her husband who punched and hit her. She left the surgery with a prescription for depression: valium and sleeping tablets.

Fear of the attacker or embarrassment at having to disclose the cause of injuries, or fearing the doctor would guess, often prevented women victims from going for help. Jean Selberg wrote:

I was hit so hard on one occasion my head smashed a glass divider; on another occasion he put my shoulder through a fibro wall in my hallway. Knife held to my throat and choking. Tried to push me over the high back and front verandahs. On one occasion when I had been beaten and kicked on a Saturday night I felt sure I had a couple of ribs cracked but even though I drove to the hospital on Sunday I felt too embarrassed to go in, even though I was in a great deal of pain.

After thirty-three years of marriage involving bitter, stormy rows with silences lasting up to eight weeks, but no other violence, Sonia Darrow was thrown to the floor by her husband Ron, smashing her left hip in several places. She allowed no one to call a doctor or take her to hospital. (Her daughter was present at the time.) She suffered for three days before finally being taken to hospital. Her hip was so badly broken a complete plastic joint was needed to replace it. She was hospitalised for three weeks and many trips back to the doctor were necessary after release. She will never be able to walk properly again. In the three years since the attack she has suffered constant agony, both mental and physical. Her husband's violent rages continue. Sonia Darrow talked to her doctor of fear of another attack, to no avail.

After the 'accident' when I feared a recurrence I went to talk to our family doctor, and he advised me to get my husband to come in and see him, but this just makes my husband angry every time I raise it, and he won't go. I am very worried at present that he will do it again. But the doctor tends to pooh pooh my fears and thinks I am exaggerating. He gave me valium to settle my nerves and told me it was probably stress on the part of my husband and an event that was a 'once off'. He at least is confident it won't happen again . . . I am sure he thinks I really fell over when we were arguing (a normal thing for husbands and wives to do!) and that I 'imagined' my husband pushed me. But that shove was REAL and *intended*.

Seven victims of spouse assault and three victims of marital rape were advised to seek psychiatric help — for themselves. Evelyn Loftus went to hospital for treatment for burns, a scald and a broken nose. Her family doctor treated her for nerves by giving her valium and recommending a psychiatrist. After psychiatric treatment, she wrote: 'I ended up believing I was mad, and my husband was sane, almost!' Robyn Nelson was also advised to visit a psychiatrist.

After I went to the local doctor I thought it was better to get out of the way of my husband, at least temporarily so I could think properly of what to do. My father said I could return to the family home and I did, but a few nights told me I didn't really fit in there any more. It put everyone out too much. They had regrouped without me there. My sister advised me to go to marriage guidance. They implied it was my fault and not my husband's. They said I had to sort myself out and advised a psychiatrist. The doctor had said this, and I thought they were right so remained with my husband and actually visited a psychiatrist for two years. I didn't feel helped at all, but kept on with it. The psychiatrist said I had problems arising out of my childhood, although I had thought my childhood happy. Finally I realised that it was my husband that should be seeing the psychiatrist if anyone should, not me and that it was getting a job and getting out of an unsatisfactory marriage with an abusive husband that would save my sanity, not lying on a couch talking to someone who knew less about life than even I did.

Child Victims

Child victims of abuse and sexual attacks had less scope in seeking help from family members or outside family support services. Where they were beaten by one parent — usually the father — they often believed it was no use to seek help from the other parent; mothers were seen by children to be impotent against the wrath of fathers. Where abuse involved violence only, children sought no help from family members, probably because the abuse was obvious for all immediate family members at least to see, so victims did not need to request help directly. Danielle Anderson said that if her mother had been able to help she would have done so, without Danielle herself asking. As it was, her mother connived with Danielle and the other children to cover up the abuse from outsiders, including neighbours, friends, and extended family. Rosemary Page saw no value in approaching her mother for help. As she saw the family situation, her father blamed Rosemary, the eldest child, for being the major object of her mother's affection; in turn, her mother blamed Rosemary for the resultant bad feeling. She felt she could expect help from neither parent in relation to the other. Other child victims were terrified of their father's anger and sensed fright on the part of mothers also. 'It would do no good to ask mum for help', wrote Laurel Trevor. 'She was beaten by my father too, and running crying to her meant she got belted same time as us.' Both Chris Denton's parents abused her, so she sought help from neither. Nor did she look to any other relatives or outside agencies, neighbours, or friends: 'I was too young to know what to do . . . I was as quiet as I could and avoided mum and dad as much as possible', she said.

Some incest victims said shame and disgust with themselves often prevented them from going to a mother or other relative. Some did articulate the problem within the family circle. The reason for incest victims complaining, whilst no victims of physical abuse complained directly to family members, was probably that because of their clandestine nature, unless someone discovered sexual molestation taking place, the acts could continue indefinitely without drawing attention. Victims complained most often to mothers and sometimes grandmothers. On a few occasions children ran to neighbours for help, although this was rare and involved other physical abuse as well as the sexual exploitation.

When agencies were brought into the conflict, they rarely came through direct contact by child victims. In most cases a mother abusing her child sought help from Parents Anonymous, a medical practitioner, or a psychiatrist. Janine Renault approached the university counselling service, family counsellors, and friends. She gained the simple 'comfort' that 'many parents have a difficult relationship with a particular child'. She was afraid, however, that the 'difficult relationship' would lead to severe abuse on her part, rather than the 'normal' family slanging matches accepted by those giving counsel. On her initiative, she and the child went to a psychiatric counsellor. His approach confirmed that Janine Renault and her eldest child, together with the other two children (not victims of her abuse), made up a 'normal family':

The child who was victimised by me always seemed to laugh off the incidents for the counsellor's benefit (I suppose) and the counsellor kept saying there was nothing to worry about, that it was all 'normal' and that it was ordinary to have conflicts like mine and my daughter's in families. I was terrified I would do something serious and no one would take me seriously. Most of my friends took the attitude that it happens all the time, but I noticed they didn't like their children to play with mine and they stopped

them coming around to our place. Despite their attitude they seemed
terrified I would hurt a child eventually, probably theirs, which was
ridiculous because it was my child I was attacking and my child whose life
was in danger from me, not theirs. I couldn't have cared less about their kids.

No child went to any religious body because of abuse, although
Sylvia Clancy attended Sunday school regularly, becoming a regular
churchgoer and a Sunday school teacher as she grew older, while the
abuse from her father continued. When grown up and free of abuse,
a number of victims talked to ministers or priests about their
experiences. Invariably the family unit philosophy was upheld,
placing emphasis on the right of a father to control his brood (even
by sexual exploitation), and the need for children to subdue their
spirits and keep in their place. Julie Ludgate didn't know what to do
to prevent her father's sexually abusive acts during her childhood.
As an adult she wrote:

In later life I went to my minister for help. He said I had to be understanding
of my father and of men's sexual needs. He said that little girls are often
sexual and provocative and invite sexual attention from men. He made me
feel more guilty than ever, so I shut it away until we all found out about my
father and his grandchildren. They were only little and not 'provocative'.
This now makes me realise that our minister was wrong and only protecting
another man and not caring about *me* when *I* was the one seeking help!

Ministers and priests contributed to anti-family feelings of victims,
and to the criminal activity of fathers against their children, by
enforcing a view of a family unit wherein fathers can do no wrong,
and whatever occurs within it, the unit must be kept together in
pursuit of social and religious dogma. Ministers and priests also
enabled men to continue their anti-social and criminal activities
when their children produced a second generation of victims conveniently placed for exploitation within the family unit. Complaining
to them availed child victims nothing.

Men Victims

Only one male victim of spouse assault went to relatives for help.
Dan Summers spoke with his mother, who sympathised with his
problem. As his wife had already left him, his mother moved in to
look after the children. She was fully supportive, especially with

child care, which was more than women victims received from their parents. Two male victims talked with friends. Andrew Travers's wife Christine bit and scratched him, and his friends said it was 'not really so important, because this sort of thing happens all the time with spirited people'. Kingsley Samuel consulted a counsellor at his wife's training college, who thought his wife was 'probably overdoing her studies'. Sam Trewin complained of his wife's sexual attacks to numerous agencies, as well as his mother, who, like Dan Summers's mother helped emotionally and practically. She offered child care and housekeeping support.

Although S. K. Steinmetz[4] suggests the stigma attached to domestic violence 'which is embarrassing for beaten wives, is doubly so for beaten husbands', no male victim in the study expressed any embarrassment about seeking medical help. In three cases the husband chose not to seek medical aid because it was unnecessary: the damage was confined to scratches and bruises, or there was no damage. One husband went to outpatients in company with his wife, seeking treatment for her, not for himself: when she had attacked him, on a sole occasion he retaliated with fists, so that she required medical attention. Another went for treatment to cuts, but he did not inform outpatients of how he received his injuries — however, neither did any woman victim. Where men consulted medical practitioners, none was given valium to help him endure abuse more peacefully. Rather, doctors took action against wives. Of the eight, one victim had his wife undergo psychiatric treatment after seeking his doctor's help, and three had their wives confined to mental institutions. Of his wife Carole, Kingsley Samuel wrote: 'I solved my problem by removing the cause from my life. She is now confined in a mental institution. However, now someone else will probably suffer because of my actions, as the problem has not been cured, just been removed to where it can't touch me.' Rather than Sam Browne being placed on valium, he had his wife June go to a medical practitioner. She was prescribed valium and other tranquilisers. On her family doctor's advice she began attending a psychiatrist. Shortly after she was committed to a mental institution. Another abusive wife went the same way. This is a startling contrast to the approach of psychiatrists in cases involving abusive husbands and victimised wives. Where wives were beaten they, not their husband, received psychiatric treatment, sometimes for years.

Although in three of the one hundred and nineteen cases of husbands beating wives and the fifty-seven cases of husbands raping wives a psychiatric assessment was made of the husband, with a recommendation that he seek psychiatric treatment, in no case did treatment eventuate. In no case of a husband bashing or raping his wife did the husband end in a mental institution because of it. Yet the damage husbands wrought on wives far outweighed that on a husband by any wife in the survey. Psychiatrists apparently adhere to a philosophy that abusive husbands are acting 'normally', whilst abusive wives are acting 'abnormally', so requiring psychiatric care. The ease with which women were committed to mental institutions gives grave warning to any woman who decides to hit back against a husband who beats her: if she fights, because she may be less physically strong and less well equipped for a fight, she may lose. Even if she wins the initial tussle, she may lose the latter — being got rid of by a husband with access to a medical system founded in partriarchal ideology. In a world where 'male' is the benchmark of psychiatric stability and 'female' is defined as 'hysterical' or 'neurotic', men run little risk of being confined to mental institutions on the complaint of a wife. Because physical violence is generally regarded as a male pastime, any woman resorting to fisticuffs can rightly fear the attitudes of psychiatrists and psychiatric hospitals.

Social Attitudes and Family Support

Whatever the reality of families today, support systems bolster the ideal of a family in which life is companionably lived out through the years, father, mother and children growing together, parents eventually growing old and becoming doting grandparents to a new set of dependent children. If the unit does not live up to the ideal, support systems set out to persuade whatever part of the unit that is 'failing' to reorder itself into the accepted mode. Women not wanting to confine themselves to the wife/mother role without any outside identity in the paid workforce are gently — or more roughly — persuaded that their central task is providing the foundation of the home. Without a wife/mother in the family home, they are persuaded the house will virtually collapse. Today women in the paid work world are vocal and cannot be ignored as a vital part of the economy, so in order that the family can live up to its ideal, women continue to be forced to accept their central role in the home; outside activities are made subsidiary. They are 'supplementing' the 'family income', 'helping' the breadwinner win those few crumbs which might make living easier, but are not 'essential'. Although today women's paid role is vital to family upkeep, as it often has been in the past (paying the grocery bill, some of the mortgage, the electricity, gas and water bills, supplementing the entertainment slush-fund or providing all the entertainment allowance), this reality is ignored by most support services. It is ignored by most of the community. Although many households today are headed by women alone, or in many the man is out of a paid job and the home is kept going by the woman's wage, we continue building services and philosophies around the 'traditional' model. The traditional model has not reigned without challenge over the years. In the past, families did not always consist of wife/mother, husband/father, two or three children, a cat and a dog. Some families have always been headed by women; some households have always consisted of single persons living with others or alone; some children have always lived without parents, or without a mother or a father. These households have been ignored in the push to confine as much of the population as possible to a way of living that stultifies the talents of some members of the unit and confines the talents of others to specific areas. The family existing in traditional form prevents women from making full use, or any use, of their talents. It acts as a means of social and political control, preventing women from becoming independent human beings. It confines men's talents to narrow limits, making them believe their identity can be realised only if they are the major income earners, if they follow certain specified paths as a means of identifying themselves as 'male' and, therefore, superficially in charge (in reality there are other men outside far more powerful than most of them), rather than 'female' and undeniably oppressed. This model for living oppresses both women and men.

Confining women and men to narrow roles in itself promotes domestic violence. It allows men to use their more developed physical skills in an abusive way on women trapped in a economically and socially dependent position. It prevents women from being economically, socially and politically equal with men and, therefore, capable of escaping from the abusive men they have married. It limits avenues of escape for women through friends, relatives, and other acquaintances. Led to believe that women who have married should remain so, whatever the circumstances of that marriage, friends, relatives and others are ill-equipped to support women wishing to escape. Because they believe, on one level at least, that families are oases in a cruel world, they disbelieve women who say they are being beaten and abused. They may accept that women are victims of arguments, of 'slight' beatings, but they do not acknowledge the extent of the abuse. They think women should tolerate arguments and 'slight' beatings, because they have no conception of a world where women and men can live together without disharmony. If a woman complains, she is exaggerating; if she does not, she likes her oppression.

Children are equally ill-served. How foolish to suggest that children who are suffering beatings and bashings from family members should approach those same members for help and protection from the abuse. How wrong to assume they can gain assistance from members of the family who are not the abusers but are living with them. How can they be helped by other relatives, family friends, or neighbours? They too believe children are owned by their parents, deserve discipline, and should remain with their parents. If they do think the 'discipline' is too strict, they are often constrained by ideas of family privacy, parental rights, and simple embarrassment, so they fail to intervene. Children, being raised on a diet of the 'perfect family', are often too ashamed to admit to outsiders that they come from something less, and that their parents are not the perfect couple of television programmes.

These attitudes are replicated in the world of strangers. Our society not only sees the family as a stable unit defying outside intervention, even where that intervention might be made by relatives or friends, but also fiercely guards the idea that what happens between family members is not a matter for criticism by outsiders. Thus Denise Briggs found no sympathy from her mother when she was beaten by her *de facto* husband. When he attacked her in a public place, similarly she received no help: 'Once at the hotel he punched me in the back, calling me all sorts of names, and no one stopped him.' No one wants to interfere between a husband and *his* wife, or father (or mother) and *his* (or *her*) children. No one wants to be contaminated by the victims. Those outside the immediate family unit often draw back, not only because they are afraid of 'becoming involved', but also because they are afraid they will be coupled with the victim of abuse, and perhaps their 'bad luck' will rub off. As in wider battles, it is the victor who is treated to attention and adulation, not the vanquished; so Patricia Collins and her daughter Patsy discovered: 'No one came near myself or my child. I was badly battered, and she was in an extreme case of shock, by everyone invited my husband out for tea and sympathy, presumably because he had no bruises and did not upset their nice lives.'

In seeking help from family, friends, relatives, or family support systems, males in the study almost invariably found right was on their side. Women had little to help them extricate themselves from the abusive family unit. Even where friends were not overly sympathetic to men, in concrete terms men were well served: they had little need of economic or employment opportunities or advice from friends, relatives, neighbours, or family support services, for they already had jobs. Men might have wanted sympathy and sometimes missed it; women wanted sympathy and frequently it evaded them. Women also needed economic and employment advice, and opportunities to help them escape from their oppressed family position. Family, friends, neighbours, and support systems did not back them. Women needed child care from relatives, friends, the community to gain economic independence, and freedom from bashings and rape. They did not get it. The men who sought such help got it. Women were confirmed by support services in their belief that the fault was theirs for not coping with 'family life', or for precipitating the violence. Similarly doctors, psychiatrists, priests, family, and friends mostly told them they should learn to cope with family life as it was, not with life as they might have wished it to be — with themselves free of abusive live-in mates, economically independent, and free to make their own judgments about companionate living. The child's view of a life free from abuse was even more remote. With family, friends, neighbours, and supports like these, the surprising thing is that any women and children escaped the abuses of their limited family lives.

CHAPTER 9   THE POLICE

In your memory stretches a dark series of scenes. Your step-father drunk and violent, your mother crouched against the wall shielding her head with her hands and screaming for you to run for the police. You can't even calculate the number of times you ran in your pyjamas to the police station, only to be left loitering in the lobby while the policemen drank another cup of tea before setting out to deal with another 'domestic'. You remember the times you were brought home from the police station, trotting to keep pace with some tall silent constable who held your hand.

'What if mum's dead?' you used to ask yourself... There was always the same scene when you got back to the house; the policeman standing calm and disinterested in the hallway, while angry man and distraught woman made long and involved accusations against each other. Then the policeman would say that he wasn't going to take sides, but that there'd better not be any more disturbance.

Sometimes, when the policeman had gone, Stanislav gave your mother a few more hits around the face, but mostly he just called her some names that you didn't exactly understand and then he stormed out of the house.

Peter Kocan, *The Treatment*,
Angus and Robertson, Sydney, 1980, p.42.

'Go ask a policeman.' Since they were young, boys and girls have been taught that their remedy when in trouble is to seek police help. In some communities, police are feared, but even here, when someone is battered or beaten, raped or robbed on the street the frequently conditioned response is to run to the nearest police station or to dial 000. Where violence is dealt out at home by members of the family, the response of many victims is to seek help. But many endure severe abuse before resorting to a law enforcement agency;

many are too young to dial, or too young to run. Some victims cannot speak the language, or simply cannot speak. Some victims do not know they have a right to ask police to intervene. But whatever the characteristics of victims of domestic violence, upon calling the police, the majority discover their childhood indoctrination fails them: police are unable or unwilling to stop the abuse.

Where an assault or homicide occurs, in at least 85 per cent of cases police have been called at least once before to the home ground. In 50 per cent of cases, police have been called five or more times. In any instance of domestic assault or homicide, the arrest of the aggressor is likely to be the culmination of serial interventions by police.[1] That law enforcement officers have been called time and again to intervene in family violence, yet depart only to return again when another bout ends in a terrified phone call from a victim, a distressed cry from a child who cannot bear to see mummy hurt, worried calls from passersby or angry shouts from neighbours to make them shut up and stop the noise, demands that we should ask 'why'. Police constantly receive timely warning of potential homicides of family members, yet assaults and killings continue. If some victims do not call on the law for assistance, their reservations may have a strong foundation. If victims do look to the law for help, why does that help fail them?

Women Victims: To Ask or Not To Ask?

Almost half of the adult respondents in the present study — victims of bashing, beating, punching, kicking, stabbing, threatening with knives and guns, being run down by cars or smothered with pillows — did not seek police assistance. In the case of domestic rape, no woman called the police unless explicit physical abuse over and above coerced sex occurred. Reasons for not doing so varied. Some women were terrified to speak to anyone about the violence, fearing attacks would intensify if the police were called. Rosemary King endured violence 'about once every three or four months' throughout the first five years of a twenty-eight year marriage. She was slapped, hit, kicked in the stomach and hit around shoulders and head. She miscarried during the third month of her second pregnancy when her husband threw her on the floor and kicked her in the stomach and back 'because I burned the roast'. She concealed the attacks from neighbours and friends, being 'too scared to come right out and tell anyone'.

I was scared of what he might do next. I couldn't get away and if I told anyone, he might find out and then it would be worse for us all. I thought about the police but that would have made him madder. Everything was done in a secret way. He belted me up in the bedroom that was next to an empty block, and if the telephone rang or the doorbell during it, he was as nice as pie until he could come back and belt me some more. Once I threatened to go to the police and he went white in the face and nearly strangled me. He said if I went to them, that was the end of me and the kids. He threatened us all regularly after that, and even took out the gun and shoved it at the littlies and told them I would get shot if ever they or anyone went to the police about him.

Evelyn Loftus 'sometimes thought about' calling the police, but could never 'pluck up the courage'. Her husband's violence started with furious tempers, grew into day-long events about three times a year, then became more regular. She 'sometimes had fantasies about police driving up in a car with the siren blaring, blue lights flashing and dragging him out to prison, and was greatly tempted to ring them.'

Carmen West thought forced acts of sexual intercourse during her three years of marriage 'were not really rape', so the police would be of no use. Gail Small complained to no one, as she 'couldn't discuss it', and the police 'were the last people I'd go to for help in a thing like that, and besides they're all men too, so what use would they be?' Other women, whether victims of beatings and bashings or rape, or both, declined to seek police assistance because they did not think the police would be able to help. Some said the police had a reputation for incompetence in handling family violence; therefore they did not waste time in contacting them. 'No, I didn't call the police or visit them', wrote Sandra Cox. 'They don't do anything about domestics that is well known by most women who get beaten up that's why I didn't bother.'

Women Victims: Calling for Help

If Evelyn Loftus had plucked up the courage to call the police, would they have come, as she hoped, sirens blaring, lights flashing, to take away the husband who was assaulting her? Eleven women who were raped by their husbands called the police; sixty-three women victims of assault in the home did so. In few instances did the police come immediately. When they did, women forced to utilise a system ostensibly established to protect all citizens needing protection were humbly grateful for what attention they received. Christine Wheeler called the police three times during her tempestuous marriage. They came promptly each time. Although the violence resulted in a disc lesion, bruises, and an injured back requiring traction and physiotherapy, with weekly visits to hospital, the police advised 'marriage guidance'. 'They were not angry with me for calling them', wrote Christine Wheeler. Margaret Fisher called nine times for police help, and they came each time: 'I was grateful because they probably had other jobs they should have gone to,' she said. Margaret Fisher spent two weeks over all in hospital with a smashed face, bruises, nerve damage, and a miscarriage.

In every other case, although they eventually arrived at least once upon receiving a call from the particular household, police took their time coming. Joyce Reynolds sought their help only once. The police came one and a half hours after she telephoned.

They said that the situation was not good for the child. I could have my husband removed and prefer charges, although they preferred not to act in such situations. Their attitude was sympathetic and helpful towards me, and fairly firm towards him, signifying he was engaging in unacceptable behaviour . . . The police reaction I experienced seems out of keeping with other reports I've heard regarding their attitude.

When Olive Smith's husband Arnold attacked her, she thought the police should help, calling them 'many times'. They did not come every time and when they did, it was hours after the event.

When they came he'd usually calmed down a bit and could talk to them properly like nothing happened. Once he went off in the middle of it and stuck his head under the back tap. Then he was a bit more reasonable. The police were good and stayed for a bit talking to us. They were okay towards me and were firm with him, I suppose. It was better when they did come because if they didn't he used to laugh at me and tell me there was no hope for me and that the police had given up on me because I wouldn't do anything about leaving him.

Olive Smith suffered a broken collar bone, broken arm, bruises, cuts
from a broken bottle and often went to the outpatients clinic for
treatment, as well as spending weeks in hospital at various intervals
as a result of the violence. Her marriage lasted twenty-five years,
during which she, together with her five children of varying ages,
left her husband at least five or six times.

Having been bludgeoned into submission by punching, kicking,
threats, knifings, pushing against walls and downstairs, shoving and
bashing against tables, women victims respond in the only way they
know how, with little recognition of the way society should be serving
their needs. A man battered and beaten on the street would not
accept that the police might or might not come if he found a telephone and called for help. He would expect help as a matter of right.
Workers pay taxes for community services. The police force is one.
A man attacked in a car park, so that he required hospitalisation for
weeks, would not accept that police should linger in the station
drinking cups of tea whilst his attacker finishes the job; when they
arrived, he would hardly expect them to be 'angry' with him for
seeking their assistance. After being robbed at gun point and beaten
over the head with the weapon when he resisted, no man would
think the police 'sympathetic and helpful' to him as victim, nor
'fairly firm' with the attacker if they told him he could have the
robber removed and prefer charges, 'although they preferred not to
act in such situations'. Would he consider this properly signified to
the assailant he was 'engaging in unacceptable behaviour'? Would
any man be satisfied if the police simply 'stayed for a bit' at the
scene of the crime, talking to the victim together with his attacker?
No one would think police had an option of coming or not coming
to assist the victim and dealing with the offender by arrest. Yet
women who are victims of serious abuse in the home often think
they have no right to police help; most accept that the police have
a right to come late, or not at all, and to leave the scene without
doing more than 'having a talk to' the husband who has beaten or
raped, or beaten and raped, them, or perhaps talking to them *both*
'firmly'. Women are forced into submission not only by their husband's abusive acts, but also by the abuse they suffer from police
who fail to use their authority in any way meaningful to victims of
domestic assault. Women submit to their husband's abuse because

they can see no other choice; they submit to the abuse of police because they can do nothing else.[2]

Although Evelyn Loftus fantasised that, if she telephoned, the police would come to take her husband away, for only seven of the seventy-four women victims calling police was this so. Nora Simpson was attacked by her husband Tony after weeks of intensive abuse. He punched and kicked her, then chased her around the house. Her daughter Fiona ran for help to a neighbour's home and she followed, her husband behind her, knife in hand.

I was terrified. I was at the neighbours who had a telephone and I ran there to safety after Fiona had run out to them to ring the police. Tony chased me over and the neighbours saved me. The sergeant asked if I was going to charge him and if I didn't, he said the police would never come again. I said if I charged him would we be safe for the night and he said no, Tony could be bailed out within half an hour. When I said that was no help to me he said it was my decision, I had to make up my mind, but emphasised I'd get no more help from them. His attitude was very upsetting. I said I would charge him and rang a friend who came and took me and Fiona to her place for the night. I rang my solicitor from my friend's place, who then contacted the police and Tony was not to be allowed bail until the following morning. The police were very abrupt until they were spoken to by my solicitor, then they were more civil. They were pleasant towards my husband. They were friendly to him and were almost apologetic to him. I was hysterical. My husband went home and showered while the sergeant was talking with us and came back far more sober.

June Meister called the police three or four times. They came when she called but told her there was nothing much they could do 'unless he kills or rapes or maims someone'. Yet 'he was raping me', she wrote. 'What sort of rape did they want? According to them it's not rape if it's your wife and it isn't maiming, either.' They inferred that June and Hans Meister should 'sort out things between ourselves'. Once, they took Hans Meister away, but this did not reestablish her confidence in them or in the legal system.

They usually talked to him in the same way they talked to me, as if I had done just as much wrong as him. Even when they took him away that once, I knew I really would never have any protection from the law and they would lose out. That's why I often thought to take action, but next day thought about it, that it was not worth it and changed my mind. The police kept saying it's a civil matter, not a criminal matter. Also when my daughter was raped the police made the following comment: 'it's like eating lollies to kids these days'. This didn't improve my thoughts about how they could help or understand what the problem was in my abusive relationship with my husband. At the moment it seems there is no law against wife abuse and it doesn't seem to be a crime at the moment. At least, this is the impression I got from the police and everyone else that I tried to talk to about it.

Women did not telephone the police station at every argument, or on every occasion that violence was used. When they did, it was because the violence had risen to a new high, or had returned, after weeks or months of lesser bashings, to a level forcing them to seek outside help. Over a thirteen year marriage, Jean Selberg saw the violence of her husband Jack increase from isolated incidents to approximately once a month in the last few years she stayed with him. The incidents varied in intensity. She commented:

I thought the police should help, but they were of no help. They simply stated 'you've been fighting for years' or 'you should get yourselves together and sort it out'. Because of the humiliation received at the hands of the police I only called them when he was most violent. Sometimes my children called them, but not at my request. I had forbidden the children to do so. I would have called them, plus the children, a couple of times a year. They came every time called. However they did take their time. It would take from half an hour to three-quarters of an hour before they would arrive. The police station is only five minutes drive. They said they could not charge my husband with an assault. I would have to go to a solicitor to do this. They didn't ever take him away. They just told him to quieten down and behave himself. They acted casually toward my husband and contemptuously toward me.

Ursula Cranitch also rationed her calls to the law. She phoned twice, once when Denzil Cranitch had beaten her and destroyed furniture and clothing, tearing up her dresses and throwing them out into the rain, and again when he threw crockery, after banging her head repeatedly on the dining room table, and left her with deep cuts in the arm and leg. Rather than taking away her husband, the police took her away to the local women's refuge: 'They were not even interested in waiting to see if I got in, seeing I wouldn't lay charges. They said they would take him away if I would lay charges. They were concerned to begin with, but they were slightly bullying and were totally uninterested in the whole thing when I wouldn't do anything about the charges.'

Yet in rationing their calls for help and leaving contacting the police to times a husband attacked them most seriously, women left themselves open to jibes often made by police that 'you wouldn't have stayed if you hadn't liked it' or 'you've put up with it for years, what's the problem now?' Marjorie Christensen blamed herself for not taking action or leaving her husband sooner than she did. Self-blame was instigated or reinforced by the comments of police officers who were called on the many occasions. Lars Christensen used weapons on his wife rather than the fists she endured without seeking police intervention. She wrote:

If I had done something earlier perhaps I could have prevented what eventually happened . . . on the other hand I did all in my power at the time, with the usual results. Police were called, but he would lay on the charm (he was a most convincing liar) and convince them I was exaggerating. They would tell me to leave if things were so bad, no amount of explaining how impossible it was to do that with six children and no housekeeping money to even pay their train fare as far as my mother's got me anywhere, just if it's so bad you will get the money some how. I had six children in ten years, so for years I find I put up with abuse, bashing, terrorisation of myself and the children. I thought the police should help, but was told no help was available in domestic matters. They said you don't have a problem, sort it out yourselves. They came every time except the last time and I was always told that if it was all that bad I'd find money some how and leave. Do not bother us again, they said. Their attitude toward me was firm and patronising. Their attitude to my husband was friendly and co-operative, laughing even. They said it was a civil matter, not a criminal matter for them.

Child Victims

No beaten children called upon the police for help; some were too young to do so. For many, the abuse continued into the early teenage years; even then they did not call in the police. Where abuse continued into late teenage, as in a number of cases, no victim voluntarily approached the law for help. Three respondents alluding to the police said it never occurred to them that police might usefully be called. Beryl Saunders commented she 'never thought of going to the police'. Chris Denton wrote: 'I sought no help during periods of abuse. I was frightened to talk to anyone, and was unaware of agencies available. The police never crossed my mind. I was scared of my parents and scared of any authority figures, so they were last on my list.'

In seven cases the children's mother sought police help. In six of these, violence was directed at the entire family, mother included. Some mothers called the police several times. Ros Newbold was institutionalised as a 'neglected child' when her mother rang for help. Yet her mother's care was loving and attentive, and in her own words she would have been 'far happier if dad *had* neglected me. Unfortunately he didn't. He belted me whenever he got the chance, like he did to my brother. That's why mum called in the cops in the first place.' Cheryl James's experience was similar:

The first abuse I can remember was when I was six my father belted my mother up and all of us kids and we were put in a home for about eight months, my brothers and me. When the police came they took us away and left dad alone. When we got back together again with my mother and father we never called the police because we were scared it would happen to us again.

Therese Sullivan's sister left to escape her father's bashing and bullying, but 'the police brought her back by force because she wasn't sixteen then. Next time she ran away they didn't catch her and she got as far as Brisbane where dad couldn't get after her and the police didn't jump to his tune that time.'

Victims of incest suffered similarly. All but two were unable, owing to extreme youth at the time of the attacks, or because of fear, shyness or feelings of guilt, to contemplate seeking police assistance. Lynda Messer went to the police, however: 'I'm not sure of the reason but eventually I realized all these things were bad and finally got the courage to visit the police station. The end was that I was sent to an institution then into a foster home. I went from children's homes to foster families back and forth.' In four cases, the children's mother approached the police. Mary David wrote:

Mum went to the police when she found out what my father was doing to my sister and tried to do to me. We stayed with my nanna. Mum was taking him to court. My sister and myself were interviewed by two detectives.

Mum dropped the charges as she said she didn't want our names dragged through the court and we had to grow up in the town. Finally mum left town with us and in the end got divorced from my father.

The seemingly traditional way police handled those few cases of child abuse or sexual molestation did not help the victims. Those brought back to the family home felt wronged, and justifiably so: making an effort to escape an aggressive father, they were thwarted by those 'in authority'. Some whose mothers tried to stop the abuse through agents of the law succeeded only in having their children committed to institutional care. Some who declined to seek police help recognised clearly that the problem at home involved an abuse of authority — and concluded that a change of authority figure from father to police officer would not help.

Men Victims

Few women found police of assistance when called on. Fewer children did so. Erin Pizzey's explanation is that policemen, like other men, may beat their wives. Some at least are, therefore, unlikely to be sympathetic to the plight of the battered woman.[3] Some policemen, like other men, beat their children, both physically and sexually; they are therefore unlikely to see any need to help. As for men victims of domestic violence, it is suggested they suffer even more disadvantage at the hands of police than do women victims,[4] for different reasons: they may be easily embarrased and humiliated, and the police may treat them with the contempt a male-dominated society reserves for those who are unable to live up to the masculine prototype.

Most of the nine husbands attacked by their wives did not seek police help, just as many wives did not. No husbands, contrary to wives, wrote of fear preventing them from doing so. Of the two male victims calling on police for help, one received a positive response; the other was badly treated. Only one called the police to the scene during a domestic argument; both visited the local police station.

Sam Browne called the police twice during his wife's attacks. On neither occasion did the police attend. His wife attacked him with the kitchen knife on the second occasion. When the police did not arrive, he went to them. They were unsympathetic, saying he had no

problem, and that he should sort it out with his wife. Their attitude
was one of 'laughing unbelief'. They took no action against June
Browne, his wife: 'They didn't believe me, and told me basically
"what a weak man you are to allow a woman to beat you up". They
virtually told me to get out of the station and stop wasting their
time.' Dan Summers went to the authorities because relatives and
friends advised him to, at the same time saying he should visit the
local magistrate, see a solicitor, call on a social worker, and go in
to the nearby welfare office:

Some people believed me when I talked to them about it, e.g. my mother,
the police, the solicitor. Some didn't, e.g. the welfare worker. I went to the
station to see the police and they were very good indeed. They were sympathetic to the problem and advised me to see the magistrate. Their attitude
was friendly and jocular. One said he had trouble like that with his wife,
and the others laughed and said they had the same complaint.

Comparing wives and husbands as victims, one male victim had
problems similar to those of female victims: domestic violence was
not given serious consideration by the police. But contrary to popular
views of husband-victims' treatment by police, the second male
victim was well served. An *esprit de corps* was established between
himself and the police. Women victims of violence have found their
attacker-husbands similarly striking up a rapport with police officers.
No attacker-wife struck up a rapport with police. Betty Samuels
called the police twice. On the first occasion they arrived one and
a half hours later saying they could do nothing. After their departure,
Bob Samuels 'got all stirred up again and threatened me with a gun'.

Then I got on the telephone again and got the police again. They took
three hours to come this time. They said I had to charge him if it was all
true, and they were hard on me and looked as if they thought it was all
made up and acted as if I was a nuisance. They were more friendly to my
husband, talking and laughing. He was saying that I was a bit hard to live
with. I think they ended up talking about the dogs at Harold Park, because
he'd been out on the grog after he had a win.

One woman sought police help following a separation from her
husband which he refused to accept. The rapport between her husband and the police was sufficient to place her in danger. 'My husband
has friends in the police department and it was no use. When he

came round after I separated from him the police just talked to him
and it turned out they knew his friends. They even gave him my
silent phone numbers every time I moved and then he used to
ring me up at all hours whenever I thought I'd got away from him
completely.' Some women victims discovered their husbands used
the occasion of a police visit to complain of their wives' conduct.
In several instances husbands simulated an attack by the wife. Rose
Randell was so frightened at one outburst of rage, when her husband
struck her and tore her clothes, that she called the police: 'When
they came (at last!) he told them *I* had physically attacked *him*! This
is absurd! I am 5 foot 3 inches and seven and a half stone. He is
6 foot and twelve stone!'

Twice when Margaret Fisher was attacked by her husband, she
was provoked into hitting back.

My feeble pats on the chest didn't affect him. But he immediately hit his
head against the wall to make his nose bleed and went to the police to complain. He got two of them to come back with him to frighten me. They
left the police car outside and came in with him as if *I* was the dangerous
one. There was never a chance I'd do that to him and if they had any sense
they'd see it. But the damage he did to me was a lot worse than a nose bleed,
which is what he did to himself anyway.

Why persist with the idea that male victims of domestic violence are
in a worse position than female victims? Because police and male
victims are 'men together', the beaten husband may obtain sympathy
and advice on how to relieve himself of the burden of his wife.
Women can never establish this comradeship with police officers,
who are almost always male.[5] Their sympathy, rather than being
with the abused wife, may well be with abused and abusive husbands.

Legal Duties of Police

Police officers are expected not to be influenced by their personal
lives in dealings with the public and treatment of crime. Whether
male or female, whether married or not, whether they beat their
own wives (or husbands), law enforcement officers have a duty to
uphold the law. Their duty is to protect people and property, whether
harmed by criminal acts or not. Police may arrest any person they
reasonably believe has committed a serious crime. They may arrest

anyone they reasonably believe has stabbed someone else, has
punched and wounded someone, has battered and bruised them.
They may arrest anyone they reasonably believe is about to commit
a serious crime. Police are empowered to arrest any person they
reasonably believe is about to commit a breach of the peace, or is
about to renew that breach. They may arrest any person committing
a breach of the peace in their presence. Police have a power to enter
onto private property in order to arrest anyone they are empowered
to arrest, if they reasonably believe that person is on the premises.[6]

Although this is the law, police in Australia often seem to be
unaware of it — at least where the crime or damage is done within
the four walls of a private home. When interviewed, police officers
take differing positions. A Queensland police officer stated police
had no power to arrest any man who beat his wife and that the wife
must take action herself. In New South Wales, one police officer
acknowledged police have powers of arrest and power to enter on to
premises, but declared it was 'too difficult' for the police to intervene in family 'disputes'. A second New South Wales officer took
the contrary stance: he claimed the law gave him no power to enter
on to private property, even where he suspected a wife might be
killed by her husband! Victorian police declared they required an
increase in their powers to enable them to arrest men who beat their
wives:

We get phone call after phone call from women who say their husbands are
abusing them, or are drunk and scaring the daylights out of them. We can't
do a thing except maybe go out there and talk them into calming down.
Mostly you find the wives just want someone to take the heat off. They
don't want hubby taken in, and we can't do anything about it if the wives
won't help themselves.

Police in New South Wales, Victoria, Queensland and Tasmania
stated 'we don't like getting involved in family arguments.'[7]

Despite all seventy-four women victims who called the police
suffering from severe attacks by their husbands, on only seven
occasions did police exercise their right of arrest, even though the
attacks qualified as 'serious' or 'felonious' in law. On two of the
seven occasions, police did not arrest because the man had beaten his
wife. They told the wife they were unable to arrest, although they
had had direct contact with the family on a number of previous

occasions and in both cases knew the wife had suffered abuse and had been to the local chamber magistrate. They knew severe bruising had occurred and that one woman had once had her collarbone broken by her husband. At the time of arrest, they were aware the wife was a victim of severe domestic violence, because in conjunction with the circumstances surrounding their coming into the home, bruising was visible on both women. Elizabeth Benson fled with her four children after a particularly violent bout of abuse. Her father then took her to the police station. The police told her she should see a solicitor and declined to visit her husband at home, yet both her eyes were blackened and her arms severely bruised. Later that year she telephone police twice. They came each time and on the first occasion told Elizabeth Benson she should see a magistrate. The second time, bruising was apparent and she had obviously been severely hurt in the lower back region.

This time they went away after speaking strongly to my husband. I begged them to take him away because I didn't know how bad he would get this time and besides myself I was scared about the children. He was always gentle with them, except when he was angry with me and then it was impossible to guess what he was likely to do. They were kind and sympathetic to me and firm and unfriendly to him but that wasn't much help. The first time they escorted him off the property but he returned as soon as they left. The second time, finally they came back and arrested him for non-payment of traffic fines and advised me to leave town. If I hadn't been so upset at the time and just so grateful that he was finally being taken away to be locked up, at least for a while, I would have laughed. They told me they couldn't arrest him and lock him up for nearly beating the life out of me, but they arrested him for forgetting to pay his parking tickets!

Elizabeth Benson's story is not unique: Lyn Stanford was almost strangled by her husband. When the police came, three hours after her call, her throat was bruised and red. She had a large bruise on one thigh. The police were firm with her husband and sympathetic to her, and officers from the same station had been called in three times before. She told them she was terrified that her husband might become more violent if they did not take him away. They departed with strong words to him, returning half an hour later to arrest him — for non-payment of traffic fines. They (wrongly) told her they could not arrest him for his violence toward her.

For some women, not only were police slow in attending, but they were also affected by the status of the abuser. Kitty Jordan called the police once during an eighteen year marriage, sixteen years of which were clouded by slapping, kicking, biting, pushing, throwing across the room, threatening with guns and with war knives. They arrived 30 minutes later. She wrote:

They seemed sheepish and were deferential to my husband and wouldn't look me in the eyes. They were embarrassed because we lived in Turramurra and have a pretentious house on a huge block (which means that even if I screamed *loudly* the neighbours wouldn't hear). They ended up going away telling us how busy they were.

My husband put on a big act and told them I was hysterical and under psychiatric care. He can be very charming when he wants, and the fact that he is a Q.C. had the police almost touching the proverbial forelock.

After they left he was furiously angry, spitting at me 'you wait', then he just went out and didn't come back for a couple of days. He never told me where he went (he didn't anyway) but it was probably the club and we hardly spoke for weeks after that. At least there was something positive from it all. I never called the police again.

Living on the north shore has its disadvantages.

Although it is not the law that a victim of an assault must lay charges against her attacker because police 'have no power' to do so, officers in every state, when questioned about their response to domestic disputes, claimed they were unable to take action. A Queensland officer stated: 'It's up to the woman to charge her husband, and if she won't, she can't expect us to hold the bag for her. We end up in court and she doesn't turn up. She has to take action, we don't.' Rather more euphemistically in Tasmania it has been said:

Although there are many options available to police to enable them to handle violent domestic disputes, the choices are not always easy to make because of the conflicting public expectations . . . [Police] know themselves that their efforts often have little or no lasting effect on the participants and they frequently set out to do nothing more than to effect only those things which will facilitate a prosecution or which may be referred elsewhere. It is this frustration with their [*sic*] predicament which sometimes expresses itself in lack of interest by police in family disputes except to cool them down and get out.[8]

Every woman calling for police help was told that the police had no power to intervene because the matter was civil, not criminal, or that if she wanted action taken she would have to lay charges against her husband, or both. An assault *is* a crime. The police exist to deal with crimes. Where an attack qualifies as *serious* or *felonious*, that is, where the skin has been broken, there are bruises, there is blood, where bones have been broken or the like, it is the police role to charge the assailant. With *common* or *simple* assault (a *misdemeanour*), that is, where no skin has been broken, no bruises have appeared following the attack, there is no blood, no bones are broken, the victim should take action. However, even here police are obliged to lay the charge if the victim is aged, frail, or *otherwise unable to do so*. Many women, victims of their husband's abuse for weeks, or months, or years, are unable to initiate action because they are socially depressed, economically deprived, politically oppressed. Women victims are unable to get to the chamber magistrate, or to the police station, because they cannot pay the bus fare; because they cannot pay for child care in order to free themselves for laying charges; because they are terrified to do so; because they have been socialised into accepting that they are their husband's property; or because they are sufficiently pragmatic to know that where they have been victims of male domination in the family home, a male-dominated court system will not assist them.

Susan Davey's case shows lack of police awareness or deliberate failure to acknowledge their role. Susan Davey was attacked whenever her husband lost his temper. She was flung against walls, pushed across the room, and hit and punched so that the blows would 'leave no marks'. Despite her husband's tactics, she suffered numerous bruises, which on at least one occasion took more than two weeks to disappear:

I called the police several times. Sometimes I went to the police station. They didn't come every time I called. They told me they didn't like being involved in domestic violence. They told me there was nothing they could do. They told me to tell my lawyers to get off their bums and do something (I had a court injunction to protect me from violence, etc.!!) Often my husband had fled the scene by the time they arrived. He conveniently came back every time when they left. They obviously didn't want to involve themselves. I was usually sporting huge bruises whenever I saw them, and once my step-daughter came home in the middle of it and rang the police herself, but even that didn't make any difference. They still said they couldn't arrest him, or charge him with anything or do anything at all. I began to wonder what the police are for.

Like Susan Davey, women calling the police often found injunctions or restraining orders were of no help. Some said that when police came, they refused to do anything, saying the women 'should take out an injunction' against the husband. Some women did so. Police were then called when the husband began harrassing their wives in contravention of the order. The response was 'we can't do anything about it; it's a Family Court order and that is a Commonwealth matter'.[9] Some women took out restraining orders by way of a quasi-criminal procedure, but they had to be beaten before a restraining order was awarded. If they sought police help, they did so because the order had been broken, and they had been beaten again. In some cases, police removed the abusive husband, but this did not prevent him from returning later. Husbands sneered at the orders, saying 'it's only a bit of paper'. Women taking out orders had been victims of violence for years in all but one case, finally resorting to the legal process for help. Sonia Darrow had a restraining order. The police took her husband outside 'and I think they thumped him one', she wrote: 'He disappeared for a few hours down the road, but . . . he blamed me because they bashed him, and took it out on me again. That time I didn't ring them, because what was the use. They only made it worse, not better, so I got no more orders.'

Where a woman is being beaten, it is irrelevant to whether a crime is being committed (giving police power to arrest) that she does or does not have a Family Court injunction or restraining order. Beating is criminal, and the beatings to which women were subjected in the present study gave the police power to arrest.

Police Training

Other Australian surveys of family violence replicate the findings of the present study. The Victorian Western Women's Refuge Group found police often ignored a call made by the victim herself but came when called by a child or relative; police allowed substantial periods of time to elapse between the phone call and arrival at the scene.

Of forty-one cases studied, each involving serious damage to the victim, arrest resulted in only seven cases; only one husband was detained by the police; only three were charged. Twenty-six were 'warned', and 'nothing happened' in four cases. Women said police 'wiped their feet on me; that was the impression I got'; 'they didn't want to know about me'; 'I think they thought I was just a woman'. Police said: 'we don't like getting involved in domestic arguments'; 'find somewhere to go'; 'you should leave' — but they had no suggestions as to where the woman should go, or where she could stay, with no money and three children under the age of seven. One woman said: 'they just wanted to fill out official forms. I was hiding under the bed when they came. My husband had broken every window in the house and I felt as if I was in an extremely vulnerable situation. I had no where to go and they were more interested in their forms than me and what he had done to me and the house.'

Women who are victims of domestic violence are dissatisfied with police handling of the matter, and rightly so. Looking at the lack of assistance children in the study received from police, or their failure to call upon the police for help, abused children are not well-served by law enforcement authorities. Some men, too, suffering violence in the home fail to receive an adequate police response. Why is there this manifest dissatisfaction with the police response, and why are the police unable to handle crime in the family?

Not all police are incompetent or inadequate in coping with domestic violence, but on the evidence, most are. The reason lies primarily in community attitudes toward domestic abuse, which are founded in patriarchal ideology, and in the way those attitudes are translated into police training manuals. The Tasmanian police manual, typical of its type, begins with the statement that the 'primary object' of the police is 'the prevention of crime; the detection, arrest and bringing to justice of offenders'. It then differentiates this activity — 'legitimate police business' — from family disputes:

Due to the increasing complexities of today's society, more demands are being made of the Police Officer *extraneous to his primary functions*. Police are invariably requested to involve themselves in situations, where strictly speaking, they are not empowered to do so. Such a situation would be where Police are called to a 'domestic disturbance' where no offence has been disclosed, but other circumstances are such that remedial action is warranted and necessary.[10]

In similar vein, the Victorian police manual commences:

The term 'domestic crisis' may be translated to mean a *dangerous* family affair in the home. This definition would describe the majority of domestic crises handled by the Police Service. *Although police may regret the social service component of their work*, they accept that there is no other community resource capable of responding as effectively. It would appear that for a variety of reasons domestic crisis intervention is the role of the police.[11]

The entire thrust is to persuade trainee police officers (some of whom, despite the manuals' not disclosing it, are female) that 'domestic disturbances' are outside the core role of 'police work', not involving 'crimes' but being 'social service' work. As it is estimated that 'domestic disturbances' take up to 40 per cent, 50 per cent, even 70 or 80 per cent of police time, why is the message of the manuals so deceptive? As so many 'domestic disturbances' involve the commission of crimes, frequently very serious crimes, it is disturbing that trainees are told domestic disputes are not criminal, but social service matters only.

It is also questionable that police 'are not empowered' to enter into 'domestic disturbances'. If police were not entitled to do so, both manuals and their counterparts in effect advise them to break the law. The truth is, however, that police do have powers of entry where violence is occurring or about to occur, or has occurred, whether premises are 'private' or 'public'. The question of police entry on to premises is fundamental to the problems suffered by victims of domestic violence, through inadequate police training combined with community attitudes. English law — which is the basis of Australian law — begins with the premise that a man's home is his castle. (It does not mention a woman's home.) It does not contemplate that, if a man and woman are living in a house in a married or *de facto* relationship, both should have equal rights and entitlements to that property, or that both have equal rights as to who enters in, and what occurs within the home. The law does not grant men and women equal rights, particularly in personal relationships. The legal position is bolstered by the prevailing community attitude that *men own property*: they make the money, act as the 'breadwinner', pay the mortgage, 'rule the roost'. Whatever the reality, in common thought women are dependants, do not 'work' (or if they do, it is not 'serious', not 'a career'), are minders of children, homemakers (but not house owners), housewives (owned by houses, not owning houses), remaining in the home as attachments to the owner, their husband. When having to enter on to property because a woman is being beaten or a child bashed, this ideology interferes with the duty of police to protect them. If a woman telephones a police station and the police follow up the call, they are too easily persuaded that the man owns the property and that what he says goes, not to enter if he orders them not to, or to go if he orders them out. If a crime occurs, has occurred, or will occur, and the police reasonably suspect so, they have a right and a duty to be there. But the idea of women and children being the property of husband and father intrudes, and with the teachings of the manuals that such matters are not crimes and that the men are not offenders, prevents the police from acting. Teaching that when the owner says 'go', they must go, means that whenever the 'man of the house' says depart, the risk is high that police will leave. They do not comprehend that, as a partner in a marriage, a woman might have equal property rights with a man and therefore an equal right to say 'stay'; nor do they ever contemplate that the woman may own the home fully in her own right.[12] Thus when she called the police, Merrilee Sadka found:

It's worse if your husband assaults you than if a stranger does it, because you live in the same house and chances are your children will see it. The only way to get away is to give up your home and friends and move and hope the law supports you and your children. The police didn't have any effect when I called them in and did nothing to help. They kept saying that I had to leave and that that was the only solution. They didn't see that the house was the only house we had to live in and that if I went away with the children we wouldn't have anywhere to live. Therefore I think the only escape is to go away, but as for the support of the law, if they won't support you when you're in your own home, where will they support you?

After explaining that domestic crises are not crimes and police intervening are engaged in social work, the manuals immediately reveal a certain schizophrenia:

Perhaps more important than the precise proportion of police work which can be labelled domestic crisis intervention is *the danger inherent in this part of the police officer's roles*. Various studies in Canada and the United States indicate that more police injuries and homicides occur in domestic disputes than in any other police activity. The risk of injury or death is even greater for the participants of these disputes. 43% of Canada's 675 murder victims between 1967–1971 were killed by members of their own family or close acquaintances. For the year 1978, Victoria had a total of fifty-one murders, thirty-two of which were the result of a domestic situation. Police intervention in domestic crisis or disturbance situations is, therefore, an extremely dangerous task for police officers involved.[13]

First observing that more *citizens* are killed or injured in the course of domestic 'situations' (which we have earlier learned are not real police work), the manuals go on to show greater concern for the police! Police safety always comes first: 'it is necessary that the intervening officer make a quick analysis of the situation, paying close attention to the possibility of the use of weapons, and the emotional actions of the parties involved. This is a primary function of officers *for their own safety* and the safety of others who may be present.'[14] Trainees are told that the aim of the manual is to 'better equip members engaged in Domestic Crisis Intervention duties . . . The effects of such training are expected to: —
(a) Reduce police injuries.
(b) Reduce police attendance time in Domestic Crisis intervention.
(c) Enhance good public relations.'[15]
No mention whatever of any need to protect the victims!

It is wrong that police are more frequently killed or injured when intervening in domestic arguments than in other crimes. Even if it were true, more members of the domestic circle are maimed or murdered than are visiting members of the police force. It is no argument against police intervention in bank robberies that a number of police are killed or injured during these offences. The community would not sit back and accept a statement in a police training manual that, because the death rate of officers during car chases, drug raids, and bank stake outs was high, the police need not attend. Nor would any society accept that, in order to lessen the danger, police should adopt a social worker role, their primary concerns being to reduce police injuries, reduce police attendance time during chases, raids and stake outs, and finally to enhance public relations whilst these crimes are in train. Yet this is what manuals tell rooky cops, and this is what our culture accepts as proper and realistic for police 'training' in 'domestic intervention'.

No wonder women in the Victorian refuge group survey of police reactions to domestic violence commented upon the emphasis officers placed upon 'the legalities', filling out forms rather than paying attention to what had happened. The Victorian manual asserts: 'As part of *his* general training in police work, the officer is constantly reminded of the need for gathering basic facts about the person or situation with which *he* is dealing. Thus, in coping with family problems, the officer must have a knowledge of the basic family structure and background.'[16] Then follows a list of seven items which 'seem important to the officers in understanding the basic family structure' and 'should be gathered ... as well as any other points of information which seem important'. A battered woman in Victoria — and in other states in which police manuals say that knowing about family relationships is more important than protecting lives — is then faced with a battery of questions about the legal status of the relationship: is it a validated marriage? 'common law situation'? boy friend-girl friend? What is the relationship of the parties involved: husband-wife? parent-child? uncle, nephew, niece and so on. What are the names and addresses of the parties, their ages, their ethnic backgrounds, occupations, if employed, or income status if not employed? is someone a recipient of a pension? What is the length of residence in the present home? How many years have the parties been living together? if separated, how long have they been separated? do legal custody rights apply to the children? Where children are involved, trainee officers are admonished to ask their ages, their relationship to the participants as regards parentage: are they 'the products of the same marriage, or a combination of different relationships?' Police are asked to establish 'through questioning' if there has been prior police intervention, and if so, how many times. 'Where applicable' they must ascertain where the parties were born or raised and their educational background.

The relationship between the parties is vital, to some police officers, in determining how violence will be dealt with. Although a marriage licence has been described as a 'hitting licence', a man does not have to marry to gain a 'right' to hit. Marilyn Kennedy wrote:

My boyfriend knocked my teeth out of place, but when I went to the police they were going to do something, then my boyfriend followed me and came in and he told them we were living at the same address. That was a lie because he was around the street from me but they didn't believe me. They believed him and told us to go home and leave them to get on with their own work and not to bother them again with it.

Leaving a man, once having lived with him, is also insufficient to guarantee rights to women. Trudy Smart sought police help:

I had two injunctions and they were no help. The police advised me to move away with the children. They were abrupt with me and friendly with him. They said it happens all the time, that it's a civil matter, not criminal. He would convince the police he still lived at home and they would ignore the court injunction and tell me to let him back inside. They kept saying it's a domestic. They ignored my distress completely. So now I'm convinced men *know* they are free to abuse women 'by law' so they do. Now I don't have trust in a man's intentions or manner and expect aggression. My husband used to become uncontrollable and even when he didn't live with me, they never came and took him away.

It is not for police to say that, because parties are living or have been living in an intimate relationship, the legal approach should be different from the approach taken if strangers bash and abuse each other. The relationship between parties is irrelevant to the determination of whether or not a crime has occurred. If a crime is committed, the police should be trained to intervene, rather than questioning the parties about the relationship. The relationship of the parties may be relevant to whether a crime *will* occur. Although this likelihood is well documented, the irony is that when police question the parties as to their relationship it is not because they intend using the information as an indicator of the future probability of severe injury or death (if that has not already occurred).

In South Australia, the Police Commissioner has said that 'over the years' the claim 'has occasionally been made' of police failing to arrest where crimes occur in the home. (Perhaps the claim, *frequently made*, is not often heard by police.) 'Arrest and imprisonment', he comments, 'are not always seen by the aggrieved spouse to be the appropriate remedy'.[17] Yet rather than simply an 'aggrieved spouse', a woman who has been beaten by her husband is the victim of a criminal act; the victim of a crime has no right to prevent the law from taking its course. Where a felony is committed, anyone aware of the circumstances of that crime who refuses to give the police information about its commission may be charged with misprison of felony: it is an offence not to reveal such information.[18] Some acts are classed as crimes because the state considers those acts so serious as to warrant community condemnation. The victim is not the only loser where a crime is committed. Society is threatened when citizens are beaten, bashed and abused. Criminal law recognises that threat by outlawing the activity. Because the community as a whole is threatened, the victim has no right to protest that she, or he, prefers to ignore the crime. Yet police are told by their superiors that the wish of the victim should prevail in domestic violence cases.

The police frequently report that women do not wish their attackers to be dealt with by criminal law. Often their 'wishes' are forced upon them by police who are *themselves* reluctant to act. Women are told by police that crimes committed on them in the home are not criminal. Women are constant in their tale that police say they are impotent in the face of violence occurring in family surrounds. It may be less a problem of women not wishing the husbands beating and raping them to be charged and prosecuted, and more a problem of male police officers not wishing to exercise their powers of arrest and prosecution over men committing criminal offences against their wives. Police often tell women to leave the family home; they infrequently remove men who have beaten. It is convenient for a force that is reluctant to use its powers to control violence against women (who happen to be wives) to use them as scapegoats: 'There's nothing we can do; the women won't co-operate; they don't want their husbands charged.' Yet Emma Fitzhugh reported her husband's assaults, rapes and forced buggery, displaying ample bruising, medical reports, and neighbours' observations of the attack. The police refused to take action, and refused to allow her to sign the charge book so she could take action, although she asked to do so. As Susan Davey said, after her husband Jack had dealt her severe blows about the head and shoulders, and pushed her down stairs and against walls:

I think spouse assault is and most definitely should remain a crime. No! It should not be a civil matter. I think police should be empowered to take action, especially where a man attacks a woman. Everyone must agree that, except in very exceptional circumstances, a woman is physically outmatched by a man. I think the punishment should be the same for strangers and husbands who assault women and wives.

Those women in the study who chose not to call the police did so, in the main, because they thought the police would do nothing. Those who called desired the police to take action; it was the police, not the women, who failed to take that action.

Conclusion

Where police are called in to domestic violence cases, they are confronted by conflicting views of their job. Part of society regards woman bashing as criminal activity; part of society takes it to be a man's right to do as he wishes with his wife. Part of society thinks whatever happens within the confines of the home is a private matter; part of society believes that where crimes happen at home, those crimes are a matter for public scrutiny. The view most often enshrined in police training manuals is not that crimes committed in the home are a matter for public concern; the manuals most often depict those acts as non-criminal, civil, 'domestic'. They are outside the 'real' scope of policing.

The police force is one of the most well-resourced strongholds of male dominance. It is in the forefront of the enforcement of the patriarchal structure. Women asking the police to help are appealing from Caesar to Caesar. They appeal from a private male individual who oppresses them, to a public body of men playing a key role in that oppression. Even if women police officers were employed in equal numbers in the force, and if manuals, promotion lists, job listings, areas of work recognised equally the existence of women workers alongside men workers, it is doubtful that the police force would be a useful tool in ending abuse in Australian homes. A police force recognising women as equal with men might, however, play a prominent part in changing attitudes and behaviour supporting violence at home. If women became equal in the police force, this would indicate a radical change within a significant social and political institution. As a temporary measure, efficient and effective policing of men who beat their wives and children may bring about a temporary freedom for those victims. Whilst temporarily free, if other resources exist to give women and children a real chance to establish their own lives independent of the men who have abused them, victims of domestic violence may create a society in which they are no longer vulnerable to men who have learned that women and children are for beating.

CHAPTER 10   THE COURTS

The judicial response to violence against wives generally reflects the same pattern of indifference, official inaction, and occasional unofficial reaction exhibited by police departments. Very often police departments use the judicial system as a means of appeasing the woman or discouraging her from pursuing complaints against her husband. Rather than arrest the husband when this action is clearly warranted, police officers will tell the woman that her problems are really personal and/or civil and not criminal but that if she wishes to press criminal charges she can go to the district attorney's office (magistrate's court in England) and attempt to file a complaint. The woman must appear before the magistrate or public prosecutor the following morning and request that criminal proceedings be brought against her husband.

> R. Emerson Dobash and Rusell Dobash, *Violence Against Wives*,
> The Free Press, New York, 1979, pp.217–218.

Courtrooms and judges have an air of authority about them, and this rubs off on the lowliest level of the judicial system, the magistrates' courts. Often women and men, boys and girls are unable to distinguish between judges and magistrates; they are awed by them equally. The High Court, Supreme Courts, District Court and County Courts, magistrates courts are as one: large, high-ceilinged rooms located in large, darkly forbidding buildings in the centre of town; frequently they are the oldest and most impressive buildings in country centres.

Although most people are impressed by the majesty of the law, women may be more likely to be impressed than men. Women are often less familiar with the workings of the law and the operation of the courts. Lack of familiarity breeds awe. Women go less frequently to court than men. Women are rarely judges, magistrates or lawyers. Women are rarely brought before the courts on criminal charges. Women rarely appear as plaintiffs or respondents in corporate matters. Legal jargon comes less easily to women, because they come into contact less often with lawyers and legal writing, because they are not in court to hear judicial pronouncements. They, perhaps more so than men, believe implicitly in 'fairness' and that the courts are there to right wrongs. When they are wronged — beaten, abused and raped by their husbands — some women think the courts will help. They assume the criminal law and the judicial system are designed to protect the abused from the abuser. Yet when they finally come before the magistrates, when they appeal to the prosecutors, when they turn to the judges, this notion is too often dispelled. They meet with a judicial system impervious to their needs, and to the needs of their children.

Women Victims: Asking for Help

Of the women who were abused in isolated instances, few thought of court action. Only one woman left immediately and sought a divorce. The remainder stayed with the abuser because they 'hoped it would never happen again' or found it 'so foreign' to the man's 'normal' temperament that they believed it was a momentary lapse not requiring court attention. About half the victims of continuing spouse assault took no court action. Sometimes fear prevented them from approaching courts for help; sometimes it was shame; in some instances women had no belief courts would help; some women did not know they had a right to protection from abuse by court intervention. Virginia Williamson was slapped and punched by Gerrard Birch, her *de facto* spouse. One eye closed and the bruises took weeks to disappear. She was too ashamed to go to court, and was scared of Gerrard's reaction. She tried to escape his attacks, but said 'I can't go to court about him yet I live in fear deep down that there is no real help for me and I will be at his mercy for as long as I live.' Christine Wheeler was 'too sick to cope with court proceedings'. She was bashed, kicked and 'treated worse than a dog'. Thomas, her husband, constantly threatened her with further beatings if she approached a court for help. If she went to court, she said, 'he would only do it again and I couldn't cope with life at all'.

Wives who are raped in marriage more often said shame and disgust with themselves prevented their seeking help from the courts. June Graham commented legal action 'wasn't an option as far as I was concerned . . . I was too ashamed to seek help from anyone, much less the courts of law. I just made long range plans to leave with enough money for security for myself and the children. Now I am angry about the rape. Then I was too mortified to speak about it to my mother or sisters, never mind any magistrate.' Valerie Roberts told no one she was threatened and pushed around when her husband demanded she submit to his abusive acts of intercourse. She did not complain, because she believed it was her husband's right. That courts might assist her never entered her head. She wanted 'peace at any price', and court intervention would intrude on that peace although her twenty-five year marriage was continuously interrupted by Tom Roberts's sexually abusive threats and a continuing pattern of rape.

Some women victims of assault and of rape considered taking court action but changed their minds. Rose Randell said it was 'unacceptable for anyone in our family to go to court about such a matter'. Jennifer Jones's husband Dennis forced her to change her mind about court action: 'Once I was going to take action but changed my mind. When I rang the police once and talked to detectives about charging him and taking him to court so that everyone could see what he was doing to me, he sneaked back into the room. He held a knife at me while the detectives talked to me on the phone.' Maxine Harris was slapped, hit, thrown downstairs and pushed out of the family car by her husband Peter. Her body was constantly bruised and aching. She wrote:

I came to the point of getting an injunction to have him removed from the house three times but backed down each time because he promised he would be reasonable. Several times I thought it was not worth any police action or court action, as he was only bad sometimes. I was afraid of him. I was ever hopeful that he would be a little more reasonable and easy to get along with. I was prepared to go to any length *not* to break up our family.

Roseanne Grant, Lyn Stanford and Noreen Connors each thought the violence was a momentary aberration, although it went on for years. For four years Janet Coney was beaten and abused by her *de facto* husband Len. Sometimes she thought she should go to the police and get to a court for help 'but never did because I wouldn't want to hurt him. I love him and want to stay with him.'

Women Victims: Going to Court

When women call the police, often they believe the police will come, remove the abusive husband, take him away, and put him before a court. They think the court will properly find the man has beaten and maimed, and that he will be dealt with as others committing criminal acts, by being sent to prison. In the present study court proceedings did not progress naturally from a telephone call to police. Where women went to solicitors for advice and assistance, court action against the man who had beaten and abused was rarely taken. Where men were taken before courts, the results gave little comfort to abused wives. Few men were imprisoned; most were not even punished.

On the advice of police, Trudy Smart gained two court injunctions from the magistrate's court, requiring her husband to leave the family home and to cease assaulting Trudy and the children. On both occasions he ignored the injunction, came home and recommenced beating his wife. She returned to court to enforce the orders; the court reissued them. Her husband returned once more. Trudy Smart returned to court. Her husband has not been served with papers relating to the latest assault, for he is 'deliberately avoiding this, owing to a suspended sentence from his previous contempt of the injunction'. Olive Smith was often advised by police to take action against her husband, because, they said, they could do nothing until she acted. She was confused by their approach, for as she wrote, she frequently took action against her abusive husband, but this did not assist her:

I sought help so many times I can't remember the details. So many people said so many things for so long that I just can't remember whether I was told to seek help from an agency or what it was that they were saying to me. The police kept telling me I had to do something about him and they couldn't do anything for me. I took out many restraining orders against him but it didn't help. Many times I thought I should take some action but thought it would not be worth it the next morning because I kept going to court and getting a restraining order but he kept belting me up and tearing up the paper. He said it was only a paper law so in the end I stopped doing anything.

Following her neighbours' advice, Ursula Bendall went to a magistrate, securing two injunctions. Her husband disappeared for weeks after the first order was issued, but he eventually returned to continue the abuse. Ursula Bendall said 'the magistrate treated me as if I was exaggerating and we should kiss and make up. I felt as if the law wouldn't protect me, and it didn't.' Rosalyn Tenby went to a magistrate after a friend told her she should. She took out an injunction but, she wrote, 'my husband said it was just a bit of paper and beat me up more'.[1]

The quality of assistance and advice given to beaten women by lawyers was variable. Nora Simpson's solicitor was helpful, but the police refused to co-operate.

I went to a doctor after I went to my solicitor. The doctor examined bruises on my breasts, ribs and stomach and wrote a certificate of what he saw. I showed this to the Gunnedah court. I got an injunction for assault through the court. He came back and did it again, then in March 1977 I dropped the case as I knew that once we went to court again the marriage was finished and at that stage I still cared. In February 1978 our solicitors settled out of court as I couldn't stand the idea of relating everything in court especially with Tony's ability at lying so well.

Then it all started up again and finally I had to leave and take my daughter away. The day after we left the house Fiona and I needed to get back and get some underwear and clothes. I also wanted to check that the dogs and cat were alright. My solicitor told me to go to the Police Station and ask to be taken to the house by someone there as I was scared of Tony being home, because I knew he hadn't gone to work. The sergeant was very rude and said my solicitor didn't run the police station and they weren't marriage guidance officers. In the car he said he bet $100 after all the fuss I was causing that I would be back with him within the week. I was annoyed and said I would take him on and he said he wasn't a betting man. Tony wasn't home and the sergeant said I should have ridden down on my bike first to see if he was home before I bothered him. He made some comments about my solicitor, saying solicitors were too smart for their own good. I told my solicitor what he said but he didn't seem to be able to do anything. He likely thought I was making another fuss about nothing too.

Marjorie Christensen suffered years of extreme abuse, often involving guns and other weapons. A solicitor advised her 'to give him time to consider the case — even though my position was desperate'.

No one wanted to give me shelter in case my husband caused trouble for them as he was chasing me. I had to smuggle the children aboard a train at midnight. He came along the train with a guard and we hid in the toilet.

My father introduced me to the local MP who sent me to the police where I filled in papers for aid. I was granted $8.00 per week for myself and four children. I was given a free rail pass to travel from my mother's place in Tammin to Northam for court proceedings of which there were five. Also to help in obtaining a pension and commission home. I had to wait six months for this to come through. An interim order was granted at the first hearing for money and a place to live but my husband never complied with this order in any way. No other help was available.

Once I left I went through with the maintenance as advised by my solicitor and the police inspector who interviewed me. I feel that solicitors are overrated because all the 'help' I got from mine I got from the police inspector, so needn't have paid my solicitor anything.

Some women were poorly advised of their legal rights, although they sought help from trained lawyers.[2] Merrilee Sadka's solicitor 'gave me inaccurate advice and the welfare officer put me right relating to access and court action about divorce, maintenance and property'. Lesley Morgan went to a solicitor who advised her to wait for the new *Family Law Act* to be passed as divorce would be cheaper. She was disillusioned by the court process:

I now think, with the benefit of hindsight and new information from women's groups, that spouse assault should be a crime. I think it deserves more severe punishment than does assault by a stranger, for there is an element of trust in an intimate relationship. But now my place in the family because of bad legal advice from a solicitor is no more. My children now reside unhappily with their schizophrenic father. Because of the bad legal advice I received I have lost custody of my children. My husband embezzled the funds from our joint business account. There appears to be no redress for me on either account. So I'm thoroughly disgusted with the law. Male legal personnel trivialised me, they paid no heed to anything I said — they totally disregarded me — even though I was paying *them* to represent *me*.

Jane Robbins was bashed by her husband over about five years. He brutally attacked her with a broken chair on an Easter weekend, and she finally went to a lawyer for assistance. She requested that the lawyer have her husband charged, as she had had him charged four

times before and hoped on this occasion the law might have some
effect. When the case was scheduled to come on, as she sat waiting in
the witnesses' room, the barrister employed to act for her talked to
her, telling her she should go home, lose some weight and put on
some make-up, go back to her husband 'and he would still love her or
start to love her again'. He forcefully persuaded her to confer with
her husband, brought Des Robbins into the room, then negotiated a
'reconciliation' between them. Jane Robbins dropped the charges.
Her husband did not, however, cease beating her. His attacks grew
worse.

Other women wrote of their difficulties in dealing with solicitors
who failed to adhere to ethical standards. After twenty years of
violence, Caroline McHale made an appointment with a lawyer to
begin divorce and custody arrangements. Arriving at the appointed
hour of 2.00 pm, her lawyer told her he knew 'all about her problem
because her husband had come in that morning and talked about it
all to him'. Janet Broady escaped from home to a women's refuge,
finally moving out to a housing commission area. She explained
clearly to her solicitor that she had suffered years of abuse and sexual
assault by her husband Jim. She asked her lawyer not to reveal her
address to him, fearing he would visit and attack her. Her lawyer
ignored the plea and gave Jim Broady her address.

I felt as if the whole world was against me. There was I trying to pull myself
together and get away from Jim to start a new life, and my solicitor who I
had trusted getting on Jim's side. I felt as if no one would help me and that
no one was going to take my part. I lost faith in the law and the legal
profession. The whole system is against me and against women like me.

Women Victims in Court

Susan Davey was helped through the court process by her solicitor,
her step-daughter, and her medical practitioner. Her solicitor made
good use of the evidence given by Jan Davey, witness to her father's
attacks not only on Susan Davey but also on his former wife Patricia.
The medical evidence was strong proof of Jack Davey's vicious
attacks. Jack was not sent to prison, although attempts had been
made to crush Susan Davey's skull, she had been pushed and flung
across the room, hit and punched, and suffered severe bruises and

abrasions. The evidence was used to support her claim for a non-molestation order. Later, she went through the Family Court in an effort to distance herself completely from her husband's claims of ownership and his assertion that he could 'do as he liked with her'.

Finally taking the advice of police, Renate Warne went to a magistrate and charged her husband with assault. She wrote:

The magistrate said that if I really cared about the kiddies I wouldn't let him do it to me and that if I stayed I must want to stay. He didn't tell me how I was going to leave with three children and one retarded and a burden completely and the reason I was coming to him was to try and get away from him or to stop him from getting at me and finally the magistrate said to me that it was foolish of me to think that I could live by myself alone with the children, and the one retarded, and how did I think I was going to get money to live on. And so the end was that I went back home and the magistrate didn't help me except that I told the police next time that he was no use.

Jean Selberg said the court's view of her position was totally un-realistic. Over thirteen years of marriage to her husband Jack, violence increased from isolated incidents to approximately once a month in the last few years. The incidents varied in intensity, involving slapping, hitting, punching; hitting with a chair and a broom; pulling hair; kicking with steel-capped boots; attacks with a table knife; threats with a gun; attempts to throw her down stairs; and violent kicking so that she was thrust out of bed and on to the floor nightly. She suffered split lips, 'very bad bruises', a gashed forehead, and eyes 'so bruised they closed for days'. When she told the court her husband had assaulted her, the judge stated 'that I had put up with it for thirteen years and a little while longer wouldn't hurt until we had been counselled by a marriage counsellor. What the judge didn't seem to understand was that I feared for my life *every day*.' Going to court did not really assist Jean Selberg; rather, it supported her husband in his view that he had a right to do as he did.

On the first occasion I had him charged with assault, my parents took me to the police station, where they refused to charge him and told me to go to a solicitor. However on the second occasion, the University Legal Aid rang the police and asked them if they would charge him if I laid a complaint, which they did. An interesting point was that when I had him charged through a solicitor, it took approximately six weeks for the case to be heard. When the police handled the matter my husband was charged the next day.

However on the first charge of assault he was fined $200 but put on a good behaviour bond for 12 months. On being charged a second time he was fined only $100. An additional note to the first time is that he was warned never to appear in court again on this charge or he would be dealt with far more severely. Yet he was given a much lighter penalty and came home feeling the law was on his side.

Although women are advised to take court action on their own initiative, this advice is unrealistic if the courts fail to have regard to the abuse the women suffer. It can only promote violence in the family if courts appear to support abusers and can only increase the despair of victims if they find that courts fail to stop family crime and pay little or no account to victims who happen to be wives, even though courts are established to control crime and stop victimisation.

Child Victims

If courts were little better than useless in attacking the problem of wife beating, they were worse in the field of child abuse. The courts rarely assisted child victims of violence or sexual molestation. Most respondents did not contemplate seeking help from the criminal justice system through the courts. Particularly with incest, victims were too scared to tell anyone in authority. Kerrie Senior wrote that she was terrified at the time and could think of no way to seek help: 'The courts were far from my mind.' A number of victims were threatened with court action against themselves. Mary Moore was sexually abused by her father. At the same time, he molested his young sister-in-law Sally, threatening them both. He said that if Mary or Sally told anyone, he would have Sally sent away to a girls home. Rather than the abusive father, step-father or uncle going through the courts, victims passed through the children's court if they ran away or sought official help to escape molestation. Maureen Hamilton was placed in Parramatta Girls Home for five years after a children's court decided she was in moral danger. The step-father, who had sexually abused her from the time she was 10 years old until she turned 14 and was committed, remained free to molest his own daughter. At no time did he run any risk of censure by any court. Rhonda Gardner was victimised by her own father for more than five years, beginning in her early teens, and was finally committed to an institution as incorrigible and a truant. Her father remained to abuse his other daughters, and no court enquired into his unlawful activities.

The picture for victims of violence is similar. Few victims sought the help of courts. Where courts were involved, almost invariably it was the children's court intervening to commit a runaway child, ignoring the abusive parent who caused the running. In a few cases, the mother looked for assistance from a magistrate. Irene Tanner was terrified for the safety of her children after they had been continually beaten and abused by their father. She gained a non-molestation order for herself and the children, but this did not prevent her husband from continuing to terrorise them. Maxine Thompson wrote: 'A New Zealand doctor once advised me to lay charges against my husband (after a vicious assault on our eldest son) but the position at home would have become quite dreadful.'

In no child abuse cases was court action instituted and successfully concluded. In a few incest cases, court action was commenced. In even fewer was that court action successfully concluded. Lynda Messer was placed in institutions and foster homes as a result of court action. Her father was prosecuted but 'he got off scot free'. She believed her mother supported her father, so the court took the 'family orientated approach': of condemning the victim and 'keeping the family together' (minus the victim, of course).

Paula Mendelsohn and Prudence Murphy each successfully instituted actions against a husband who interfered sexually with their daughters. Thomas Mendelsohn was gaoled for six and a half years on a charge of unlawful carnal knowledge of his daughter Jess, aged 7 at the time. Prudence Murphy found her husband attempting to rape their eldest daughter Susan, then 5 years old. Together with the children, Prudence Murphy left the matrimonial home. Her husband Trevor scoffed at her as she left, saying she would be too scared to take any action 'and anyway, no one would believe me, and if they did, he would kill me and the kids'. After talking with friends, she went to the police and proceedings were commenced. In court, Trevor Murphy admitted he had committed acts of incest upon his daughter not once but three times. He was gaoled for six years and served four. The maximum penalty for unlawful carnal knowledge of a girl under 10 years in New South Wales, where the crime was committed, was life imprisonment. The penalty for rape was life imprisonment as maximum; for attempted rape, a maximum of fourteen years.

Men Victims

Only one of the eight male victims of domestic assault went to the courts for help. On the advice of relatives, friends and police, Dan Summers went to a magistrate. He had suffered seven years of slapping, hitting and punching; hitting with a broom; hair pulling, scratching, biting and kicking; and threats with a kitchen knife. He suffered bruises and abrasions. The magistrate awarded him a non-molestation order against his wife. Dan Summers found no difficulty in obtaining the order. Sam Trewin, victim of 'attempted rape' was also helped at the magistrates' court.

The Family Court

Adult victims made more frequent use of the Family Court for divorce as a solution, than of criminal or quasi-criminal court procedures. Divorce was also an escape route for children suffering abuse, when the non-abusive parent (almost without exception the mother) left home with the children. The victims' hopes that divorce would end the abuse were often erroneous, however. As well as assaults and harassment continuing after divorce, victims felt abused by the court processes themselves.[3]

When Jennifer Brown's neighbours suggested she take court action against her husband's abuse, she left Rob Brown. Determined to end the relationship through divorce action, she waited out the twelve months qualifying period in rented accommodation, fearing he would come after her. Iris Fenton did not have the necessary stamina, however. She commenced divorce proceedings in 1975 but later dropped them, finding it too difficult to live alone during the twelve month waiting period, to make a separate home for her three children and start a new life. No one she spoke to had much support for her action. She often heard of women seeking maintenance for the children from the children's father, but maintenance was never paid.

About two-thirds of adult victims in the present study were divorced or seeking divorce as a result of the violence. Of those who had gone through the Family Court, none expressing a view of procedures was satisfied with the outcome. Some had reservations about Family Court counsellors. Marilyn Bennet said 'Most of the Family Court personnel seemed to have the attitude that being beaten up regularly was all okay.' She emerged from the divorce proceedings believing the courts 'are corrupt as the police if not worse' because they hold more authority generally. She thought the law 'was no place for people to go for help — particularly the Family Court'.

Lesley Morgan left her husband, went to the Family Court, and sought a divorce and custody of her children, a boy and a girl:

The psychiatrist made a report to the court that I was brought up to compensate for the loss of a son and was therefore 'mannish' and competitive with men! He saw this as one of the reasons for my marriage failure. My ex-husband's solicitor used this against me in the custody battle. I believe my parents brought me up to be a compassionate, competent human being — and would have done so irrespective of my gender. So in fact *yes* my childhood did have an effect on my current situation — it influenced the *male professionals* who sat in judgment of me.

Rose Hogg lost custody of her son after going through the Family Court. Her husband Roger beat her every week during their two year marriage, yet their child was left in his care. Rose Hogg was slapped, punched and her hair was pulled. She wrote:

I changed my mind often about going to get a divorce because I had no confidence and thought that I would not be able to survive alone. The fear made me fail to take action. But finally I felt, and after I left, the Family Court counsellor thought I was unfit to get custody of my child because I was so depressed and nervous. Yet my husband who was the reason for me being so depressed and nervous got custody. Now I distrust the law and have no faith in counsellors. I am now very angry at society and get more depressed and sometimes suicidal. My health has gone. I have no home and I have lost my child. If it wasn't for the fact that I see my son once a week I would kill myself.

Women divorcing because they did not wish their children to suffer from continuing violence were often surprised that custody was awarded to the abusive husband, or that access was allowed despite abuse of the children when they were living as a family. Women leaving because they discovered the husband sexually molesting the children, or who left when the children complained, similarly expressed concern at access being ordered by the court. Janice Rowe left her husband when she discovered him molesting their daughter at age four. She took the child with her, but despite explaining the situation to the Family Court, access was allowed to her husband. The molestation continued during access times, but finally Donald Rowe grew tired of entertaining his daughter, and the abuse ceased when he failed to take advantage of the Court's access order. Miriam Rosen's experience was similar. Of her daughter's exploitation she wrote:

I can't tell what effect it has had. She didn't want to go on access (which is not surprising considering he was still carrying on with it) but the counsellors and judge at the court thought otherwise. The idea of a father's rights outweighed the child's distress. She really didn't want to go alone with him and that was clear enough. With me there it was alright. The judge just didn't believe it when I told him that her father was making her touch his thing and putting his finger in her privates.

Women were also disillusioned by the Court's attitude toward their claims for recognition of their contribution toward the family assets.[4] Overwhelmingly, women victims found that when it came to divorce, their efforts put into the family home, child bearing and child raising, providing creature comforts for their husbands, despite the abusive conditions under which they lived, were not adequately recognised in dividing up the property. Mandy Salmon and her husband worked together in a smallgoods business throughout their marriage. However, after divorce and property settlement she commented:

I'm certainly cynical about the Family Law Act and do not anticipate ever marrying again. I'm also very angry that all my years of 'service' to the state (through childcare/husbandcare etc.) seem to be of no consequence. Maintenance of $100 a month for me and the children was all we got, because he took out mortgages over the business and also put it in another woman's name.

Sandra Cox had been trying to get a property settlement through the Family Court 'for the past five years' with no success; Cheryl Davies's present occupation was 'trying to get a fair property settlement so that me and the children can live without thinking where every penny is coming from'. Although Sondra Lemmert was awarded maintenance after leaving her husband, the maintenance was never paid. She wrote: 'I'm very sick and haven't got enough money to live on. I'm too old to get a job at my age and because of all his violence I can't work at anything. Also I'm very confused about the law giving my husband access to my daughter when he doesn't pay any money and when he has her he isn't very nice to her.'

Women were generally disenchanted by the court system after their experiences with the Family Court. One woman said 'the only rude ones was them at the Family Court'. Mary Dunn considered 'all the people in the courts are "woman haters" . . . They took my house and let my husband live in it. Where's the law there? I think all the court people need a flogging and sent to school to learn some humanity and manners.' Others were distressed by the variable nature of decisions at the Court. Some went through the appeals process but were advised by their lawyers that the discretionary powers of the judges enabled them to make 'virtually any decisions they choose',[5] as long as it ostensibly conformed with the requirements of the *Family Law Act*. Eunice Georgevic, victim of her husband's abuse throughout their four year marriage and a continuing victim whenever he visits the family, went through the Family Court system and summed up the situation as it was for many women in the study.

All my assets were tied up jointly with his, so it was too difficult at first to take the child and start a new life. When the police came they told me to see a magistrate and welfare agency or go to the Family Court for a divorce. But it was too important that he had all the money and assets and I had control of nothing, even though I had worked hard and put all my money into the house. It is not fair that the woman has to leave and go off without any idea of whether she will get anything back that she put into it.

When it came to the final thing and I left him with the children the police, magistrate and welfare agency believed me about the abuse I was suffering. But the Family Court judge at the access and custody hearing did not believe I was a victim of abuse or that it was affecting the children the way he carried on. After going through the Family Court and the property settlement when they seemed to think I was in it for myself and not to see that I put as much into it all as he did, I am very aware that the laws in Australia are more concerned with protecting the following groups:

1. men
2. rich
3. middle class
4. mad
5. liars
6. rapists
7. child molesters

at the expense of :
1. women
2. poor
3. working class
4. sane
5. truthful
6. victims
7. children

Legal Training and Judicial Attitudes

The police are not trained to deal with family violence, and such violence is considered not to be 'serious police work'. Similarly lawyers are not educated, and the court system is not encouraged, to take complaints of domestic violence seriously. Because assault is a crime, and crimes are in the normal course dealt with through the criminal justice system, law school curricula should include domestic assaults in criminal law courses. Traditionally, no law courses include lectures on family violence as a 'normal' part of the criminal law jurisdiction. In the past, students of law were taught that spouse assault was in fact no crime. Originally a man had a legal right to beat his wife. In 1891, the English House of Lords held that a man no longer had a right to beat his wife or detain her against her will.[6] Lord Esher denied that an English wife was 'the abject slave' of her husband and that he had custody of her, 'the same sort of custody as a gaoler has of a prisoner'.[7] But he thought there might well be matters on both sides which 'might more or less furnish excuses for what was done' in a marriage. His comments are not so far removed from the comments of some present day judges, law professors, and law officials. A former ombudsofficer, in discussing complaints against the police for failing to intervene in domestic disputes, stated that their refusal could be justified, for 'the wife may have provoked the husband . . . in so many cases, if not all, this happens'. Yet it is not up to the police to say that a woman has 'provoked' her husband. That determination is for the courts. Provocation does not make a crime 'no crime' because police say so. Yet those who should know better speak to the contrary. These attitudes find their way into law schools of the present day and influence law students — future lawyers, magistrates, judges — in their treatment of women coming to them as victims of marital assault.

In rape cases, the law promotes the idea of woman as a chattel who cannot be helped by the legal system. The predominant thought amongst lawyers and in Australian schools of law is that marital rape is one of the 'natural' accompaniments of marriage, every married man's entitlement. With this formal refusal to acknowledge that married women have sexual rights comes an informal acceptance of married woman as having no personal rights so long as the marriage subsists, and sometimes, even when parties are separated.[9]

Patriarchal values are not only reflected in courts of criminal law. They provide foundation for the family jurisdiction. Judges, counsellors, and lawyers working through the Family Court of Australia have been trained, like criminal law lawyers, magistrates, and judges, in law schools steeped in the ancient regime of woman as property, woman as secondary to man. It is little wonder that women who attempted to escape from their abusive husbands by divorce were disillusioned and frequently disgusted by the views expressed by judges, magistrates, and practitioners, and dissatisfied with the outcome of their case.

Frequently the question asked of battered women is 'why do they stay?' Battered women may ask in vain, 'why shouldn't we stay?' Why shouldn't we stay in our own homes, in homes we built up, through our own efforts equally with our husbands, and to which we have an equal entitlement and attachment? Why shouldn't we stay in our own neighbourhood, with the children's school nearby, with friends and neighbours we know, with shopping centres close by, in familiar surroundings? Why should we have to move house, find bond money for rental accommodation, to have the electricity put on, the phone connected (if we can afford it — which most of us cannot)? Why should *we* have to go? The problem is that women have few means of establishing rights to property in the present system, which would enable them to keep a foothold on the neighbourhood where the family home is situated. In the Family Court, judges have a discretion to award a woman part of the 'family assets'. The exercise of discretion in a patriarchal system can never be favourable to women, against whom the system is designed to discriminate.[10]

Just as discretion is exercised by the police so that they decide not to use the powers they have to take action against men who beat, batter, bash and rape women living in the household of the beater, the batterer, the basher, the rapist, so discretion is exercised by judges and lawyers in the criminal justice system and in the Family Court. That discretion is exercised when lawyers, against all ethical standards, 'persuade' women to return to their abusive husbands. It is exercised by lawyers who 'persuade' women to accept unfair property settlements, which result in women living poorly, victims to their husbands if those husbands wish to chase and harass them. Without adequate assets, it is difficult to stand and fight, for the system favours the property-owner, not the propertyless. Judicial discretion is exercised against women when it fails to acknowledge that women's efforts in building up marital assets are equal to those of men, and that 'marital assets' is not confined to the family home, but extends to *all* property accumulated during the course of the marriage. No man could build up a medical practice, a legal practice, a pharmacy, a green grocery, an orchard, a farm, a construction business without his wife taking on herself major responsibility for the upbringing of the children they decided together to have, the upkeep of the home they consider to be 'theirs', the garden that surrounds the home.[11] If a man could do this, then women should ask why they are expected to put in constant efforts in keeping up the home ground, constant efforts in caring for the children, constant efforts in cooking, washing, cleaning up *his* share of the food, the dishes, the clothes, the bathroom, the toilet, the bedroom, the lounge. If women are superfluous in the home and their efforts not equal to those of the man working in the world of paid employment, why has society dictated to them that they should spend their lives in superfluity? If society has dictated they should be superfluous, should not that part of society in the power position, namely men, pay for conditioning women to exist on a superficial level. Recompense would give women some means of elevating themselves out of a surface existence into a more fulfilling level; without it, they remain on the surface with nothing and no way out.

Until law schools around the country drag themselves into a world where 'justice' has some meaning, and where fairness extends to both women and men, then discrimination through the legal system will continue to ensure that women who are victims of domestic violence find little help in the process of going to court. Similarly, until law schools begin teaching students that children have real rights, rather than being chattels of their parents, courts will fail to ensure that children have access to legal protections extending to adult males, namely, the right not to be assaulted or sexually abused and, where this happens, to have the aggressors dealt with by ordinary legal processess. As for those who have already been trained in the system and who may not be too old to change, there is a clear obligation upon those holding power to require judges and lawyers trained in the style of the patriarchy to undergo retraining. Where they are unable to retrain and gain an equilibrium which sees women and children as people with rights equal to those of men, then they must be pensioned off. For as long as such individuals remain in the criminal justice system and in the family law system, women and children will continue to be abused, while the courts that exist ostensibly to protect individuals from criminal acts and from discrimination in civil proceedings will fail miserably in their task.

CHAPTER 11   THE REFUGES

The concept of a refuge for women is not unique... However Women's Liberation refuges are unique in that we aim to do more than merely provide assistance to women and children in distress. We are feminist collectives working towards eliminating the oppressions which cause women to be poor and desperate. We identify the need for such places as the Halfway House as a direct result of the exploitative sexist, racist, class base of this society. That is, we do not see that the many intolerable situations faced by the women who come to the Halfway House will be eliminated or changed without an overall change in the oppressive nature of this society. Least of all do we consider that both the problem and the solution are in the hands of any one individual or even that women supporting women creates a situation where we can rise above our social context... we do not quietly provide assistance to women. We aim to make the problems we encounter public knowledge; to make the government and uninformed public feel responsible for the sufferings of women; to expose the fact that charitable institutions and the social welfare system simply perpetuate inequalities, and the powerlessness of the vast majority of people; and make more women aware that we must demand and struggle for changes in the system and the society which oppresses us.

Herstory of the Halfway House 1974–1976
Women's Liberation Halfway House Collective, Melbourne, 1976, pp. 4–5.

In 1974 the Melbourne Ladies' Welfare Society reported:

From our past records we find that deserted wives were as prevalent in the last century as they are today, but there is a great difference, for in those days pensions were unheard of and work was not available to the weaker sex.

During the 1830s, women with children were drifting about seeking a roof to cover them. At this critical period, the Society decided to rent a nine roomed house in Fitzroy Street, Fitzroy, to protect the homeless women and children. To help finance this community home, orders for any sort of laundry, fine sewing, embroidery, knitting, crochet, etc. were taken.

Very soon it was necessary to rent a second house as applicants increased.[1]

In 1974 the first feminist-run women's refuge was established in Sydney by the Elsie collective.[2] The collective did not euphemistically refer to women seeking refuge as 'deserted wives'. They recognised that women seeking shelter were victims of batterings and bashings by husbands who believed that, because they had married them, wives were there for the beating. Soon after, Warrina Women's Refuge was funded by government grant in Fremantle, Western Australia, to open its doors to women victims of domestic violence. In 1975 the federal Labor government recognised the fundamental importance of women's refuges and began funding at the rate of 75 per cent of operating costs and 50 per cent of capital costs. State governments were expected to make up the shortfall.

Since that time, the number of women's refuges in Australia has grown to almost a hundred, about thirty of which operate in New South Wales. Federal funding has fallen until in 1981 the federal Liberal government absolved itself from all responsibility for women's refuges. Women have demonstrated time and again on the steps of Parliament House and in Kings Hall in protest. Women and children have been dragged by the hair from parliamentary precincts during these demonstrations, without regard to their safety, or to the safety of women seeking shelter in refuges. Feminist-run refuges have been charged with being 'political'. They are. The women's refuge movement was founded not on the basis that battered women wanted tea and sympathy alone, nor that they should be provided for by tatting and knitting and ironing, the tasks for which women have traditionally 'been suited' and which have led to women's oppression. The women's refuge movement is a political movement standing against patriarchal attitudes and ideals that provide the foundation and cover for men who bash the women they marry. The movement believes that crime in the family will not cease until all masculine idealism is eradicated from our political, social and economic structures. The women's refuge movement does not exist to teach women how better to cope with their husband's violence; it does not continue to shore up abusive marriages. Its purpose is to alter power structures so that all women are, and are recognised as being, politically, socially and economically equal with all men.

Women Victims

Six women victims of spouse assault and two victims of marital rape said they would have gone to a women's refuge had refuges existed during the worst times of their abusive marriages. Their comments are important in that twenty, forty, fifty years ago various church-orientated bodies *were* operating shelters for homeless men and also provided (though in fewer numbers) accommodation for the 'deserted wives' the Melbourne Ladies' Welfare Society and similar bodies noted. None of the women in the study wrote of finding shelter with a welfare or church-run organisation, nor of wishing to had they been able to find one. Lorrie Richards, whose husband slapped, hit and punched her from the time of their marriage in the mid 1950s, remained 'because there was no place to go to . . . I had no where to go with my children — there were no women's refuges in those days. One had simply to remain in the situation and accept it as one's lot. Unless of course one had some financial independence — not many women had, despite the "married women's property acts" etc.' Dorothy Sands, beaten by her husband David throughout a seventeen year marriage begun in 1959, could see no way out and had no one to go to: 'If only current services and women's refuges existed then, me and the children wouldn't have horrible memories of a nightmare in our lives.'

Seven women recorded appreciation of the help given them by women's refuge workers when they were forced to run from battering husbands. Susan Davey was grateful for the existence of a women's shelter in an Adelaide suburb. She went to outsiders rather than friends 'who were angry because I had given my husband a second and third chance'.

As well, for some reason I felt ashamed to let my friends know I was trapped in such a violent situation and was still trying to make the marriage work. When I got to the shelter after hearing about it on a radio talk-back programme, I did not find the shying away from me that I got if ever I tried to talk about it to anyone before. They did not treat me as if I was weak because I had given Jack chances before. For the first time I felt as if someone really understood and as if I wasn't the only one it had ever happened to. They did not tell me I should see my husband's point of view, which is what marriage guidance kept on with. They said that a man who bashes his wife doesn't deserve a point of view, and anyway doesn't deserve a wife to stay around to try to see what it is. For once I felt as if someone was on my side.

Although Ursula Cranitch had been managing the finances of her husband's companies, her husband's attacks and continually derogatory remarks had destroyed her self-esteem. She spent several nights on two occasions at a women's refuge in Hobart and decided to leave her husband for good.

I began to see that I *did* have some talents. I certainly didn't end up a 'new woman' just from a few nights at the refuge, but talking to the workers there made me see that I had some brains and that I couldn't be a secondary school teacher with two degrees if I was the idiot Denzil tried to make out. I had to remake my life and really remake myself as a person, but they let me see there was a real person underneath that quivering jelly of nerves and self-hate.

Women going to refuges emphasised the assistance received in understanding the welfare system and how to obtain their rightful benefits; they appreciated the encouragement refuge workers gave them to be independent and to develop their own skills in talking to bureaucratic agencies, real estate agents and child care centre workers, without leaving them to cope on their own. Helen Trent consulted her mother, a friend, a doctor and marriage counsellor during the course of her marriage to Samuel, whom she classed a sadistic wife-beater after he spent ten years of their twelve year marriage slapping, hitting, punching, scratching, biting and kicking her, as well as throwing her down stairs, pushing her out of the car, chasing her in the car, and pulling her hair. She went to a women's refuge in Sydney.

When I finally decided to leave I went to a refuge. My husband went interstate on a trip and I got away. My mother helped me to pack our clothes, but I didn't want to go to her home because I knew that wouldn't work. We had to be somewhere independent, where I could get us away from him. Also I didn't want my mother to get mixed up in it all and to be plagued by him. If you don't object to women's libbers, refuges are the best way. I don't object to anything. The refuge workers were tremendous. They helped me with legal aid. Advised me to get legal help immediately. They organised custody. It was heaven. They organised medical assistance and for the children a child psychologist. Y.A.C.S. (Youth and Community Services Department) cheque. Organised counselling for me. Got more of my belongings, etc. from the house.

Before taking the final step, Helen Trent felt most people didn't want to hear of her husband's excesses. The doctor she attended 'didn't really want to know the case — seemed to be shocked at the thought'. After the refuge, Helen Trent found accommodation with another divorced woman and rebuilt her life. 'I now appreciate the feminist movement', she wrote, 'and in particular the strength and support of the refuge workers.' Other women wrote similarly.

Although Hope Begg was unable to make use of women's refuges, as they appeared after her marriage ended, she wrote:

Although I finally divorced John without getting help from outside, I know that it is the women's movement that helped me to see that as the solution. It also made me see that I had to recover my own identity and find out who I was, not just be a target for a man's frustrations and power plays. At the age of 58 I find my entire philosophy changed. I have complete sympathy with the feminist movement. I also have no faith in the current political and legal systems. I could write tomes on this, but I won't.

Reports of help from doctors, friends, neighbours, family, marriage guidance counsellors and others varied from the appreciative to the despairing. With women's refuges, in every case where she looked for their help the woman's response was positive. No respondent said refuge workers 'averted their eyes'; that they 'did not want to talk about it'; that they 'wanted to help but couldn't'; that they 'made me feel as if I was in the way'; or that it was 'too much trouble for them'. These comments were frequently made about other sources of possible 'help' for bashed women.

Child Victims

Youth refuges have been established only recently. In the past, children running away from home had nowhere to run. If caught, they were sent back to an abusive household, or shunted off to an institution where abuse might be an everyday occurrence.[3] If they were not caught, children remained in fear of discovery by police and being returned home or institutionalised. They depended on illegal means for their livelihood: children under 16 years of age are status offenders if they truant; generally they are not legally entitled to a paid job; they are not entitled to receive child endowment, a family allowance, or unemployment benefits.[4]

None of the respondents battered by parents or sexually abused left home to enter a youth refuge. Most who left home were brought back or institutionalised. Some young girls left home by marrying and often found themselves victims of equally severe battering and bashing or sexual abuse as had occurred in their parents' home. Some said marriage was worse, and no escape, for at least a child grows up and is entitled eventually to leave the parental home; when married, the expectation is that the wife will remain with her husband 'till death us do part'. Children are born cementing the relationship further and making it economically more difficult for the abused woman to escape.

Child victims in the present study running away from home would have been assisted by youth refuges. If Pamela Mawson had left behind her father's attacks with an electric cord, hitting with a strap, a belt, a piece of wood; his forced feeding; locking in an outside shed and holding her head under a backgarden tap, she would not have gone from home at 17 to marry as an escape — thus subjecting herself to beatings and sexual abuse from her husband. Lindy Mason was sexually abused by her father and actively tried to get away to her grandmother's home as often as she could to escape; she went to her grandparents' for holidays whenever the opportunity arose; after school she stayed as long as she could playing with friends, at their homes. If youth refuges had been opened with government support, her time might better have been spent on school work, on enjoying herself playing with school friends, rather than using her time planning ways to escape her father's exploitative and abusive attacks upon her. Had Ellen Longmore an opportunity to go to a youth refuge, together with her sister Celia, she would not be obliged to remain in her step-father's home, enduring his fondling of her breasts; touching her genitals; having to touch his genitals, rub his penis; submit to full intercourse. She would not have to remain through fear of Rick Longmore transferring his attention to Celia if she ran away to escape. Celia and Ellen could have gone together, without fear of being returned.

For very young children, youth refuges would not suffice. Yet evidently the mothers of abused children, doing their best to keep the children out of the way by sending them to bed early, before father's arrival home to beat them; having them tiptoe around the house so he was not sparked off into a rage; sending them off to grandparents for weekends, after school, school holidays; booking them into boarding schools to begin as soon as they were five or six years old, would have appreciated freely available day-care centres, community centres and neighbourhood centres. Mothers who needed to join the workforce for financial reasons, or demanded the intellectual stimulation of the office, university, executive work, work in the park or on a delivery run, would have been helped in being able to leave their children in nearby child care centres, or after-school play centres, and not had to fear their being alone in the house with a potentially abusive father or *de facto* spouse. Those mothers abusing their own children would be helped by youth care centres or child care centres located within easy distance of their homes. Trisha Maine, alone in suburban isolation with her prematurely born first child, would have been saved memories of bashing that child had community care for youngsters been available in her neighbourhood. Janine Renault would have been 'more tolerant', 'in control' of herself, and not a screaming, hitting mother had her child been able to go to a nearby centre whilst Janine developed her own talents and skills free from a constant, twenty-four hour a day responsibility for Suzanne Renault from birth.

Men Victims

'Women's refuges have been established and funded by Governments; but not only wives are victims of bashing. What about poor old hubby?'[5] In the United States concern about victims of abusive husbands has been replicated by concern for victims of abusive wives. A real concern for all victims is important, whether wives or husbands. Yet suggestions that men victims of domestic violence are ignored accords little with reality. Since Australia was founded by an influx of migrants from Britain in the late eighteenth century men, whether victims or not, have been relatively well catered for. The population was predominantly male for years after the first white settlement, and it is only recently that women have exceeded men in population figures. Because men were superior in crude numbers, as well as dominating parliaments, the judiciary, corporations, primary, secondary and tertiary industry, indeed every aspect of eighteen, nineteenth and twentieth century living, services and facilities in this country have been designed with men, not women, in mind. The women's refuge movement was begun to correct the gross imbalance of facilities for homeless women in Australia. Homeless men have been provided with rooming houses, kitchens, and welfare benefits from before gold rush days.[6] Those in the more affluent categories have had their pubs and clubs to retreat to for solace, if set upon by an abusive wife.

In the present study, of the eight male victims of violence, none lamented a lack of facilities for escape. Indeed, none saw any need for escape. Three had their wives committed to mental institutions. They did not need to abandon their homes. They remained, sole owner in fact and probably in law. Why abandon a three-bedroom, family home for one room, probably shared with one's children and probably another single parent family, in a refuge, as women do? In Dan Summers's case, his wife Maureen left the family home, not he. Christine Travers left husband Andrew at home when she divorced him. Ronald Jackson had no need for a refuge: his wife Margaret hit him only once during their marriage, and both remained living in the family home. Graham Gordon and his *de facto* spouse Shirley Weston split up, eventually, after seven years of living together. There was only one serious bout of violence during the marriage, when Shirley Weston, not Graham Gordon, required medical attention. Graham Gordon did not seek, and did not need, alternative accommodation in a male equivalent of a women's refuge.

Refuges as a Solution?

Can women's, children's and men's refuges provide a solution to domestic violence? Some criticism has been voiced about youth refuges. Critics say children are unable to look after themselves and should not be given governmental encouragement to leave home to set up in a youth refuge in a semi-independent state. Critics aver that youth refuges will lead to an escalation of family breakdown, of youth involvement in crime, and of youth promiscuity, general precociousness, and incorrigibility. Yet without youth refuges, families will continue to breakdown as girls and boys leave home without leaving a forwarding address. Girls and boys will continue to engage in crime and sexual relationships, whether or not there are youth refuges. Girls and boys will be classed 'incorrigible' or 'in moral danger' when found without support, perhaps running from an unsatisfactory home life,[7] whether or not youth refuges are funded by government. If youth refuges are funded, perhaps fewer will be caught and labelled by the authorities in this way. A positive outcome of funding youth refuges would be that those departing an abusive household, those escaping the sexual assaults of a father or step-father, an uncle, or mother's *de facto* husband, will have a relatively safe haven to run to. Crimes committed by parents on teenage children might not cease, but they would be repeated less often: the victim of the initial crime could leave safely, and not become a victim of continuing criminal acts.

Youth refuges and community child care are part of a philosophical development gaining force with the resurgence of the women's liberation movement in the late 1960s and finding its most obvious expression in the women's refuge movement: the belief that every human being, regardless of sex, age, or socio-economic class, has a right to full and free development without interference from those standing in a superior position of physical or economic strength. The youth refuge movement recognises that children, like women, are people. The child-care movement recognises that infants and young children need the freedom to mix with those of the same age; that they should not be fully dependent upon their mothers (or fathers), and that such dependency is detrimental to their proper physical and mental development; that mothers, like fathers, have an identity apart from their parental role and have a right to time to develop that identity.

What of refuges for men? Women and men victims of violence differ, in that men victims do not think they should remove themselves from the family home. They believe the aggressor should calm down or get out. Women victims talk constantly of escape but frequently have nowhere to go. Women's refuges are not sufficient to fill the need: women and children are turned away from refuges through lack of accommodation.[8] If there were more women's refuges, they would easily be filled by women seeking to extricate themselves from violent marriages. Women victims do not emulate their male counterparts by sitting tight in the family home, waiting for the aggressor to leave voluntarily to seek accommodation elsewhere and divorce, or to be removed by force and taken to a mental hospital. If battered men need refuges, refuges must be provided — not by women, who have few facilities and fewer funds for the greater needs of women victimised by husbands. If men need refuges, men should come forward, make applications for funding, and set them up. That no men have as yet made 'new wave' applications for funding men's refuges of the type women have established means that facilities, if needed, are already well established. It also means that men are less often beaten than women, and less in need of somewhere to go; it means that where men are beaten, with access to funds and a regular income, something women far less frequently have, they have no need to fall upon charitable avenues for assistance. They retain their economic independence, whether batterer or battered.

And what of women's refuges? The women's liberation movement does not see women's refuges as an *answer* to woman bashing. As the Naomi Women's Shelter, established in Adelaide in 1975, points out in its 1976–1977 Report:

The Shelter's existence is a small acknowledgement that women are being bashed, abused and kept in ignorance, but that is not enough! The fact is that women do have acute homelessness, drinking, drug abuse and mental traumas and other associated problems. These result from years and years of not being allowed to know the truth about their own bodies, of being bashed, humiliated, abused, treated as slaves, of raising families (which are often unwanted) and coping with insane, alcoholic and straight out bastards of husbands. This does not mean that we are unaware of the overall political and social reasons why they, the husbands, are such bastards, only that they are; and that in itself contributes to the continuing and lasting oppression of women.[9]

Women's refuges were established with a dual purpose: to provide shelter for women in need and to draw attention to the daily battering of Australian women by their husbands. They were set up not to provide 'welfare services' on an ongoing basis, which would serve only to keep women oppressed, by not enabling women to escape a day-to-day existence in which they are dependent on government 'handouts', or must return to abusive husbands because they see no other way out. Rather, women's refuges were set up to help women see our own oppression and to assist women in recognising that the personal is political. They aim to drive home to every woman who is beaten, every woman who is bashed and raped that she is not

alone; her husband is not operating in a vacuum, isolated from the rest
of the masculine world where men treat 'their' wives with contempt,
disdain and abuse. By bringing women together to talk about their
lives, women would be given new strength to work together to
combat anti-woman feelings that reveal themselves to greater and
lesser degrees in most marriages.

In the debate on the women's refuge movement, charges have been
made that feminist refuges are so political that they ignore the needs
of women victims. Allegations are that the collectives keeping
refuges operating are so imbued with their own vision of the world
— one in which men have the upper hand and women are subser-
vient — that they are unable to cater for battered women who do not
have any political analysis of their own situation and who do not
want to be provided with one. The allegations are not borne out by
the facts. Women in the present study mentioning refuges strongly
stressed the refuges' importance in helping them to escape from
abusive marriages; some had first-hand knowledge, others expressed
a wish that they could have had first hand knowledge.

A reassessment of the women's refuge movement is going on
within the movement itself. Funding that was never adequate is now
on the way out. In states such as Queensland and Western Australia,
where state governments have never been sympathetic to the plight
of battered women, or to those attempting to change their situation,
funding has nearly dried up. In April, 1982 all around Australia
refuge workers went on strike to publicise present difficulties faced
through lack of funding and an increasing call on the services by
women waking up to the regime of terror they have been forced,
silently, to endure through years of wedded bliss. Refuge workers
and sympathisers around Australia demonstrated before every state
Parliament and on the lawns outside federal Parliament. Despite
their demands and despite the very real need the refuge movement
has uncovered, these demonstrations were ignored. State and federal
governments seem determined to let the movement languish for lack
of resources, or to force women once more to take an entirely volun-
tary role in the operation of women's refuges.[10] At a time when
refuge workers have unionised to demand adequate wages, where
previously they were dividing one small salary between two or three
workers, most governments are choosing to forget that refuges are
an essential part of the Australian scene and a necessary item in

every government budget, local, state, and federal, because all over Australia women are beaten every day — and every night — by Australian husbands.

In 1979 at the International Women's Decade Conference in Copenhagen, the then Minister for Women's Affairs delivered a speech extolling the virtues of his government in 'establishing' the women's refuge movement in Australia; providing the impetus (!) for the setting up of women's health centres — indeed, virtually creating the resurgence of the women's liberation movement in Australia. 'We provide funds', he said, 'for the operation of ninety-nine refuges which in the past year provided shelter for 12 000 women and their 15 000 children in domestic crisis ... There is also an extensive program for the provision of child care facilities.'[11] In 1982 the federal Liberal government does not fund women's refuges. It has produced a policy document aimed at curtailing the 'extensive' program for child care — never sufficiently extensive to enable all children requiring care to be adequately catered for.[12]

The value of the women's refuge movement, apart from the very basic role of providing shelter for the proportionately few beaten women who find their way to their doors, is that it has awakened in many women and women's organisations a political recognition of the oppression of women in our society. However, it may be time for a change in approach. Women should now demand the right to remain in occupation of their own homes. Women should not be driven from them by abusive men. Their right to own property in the family home should be granted immediate recognition under the *Family Law Act* and under the *Marriage Act* — effectively rather than nominally.[13] As well as funding for refuges, to give women greater choice, funds should be provided for teams of trouble shooters, feminists who, like women's refuge workers, are fully acquainted with the workings of the bureaucracy and of the court system. Whenever a woman calls and wants their help, the team would visit to inform her of her rights, how to go about a legal clarification of her rights in the family property, how to gain sole custody of the children, and if necessary, how to prevent her husband from continuing to abuse and harass her in her own home. They would put her in contact with other women, living in their own homes, who were victims of domestic violence, or who were sympathetic to the position of women battered by men. A community could be built up between battered women and empathisers much as it is built up in women's refuges today — but all women would have their own piece of land, their own homes to remain in. Trouble shooters would assist them through the maze of relevant community welfare departments to discover what benefits are available to them for rent payments, or mortgage payments, electricity and rates payments, so the family home or lease could be kept on in their name. The team would talk with any woman who wished about the nature of a society which placed her in a position of subservience to a man who took it upon himself to beat her regularly — or irregularly — until she could take no more and begged — or demanded — help.

The foundation for this idea was articulated early in a letter from the Queanbeyan women's refuge, named 'Louisa' for Louisa Lawson, publisher, journalist, writer, poet. It was prompted by a Sydney Women's Electoral Lobby initiative, begun in the debate on equal property rights for women.

15th May, 1981
To all N.S.W. Women's Refuges and Victorian Women's Refuges.
Dear Sisters,

LAND RIGHTS FOR WOMEN : WHAT ARE THE ISSUES?

Land rights for women — or as it may be called, 'community of property rights' or a 'property regime' will soon be a major topic of debate in Australia. The Federal government is setting up a committee of enquiry as a result of the Select Committee on the Family Law Act which reported last year to Parliament. We are concerned that *all* women as far as possible should have a say in this question. We are particularly concerned that women in the refuge movement should have a say, and should know what the debate is about. We outline the issues as we see them. We will be sending further information around the networks.

One of the most fundamental reasons for women's oppression is our lack of access to facilities, our lack of rights as regards finance, the lack of any real recognition, in law, that we have a right to occupy our own homes. This is evidenced by many aspects of our society and in particular by the number of women who are forced to seek refuge in women's shelters. Why are women driven from what are our own homes? Why is it that the men who are bashing and beating us end up in the homes like lords of the manor whilst women have to 'make do' with a room — often shared with her children — in one of the very few refuges that the women's movement has managed to get, grudgingly, out of the government. (And these, no doubt, will soon go unless we set up cake stalls and hold endless lamington drives to keep the payments up, to keep the places going . . .)

Women are continuing to marry without thinking about the future. If women think about divorce or about wife beating, so many always think 'it won't happen to me'. Women continue to be the major carers of children, and even when they combine child raising with a paid job the jobs women get are lower paid than those of their husbands or de facto spouses. All the money coming into the home is considered so often to be that of the husband, women thinking they have no real right to that money and are 'lucky' for what is 'given' by a 'generous' husband. When the woman works for money, she frequently uses her money for food, clothing for the children, etc. whilst the husband's money goes on substantial items — like the house payments, boat, car, etc. even the television set. He acts as if it all belongs to him. When a woman leaves to seek refuge from his bashing, she goes with nothing and doesn't consider she has any real right to own anything. In so many cases women buy on 'pay by the week' finance from Lawtons (see and where possible buy *The Last Resort* by Vivienne Johnson and the Marrickville Women's Refuge Collective) — many have furniture and bedding, children's clothes, their own clothes, that they leave behind when they are driven from home. Even if she does want to get something back, it's tough. *She* has to get a lawyer (how — no money!), has to beg for legal aid, to find out where any property is and to try to prise out of him what should rightfully be hers.

How can this and equally horrific problems be overcome, in some small way? (Note: This is not the answer to everything, but may be part of the answer and a step on the way.)

We believe that equal marital property rights may be one way. Here, right from the time of marriage all property would be taken to be owned equally by both parties. This would be so throughout the marriage, whether both were in paid employment or the wife (as so often) left the paid workforce to care for the children. Both would have an equal say, *by law* as to what was done with the property and money during the marriage. A husband couldn't come home and say he had gone and spent the money on an electric mowing machine when they hadn't discussed it, and the wife desperately needed warm blankets for the children or a washing machine, etc. He couldn't just throw her a mingey part of the wages and say get food, clothes etc. etc. and everything on that while I do with most of the money what I choose to do with it.

On divorce, there would be a 50–50 breakdown of EVERYTHING — including any business assets (that at the moment he says all belong to him), family car, pots and pans, electric jug, etc. Where there were children, a certain percentage of the property would be held in trust to be used for the children by the person (usually the mother) having custody and care. There would have to be an arrangement — as at present — where the person with custody of the children retained full possession of the family home until the children were grown up. Where there were no large assets like the family home, car, etc. or money to be put in trust, then the party not having custody would have to put some part of the 50% he/she got, into the hands of the party with custody, or agree to pay as maintenance a reasonable part of his/her income to help keep the children.

REMEMBER: 50% OF SOMETHING IS BETTER THAN 100% OF NOTHING. NOTHING IS WHAT MANY WOMEN ARE CURRENTLY GETTING WHEY THEY LEAVE THEIR HOMES, AND TO GET ANYTHING BACK HAVE TO PAY SOME OF THEIR NOTHING FOR LAWYERS . . .

If people don't want to be under this system, then they would make up contracts on marriage setting out clearly what they wanted to have separately and what (if anything) they wanted to own together.

Women would be clear about their position re property: a husband (i.e. potential husband) would have to spell out what of his 'wordly goods' of now or in the future he truly on her bestowed! If he knew that half of 'his' would be hers, he might think twice about holding her in a position of slavery, and encourage her to become an independent member of the paid workforce — he might even think about participating equally in household work, childcare etc.

Women would know what the man's attitude toward her position was and whether the man was prepared to pay for putting a woman into the position of a slave in the home.

Men might wake up and realise that if they married, kept the wife down, didn't 'let' her get on in her career or in learning job skills and did nothing in the childcare department, etc. that when they wanted to beat her up and she left, she would be rightly taking 50% of everything. She might more effectively kick him out of HER house — just as much hers as his. Knowing the money coming in and what it bought did not belong solely to the husband, her position might be stronger (it certainly couldn't be any weaker than it is at present) . . .

REMEMBER — THIS SYSTEM IS DESIGNED FOR THOSE WOMEN WHO GO INTO MARRIAGE NOT THINKING ABOUT WHAT THEIR PROPERTY RIGHTS WON'T BE. FOR THOSE WOMEN WHO HAVE INDEPENDENCE AND PAID JOBS, ETC. AS WELL AS MORE EDUCATION TO REALISE THE CONSEQUENCES (FINANCIAL ETC.) OF MARRIAGE WOULD KNOW THEY COULD MAKE A CONTRACT TO KEEP THEIR OWN PROPERTY SEPARATE FROM THE HUSBAND'S AND HE WOULD BE ABLE TO KEEP HIS SEPARATE.

THERE WOULD HAVE TO BE NOTIFICATION BEFORE MARRIAGE AND BEFORE ANYONE COULD ENTER INTO MARRIAGE OF HOW MARRIAGE NOW CHANGES ECONOMICALLY THE POSITION OF THE PARTIES.

THE ISSUE IS, EVERYONE GETTING MARRIED WOULD KNOW WHERE THEY STOOD RE PROPERTY IN MARRIAGE AND HOW DISADVANTAGED OR NOT DISADVANTAGED THEY MIGHT BE BY ANY CONTRACT THEY MADE THAT TOOK THEM OUT OF THE SYSTEM WHERE ALL PROPERTY WAS RECOGNISED AS BEING OWNED 50–50.

REMEMBER: 50% OF SOMETHING IS BETTER THAN 100% OF NOTHING!

In sisterhood.[14]

As the Louisa Refuge knows, talk of fundamental happiness through independence for women is empty of meaning unless women have economic rights. Although in many areas women have formal equal rights with men as regards entry into professions, trades and other paid employment (although still formal equality is lacking in some areas),[15] in real terms such equality is elusive. Some professions, trades and other areas of paid employment continue to perpetuate discriminatory rules and regulations keeping women out. In practice, many women are kept out owing to sexism, lack of child care, discrimination in education. A woman who is being beaten cannot free herself if she has no economic independence. If she were tied socially, economic freedom would help her break that knot. The entire debate on crime in the family will be diverted into side issues unless the major question is faced squarely: until women have land rights — the economic ownership of 50 per cent of the entire wealth of this country — women will continue to be beaten by husbands, and children, at the bottom of the economic, political and social ladder, will continue to be beaten by parents. When the wealth in Australia is shared out equally between all women and all men, crime in the family will cease. Until that time, abuses at the family hearth will continue, when men who consider themselves to be inadequate and powerless in some part of their lives assuage those inadequacies and utilise their powerfulness against women and children, who are powerless to resist.

CHAPTER 12   ENDING CRIME
IN THE FAMILY

Under patriarchy, no woman is safe to live her life, or to love, or to mother children. Under patriarchy, every woman is a victim, past, present, and future. Under patriarchy, every woman's daughter is a victim, past, present, and future. Under patriarchy, every woman's son is her potential betrayer and also the inevitable rapist or exploiter of another woman.

Andrea Dworkin, 'Remembering the Witches' in *Our Blood — Prophecies and Discourses on Sexual Politics*, The Women's Press, London, 1982, 15, p. 20.

Casting back over the litany of crimes committed within the family. it is remarkable that, in the main, victims are women or girl children, and in the main, attackers are men. Rather than ignore this fact, in the fear that if it is acknowledged that men abuse we run the risk of being labelled men haters, it is important for women to face up to the reality of present male-female relationships. It is even more important for men to confront their own actions. Why should it be that, whether the victim is beaten or battered by a parent, sexually molested, bashed by a spouse, raped or murdered, almost inevitably the attacker is a father, husband, grandfather, uncle, step-father? Why is it also that today, more and more frequently, newspaper reports tell lurid stories of *women* who beat, bash and abuse their husbands? The evidence shows that whatever aggression a comparatively few women mete out on men in the home, it does not begin to equate with that meted out by men on women, inside and outside the home. To contend that women are equally abusive to their husbands as men to their wives, or even more abusive, enables society to cope with a form of violence repugnant to the fictionalised account of marriage and family life to which most people pay lip service. It allows us to laugh off seriously destructive behaviour in the form of the joke about ma waiting behind the kitchen door with the rolling-pin. It leads to the leavening approach, the idea that, if women are being beaten, men are also being beaten, so let them fight it out together, each giving as good as she or he gets, rather than intervening with the whole panoply of the law and demands for social change.

This coping mechanism also occurs where sexual crimes are committed against children at home. For decades society has concentrated upon 'stranger danger' — the idea that children are at risk of sexual exploitation by persons unknown to them, rather than men known to them well which is far more frequent. By building up a picture of a sexual attacker lurking in an alley or at the children's playground, sometimes tinged with the horror of approaching young boys as often as girls, we are lulled into a false sense of security. It is possible to warn our children not to speak to strangers or accept sweets from them; to play in groups and not wander off alone; to come straight home from school. These safeguards are enforceable. We can believe that *our* child will not be one of the unlucky few upon whom the stranger's eye falls. The lurking stranger is seen as a sexual deviate and a madman — without acknowledgement that he often lives a 'normal' life at home with his own family; and that many men who are not 'mad', live 'ordinary' lives whilst occasionally, or monthly, or weekly, or daily, molesting their own daughters, nieces, step-daughters, and sometimes their sons.

Whatever form the abuse takes, inequality is inherent in the structure of the relevant relationship. Women who are politically, socially and economically oppressed are battered and killed by men who are, comparative to them, politically, socially and economically dominant. Those men who are bashed and killed by their wives often themselves beat and abuse, almost kill, and oppress in other ways — through greater political power, through support from social structures classifying men as 'more equal' than women, by a comparatively higher income, or an income he classes 'his', while she waits for handouts in the form of housekeeping allowance, or whatever she can filch from his trouser pockets in order to keep the household going. Girl children — and some boy children — are sexually exploited by men who, as well as benefitting from present social, economic and political structures, are more powerful because of strength, age, authority position; with girl children, the fact that females are from birth indoctrinated to standards of femininity commanding them to submit to male dominance cannot be ignored. Where women exploit children sexually — and on the evidence, this is rare — they too profit from adulthood and authority, although on a lesser scale than men. Children are vulnerable because they are comparatively weak, economically dependent, lack adult social standing, and have no political rights. They are beaten and abused by fathers and mothers who are more powerful and thus comparatively free to vent their frustrations and aggressions on those who are unable to effectively retaliate or realistically escape. Mothers who beat and abuse are in turn locked into a position of inferiority: without access to funds for child care, without support in their responsibility for care of the children, with little relief from the tiring task (often carried out on a 24 hour basis) of parenthood.

In support of crime in the family, society has manufactured convenient myths which are backed by social attitudes. The myth of the 'willing victim' is apparent in 'analyses' of crimes against women and against young girls. The wife who is bashed 'asked for it'; the girl who is sexually molested 'wanted it'. Despite the incontrovertible evidence that women hate being hurt, just as men do not enjoy being belted or bashed, the myth of masochism persists. Despite a wealth of evidence from young girls, and young girls now grown old, that their father's, or uncle's, sexual fumblings seared their minds or iced over their souls, psychologists, psychiatrists and other 'responsible' members of the community continue to push the idea that victims of incest enjoy the activity and would be damaged by the molester's removal. Despite the physical and psychological ravages of rape at an early age by a father, courts continue to follow a policy of 'rehabilitating the family', meaning that the attacker will be left in the home... to attack again.[1] Acceptance of the adage that children should be seen and not heard is waning, but parents continue to believe, and to be supported, in 'disciplining' noisy, disobedient, or just plain 'normal' children, by the strap, hand lifted in anger, banishment to the bedroom. The view that 'children need a firm hand' too often translates into 'a firm thump', beltings with the curtain rod, head shoved under the garden tap, being forced to eat grass because they won't eat liver... or peas... or tomatoes. It translates into a child having his head shaved, dolloped with red paint, and being led off to school on a dog leash.

The myth is that women who are beaten don't leave because they love it; the myth of those who kill from despair at being constantly beaten, or as the only recognisable means of escape, is that they diabolically set out to murder. Often a 'motive' is erected out of a minor financial gain, such as an insurance policy, or a mortgaged home. Often such women are told they have no excuse: why didn't they call the police? go to a magistrate? leave? Where women are raped by their husbands they are castigated for constant child bearing; fanatics deny them a right to choose an abortion. Where they protest the rape, wives are charged with being frigid and denying their husband's rights. Even before they protest, stories that wives will falsely complain render hopeless any thought of reporting to the police.

The myth of the man's castle and woman's place permanently in it underlies all family-centred abuse. Within *his* own four walls any man can do as he chooses — and any woman must submit to his choice. Despite their powers, police will not enter; despite the violence, priests, ministers, professionals, neighbours, other family members respect the privacy of a man to do as he wishes to *his* family, inside *his* home. Protestations that marriage is a partnership and women and men have equal rights within it are empty in the face of a primitive allegiance to a belief, based on the Roman slave unit, that a man is head of *his* household. And mothers, left alone so often during the day with young, vulnerable children, are enslaved — yet free to pinch, and shove, and shake, and beat with little fear that the neighbours will hear — or that, if they do, they will intervene by breaking into *his* household. (Where mothers live alone with their children, the 'castle' is less secure; social security officials, police, social workers all come through the door.)

We know so little about what makes a man beat his wife, it is said — or his children, or sexually molest his daughter, or niece, or his wife's daughter — and 'information about what stops him beating her is even more scarce'. Donna Moore[2] suggests that changing any of the conditions 'leading' to spouse abuse — frustration, learned violent behaviour, sex-role expectations, low self-esteem — would stop the beating. She comes down on the side of therapy. A decrease

in the amount of battering in the home would occur, Moore
contends:

if we can teach the batterer to use behaviours other than violence when
responding to frustration or stress, if we can help him understand that
traditional sex roles are not the only way (or even the most effective way) to
relate to a woman and to one's self as a man, if we can help him elevate his
self-esteem, and if we teach him to control his alcohol use.[3]

Although this stance is preferable to that of blaming the victim,
the analysis is inadequate. Moore turns what is a political issue,
extending beyond the actions of individuals, into a problem going no
further than the personal. Teaching a man to control his consump-
tion of alcohol use will *not* end spouse assault. Teaching him to use
'other behaviours' will not necessarily end abusive acts toward his
wife (or children): rather, he may resort to or expand psychological
methods of indulging his violence against her. Teaching him to
change his attitude toward sex role expectations is insufficient: *every*
man must be positively encouraged to participate equally with
women in traditional 'female' tasks — child rearing, housework,
cooking. Not only identified abusers must change; all men must alter
their attitudes towards women and the behaviour that supports
and ultimately leads to aggressive acts against women, and against
other defenceless human beings, the children.

Today, governments have become caught up in the fashionable
notion that domestic violence requires action. Women's efforts to
combat male violence have begun a movement that has been taken
up by officialdom. Domestic violence is seen as a vote catcher.
Around Australia, official phone-ins are held; government reports
are written; legislation is drafted and passed; members of Parliament
pontificate about the desperate position of women and children and
the need for more women's refuges — although funds are rarely
forthcoming; and bureaucrats preserve and expand their empires
mouthing catch-phrases about injunctions, powers of arrest, police
powers of entry. Police powers are increased in the belief that some
how, although police do not use the powers they already have, they
will use to the advantage of women and children new and expanded
powers.

Meanwhile, courts continue in past patterns of ignorance about
the truth of violence in the home; doctors continue to hand out the

valium; social workers attempt to 'conciliate'; psychiatrists label victims neurotic, or just plain mad, and commit them to institutions, where they take their place beside the few angry women who have lashed out at their oppressors. Meanwhile, women and children continue to be abused; few are able to run — there is little to run to. Laws already in existence which would, if applied with non-sexist neutrality, protect victims of domestic violence, lie in abeyance, or are used to disadvantage women and children. The stranglehold that men have on power, property, prestige, jobs and money continues, despite any economic downturn. Some women continue to see their only escape as going interstate; being bundled from one women's refuge to the next; looking back over their shoulders in fear; living like outlaws in a society that ignores their contribution and denies them rights equal to their male counterparts. Some women escape only by killing the abuser. Some escape only through death.

As long as some people in our society (men) have more rights than other people in society (women and children), domestic violence in all its forms will continue. Women have lobbied hard for services that would ultimately lead to the conferring of rights upon children. They have lobbied hard for services that would assist women to gain equal place with men, and to exercise equal rights, as an essential part of a truly democratic society. Yet these services are provided on a minimal budget that must be reapplied for year after year. In 1982 government budgets in the 'women's services' area are being cut more severely than in any other area. Child care services are also subject to severe cuts. Even where they are provided, the practice of child care is unequal between women and men. Women, not men, organise the children to go to child care facilities. Women, not men, pay the expenses of child care. Women, not men, take the major responsibility for child care. Where men involve themselves in this activity, they 'help' their wives; men now 'allow' women (their wives) to participate in the paid workforce, 'so long as you make satisfactory arrangements for the children, dear'.

To stop abuse in the home, inequalities in the relationships making-up the family unit must be eliminated. If women and men become equal in personal relationships, no man will any longer have the doubtful privilege of owning his private punching bag. Deprived of this, he must look outward at the frustrating and competitive world that forces him into resentment, aggression and anger. At the same time, in a marriage of equality no woman will be forced to work alone: husband and wife will recognise that cleaning up after oneself is a task for all; that cooking is not a sex-linked capability. No man will beat his wife because *she* has cooked *his* dinner badly or failed to iron *his* shirts. No woman will beat her husband while *he* sits ruminating or watching television whilst *she* cooks *his* dinner and irons *his* clothes: he will be cooking and ironing for himself. Beating will not erupt out of disagreements over responsibilities for child care and child rearing: mother and father will recognise that caring for children is a responsibility and privilege for men and women equally, and the theory will become the practice.

To eradicate the exploitation and oppression of child abuse, child sexual molestation, spouse assault, marital rape and marital murder, women must gain public and private autonomy, and children must be recognised as human beings with rights. To gain children's rights and women's public and private autonomy, women must have equal choices with men about our private and public activities. Women must have equal rights and equal responsibilities in determining life-style, relationships, work. Yet changes so far brought about by legislation and administrative action have resulted in women being made more responsible politically, economically and socially but have not conferred upon women rights equal to those responsibilities. Women today are equally responsible with men for the maintenance of their children. But the children they are called upon equally to maintain are too often born as a result of lack of autonomy on the part of the woman, who has no effective choice to participate freely, or to freely refuse, sexual intercourse with a husband, *de facto* husband, or boyfriend. The economic ability of women to maintain their children is less than that of men. The right to engage in paid work is, for women, circumscribed by restrictive laws, or by restrictive patterns and practices; it is threatened by media campaigns and governmental policies. Women in employment have restricted incomes, access to promotion, and access to positions of authority, despite anti-discrimination and equal opportunity legislation in some states. Women today are held equally responsible with men for the legislative programs of governments, because they have an equal formal right to enter Parliament and have an equal right to vote. Yet women are rarely elected to Parliament to have an input into legislation and policies, because they are rarely selected by the major political parties for safe or winnable seats. Women are equally responsible for their own maintenance before, during and after marriage, and while living in *de facto* relationships. Yet too few women have the economic resources to carry out these responsibilities. Where they have economic resources, these are less than the economic resources of their husbands or *de factos*. The right of choice as to relationships is closed to women, owing to the boring and debilitating nature of the work usually assigned to women, which means young women continue to think of marriage as an essential part of their lives and their jobs as simply 'filling in'. Older women know of the unpleasant and unrewarding nature of most jobs open to them and so remain in dreaded relationships without the real possibility of serene escape.

When equal rights in the home are established, both partners will look out to the greater world as a source of the frustration and conditions that give rise to hatred and aggression. That world will have to be changed. In turn, changing outside aspects of living which dominate family life will inevitably enhance personal living relationships. The pressures of the outside world interact with the family unit to exacerbate role domination and role submission between women and men. Both interpersonal relationships and the broader society must change to stop violence in the home. The unequal relationships between women and men in the private and the public world, which are consolidated by the dependency of children and inevitably lead to violence in too many marriages and *de facto* relationships, will be changed only when economic relationships between the two sexes, and between men and men, change. Economic inequality lies at the base of unequal political and social power; it founds our sexist and classist society.

In the early 1970s, 22 per cent of all the wealth in Australia was owned by the top 1 per cent of the population; 72 per cent was owned by 20 per cent of the population.[4] Women took their place in the lower levels of wage earners and property owners — if they came into these categories at all. In the intervening years women's position in the economic hierarchy has fallen rather than risen. Disparities in income and property ownership between women and men, and men and men have intensified over the years from 1975 to 1982, so that those men at the top have accrued more power, through more wealth, more income, and less taxes.[5] The existence of a ruling class is perpetuated by the ideology that certain men — or families (meaning fathers and their sons) — are born to rule because of birth and/or money. Our parliaments are populated by men whose fathers, grandfathers or uncles preceded them; sometimes all three. The judiciary, the legal profession generally, the large corporations are similarly crowded. This system promotes amongst men the notion that sex, birth, and wealth are intrinsic to the right to govern in various capacities. All men are seduced into supporting the system because, however lowly their birth, however low their economic standing, each one of them has his own small kingdom, populated by those having less wealth, less standing than he — his wife and children. Competition is promoted amongst men as a further means of keeping them in their place on the hierarchy: in the paid work world each competes against the other, hoping that he will be sufficiently lucky to 'win', and thus take his place amongst the fortunate few at the top; in the world of the home, the 'competition' is loaded in the man's favour — no woman or child is supposed to win against his superiority. Rather than men in the home belting their children, bashing their wives, sexually invading the lives of their daughters because they lack power, they do it because it is within the home that they *are* powerful and are able to indulge that power without the operation of external controls. If men and women owned property equally in marriage, an important plank in maintaining the capitalist patriarchy would be destroyed. If all property in Australia were redistributed equally amongst all men and all women, capitalism and the patriarchy would be destroyed, and with them would go the conditions necessary for the continuation of brutality and exploitation behind closed doors.

Looking back over two hundred years of agitation to alter the oppressed life of all women in Australia, and thereby to release women, children and ultimately men from inhumane economic and class structures, the conclusion is that women's power to change is hampered by our fundamental lack of power. We are powerful in ourselves, but the power to alter economic relationships, and therefore to eradicate accompanying inequities and inequalities, of which the most brutal is violence at home, lies in the hands of those controlling the economy and controlling the relationships. As Betty Moss wrote of her twenty-four year marriage, during which she endured twenty years of continuing violence: 'I felt like a slave in prison.'

Ultimate power to change any system of slavery, any prison system, any system promoting, encouraging or simply tolerating beating in the home lies not with those who are the enslaved, the imprisoned or the beaten. The key remains with those who are the head of the slave-camp, the gaol or the home, and with those representing the heads in every political, social and economic institution. As militant feminist Christabel Pankhurst wrote of the trade in women: 'Men have a simple remedy for this state of things. They can alter their way of life.'[6] For women and children battered, brutalised and exploited in their own homes, the remedy is the same. Men must alter their way of life.

CHAPTER 13   THE POLITICS OF VIOLENCE

Try thinking without apology with what you know from being victimised . . .
Look for the deepest meanings in the least elevated places. Be more radical than
anyone has ever been about the unknown, because what has never been asked
is probably what we most need to know. Take the unknowable more seriously
than anyone ever has, because most women have died without a trace; but invent
the capacity to act, because otherwise women will continue to.

Catharine Mackinnon, *Feminism Unmodified – Discourses on Life and Law*,
1987, Harvard University Press, Mass., p.9.

They said, 'You are a savage and dangerous woman.' [I said] 'I am speaking
the truth. And the truth is savage and dangerous.'

Nawal El Saadawi, *Woman at Point Zero*, 1983, Beacon Press, Boston

In Australia at the close of the 1980s and into the 1990s, violence
gained a recognised place on the political agenda. The Human Rights
and Equal Opportunity Commission held public hearings on racism,
enquired into ethnophobia, and reported on 'street kids', exposing a
welter of aggression and abuse. A national committee on violence was
established by the federal government; in Victoria a parliamentary
committee deliberated on violence, and in its wake a community committee on violence was appointed by the state government. (The *modus
operandi* of the latter was novel: on one occasion members disported
themselves at nightclubs, a panoply of television cameras in tow,
studying, they said, the problems of violent nightlife in Melbourne
city.) Every state passed 'domestic violence laws', granting police greater

powers. Yet still the cry for more police powers was generated, the national committee on violence recommending in a 1990 report that federal (rather than state) laws should cover criminal assault at home, giving police yet more authority to deal with it.

Women continued to speak out against violence. Having escaped from beating and brutality at home, in 1989 women staged a rally in Melbourne's city square, reading poetry and prose written from their experiences. The Coalition Against Family Violence held a day of commemoration 'for all women and children killed by the man in their life'. Hundreds attended at Melbourne Town Hall to hear the relatives of the dead declare their anger at a system that not only allows women and children to die at the hands of husband and father, but condones the killing by labelling it manslaughter rather than the murderous womanslaughter it truly is. In Darwin the Women's Consultative Council held public meetings to bring out of doors the violence that too often remains hidden. In Townsville members of diverse women's groups joined together in a conference of some three hundred women on the theme of ending violence against women, and gaining women equal dignity and autonomous rights. In Adelaide in 1984 at the Young Women's Christian Association headquarters a conference of some 200 participants comprising mainly women, but some men, demanded the recognition of the reality of male violence, and acknowledgment of the paucity of resources made available to women bashed and battered. In 1990 in Western Australia the National Women's Refuge Conference held a public meeting to deplore the conviction of a woman, named only as "Nina", for murder of her husband who had, amongst other matters, shortly before his death confessed to her of his rape and abuse of their daughters. Such meetings, conferences and speak outs were replicated elsewhere.

In 1988 the federal government's national social survey of community attitudes towards criminal assault at home recorded that the great majority (85 per cent) of people 'rate domestic violence as a serious issue', 75 per cent 'think[ing] that at least a moderate number of families are affected by it'. The survey found 'nearly half the population personally knows either a perpetrator or a victim of domestic violence'. Yet one in five (19 per cent) told survey workers that the use of physical force by a man against his wife is acceptable under some circumstances. Seventeen per cent of women and 22 per cent of men held this view. More than half (57 per cent) considered it justifiable for a man to yell abuse at his wife. One in five thought that threatening to hit can be justified, whilst one in ten considered slapping or smacking justified. The survey continues:

Six per cent even think that there can be justification for extreme forms of violence including threatening or using a weapon on one's wife. There is a close relationship between not classing an action as domestic violence and considering that the act can be justified. However, many of the people who justify actions involving physical force also classify them as domestic violence.

About six in ten people think that it can be justified for a parent to threaten to hit or to slap or smack a child. The more extreme forms of violence against children (kicking, beating threatening or using [a] weapon) are considered justifiable by about one in twenty people.[1]

In 1990, criminal assault at home remained the subject of 'light hearted' comment, or 'jokes'. In the *Sunday Age* of 8 April 1990 the coach of a prominent football team in the Australian Football League, asked to comment upon 'what it's like' to work as coach, was reported to have said:

It's more mentally draining than playing and more frustrating because you can't do anything about it.

I was a bit down when I got home. My wife had a friend with her, which was probably just as well. No, I don't have a dog to kick.

Spouse Assault, Police Powers and the Courts

In 1982 the New South Wales' Task Force on Domestic Violence recommended an increase in police powers, ostensibly to deal with criminal assault at home. Consequently the *Crimes (Domestic Violence) Act* 1983 (N.S.W.) was passed, amending the Crimes Act to include section 547AA. Orders can be made by a court, on the application of a woman (or other family member) who apprehends violence against herself by her husband, or harassment or molestation:

■ prohibiting or restricting approaches by the defendant to the spouse (or family member) aggrieved;

■ prohibiting or restricting access by the defendant to any specified premises occupied by, or the workplace, or places frequented by, the spouse;

■ prohibiting or restricting specified behaviour by the defendant which might affect the spouse of the defendant.[2]

Orders may be applied for by a police officer on behalf of the victim of apprehended violence. Orders may exclude the defendant from premises albeit he has a property interest in them.

The New South Wales' legislation was swiftly followed by similar laws being introduced elsewhere in Australia, the Northern Territory being last, passing its Act in 1989. The laws are similar to those existing under the *Family Law Act*, where section 114 provides for an injunction to be issued by the Family Court:

■ for the personal protection of a party to the marriage or of a child of a marriage;
■ restraining a party to the marriage from entering or remaining in the matrimonial home or the premises in which the other party to the marriage resides, or restraining a party to the marriage from entering or remaining in a specified area, being an area in which the matrimonial home is, or the premises in which the other party to the marriage resides are, situated;
■ restraining a party to the marriage from entering the place of work of the other party to the marriage or restraining a party to the marriage from entering the place of work or the place of education of a child of the marriage;
■ for the protection of the marital relationship;
■ in relation to the property of a party to the marriage;
■ relating to the use or occupancy of the matrimonial home.

However, police have no role in applying for a Family Court order. It remains a matter between parties to a marriage, so that applications must be made by a marriage partner. (Although state and federal police have duties in the enforcement of Family Court orders.) Further, unlike the state laws, the *Family Law Act* requires a specific request to the court for attachment of a power of arrest. In 1983 the Act was amended so that a power of arrest could be attached, at the discretion of the judge by whom the case is heard, to an injunction. The judge may do so only where satisfied that:

■ the person against whom the order is made has caused bodily harm to the spouse or a child of the marriage;
■ the person is likely to cause bodily harm to the spouse or a child of the marriage; and
■ notice of an intention to apply for attachment of a power or arrest has been served on the person or that, in the circumstances of the

case, an order may appropriately be made without notifying that person; or

■ the person has threatened to cause bodily harm to the spouse or a child of the marriage;

■ the person is likely to cause bodily harm to the spouse or a child of the marriage; and

■ notice of intention to apply for an order has been served on the person.

It is argued by some that the 'new' laws advantage women victimised on the home ground. Yet this is far from the case. Women refuge workers and radical women lawyers acknowledge the relative ineffectiveness of the restraining order process, and of the accompanying increase of police powers. In January 1985 New South Wales' women's refuges joined in a letter of complaint to the editor of the *Sydney Morning Herald* making the point that police continued to fail to act effectively where women are beaten by husbands, despite changes to the law. The Women's Legal Resource Group in Victoria wrote similarly to the editor of the *Age* on 17 February 1989:

... Despite the introduction of the Crimes (Family Violence) Act in December 1987 to increase protection for victims of family violence and encourage police involvement in these matters, [police remain] reluctant to involve themselves because it is not considered 'real' police work.

Recent interviews of senior police showed that their major concerns were with property crimes — domestic violence didn't rate a mention. Police receive at least 50,000 calls annually for assistance at domestic disputes. Such attitudes are disturbing, given the life-threatening nature of many of these assaults and that domestic murders comprise 60 per cent of all homicides.

Criminal assault in the home is the result of intrinsic power differences between men and women. Consequently, any measures aimed at eradicating this most serious and common crime must address women's inferior economic, social and political status ...

The number of orders issued by courts is ludicrously low in comparison with the number of disputes coming to attention of police, and with the estimated level of violence by husbands against wives. In New South Wales Julie Stubbs' analysis of the operation of the 'apprehended domestic violence' laws showed 172 orders made in a thirty-seven week period in 1983; 423 orders made for the whole of 1984; and 283 orders for twenty-six weeks of 1985. More than 90 per cent of the orders were initiated by the victims themselves. This means little has changed from the previous approach of police, which was to inform the woman (wrongly) that the onus lay upon her to take action against her violent husband. As for police taking action by apprehending a man where he breaches an order, police activity is again minimal. In 1984 there were 26 cases before New South Wales courts for breaches of apprehended domestic violence orders. Twenty-two of these were instituted by police charging the offenders. In four cases the matter was instituted by summons. Seventeen of the accused were found guilty of breach.[3] A 1985 report of the New South Wales' Domestic Violence Committee noted that only seven breaches of orders were charged, despite reports from women's refuges, and from legal centres, that breaches were frequent.[4] Police had consistently met demands for their intervention in 'domestics' prior to the introduction of the new laws with the excuse that they were precluded from going onto private property when receiving a complaint, because the owner refused them entry. This is no excuse: police have a duty to enter onto property, private or otherwise, where they have a reasonable apprehension that a criminal offence has occurred or is occurring, or a breach of the peace is likely to recur. Nonetheless, the law was altered to give police power to secure a 'telephone warrant' in such cases: the procedure is to telephone a justice of the peace to obtain a warrant granting police authority to enter private property. In 1984, only six such warrants were requested by police. This could mean that there was a minimum number of domestic altercations to which police were called that year. The more likely reality is that rarely are police refused entry — or that even with the telephone warrant facility, they decline to act.

For Wangaratta, an area of country Victoria, in 1990 it was reported that on average eight complaints per day were made since introduction of the *Crimes (Family Violence) Act* in 1987, yet approximately 50 final orders only were made each year. Approximately two warrants for arrest for breach of an order issue per year. An estimate was made of 500 to 600 orders overall having been made by magistrates courts in the region in some two-and-a-half years: this includes *ex parte* (where the abused woman alone appears, the urgency of the application accepted as precluding serving papers on the husband), interim (temporary orders, which may be made final at a later hearing), and final orders. This does not mean that 500 to 600 wife beaters have appeared before the courts: final orders are likely to relate to men against whom an ex parte or interim order has been issued; and a woman may apply for an order against her husband, then re-apply at a later date, thus appearing twice or more in the statistics. If the woman makes her own application rather than a police officer applying on her behalf, or being legally represented, she has to overcome the hurdle of the clerk of courts determining whether or not her application is sound. Efforts have been made to educate clerks throughout Victoria, but clerks will have varying views of the aptness of an application.

Police and magistrates have varying views, too: in the first week of operation of the Northern Territory law, a woman who called police for assistance was herself removed from the home, and police obtained a restraining order against her. Her face was bruised from her husband's attack with a torch; her husband's knuckles were grazed when she, waiting for the police to come, threw a knife at him after her husband attacked her again in the interim three-quarters of an hour. Mary Jansen said that when police finally arrived 'they did not speak to her and, after listening to her de facto husband's side of the story, sought and obtained a restraining order against her, leaving her nine year old daughter with the man':

'I've got no faith in the system,' she said. It's just who can tell the best lies. Aren't you supposed to defend yourself? Or do you just get beaten?'[5]

The figures for South Australian orders were substantially higher. In the first three years of operation of the law, approximately 4,500 persons (mainly women) obtained a restraining order. An estimated 60 per cent related to 'marital/family' disputes. Almost 25 per cent of the orders were withdrawn for various reasons, but of the remainder almost 780 apprehensions for breaches took place. There is little reason to believe men in South Australia are more violent than those in New South Wales or Victoria. The difference seems to lie in the (moderate) activity and (in)activity of the respective police forces. Indeed, in South Australia the majority of orders were sought by police on behalf of beaten women.[6]

The issue remains of why police action on criminal assault at home is inadequate, despite long existing, and more recent, laws. The New South Wales' committee in 1985 saw the problem lying in entrenched police practice: 'the appropriate way [according to police] to handle domestic violence disputes is to mediate, to settle situations down and to take action in extreme circumstances only'. This highlights the error into which some proponents of the need to end assault at the hearth have fallen. Just as the 1974 New South Wales' Bureau of Crime Statistics and Research report showed women being required, by police (contrary to law), to initiate their own actions despite suffering substantial and extensive injury, the 1980s police approach shows a continuing adherence to the view that if its not 'extreme' then 'there's nothing we (or you) can do about it'.[7] Yet the position instigated in the 1980s is even more serious: what is occurring through the implementation of the new *civilly based* laws of apprehended domestic violence orders, non-molestation orders, or injunctions, is the decriminalisation of wife assault. This decriminalisation is not, as it was in the 1970s, simply a matter of police discretion or court failure. It (and the inaction of police and courts) now has the imprimatur of the legislature.

Prior to the passage of the new laws, police were under a duty to arrest and prosecute any man who beat and abused the woman whom he wed, or with whom he lived or had lived in an intimate relationship. If the assault was serious (indicated by blood, bruises, broken bones or the like), laying charges was the responsibility of police. If it was simple assault, but the woman did not have the physical or psychological resources to initiate the charge, that task again fell to police. Rarely did police act upon the duty. (Police remain under the duty, and continue to act upon it rarely.) At the same time courts had (as they continue to have) a role in finding a man guilty of criminal assault if the prosecution proved, beyond a reasonable doubt, that he had committed the offence upon his wife or ex-wife, fiance or ex-fiance, or woman friend. Frequently magistrates confronted with this situation found the case unproven, whatever the evidence or, despite the proof, merely admonished the couple to 'make friends'. Yet statute law was unequivocal in recognising wife bashing (like the abuse of strangers) as criminal assault.

Today, when women's refuge workers and others complain about the inaction of police, the complaint is not of a failure of police to execute criminal laws, and execute their duty according to criminal law, but of a failure to act in accordance with civil law demands. Although criminal laws (theoretically) continue to apply to men who beat their wives, that police should initiate criminal prosecution appears to have fallen, somewhat, by the wayside. The new laws have now turned criminal assault into a civil matter at law, not just in the minds of police or magistrates. These laws condone the past inactivity of police and courts, and are used as a lawful excuse from the requirement that police and courts should act according to criminal law requirements today.

When the New South Wales' law was introduced into the parliament on 9 November 1982, in the Second Reading Speech it was said:

The Government believes these reforms in themselves will contribute to the reduction of violence in New South Wales by giving the lead to the community in recognising that domestic assault is assault, and by making the police and courts more effective in dealing with the problem . . .[8]

The New South Wales' Domestic Violence Committee report of 1985, following the changes, stated that the new laws:

. . . establish that an offence of assault committed within the confines of the family should be regarded as seriously as an assault between strangers in a public place. These reforms are thus located within the criminal law, encouraging criminal charges to be laid by police where offences have been committed and consequently carrying criminal sanctions when convictions result.[9]

How it could be asserted that a civil law newly introduced would ensure criminal acts are dealt with criminally (particularly when criminal laws already existed but were unused) is difficult to see. Indeed, the facts belie the truth of parliamentary and committee statements.

In South Australia, with the introduction of the new restraining order law, the Police Commissioner issued policy circulars notifying police of their power to make an application on behalf of an abused woman. The circular also alerted them to the requirement that they arrest a man for breaching an order. Circular No. 456 of 1982 defined 'domestic violence' to indicate to police what conduct would justify their making application for an order on a woman's behalf:

. . . actual or threatened violence (including all sex offences) *generally* between people living at the same address (but not necessarily so) including married couples, de facto relationships, divorced/separated couples ex de facto relationships, child/parent or child abuse.[10]

Violence inflicted by one person, husband or not, upon another person, whether or not his wife, is criminal. The circular gives credence to a response that criminal prosecution should be ignored whilst a civil remedy is pursued. Police are told by the highest level of the force that a restraining order (a civil remedy) is appropriate for *actual violence* – including *all* sex offences! Yet these are crimes, for which criminal prosecution is the appropriate response.

The new laws mean that women suffer criminal assaults (even including sexual assaults) with police being given a legislative excuse for not prosecuting: they can advise the woman to take out an injunction or apprehended violence order, or take one out on her behalf. The next step may be that police will arrest the man for breach of the order if he returns to beat her – a second criminal offence. Yet the man will not be arrested for criminal assault. Rather, he is arrested for breaching the order. Breaching an order of a court is a contempt of court, or an offence against the court. The ethos and mechanism of this procedure conceals the reality of women's lives. Women are raped, bashed and beaten by their husbands, ex-husbands, de factos and boy'friends'. Those acts are criminal. This should be recognised clearly by the law and in the application of the law. Yet the criminality of the first offence is put to one side. The offence is not seen as criminal. Rather, it is used (if at all) as the basis for a civil action. The second crime is seen only as a breach of a court order. This places the status of courts (male institutions) above women's bodily integrity.

Traditionally, the role of police is to apply criminal laws, not to involve themselves in the application of civil laws. Criminal laws relating to offences against the person concern acts committed by a person on another person which the state affirms are unacceptable to the community as a whole. Criminal law is an affirmation that all citizens consider the act constituting the criminal offence should be policed, as being destructive of all members of society, not only the person victimised. Civil laws involve personal suits by one person against another. It is not the role of police to involve themselves in personal suits. However, the new laws have confused the application of civil laws, and given credence to the notion that brutality inflicted by a husband upon his wife is personal only, a civil law remedy being sufficient.

The act of assault has both a criminal and a civil dimension. Traditionally, the role of police is to deal with the criminal dimension whilst an individual may seek a civil remedy in respect of the same act. Thus, if a man beats his wife, the law accepts this as criminal, and requires criminal prosecution of the offence at the behest of the state. The beaten woman has rights of a personal nature at law: the right to seek damages through a civil suit; the right to seek compensation through victim compensation schemes. Rather than 'reforming' laws so that police now intrude into the civil law sphere by (sometimes) applying for a (civil) order against an errant husband, and vacate with ostensible legislative backing the criminal law sphere, it would have been preferable for lobby groups to address the need to make existing criminal and civil remedies more effective. Police continue to fail, now failing in a lesser sphere, that of civil law application; women miss out on criminal law rights, and the civil law rights of women to damages and compensation continue to atrophy.[11]

Some argue that the value of the new laws is that the proof required for a woman to obtain an injunction or apprehended violence/non-molestation order is based on the civil rather than the criminal standard. That is, an applicant need show only that, on the balance of probabilities, violence has occurred, is threatened or is apprehended. At criminal law, proof beyond a reasonable doubt is necessary. Yet the reality is that many magistrates apply the new laws using the criminal standard of proof, anyway. This is attested to by those working in the field in country and city areas.

Prejudice and sex-bias of courts is frequently encountered. Magistrates are reported as commenting 'why should she be worried (or complaining) about him following her? He's her husband, isn't he?' or 'He's got a right to try to get her back; she's his wife, after all.' Where the woman seeking an order is of non-anglo-Australian origins, she may encounter additional difficulties. In one case, the wife gave evidence of having been frequently beaten, followed and harassed when she had left the matrimonial household, threatened with a gun, and forced to travel in the husband's car with him on at least one occasion. The husband, representing himself, was allowed (over the objections of counsel representing his wife) to continually question her about her previous life in Thailand, where she had worked in a bar. Although irrelevant to the question whether or not she had been beaten and abused, and was afraid of future attacks by the man, this material was allowed in by a magistrate who apparently gained some lascivious satisfaction from the evidence and the woman's discomfort and distress. This is not an isolated instance.[12]

In New South Wales in support of the new laws it was said that the criminal laws would operate alongside, without the civil remedy of an intervention order interfering with the police role in prosecuting crimes. Yet the more likely result is that crimes continue to go uncharged and unprosecuted, whilst they show up, if at all, as civil matters only. (The frequently heard words of police in the past that 'it's a civil, not a criminal, matter' now have an even more ironic ring.)

It was said that intervention orders would be used to assist the woman who, after suffering a beating, was regaled by a remorseful husband pleading with bunches of roses his sorrow and declarations that it would 'not happen again'. It is doubtful whether any magistrate, anywhere in Australia, would issue an injunction or non-molestation order against a husband on the ground that he had sent his wife flowers. Indeed, experience in the courts reveals the difficulty in obtaining orders where substantial evidence of abuse is readily available.

Some police and some magistrates are sympathetic to the issue of criminal assault at home, and anxious to ensure that women are protected as adequately as the law is able. (Although application of the law and recognition of women's rights are what is necessary, rather than mere sympathy or 'protection'.) Some magistrates have, with some courage, held consciousness raising conferences for magistrates, with feminist speakers and refuge workers in attendance. Some police do arrest where a criminal prosecution is the appropriate response, and take appropriate prosecutorial steps. Some police forces have acquired the services of feminist trainers who have worked for many years in the field.[13] But some police who take the civil approach in criminal matters believe they are acting in accordance with legislative requirements. Some magistrates effect the civil standard of proof in applications for injunctions and intervention orders. Some express effective concern about the level of violence inflicted upon women who seek orders, or on whose behalf police take action. Yet if violence against women is to be ended, a clear adherence to the principle that assault at home is criminal is essential. Leading men to believe that the initial blows do not warrant prosecutorial intervention simply confirms them in their view that violence against women (particularly where they are wives) is 'different'; that it is less serious than violence against other human beings; that the laws will excuse at least one violent episode — at least if it is directed against a married woman, and the aggressor is her husband.

And what of all those violent episodes where the woman suffered in silence, or where her cries were ignored, where police failed to arrive, where they came — but when the brutality had died down. There can be little doubt that the beating for which the apprehended violence order is issued will not have been the first.

Child Sexual Molestation, Police and Courts

The 1980s saw an increasing emphasis on child sexual abuse, and a growing demand by feminist groups that child molestation by family members and family 'friends' be named as 'rape' rather than not being named at all, or being covered up by the term 'incest' which implies consent. Task forces, commissions and committees, established by government, deliberated around Australia, particularly concentrating upon the purported difficulties of dealing with these offences through the criminal justice system. The Family Court was also prodded (although with painful slowness) into recognising its responsibilities in the area, due to an increasing number of disputes involving access and custody applications, and allegations of (or concerns of custodial parents about) child sexual abuse by an access or divorcing parent.

Legal rules surrounding the giving of evidence by children and the need for child witnesses to appear in court if these crimes are to be prosecuted are subjected to criticism. Mothers of children sexually interfered with by family members or friends frequently meet the proposition, put by police, that the crime cannot be prosecuted without 'corroboration'. It is implied that what is essential is eye witness evidence, by an adult, of the commission of the offence. This is not a correct statement of the law. It is also said that sexual offences against children are 'too difficult to prove' due to the corroboration requirement, and to the inability of children to give sworn evidence. Yet what is more likely is that these offences are all too easy to prove, to courts applying commonsense and requisite standards of courtroom practice and proof, and to juries properly instructed by judges. There is considerable risk in prosecuting child sexual abuse cases through the courts: taking into account the incidence of the abuse, if all cases were dealt with by the criminal process, the family as it is traditionally comprised would be at serious risk. If all those who sexually molest children in the family home were prosecuted, convicted and sentenced, court lists would be even more jammed, and prisons the more crowded.

The law presumes adults are competent to give evidence on oath or affirmation. It makes no such presumption about children. A court will allow a child to give evidence as a competent witness if she or he understands the nature of the oath; testimony then comes into the category of sworn evidence. If the child does not understand the oath, the court may allow her or him to give unsworn evidence if it is of the opinion that the child is possessed of sufficient intelligence to justify the reception of the evidence, and understands the duty of speaking the truth.

But just as women are taken to be unreliable witnesses where complaining of rape and other sexual offences against them, children are considered by the courts to be unreliable. A judge is required to warn the jury, in a trial where a child is witness, that there is a risk in acting on the child's sworn evidence unless it is corroborated by other evidence. (In sexual offences, this might be medical evidence of genital damage, venereal disease or other relevant injury; it might be evidence that the child was seen going hand in hand with the accused to some secluded place at about the time of the alleged offence, etc.) With un-sworn evidence, *Evidence Acts* in the various Australian jurisdictions set a particular standard. For example, the Victorian law (s.23(2) of the *Evidence Act*) provides that a person cannot be convicted of any offence by unsworn evidence of a child under the age of fourteen years unless that evidence 'is corroborated by some other material evidence in support thereof implicating him'. The English House of Lords considers the unsworn evidence of a child must be corroborated by sworn evidence, and cannot be corroborated by the unsworn testimony of another child; the Australian Law Reform Commission, analysing the law, holds the corroboration requirement can be fulfilled by any evidence additional to that of the child not on oath, including unsworn testimony.

Various Australian states have amended evidence laws to introduce new tests for child evidence. Rather than the 'understand the oath' test, in New South Wales the criterion is 'intelligence'. In South Australia and Western Australia the criterion is 'competency'. The Australian Law Reform Commission, considering the question in its reference on evidence, found intelligence to be an unhelpful measure:

The meaning of intelligence is left at large for the judge to interpret and each judge might have a different notion of what he understands as intelli-gence . . . It would be preferable to frame a test of competency in terms of cognitive development, rather than in terms of intelligence – that is, to assess the child's actual stage of mental functioning rather than to concentrate on his potential.[14]

The competency test is based on the Australian Law Reform Commission recommendation in its 1985 *Interim Report on Evidence:*

A person who is incapable of understanding that, in giving evidence, he or she is under an obligation to give truthful evidence is not competent to give evidence.

    A person who is incapable of giving a rational reply to a question about a fact is not competent to give evidence about the fact.

In April 1976 Judge Sutcliffe at the Old Bailey in England concluded:

It is well known that women in particular and small boys are liable to be untruthful and invent stories.[15]

This was a simple restatement of adages honed by sometimes revered judges and academics such as Chief Justice Hale of seventeenth and Glanville Williams of twentieth century England. Such 'truths' have been supported by psychologists and psychiatrists, such as Brown, who included in his 1926 book *Legal Psychology* a chapter entitled 'The Child and the Woman', in which he formulated 'an excellent rule' (in his view):

It is never safe to depend either on the memory or the reason of a child. Practically the only value in a court of law of any testimony that a child might give, is that which re-enforces or is re-enforced by other testimony . . . Women are more suggestible than men, and children are more suggestible than adults . . . [16]

More recently, research has shown the fallacy of this 'theorising'. A Queensland enquiry into sexual offences involving children sought advice from psychologists, who concluded:

The assertion that children are not more suggestible than adults would have surprised early researchers. But it appears that age is not the crucial variable affecting suggestibility. If an event is interesting and understandable to both adults and children, then no age differences are found in suggestibility. But when events are vague or outside one's experience then people of all ages are suggestible . . .

Children do not consistently confuse fantasy with reality although they may have trouble discriminating their intentions (and the intentions of others) from their actions . . .

Although it is common to view children's memory capacity as improving as they advance through a series of developmental stages psychological research indicates that children's memory may, under certain circumstances, be superior to adults. Careful questioning, particularly when the situation or material to be recalled is familiar to them, can result in children's recall that is equal to or better than adults.[17]

New South Wales, Queensland, Victoria and South Australia have accepted that there should be no special rule that a child's evidence must be corroborated. The South Australian *Evidence Act* was amended by the inclusion of a new section 50:

If a young child, who is not obliged to submit to the obligation of an oath, is to give evidence before a court and —
(a) the child appears to the judge to have reached a level of cognitive development that enables the child
    (i) to understand and respond rationally to questions; and
    (ii) to give an intelligible account of his or her experiences; and
(b) the child promises to tell the truth and appears to understand the obligations entailed by that promise, unsworn evidence of the child will be treated in the same way as evidence given on oath.

However, dissatisfaction with the court approach to children has gone beyond whether or not a child's testimony is acceptable evidence. Proposals are made in the various states for the giving of evidence through video tape; with the child in a room behind a two way mirror, questioned by a specially trained and chosen 'friend'; or with the accused required to sit behind a screen whilst the child gives evidence in court. These proposals miss the point. The difficulties of sexual offence trials extend not only to children, but to all who are victims and take the role of complainant or witness in court. Children may be particularly disadvantaged due to age, but it is the process and nature of the trial and underlying assumptions which cause the greatest difficulties. These problems extend to adult women and teenagers.

The proposals also suffer from a failure to think through the nature of the complaint and the offence to which the child has been subjected. If the interview is to be taped, is the child to be told of the taping? Is the child (or guardian or custodial parent) to be given a copy of the video? What is to happen to any copies made? (Is the video to be used as a police 'training film' as occurred in at least one instance in one state.) If the child is not told, then she (or he) is being deceived − just as she or he is the victim of deception by the adult who committed the offence. Is the child to be told that the two way mirror is just that − and that a judge, the accused, and legal counsel, as well as the jury, are concealed behind it? Is the child to be informed by her questioner that the questions are being directed, through a hearing piece and electronic link, by the judge or counsel for accused and prosecution? If the child is not told, she is victim of deceit − by a person selected to build a rapport with her, to enable optimal questioning. Is the child to be told that, when she gives evidence in the courtroom, the accused is to be hidden behind a screen? Children grow up. They may be five or three or seven at trial. They do not remain so for long. And as the years go by, it is certain they will discover the deception played upon them by participants in the criminal justice system, participants who held themselves out to be trustworthy and particularly concerned with their welfare. The trauma of being sexually abused and deceived by a person who holds a central role in childhood and childhood development is compounded by the trauma of being psychologically abused and deceived by a person (and justice system) holding out to be trustworthy and dependable. And if the child is told, how more terrifying to know that her father, who sexually abused her, is secreted behind a two way mirror or screen. What fear lodges in her heart when she contemplates the possibility that 'daddy' will rise up from behind the screen, or plunge wrathfully through the mirror. That these may not be real possibilities (though the contingency surely must always be guarded against), this is no satisfaction to the child who is confronted with this artificiality. And what of the child who wants to face the man who sexually abused her, and speak out against that abuse, directly in his presence.

Disturbingly, such proposals are advanced at a time that women and children are speaking out more readily against sexual abuse, and when women have made it clear that these voices will not be silenced. Schemes for keeping witnesses out of the courtroom, to place the evidence of children in a different category from that of other witnesses, serve only to lessen the impact. Predictably, charges are now being made with increasing frequency by some lawyers and television commentators that children are being 'coached' in their evidence. Such charges are bound to increase with the introduction of 'trial by video tape'. Rather than concentrate upon a child witness as 'the problem', it would be better to look at the need to educate lawyers, courts and juries in the nature of sexual offences against children (and women) and take the first long, hard steps to eliminate the biases and reorientate the behaviour of those who dictate the nature of the courtroom process, and direct sexual offence trials.

This need is illustrated in cases involving claims for access, by non-custodial parents, to children following divorce. In 1988 the High Court of Australia heard appeals dealing with this problem, where allegations of child sexual abuse by the father were made. In *M. v. M.* and *B. v. B.* the High Court unanimously held that in access and custody cases the Family Court of Australia has a responsibility to decide in accordance with the best interests of the child. Those interests are classed as 'paramount'. If in so deciding a 'right' of a parent is seen by him to be infringed, this is not the concern of the Family Court. The Family Court does not exist to 'clear someone's name' or sit in judgment on a person accused of child sexual abuse. In both cases, the ex-wife (and mother of children the subject of access orders) applied for cessation of access on the ground of sexual interference by the father. At trial, access was denied. Each father appealed. The Full Court of the Family Court upheld the original decision, by a two-one majority. (In each case the Chief Judge dissented on the ground that an order for access should not be refused because there was 'a mere possibility that access would expose a child to sexual abuse'.) The crucial passage of Justice Gun (the trial judge in *M. v. M.*), cited by the High Court, was:

My reasons for [not being satisfied on the balance of probability that the husband had sexually abused the child] are the facts that neither Doctors Moody nor Connor was able to find any evidence that the child had been sexually abused, the conflicting evidence of the wife as to when and why she first suspected abuse, the initial refusal of the child to say that the husband had sexually abused her, to a limited extent the interrogation techniques employed by the wife and Constable Anderson, and the husband's denial.

On the other hand, I do not consider that I am in a position to say that the husband did not sexually abuse the child. Indeed the aggregate effect of the evidence of the wife, Constable Anderson, and Miss Fitzgerald [a clinical psychologist] is such as to raise in my mind the possibility that the child has been sexually abused by the husband.[18]

The High Court noted Justice Gun's conclusion was based, to a large degree, on his acceptance of Ms Fitzgerald's evidence. As for medical evidence, on physical examination, the child's vaginal entrance was open and appeared widened, the vulva reddened. 'But,' concluded the High Court, 'that was all [sic]'.

Although the decisions are valuable in affirming the right of a child not to be sent on access where there is a considered endangerment or risk of physical, sexual or emotional harm, an element of the High Court's reasoning gives reason for concern. Amongst other matters it asserted that an allegation of a parent having sexually abused a child is 'an allegation which is often easy to make, but difficult to refute'.[19]

It is extraordinary that some four centuries after Chief Justice Hale made his (in)famous statement that rape is a 'charge easily made and hard to be defended against, tho be he never so innocent' the High Court of Australia reiterates it without critical analysis. Such a charge by a child is inherently difficult to make; few listen; those who listen are all too rarely listened to (at least by 'justice' authorities, particularly the courts). The charge is almost equally difficult for the mother: traditional theorising about mothers of victims of incest asserts they collude in the crime, or their 'frigidity' or attention to matters outside the homeground somehow 'provokes' the man into it, or 'makes' or 'causes' him to sexually exploit their children. If the mother does not complain about the abuse and exploitation, she is seen as responsible for it (often, she knows nothing of it, or has sought help from numerous unresponsive quarters). If she does complain, she is likely to be seen as viciously attacking her innocent husband, attempting to 'get back at him'.

Almost 20 years ago a federal court in California critically analysed the homily that rape is a charge easily made. Giving adequate and proper attention to the reality, the court acknowledged the truth: rape (like child sexual abuse or child rape) is not easily *talked about* by the woman raped, much less drawn to the attention of authorities;

it is even more difficult for a child, and difficult again for the mother of the child who sees herself as responsible for her husband's sexuality and for her child's distress and exploitation. The Californian court said:

In light of . . . examination of the evolution of the cautionary instructions [given to the jury by the judge that 'rape is an accusation easily to be made'], and with the benefit of contemporary and empirical and theoretical analyses of the prosecution of sex-offenses in general and rape in particular, we are of the opinion that the instruction . . . has outworn its usefulness and in modern circumstances is no longer to be given mandatory application . . .

   We next examine whether such a charge is so difficult to defend against as to warrant a . . . cautionary instruction in the light of available empirical data . . . [Of] the FBI's four 'violent crime' offenses of murder, forcible rape, robbery and aggravated assault, forcible rape has the highest rate of acquittal or dismissal . . . Equally striking is the ranking of forcible rape at the bottom of the FBI's list of major crimes according to percentage of successful prosecutions of the offense charged . . . As to sex offenses other than forcible rape and prostitution, the percentage of prosecutions ending in acquittal or dismissal is almost 50 per cent higher than the average for all major crimes . . . a similar situation is indicated by California crimes statistics, which show forcible rape to have an acquittal rate second only to bookmaking, with prosecutions for other sex offenses resulting in acquittal or dismissal more frequently than the average for all felonies.[20]

That the High Court adopted seventeenth century English thought without question, rather than addressing the reality of rape and child sexual abuse in twentieth century Australia, attests only to the pressing need to require judicial training, which is accepted in the United States (and even, to some degree, in England) as essential to the good conduct of the courts.

Rape in Marriage

In the 1980s, rape laws were redrafted or the subject of proposals for amendment in all Australian states and territories. The South Australian legislature had, in 1976, introduced an amendment which purported to render rape in marriage (in certain circumstances) a crime. It was poorly drafted, as a consequence of opposition in the Legislative Council. In 1980 the National Conference on Rape Law Reform, held jointly in Hobart by the Australian Institute of Criminology, the

Tasmanian Law Reform Commission, and the University of Tasmania Law School, passed a resolution that no distinction should be made, in law, between rape between strangers and rape in marriage: husbands should no longer be immune from prosecution. In 1981 the New South Wales' parliament addressed this in amending the *Crimes Act* 1900. Victoria and Western Australia took a less happy approach, providing that a husband could be subject to a prosecution for rape of his wife, if the parties were living 'separately and apart' at the time of the offence. Predictably, this caused problems.

In 1985 a Victorian court held that a man could not be prosecuted for the rape of his wife in circumstances where he had penetrated her anally without her consent, and where she had left him, but the offence took place when she returned to collect some belongings.[21] This absurd situation arose for two reasons. First, when Victoria amended its rape laws, it provided that 'rape' covers sexual penetration of the vagina, the anus, and the mouth. Although at common law anal penetration was considered to be an offence whether or not a person consented to it (it was viewed as an offence against morality), the court said that by 'collapsing' all types of penetration into one category, the legislature had thereby extended a husband's immunity from rape to anal rape. Secondly, the court said that the parties were not living separately and apart, anyway. This appeared to be giving to the phrase 'separately and apart' a restrictive meaning, difficult to justify in the circumstances. The woman had left her husband to stay at her mother's home, with the intention of ending the marriage. The following day, having departed the matrimonial home with nothing other than the clothes she wore, she returned. She did so at a time of day her husband ordinarily was at work. Unfortunately for her, he had remained at home. He attacked her physically and committed the act after having beaten and abused her. Although the court allowed the prosecution for assault to continue (thus clearly recognising that the events leading to the rape involved force and coercion), it refused to allow the prosecution for rape to stand.

The public outcry led to immediate action on the part of the government, which drafted an amendment to the *Crimes Act* providing for no rape immunity for a husband, whether or not living 'separately and apart'. The Liberal Opposition supported the new law, which passed through the parliament within two or three weeks of the court's decision. The *Crimes (Amendment) Act* 1985 provides:

The existence of a marriage does not constitute, or raise any presumption of, consent by a person to an act of sexual penetration with another person or to an indecent assault (with or without aggravating circumstances) by another person.

In 1986 the Tasmanian parliament effected a similar reform, as did the Western Australian and South Australian parliaments, following further reviews of rape laws. The Northern Territory government, in drafting a *Criminal Code* for the territory, originally took an approach of explicitly excluding immunity of husbands from prosecution for rape. A subsequent redrafting omitted reference to rape in marriage. Queensland made several attempts to reform the law during the 1980s, and in 1989 the right of a husband to rape his wife with impunity was finally removed from the *Criminal Code*.

Women continue to be vulnerable to rape in marriage. Ironically, the crime that had, throughout the nineteenth and twentieth centuries, continued to be labelled as 'no crime' was redefined as criminal in Australia at a time that legislation was being simultaneously passed decriminalising criminal assault at home. Those groups lobbying for the civil law approach to the assaultive behaviour of husbands did not, apparently, see any illogic in lobbying at the same time for criminalising rape in marriage.

Marital Murder

The 1990s saw courts continuing to take an exculpatory approach to the unlawful killing of women by their husbands. This extended, in one English case, to the conjoint killing of the couple's child. As the *Australian* of 1 March 1990 reported:

A Royal Marine commando who blasted his wife and newborn baby to death with a shotgun walked free from court yesterday. Graham Sherman, 21, was told by Lord Dunpark at the High Court in Aberdeen, Scotland: 'You have punished yourself enough.'

The judge said the reason for the killings remained unexplained. Sherman was found guilty of the culpable homicide of his wife Michelle 23, and one-month-old son Josh, whom he shot as they slept at the family's married quarters in Abroath last November. The previous night he had been out with fellow Marines at a colleague's leaving celebration, and showed no sign of anything wrong.

After the shootings, police received a call from a sobbing man who said: 'I've just shot my wife and son.'

Lord Dunpark told Sherman after hearing the jury's verdicts: 'I'm going to do something I have never done before in a case of culpable homicide and I don't anticipate I will ever do it again. I'm going to admonish you on both charges. I will tell you why I'm taking this unusual, if not unique, course.'

He said there were a number of purposes to sentencing. 'First of all to punish, and in my opinion you have punished yourself more than enough by what you did. You will have to live with this for the rest of your life. You don't know why you did it.'

Lord Dunpark said a second purpose would be 'to deter anyone from committing a similar act'. 'That would be futile, as would imprisonment, to deter others, for no one in their right mind would have killed without reason these two people who were dearest to them in the world. But that's what you did. There's no point in deferring sentence for good behaviour. You have no previous convictions. Neither is this a case in which in my opinion a probation order would help you. It would just keep reminding you of what you have done. And the sooner you try to forget this the better. For all these reasons I admonish you on both these charges and you have my deep sympathy.'

Yet women continued to face difficulty in having distressful circumstances, involving criminal acts on the part of the dead person, taken into account in charges of unlawful killing. Thus in Western Australia in 1989 a woman who killed her husband after he had told her of his continuing acts of sexual abuse, exploitation and rape of their daughters was sentenced to a mandatory penalty of life imprisonment. She was convicted of murder, the judge refusing to allow provocation to go to the jury, on the basis that what she had heard and experienced did not amount to provocation. This contrasts starkly with the case of the man 'jailed for axe killing of his wife'. On 1 October 1983 the *Age* reported:

A man convicted of killing his wife with an axe after she refused to put drops in his eye was sentenced yesterday to six years' jail . . . Justice King, in the Criminal Court, said that Pasquale Malarbi had lost control after his wife taunted him and was overcome by rage when he picked up a small axe and struck her about the head a number of times.

Malarbi, 58, waterside worker, was acquitted of having murdered his wife Teresa at their home in McBryde Street, Fawkner, on 21 November last year, but was convicted by the jury of manslaughter. He pleaded not guilty . . . Justice King imposed a non-parole period of four-and-a-half years.

The judge said that in reaching its verdict, the jury had probably considered Malarbi's mental depression and the physical pain he was suffering at the time that he lost control. But the attack was not something lasting for a moment, carried out with a handy weapon.

The judge said the sustained attack with the axe Malarbi fetched from the backyard was an emotional explosion resulting from an accumulation of resentment at his wife's insults and humiliation over a long time.

Wifely 'insults' and 'humiliation' (and the ubiquitous 'nagging') apparently hold more concern for courts, in determining upon what is 'provocation' to go to the jury, than do sexual abuses against daughters, reported to wives and mothers who then strike out, to kill.

Women who announce an intention to leave a man, and particularly those who follow through that intention, are equally at risk as those who 'nag' or 'insult'. Judith A. Allen reports upon a case occurring in New South Wales 100 years ago:

'I left him two weeks before he shot me because he badly used me. I came to Newcastle. I met the accused in Hunter St . . . He wanted me to go back with him. I said I would not. I said I would rather work by myself than stop and be badly used by him. I had my baby in my arms. He asked me where I was stopping. I would not tell him. I heard the report and was shot.'

Christina R. lost the left side of her lower jaw as well as her hearing, and incurred permanent paralysis on the left side of her face in her attempts to escape a violent marriage in 1890. Upon charging her husband with attempted murder, police asked why he had shot her. He replied 'because my wife would not come home and look after my children'.[22]

Allen goes on to observe that of sixty-three men tried for murder, manslaughter or attempted murder of wives in late nineteenth century New South Wales, attacks took place at locations other than the marital home in twenty-nine cases. She adds: 'Generally, the man's violence precipitated such estrangements.'

In the late 1980s in Australia, that a woman had told her husband or de facto spouse she was leaving him, and did so, was a standard 'excuse' for unlawful killing, reducing a charge of murder to manslaughter, and therefore to a lesser penalty. In one celebrated Victorian case, the man approached his former de facto wife outside her place of employment. She had left him some three months before. He carried with him two knives, one a Stanley trimmer. He stabbed her to death in front of the kindergarten where she worked. At his trial, he asserted he had taken the knives not with any intention to kill, but to slash the tyres of her car. (The knives he carried were hardly suited to the stated purpose – but they did suffice in putting an end to his former lover's life.) A conviction for manslaughter resulted in a penalty of six years' imprisonment – which means release in far less, generally calculated on the basis of one-third of the stated sentence.

In South Australia in 1984 a bond was imposed where a man fired at his wife as she fled out of the house, following an altercation during which he was violent (as he had been before). He demanded that she, and a child who was present, leave the matrimonial home. As she obeyed, he raised a gun and shot her in the back. The 'provocation' was a combination of 'nagging' and (albeit in response to his demand) leaving. The outcry from women's groups led to an appeal, by the prosecution, against sentence.[23]

Six years for manslaughter was the sentence imposed in another Victorian example. The 'ground' of provocation? The parties had lived together for a time in New South Wales. Leaving him, the woman transferred to Victoria, where she lived for a time alone with their two children, a boy and a girl. The man followed her. He moved in. For most of their life together, she worked as a prostitute. Reportedly, for most of their life together, he worked little or not at all. Her money kept the household. The relationship again came to an end, at her instigation. He obtained access to the children, which took place at her home, she leaving during his presence there. On the day of the killing, she left as usual. Upon her return, he took up the gun he had brought with him and laid upon the dining room table awaiting completion of the access period, and shot her in front of the children. He asserted he was 'provoked' because she was working as a prostitute; and that he was 'afraid' the boy and girl would contract AIDS through her work.

Selected at random, these examples are not isolated. They are replicated throughout Australia.[24] Yet despite the evident differential in the treatment of women and men through the criminal justice system in the instance of marital killing, and the continuing accumulation of cases, in 1988 it was claimed in a *Discussion Paper on Homicide* produced by a law reform commission that the 'claim that provocation is gender-biased requires evidence to support it'.[25] Women activists and researchers may be excused for concluding that evidence is never sufficient, where gender bias is posed.

To determine upon gender bias, it is necessary only to look at the history of provocation rules, their application in cases where men are prosecuted, and their failure of application in cases where women are prosecuted. One of the most telling measures is the simple reflection that provocation as a mitigating factor has, through the years, concentrated upon the male perception of masculinity and threats to it. The classic case of provocation is that where a *man* finds his *wife* (or, in these enlightened times, his de facto wife or lover) in the act of adultery. Never is the 'classic' case posed in the opposite circumstance − of the *woman* who finds her *husband* or lover in that circumstance. It fails to have the same impact − just as another commonly stated ground of provocation fails to impact in the reverse: the case of the man who is charged by his wife, or lover, or a prostitute, with being *impotent*. Would the woman who claimed she shot her husband because he said she was *frigid* be so certain of claiming provocation as mitigation? Or of having such a claim taken seriously (by the legal system)? And what of the woman who claims she stabbed 'her man' because he nagged her? Or that he failed to put eye-drops in her eyes? Or that he told her he was having an affair with the woman down the street, and she was ten times a better lover than his wife?

Provocation is built on maleness and visions of masculinity, and insults to that vision. Insults to women's sense of being 'women' understandably do not fit into the classic case of provocation at law − because the world is awash with them. Standard 'humour' is based on jokes directed at women's sense of self. The 'mother-in-law joke' is a classic in the annals of (male) humour. The 'old cow' reached heady levels of promulgation on world wide television in the 1960s and 1970s. (The notion of television moguls tolerating a series starring a woman in the lead role who continually berates her husband as a 'clapped out old bull' is absurd.) Even much now acclaimed 'feminist' humour is directed against women, women's bodies and women's bodily functions. In the nineteenth century, and up to the 1960s, when men claimed provocation upon grounds of being insulted by being charged with impotence, women were regularly assailed (whether publicly or privately) with the knowledge that their sexuality was nugatory, unmentionable, non-existent, or by reason of biology or physiology 'naturally' frigid. In such a climate, it would hardly avail any woman to claim provocation at being charged with falling into any such category. Even in the late twentieth century, when women's 'right to define our own sexuality' has been a slogan of the Women's Movement, the notion that a woman might be exculpated from murder because she killed a man who said she was frigid sits ill with the interpretation of the law. And while 'nagging' remains a solidly female failing in common parlance, it belies belief that a woman could successfully claim provocation for her husband's nagging.

With self-defence, women continue to suffer potential disadvantage. Self-defence covers the case where the accused is attacked without warning by another and fights back to defend her or himself; and where the accused began the altercation, subsequently being placed in a position of having to defend her or himself against what is believed to be a murderous attack by the other person. For women, the need to qualify for the defence by (in the old formulations) 'meeting fists with fists' raises obvious difficulties.

In 1987 the High Court addressed the need to clarify the law to assist judges in their summing up, and juries in their deliberations. In *Zecevic v. Director of Public Prosecutions* the court said that when upon the evidence the question of self-defence arises, the trial judge should in charging the jury 'place the question in its factual setting, identifying those considerations which may assist the jury to reach its conclusion'. The whole of the circumstances should be considered, of which the degree of force used ('meeting fists with fists') may be only part. The primary question is whether the accused believed her or his actions (bringing about the death) were necessary in order to defend her or himself, and whether that belief was held on reasonable grounds. The court added that it 'will in many cases' be appropriate for a jury to be told that in considering this, it should also consider whether the force used by the accused was proportionate to the threat offered. But an accused is entitled to an acquittal only if the jury accepts:

- the accused 'believed upon reasonable grounds that it was necessary in self-defence to do what he did'; and
- there were reasonable grounds for that belief; or
- there is a reasonable doubt about the matter.

Effectively, the High Court in *Zecevic* removed the defence of 'excessive self-defence' which might be seen as particularly applicable to women's situation. Under the original law, if a person pleaded self-defence but was found to have used excessive force in repelling the attack, then she would not be acquitted entirely, but could be convicted of manslaughter rather than murder. For the woman attacked by her husband, meeting fists with fists is not a realistic approach. She is likely, if fighting back, to resort to some weapon, which raises a likelihood of her having been found to have used excessive force. Unless she can plead provocation in such a case, she will be convicted of murder:

A killing which is done in self-defence is done with justification or excuse and is not unlawful, though it be done with intent to kill or do grievous bodily harm. However, a person who kills with the intention of killing or of doing serious bodily harm can hardly believe on reasonable grounds that it is necessary to do so in order to defend himself unless he perceives a threat which calls for that response. A threat does not ordinarily call for that response unless it causes a reasonable apprehension, on the part of that person, of death or serious bodily harm. If the response of an accused goes beyond what he believed to be necessary to defend himself or if there were no reasonable grounds for a belief on his part that the response was necessary in defence of himself, then the occasion will not have been one which would support a plea of self-defence. That is to say, the killing will have been without justification or excuse and it will be for the jury to determine how it must be regarded. If it was done with intent to kill or to do grievous bodily harm, then unless there was provocation reducing it to manslaughter, it will be murder . . . [26]

Take the woman who is beaten and bashed, frequently, by her husband. If on the final occasion she defends herself and kills him with, say, a kitchen knife or his own gun, it may be difficult for her to assert that she had a 'reasonable apprehension of death or serious bodily harm'. What makes this situation any different from the myriad times before that her husband attacked her? On those occasions, she did not apprehend death or serious bodily harm (goes the prosecution argument), for she did nothing to fight back. She didn't call the police. If she did, they didn't arrest the man — therefore it cannot have been serious; she suffered no serious bodily harm. There was no prosecution of the husband. If it had been a serious attack, he would have been prosecuted, runs the case for the prosecution. Now she says she was in reasonable apprehension of death or serious bodily harm this time — but she put up with it on many prior occasions: same man, same ability to harm her, no prior fear on her part of death or serious injury. The difficulty is compounded if, as was shown by Bacon and Lansdowne in their study of women serving prison terms in New South Wales as a consequence of marital killing, police do not in initial interviews obtain evidence from the woman about her violent circumstances, or she fails to volunteer the information, through fear, fright, shock, nerves or compliance with authority.[27]

Some on the jury may be able to empathise with the woman's position, if the issue of repeated attacks and past violence is put into evidence. Yet the setting out by the High Court of the rules makes it clear that women pleading self-defence may well be disadvantaged. There is an implication that the murderous attack arises essentially as a 'one off', not that it may be a culmination of violence and aggression arising out of a close, continuing relationship. And there is also the question of who is the original aggressor. The High Court said of this:

There is . . . one situation which requires particular mention . . . Where an accused person raising a plea of self-defence was the original aggressor and induced or provoked the assault against which he claims the right to defend himself, it will be for the jury to consider whether the original aggression had ceased so as to have enabled the accused to form a belief, upon reasonable grounds, that his actions were necessary in self-defence.[28]

Justices Wilson, Dawson and Toohey continued:

For this purpose, it will be relevant to consider the extent to which the accused declined further conflict and quit the use of force or retreated from it, these being matters which may bear upon the nature of the occasion and the use which the accused made of it. Indeed, even in circumstances in which the accused was not the original aggressor, retreat in the face of a threat of violence before resort to force may be relevant to the belief of the accused or the reasonableness of the grounds upon which the accused based his belief. There is, however, no longer any rule that the accused must have retreated as far as possible before attempting to defend himself. It is a circumstance to be considered with all the others in determining whether the accused believed upon reasonable grounds that what he did was necessary in self-defence . . .

The woman pleading self-defence may be confronted with a prosecution asserting she was the original aggressor, provoking the attack against herself. This proposition has been pursued in a number of cases. The allegation is that the woman deliberately provokes her husband so to present herself with an 'excuse' for 'defending' herself, and killing him.[29] Where husbands frequently assert provocation as an 'excuse' for beating and abusing wives, this approach has a firm basis in folk-lore and dominates views of criminal assault at home and marital murder. It is likely to be present in courtrooms, with judges and juries, where women are accused of unlawful killing. It is equally likely to be present at trials of men for wife-killing. It discriminates against the women who kill, and against she who is killed.

Conclusion

To assert that nothing has changed since the early 1980s push for increased awareness of criminal assault at home in its many forms, and the demand for measures to eliminate it, is to ignore the work of women activists. It is to retreat from the reality: that although the moves are insufficient, and sometimes backward steps have been taken, women's demands have effected positive change.

In 1979 proposals were put to a conference of advisors to the state Premiers and the Prime Minister. They included:

Police

Police should undergo proper training programmes designed to acquaint them with the realities of domestic violence; refuge personnel and others working in the field should be involved in training programmes.

Police should be given a directive to answer every domestic call promptly.

Police should give prompt and proper support and protection to refuges.

There should be equality of opportunity – by way of appointment and promotion – within the police force; affirmative action programmes for women should immediately be introduced to bring women's participation in the police force up to equal strength with men's.

Justice Personnel

All justice personnel – ombudspersons, prosecutors, lawyers, magistrates, judges, Family Court counsellors and others who may come into contact with family violence should be required to attend training classes alerting them to the realities of domestic disputes.

Child Care
Proper and adequately funded child-care centres should be set up in the community and in courts, police stations and the like, so that persons having dealings with the legal system will not be disadvantaged where they have the care of children.

Marriage/De Facto Relationships
On marriage all individuals should be handed a booklet containing information of all types relating to marriage including procedures covering spouse assault, lists of refuge phone numbers, etc.

The Family Court of Australia should provide pre-marital counselling courses covering all facets of married life including family violence.

De facto spouses should be given like protection as married persons, and married persons should be given like protection as those unmarried. In particular there should be a clear directive from the Parliament that all forms of non-consensual sexual acts within marriage are subject to criminal law.

Other Training
Not only police and justice personnel should be trained for domestic intervention, but medical practitioners, nurses and other hospital staff should be trained in how to deal with cases resulting from family violence.

Dissemination of Information
Information relating to spouse assault and all other forms of family violence, and the legal and other methods of dealing with it should be freely and readily available at various points, for example:
- police stations
- doctors' rooms
- court enquiry counters
- neighbourhood centres
- refuges
- community health centres
- baby health centres

- Family Court of Australia – all registries
- outpatients' departments
- social welfare departments and officers

Supermarkets and Department Stores
Consideration should be given to the introduction of a poster campaign, with posters placed at strategic spots – that is, everywhere, stating 'Spouse Assault is a Crime'.[30]

Some steps have been taken to implement the majority of these proposals. Thus, around Australia police forces have introduced or improved training in dealing with criminal assault at home. Debates on equal opportunity and affirmative action in police forces have occurred, and cases have been taken to Equal Opportunity Boards and Tribunals under equal opportunity legislation. In Victoria, Jude McCulloch and the St Kilda Legal Service made application under the *Equal Opportunity Act* to the Commissioner for Equal Opportunity for an enquiry into discriminatory procedures and practices of police in failing to attend domestic violence calls, erring in not arresting men for assault, and failing to prosecute offenders. (Sadly, the Commissioner has not yet publicly reported on the application.) Women's refuges and shelters report differing relationships with police: in a number of instances, police support is prompt and positive; however, it appears to depend upon the will and behaviour of individual police officers, rather than upon any considered policy.

If these moves have not adequately addressed the inadequacies in the policing of criminal assault at home, they have at least occurred. There is noticeably less will on the part of justice personnel to comprehend their part in perpetuating the endemic problem that is violence on the homeground. Individual members of the magistracy are alert and concerned. Since 1980 most states have taken steps to ensure there is female representation in the magistracy, or an increase in women magistrates. The Chief Magistrate of the Northern Territory (Sally Thomas) is female, as is the Deputy Chief Magistrate (Sally Brown) in Victoria. A woman (Justice Mary Gaudron) sits on the High Court. Justice Jane Mathews of the New South Wales' Supreme Court has replaced the now retired Justice Roma Mitchell of the South Australian Supreme Court as the sole female Supreme Court judge in Australia. A number of women (approximately six) sit as judges of the Family

Court. One woman is member of the Federal Court of Australia. Three women sit as District (or County) Court judges: one in Western Australia (Judge Antoinette Kennedy) and two in South Australia. Women are members of various tribunals and boards (for example, the Administrative Appeals Tribunal, the Social Security Appeals Tribunal, Equal Opportunity Tribunals and Boards). Yet the face of the judiciary remains firmly male. Training classes for judges are yet to be established, although the Institute of Judicial Administration, based at Melbourne University, has discreetly proposed some form of training (without stipulating any areas of particular concern to those suffering violence at home and its (occasional) aftermath in the courts).

Child care continues to go unrecognised as an industrial issue by the Australian Industrial Relations Commission, despite the commonsense of the notion (and the reality of the paid and unpaid working lives of those with child care responsibilities), and submissions put to it by the Women's Electoral Lobby in the 1983 *National Wage case*. The Family Court has some provision for child care for litigants' children, as do some Magistrates' Courts and Social Security Appeals Tribunals. Women and child care lobby groups continue to insist on governments incorporating expanded child care programmes into their agendas. Capital works have ensured that child care places in community based centres have increased. Women's groups have taken on the question of child care as a tax rebate or deduction, pursing it through the courts under the *Income Tax Act* 1936 (Cth).[31]

In 1983 the *Marriage Act* 1961 (Cth) was amended to incorporate provisions supportive of marriage guidance counselling at all stages of married life. Yet women and men continue to marry without formal advice on the realities of married life, whether economic or as to violence at the hearth. Today husbands, like other men, can be prosecuted for rape – though rarely are they. (In Queensland, following changes to the law in 1989, the first charge in that state against a married man, for the rape of his wife, took place in May 1990, committal proceedings being adjourned to later in the year.)

In 1985 Robyn Holden of the Royal Australian Nurses Federation completed research into violence inflicted against nurses in hospitals, by patients, in circumstances having a disturbing similarity to violence inflicted against wives, at home, by husbands.[32] Medical practitioners, like lawyers, are unlikely to attend compulsory lectures and training sessions based around criminal assault at home and measures that might be taken by professionals to adequately deal with that part of the problem which is within their competence. Criminal law is often taught without any reference to sex-bias in its derivation and application. Family law is sometimes taught with reference to this bias; some lecturers do not accept this notion. Women and the law, and gender and law, courses are included in the curriculums of most law schools in Australia. There is less evidence of women and medicine or women and health courses in medical faculties. However national psychiatry and psychology conferences have sometimes included addresses and workshops on gender and sex-bias, and particular issues arising in the context of criminal assault at home. Centres Against Sexual Assault, and Domestic Violence and Incest Resource Centres or their equivalents work to assist women and children who have suffered sexual abuse, and to incorporate knowledge of this abuse into hospital and medical practice.

Poster campaigns and information dissemination began faltering-ly. Advertising campaigns were originally addressed only to victims and survivors of violence, the message being 'Domestic Violence: You Don't Have to Put Up With It', rather than confronting the reality, that this violence will stop only when men are told 'Assaulting your Wife is a Crime: You Should Stop Doing It'. In the late 1980s the New South Wales' Women's Advisory Council inadvisedly published a slogan, apparently addressed to women beaten and bashed at home: 'Don't Let [sic] Him Do it to You Again'.

In 1985 the Victorian government published its report *Criminal Assault in the Home*. Apart from this initiative, initially there was a reluctance to name criminal assault for what it is. At federal level this was, apparently, based on research which found those responding 'did not want to be told' that wife beating is criminal. Yet if courts and government refuse to tell them, who in authority will?

In 1989 booklets, posters and television advertisements at last conveyed the clear message: 'Violence in the Home is Crime'. The message was equally directed to aggressors and perpetrators of the violence. The next step must surely be to ensure that this message is not emptied of its force, by failure of a demand that police and courts label the crime for what it is.

The 1980s and 1990s led to an increased push toward counsel-ling, conciliation and mediation in numerous spheres, and not the least in matters involving gross inequalities between parties. Community

Justice Centres in New South Wales, originally established with a brief
to deal with 'neighbourhood disputes', increasingly involve themselves
in cases involving aggression, violence and disagreement between
husbands and wives. 'Diversion' programmes were introduced or proposed to 'deal with' perpetrators of sexual offences against children,
particularly where the aggressor was father to the child. Pressure is
increasingly placed on mothers to 'rehabilitate' the husbands and fathers
who have sexually molested the children, by engaging in 'family
therapy' programmes. Where a man is sentenced and actually gaoled,
rehabilitation organisations follow-up the wife and mother of the
children for whose abuse he is imprisoned, 'requesting' she visit him
(perhaps even taking the children) to assist him recover his equilibrium.
(It seems to be forgotten that her equilibrium requires cosseting, and
prison visits, particularly to him, are likely to be less than helpful.)
Just as methods and mechanisms are being pursued to keep children
out of courts at a time that children and women's voices, angry and
distressed at suffering sexual abuses, are growing louder, so programmes
are developed which serve to privatise at an official level the abuse which
is criminal assault, rape, sexual abuse and child rape at home.[33]

The combination of counselling, mediation, conciliation,
diversion, peace complaints, non-molestation orders and intervention
orders sends a message to men who rape, assault, abuse, beat and bash
women and children at home that the law does not take seriously what
they have done, and do. The 'new' non-molestation and intervention
order laws are not new in import. They contradict what women worked
hard in the late nineteenth century, and began working hard in the
1970s, to dispel: that criminal assault at home is 'just a civil matter'.
Why should police be told, as they are by the 'new' laws, that when
they receive the first call about criminal assault being committed in
a private home, the correct approach is to advise the woman to take
out a peace complaint or intervention order, or that they will do so
on her behalf, and not arrest the man who has committed a criminal
offence? Men continue to be led to believe they are free, at least once,
to 'get away' with beating their wives. Police reality that 'it's not
criminal' is confirmed (despite the television messages, advertising
campaigns, and slogans). Women are denied the acceptance of and
confirmation by the legal system that the criminal attacks to which
they have been victim were and are criminal.

Women's reality must be given credence. Without that confirmation, women stand akin to the position of women of the nineteenth and early twentieth centuries, who were told by the courts and legislatures they were not 'persons'. Although laws said any 'person' could enrol at university, enter the legal profession or medical profession, or become a notary public or hold other public office, courts held in their male wisdom that women were not persons and therefore could not attend university, enter the professions, take on public office.[34] Then, the reality of women's very existence as human beings was denied; the reality of university authorities and professors, members of Bar Associations and Law Societies, was confirmed: that women, not being men, were less than human and entitled to no recognition as members of faculties or professions or public bodies. Today, special laws for domestic violence confirm that women's reality – the reality of being victim (and survivor) of criminal assault, is false; rather, she is merely subject to an altercation classified under the heading of 'domestic violence'. And even the violence to which women are subjected is ignored, in the all-too-frequent dropping from the term of the word 'violence' – it's merely a 'domestic'. There will be no charge, no prosecution, no conviction, no sentence: it's a civil, not a criminal, matter.

The danger for women fighting for recognition of the compound wrongs concealed in the euphemism 'violence in the family' is that it is too easy to fall back into the habit of demanding piecemeal reform when the problem confronting women is far more profound. In our despair at a system that denies equal rights, equal space, equal dignity to women, it is so easy to clutch at apparent assistance. Too easy to imagine that the problem of structural opposition to women's rights, to women's right to live with equal entitlements as men, to women's right to live with laws acknowledging equal standing as men, to women's right to live free of oppression and domination, to women's right to live – can be overcome by a paper procedure which elevates court dignity in the breach of an order, above women's bodily integrity in the recognition of a crime.

Panegyrics will not deal with criminal assault at home, sexual and physical abuse of children, marital rape, violence, and murder of women, much less eliminate it. There are no panaceas for the prosecution and penalisation of women in the criminal justice system, who take the only way out that is available in too many tragic cases. All that can be said is that against every denunciation of women's position as wrong, when we plead for women's rights, when we demand equal attention, equal resources for women; against every charge that women are well dealt with, or equally dealt with as men; against every attempt to subvert our cause by tinkering with a legal system which is unresponsive to the interests of women, every woman must fight back. That fight back has to occur at every level of society, in every institution and outside every institution. And it must be done with co-operation and confidence.

The American feminist Elizabeth Janeway writes:

There is a kind of courage that's very familiar to [women]: endurance, patience, stamina, the ability to repeat everyday tasks every day, these are the forms of courage that have allowed generations of the governed to survive without losing ultimate hope. The knowledge of one's own vulnerability, the choice of restraint in the face of provocation, the ability to hear oneself described as unworthy without accepting the stigma as final — that takes courage of a high order. We do not want to lose it, simply to supplement it, for it's still a source of strength when the time comes to be patient no longer, when direct confrontation with the powerful for independent aims must be risked if not sought . . . for decisive action, something else must be added: bravery, daring, risk taking in public . . . [35]

Many brave, daring women have made a difference to the way criminal assault at home is regarded in 1990s Australia. But the next step — stopping the violence — cannot be done by women alone. It has to be done through the action of men who are capable of acknowledging the need to recognise the rights of women. These men who do not understand as we who are women do, the everyday lives of women who are exploited, oppressed, dominated, bashed, beaten, abused — and killed — must begin to learn through the courage of women what it means to stand out against the dominant culture. Against the men who exploit, oppress, dominate, bash, beat, abuse — and kill.

Violence is a way of life that must be repudiated. That repudiation is vital for the wellbeing of women, and for the saving of women and children's lives. But ultimately it is for the wellbeing of men, if only they could learn to look with their own eyes at the damage and injury they and their fellows inflict. Every man who stands by, ignoring the pain, passing over the cries, believing he is not implicated because he raises not a hand to his wife, nonetheless supports every man who inflicts the pain, beats despite the cries, bashes with crashing fist.

Every man is a supporter of violence against women, so long as he does not speak out against it. Every man benefits from the subjection of women who does not repudiate his place in the hierarchy where the rungs are measured by sex alone. Every man benefits from a world where some men bash, rape and kill, while he stands, mute, on the sidelines. For every woman who cries out against criminal assault at home, a man must do more than cry out.

Women's cries are so loud, the neighbours cannot but hear. But listening is not enough.

Notes

Chapter 1   Introduction

1. Australian Women's Weekly survey, 1980, *Women's Weekly.*
2. In 1972 the author wrote an LLM thesis on women and crime, high-lighting discrimination against women in criminology, criminal law and penology. Publications arising from the study include: 'Crime and Equality of the Sexes' (1976) 5 *Crime, Punishment and Corrections* 57; 'A Factor in Female Crime' (1974) 9 *The Criminologist* 56; 'Role Conditioning Theory: An Explanation for Disparity in Male and Female Criminality' (1976) 9 *Australian and New Zealand Journal of Criminology* 25; 'Psychiatry and the Development of the Female Criminal' (1976) 9 *Australian Journal of the Forensic Sciences* 64; 'The Politics of the "Broken Home" in the Deter-mination of Female Criminality' (1977) 49 *The Australian Quarterly* 37; 'Debunking the Theory of the Female "Masked Criminal"' (1978) 11 *Australian and New Zealand Journal of Criminology* 23; 'Crime and Sexual Politics' in *Women and Labour Conference Papers*, Vol. 4, The Politics of Sexuality, Macquarie University, 1978, 1, also in *Women, Class and History*, Elizabeth Windshuttle, editor, 1980, Fontana Books, Sydney, 531; 'The Myth of the "Chivalry Factor" in Female Crime' (1979) 14 *Australian Journal of Social Issues* 3; see also 'Sexism in Criminal Law' in *Women and Crime*, S. K. Mukherjee and Jocelynne A. Scutt, editors, 1981, George Allen and Unwin, 1.

Chapter 2   The Family In Law

1. See Frederick Engels, *The Origin of the Family, Private Property and the State*, 1942, International Publishers, New York, at p. 51; also Thorsten Sellin, *Slavery and the Penal System*, 1976, Elsevier Scientific Publishing Co., New York, at p. 32.
2. Bertrand Russell, *History of Western Philosophy*, 1969, George Allen and Unwin Ltd, London, at p. 186.
3. See Ann Jones, *Women Who Kill*, 1981, Fawcett Columbine Books, New York, at pp. 22–23; also Carl Bridenbaugh, *Vexed and Troubled Englishmen 1590–1642*, 1968, Oxford University Press, New York; Edward D. Neil, *History of the Virginia Company of London*, 1969, reprinted New York, Burt Franklin.
4. Gunnar Myrdal, *An American Dilemma*, cited Mary Daly, *Beyond God the Father — Toward a Philosophy of Women's Liberation*, 1980, Beacon Press, Boston, at p. 130.

5. Kenneth M. Stampp, *The Peculiar Institution*, 1956, Vintage Books, New York, at p. 52.

6. See Sue Jane Hunt, 'Aboriginal Women and Colonial Authority — North Western Australia 1885–1905' in *In Pursuit of Justice — Australian Women and the Law 1788–1979*, Judy Mackinolty and Heather Radi, editors, 1979, Hale and Iremonger, Sydney, 32, at p. 35.

7. G. A. Robinson, *Journal* 10 October 1829, reprinted in *Uphill All the Way — A Documentary History of Women in Australia*, Kay Daniels and Mary Murnane, eds, 1980, University of Queensland Press, St Lucia, at pp. 80–81.

8. *Blackstone's Commentaries* Bk 1, c. 15, p. 442; Bk 2, c. 29, at p. 433, 1770, 4th ed.

9. See A Wife and Mother, *What Will the Commons Do with the Divorce Bill?* 1857, James Ridgway, Piccadilly, London, at pp. 22–24; reprinted in *On the Property of Married Women and the Law of Divorce — A Collection of Documents*, Monckton Milnes, editor, William S. Hein & Co., London, repr. 1975.

10. Ibid., at p. 15.

11. *Re Ewing and Ewing* (1881) 1 Q.L.J. 15.

12. *In re Agar-Ellis* (1883) 24 Ch. D. 317, 337.

13. *A Brief Summary in Plain Language, of the Most Important Laws Concerning Women . . .* in *On the Property of Married Women and the Law of Divorce* op. cit., note 9, ante, at pp. 9–10.

14. *A Review of the Divorce Bill of 1856, with Propositions for an Amendment of the Laws Affecting Married Persons, Inscribed, by Permission, to Lord Lyndhurst*, Pamphlet, 1857, John Parker, London, reprinted Monckton Milnes, op. cit., note 9, ante.

15. Ibid.

16. Reported *Sydney Morning Herald* 6 February 1879; cited John Mackinolty, 'The Married Women's Property Acts' in *In Pursuit of Justice*, op. cit., note 6, ante, 66, at p. 74; also *Sydney Morning Herald* 3 November 1978; published Ruth Teale, *Colonial Eve — Sources on Women in Australia 1788–1914*, 1978, Oxford University Press, Melbourne, at pp. 165–166.

17. T. H. Atkinson, 'The Destitute Poor Department of South Australia' in *Proceedings of the First Australasian Conference on Charity*, 1890, reprinted in *Uphill All The Way*, op. cit., note 7, ante, at pp. 51–52. See also S. Maxted, 'The Responsibilities of Relatives' in *Proceedings of 2 July Conference on Charity*, 1891; reprinted in *Uphill all the Way*, op. cit., note 7, ante, at p. 53.

18. *Goldsmith* v. *Sands* (1907) 4 C.L.R. 1648, 1654. Higgins, J's comment appears at 1664. See also Marie B. Byles, 'The Custody and Guardianship of Infants' (1931) *Australian Law Journal* 53.

19. C. H. Currey, 'The Law of Marriage and Divorce in New South Wales

(1788–1858)' (1955) 41 (3) *Royal Australian Historical Society Journal and Proceedings* 97, at p. 109 et seq.

20. *M'Neilly* v. *M'Neilly, Town and Country Journal* 3 March 1837; reprinted in *Colonial Eve* . . . , op. cit., note 16, ante, at pp. 168–169. The remarks of James Rush, Inspector of the Police Force, appear in the same item.

21. Alfred Murray, Bishop of Sydney, Letter to the Editor, *Sydney Morning Herald*, 8 April 1886; reprinted in *Colonial Eve* . . . , op. cit., note 16, ante, at p. 169.

22. *The Dawn*, 5 November 1890; reprinted in Beverley Kingston, *The World Moves Slowly — A Documentary History of Australian Women*, 1977, Cassell Australia Limited, Sydney, at pp. 141–142.

23. Malcolm Broun, 'Historical Introduction' to Paul Toose, Ray Watson and David Benjafield, *Australian Divorce Law and Practice*, 1968, Law Book Co., Sydney, at ciii. (This Introduction draws heavily upon C. H. Currey, op. cit., note 19, ante.)

24. Ibid.

25. See for example I. Broverman, D. Broverman, F. Clarkson, P. Rosenkrantz and S. Vogel, 'Sex Roles, Stereotypes and Clinical Judgments of Mental Health' (1970) 34 *Journal of Consulting and Clinical Psychology* 5; Phyllis Chesler, *Women and Madness*, 1972, McGraw Hill, New York; Joanna Bunker Rohrbaugh, *Women: Psychology's Puzzle*, 1979, Basic Books, New York; Lesley Lynch, 'Naomi MacDonald: A Case of Madness?' in *In Pursuit of Justice* . . . , op. cit., note 6, ante, 57; Judith Bardwick, *Psychology of Women*, 1971, Harper and Row, New York.

26. *In Re W. (An Infant)* [1971] A.C. 682, 699–700. (This case involved lack of grant of consent to adoption, but the standard of the child's welfare as paramount equates with that relating to custody under divorce legislation.)

27. Women's Electoral Lobby (N.S.W.), 'When Will We Get a Fair Go Under Aussie Rules? Women and Law', in *W.E.L. International Women's Year Bulletin*, September 1975, Sydney, at p. 18.

28. Ann Jones, *Women Who Kill*, op. cit., note 3, ante, at p. 311.

29. Public Solicitor's Case Files, Series No. 1001, Box 428, 1932, File No. 3244. Public Records Office, Victoria. Quoted Marilyn Lake, 'Building Themselves Up with Aspros: Pioneer Women Re-Assessed' (1981) 7 (2) *Hecate* 7; see also Gloden Dallas, 'New Introduction' to *Maternity — Letters from Working Women*, Margaret Llewelyn Davies, editor, 1915, G. Bell & Sons, London; reprinted 1978, Virago, London; these letters show clearly that women deprived themselves whilst 'feeding up' their husbands.

30. *Women's Electoral Lobby Family Law Action Group Records*, W.E.L. Sydney, 1981.

31. H. H. Foster and D. J. Freed, 'A Bill of Rights for Children' (1972)

6 *Family Law Quarterly* 343, at 348; further on this issue, see Frank Bates, 'Redefining the Parent/Child Relationship: A Blueprint' (1975–76) 12 *University of Western Australia Law Review* 518.

32. In conducting research into the operations of the Family Court, which included sitting in on custody and access decisions and reviewing reported cases, in addition to receiving case histories of litigants, W.E.L. Family Law Action Group members observed a reluctance on the part of some members of the Court at least to give credence to suggestions that sexual molestation had occurred. Generally in society there is a reluctance to believe that children have been sexually molested by a parent, or that unwanted sexual acts occur. On this issue, see for example contributions in *Rape Law Reform*, Jocelynne A. Scutt, editor, 1980, Australian Institute of Criminology, Canberra.

33. Elizabeth Cady Stanton, *Eighty Years and More — Reminiscences 1815–1897*, 1898, T. Fisher Unwin, New York; reprinted 1971, 1975, Schocken Books Inc., New York, at p. 229.

34. Ibid., at pp. 119–200, 221.

35. Diana Leonard Barker, 'The Regulation of Marriage: Repressive Benevolence' in *Power and the State*, Garry Littlejohn, Barry Smart, John Wakeford and Nira Yuvai-Davis, editors, 1978, Croom Helm, London, 239, at pp. 239–240.

36. *W.E.L. Family Law Action Group Records*, 1981.

37. See Jocelynne A. Scutt, 'The Politics of the "Broken Home" in the Determination of Female Criminality' (1977) 49 (2) *The Australian Quarterly* 37 and sources cited therein.

Chapter 3   Child Abuse

1. Jane Connors, 'Reporting Child Abuse' in *Violence in the Family.*, Jocelynne A. Scutt, editor, 1980, Australian Institute of Criminology, Canberra, 107, at p. 117.

2. See Jean Hamory, 'Child Abuse: An Overview of Recent Developments' in *Violence in the Family*, op. cit., note 1, 27, at p. 33.

3. Ailsa Burns and Jacqueline Goodnow, *Children and Families in Australia*. 1979, George Allen and Unwin, at p. 155.

4. Royal Commission on Human Relationships, *Final Report*, Vol. 4, Australian Government Publishing Service, 1977, Canberra, A.C.T., at p. 165.

5. Ibid., at p. 165.

6. Ibid., at p. 164.

7. See J. Harper, *Fathers At Home*, 1980, Penguin, Melbourne, at p. 148;

Ann Oakley, *Becoming a Mother*, 1979, Martin Robinson, Oxford; Ann
Oakley, *Women Confined*, 1980, Martin Robinson, Oxford.

8.   See J. Harper, op. cit., note 7, ante, *passim*.

9.   Adele Horin, 'Childcare', *National Times*, September 21–27, 1980,
at p. 29.

10.   Although some children are conceived and born without the agreement of both parties, where wives are subjected to marital rape. On this
issue, see Chapter 6, *Marital Rape*.

11.   Royal Commission on Human Relationships, op. cit., note 4, ante,
at pp. 178–179.

12.   *Select Committee Report on Violence in the Family*, 1975, H.M.S.O.,
London; see also Sarah McCabe, 'Unfinished Business: Violence in Marriage
and Violence in the Family' (1977) 17 *British Journal of Criminology* 280,
at p. 282.

13.   Erin Pizzey, *Scream Quietly or the Neighbours will Hear*, 1974, Penguin,
London, 'The Child is Father to the Man'.

14.   J. J. Gayford, 'Wife Battering: A Preliminary Survey of 100 Cases'
(1975) 5951 *British Medical Journal* 194.

15.   Vivien Johnson, 'Children and Family Violence: Refuges' in *Violence
in the Family*, op. cit., note 1, ante, 195, at p. 198.

16.   Sarah McCabe, 'Unfinished Business...', op. cit., note 12, ante, at
p. 282.

Chapter 4   Child Sexual Molestation

1.   *Wigmore on Evidence* (McNaughten ed.) 1961; and see Jocelynne
A. Scutt, 'Sexism and Psychology: An Analysis of the "Scientific" Basis of
the Corroboration Rule in Rape' (1979) 5 (1) *Hecate* 35.

2.   Australian Women's Weekly Survey, *Women's Weekly*, 1980.

3.   Unpublished transcript of a talk delivered to the Children and Family
Violence seminar at the Australian Institute of Criminology, November
1979, Canberra, A.C.T. (See *Violence in the Family*, Jocelynne A. Scutt,
editor, 1980, Australian Institute of Criminology, Canberra.)

4.   See Institute of Family Studies, *Family Impact Seminar — Adelaide*,
1980, at p. 4.

5.   Naomi Refuge, South Australia, *Naomi Report*, Adelaide, 1978, at p. 52.

6.   In some families more than one victim gave information.

7.   Unpublished transcript, op. cit., note 3, ante.

8.   J. McGeorge, 'Sexual Assaults on Children' (1964) 5 *Medicine and the
Law* 248.

9. M. Singer, 'Perspective on Incest as Child Abuse' (1979) 12 *Australian and New Zealand Journal of Criminology* 3, at p. 8. (Footnotes omitted.)

10. See for example Shere Hite, *The Hite Report*, 1981, Dell, New York; William H. Masters and Virginia E. Johnson, *Human Sexual Inadequacy*, 1970, Little, Brown & Co, Boston; William H. Masters and Virginia E. Johnson, *Human Sexual Response*, 1966, Little, Brown & Co, Boston, Nancy Friday, *My Secret Garden*, 1976, Virago, New York.

Chapter 5 Spouse Assault

1. Yvonne Carnahan, Unpublished study, A.N.U., 1979; parts of the study are contained in Carnahan, 'Wives' Employment and Domestic Violence' in *National Symposium on Victimology*, P. N. Grabosky, editor, 1982, Australian Institute of Criminology, Canberra, 309.

2. Suzanne K. Steinmetz, 'The Battered Husband Syndrome' (1977–1978) 2 *Victimology* 499; see also E. Pleck, J. H. Pleck, M. Grossman and P. B. Bart, 'The Battered Data Syndrome: A Comment on Steinmetz' Article' (1977–1978) 2 *Victimology* 680; S. K. Steinmetz, 'Reply to Pleck, Pleck, Grossman and Bart' (1977–1978) 2 *Victimology* 683.

3. See G. Levinger, ed., *Divorce and Separation: Conditions, Causes and Consequences*, 1979, Basic Books, New York.

4. R. J. Gelles, *The Violent Home — A Study of Physical Aggression Between Husbands and Wives*, 1972, Sage Publications, Beverley Hills, Calif..

5. N.S.W. Bureau of Crime Statistics and Research, *Domestic Violence — Cases before Chamber Magistrates*, 1974, Department of the Attorney-General and of Justice, N.S.W., Sydney; also published in *Family Violence in Australia*, Carol O'Donnell and Jan Craney, editors, 1982, Longman Cheshire, Melbourne, 28.

6. Royal Commission on Human Relationships, *Final Report*, Vol. 4, 1977, Australian Government Publishing Service, Canberra, at p. 138.

7. Frances H. Lovejoy and Emily S. Steel, 'Staying Together for the Sake of the Children: Spouse Beating and its Effect on the Children' in *Violence in the Family*, Jocelynne A. Scutt, editor, 1980, Australian Institute of Criminology, Canberra, 41, at p. 42.

8. Ailsa Burns, *Breaking Up: Separation and Divorce in Australia*, 1980, Nelson, Sydney, at p. 96.

9. Christine Gibbeson, Unpublished study carried out for the Royal Commission on Human Relationships; see Royal Commission on Human Relationships, *Final Report*, op. cit., note 6, ante, at p. 138 and following.

10. Erin Pizzey, *Scream Quietly or the Neighbours will Hear*, 1974, Penguin, Harmondsworth.

11. Michael Hotaling, *The Social Causes of Husband-Wife Violence*, 1980, University of Minnesota Press, Minneapolis, at p. 147.

12. See also Gibbeson's study, op. cit., note 9; Royal Commission phone-in, published in Royal Commission on Human Relationships, op. cit., note 6.

13. Emphasis added. S. K. Steinmetz, op. cit., note 2, at p. 507.

14. See Jan Crancher (researcher), *Qualifications and Employment*, 1980, Women in the New South Wales Workforce series, Women's Coordination Unit, N.S.W. Premier's Department, Sydney.

15. Yvonne Carnahan, op. cit., note 1, ante.

16. Royal Commission on Human Relationships, op. cit., note 6, ante, at pp. 141–142. See also, for example Gibbeson's study, op. cit., note 9, ante; Carol O'Donnell and Jan Craney, 'Sex and Class Inequality and Domestic Violence' in *Violence in the Family*, op. cit., note 7, ante, 79; also published in *Family Violence in Australia*, op. cit., note 5, ante, 52.

17. Gibbeson's study, op. cit., note 9, ante; cited Royal Commission on Human Relationships, op. cit., note 6, ante, at pp. 140–141. See also Carol O'Donnell and Heather Saville, op. cit., note 16, ante, at pp. 9, 19, citing N.S.W. Bureau of Crime Statistics and Research study, op. cit., note 5, ante, at p. 7.

18. Joanna Downey and Jane Howell, *Wife Battering — A Review and Preliminary Enquiry into Local Incidents, Needs and Resources*, 1976, Social Policy and Research Department, United Way of Greater Vancouver and the Non-Medical Use of Drugs Directorate, National Department of Health and Welfare, Vancouver, B.C., at p. 56.

19. J. J. Gayford, 'Wife Battering: A Preliminary Survey of 100 Cases' (1975) 1 *British Medical Journal* 194; C. Gibbeson, op. cit., note 9, ante; Royal Commission on Human Relationships, op. cit., note 6, ante, pp. 139–140.

20. Carol O'Donnell and Heather Saville, op. cit., note 16, at pp. 82–83.

21. On this issue, see J. Price and J. Armstrong, 'Battered Wives: A Controlled Study of Predisposition' (1978) 12 *Australian and New Zealand Journal of Psychiatry* 43; see also Jocelynne A. Scutt, 'Spouse Assault: Closing the Doors on Criminal Acts' (1980) 54 *Australian Law Journal* 720, at pp. 727–731; Jocelynne A. Scutt, 'The Alcoholic Imperative: A Sexist Rationalisation of Rape and Domestic Violence' (1981) 7 *Hecate* 88.

22. Richard von Kraft-Ebbing, *Psychosis Menstrualis*, 1882, Vienna, cited Otto Pollack, *The Criminality of Women*, 1950, New York, at p. 128.

23. Katherine Dalton, *The Pre-menstrual Syndrome*, 1964, Charles C. Thomas, Springfield, Ill.; Katherine Dalton, *The Menstrual Cycle*, 1969, Penguin, Harmondsworth. For an extensive criticism of this position, see Jocelynne A. Scutt, 'A Factor in Female Crime' (1976) 9 *The Criminologist*

56; Jocelynne A. Scutt, 'Premenstrual Tension as an Extenuating Factor in Female Crime' (1982) 56 *Australian Law Journal* 99.

24. Katherine Dalton, *The Pre-Menstrual Syndrome*, Penguin edn, 1978, pp. 100, 101; also Katherine Dalton, *The Menstrual Cycle*, 1969, Penguin, Harmondsworth, p. 112 — the woman's menstrual cycle is blamed for 'causing' her husband's regular attacks of bronchial spasms.

25. Estelle Ramey, 'Males Cycles' in *Ms Magazine*, Spring, 1972, p. 8.

26. Karen Paige, 'Women learn to sing the menstrual blues', *Psychology Today* 7 (4) 1973 pp. 41–60; Paula Weideger, *Menstruation and Menopause — the physiology and psychology, the myth and the reality*, Penguin, Ringwood, 1977.

27. Jean Renvoize, *Web of Violence: A Study of Violence in the Family*, 1978, Routledge & Kegan Paul, London.

28. J. J. Gayford, op. cit., note 19, ante, at p. 21.

29. Karen Horney, *New Ways in Psychoanalysis*, 1939, W. W. Norton, New York; see also J. Strause, ed., *Women and Analysis*, 1976, Penguin.

30. R. J. Gelles, *The Violent Home — A Study of Physical Aggression Between Husbands and Wives*, 1972. Sage Publications, Beverley Hills, Calif., at pp. 63–64.

31. S. K. Steinmetz, *Cycle of Violence: Assertive, Aggressive and Abusive Interaction*, 1977, Praeger, New York.

32. See, for example, J. Price and J. Armstrong, op. cit., note 26, at p. 46.

33. James H. Kleckner, 'Wife Beaters and Beaten Wives: Coconspirators in Crimes of Violence' (1978) 15 (No. 1) *Psychology* 54, at pp. 54–55, 56.

34. On masochism see S. Freud, 'Femininity' in *New Introductory Lectures on Psychoanalysis*, 1932, at p. 149; reprinted in *Women and Analysis*, J. Strouse, ed., 1976, Penguin, Harmondsworth, 73.

35. See for example, Phyllis Chesler, *Women and Madness*, 1973, Avon, New York.

36. S. K. Steinmetz, op. cit., note 2, ante.

37. Jean Renvoize, op. cit., note 27, ante.

38. Donna Moore, editor, *Battered Women*, 1979, Sage Publications, Beverley Hills, Calif., at pp. 15, 16, 18.

39. Yvonne Carnahan, op. cit., note 1, ante.

40. Donna Moore, op. cit., note 38, ante, p. 19.

Chapter 6   Marital Rape

1. *Caldwell* v. *The Queen* [1976] W.A.R. 204; see also *R.* v. *Jackson* (1891) 2 Q.B. 671; *R.* v. *Clarence* (1888) 23 Q.B. 22; Jocelynne A. Scutt, 'Consent

in Rape: The Problem of the Marriage Contract' (1977) 3 *Monash Law Review* 255; Jocelynne A. Scutt, 'To Love, Honour and Rape with Impunity: Wife as Victim of Rape and the Criminal Law' in *The Victim in International Perspective*, Hans Joachim Schneider, editor, 1982, Walter de Gruyter, Berlin-New York, 423.

2. John Galsworthy, *The Forstye Saga*, Book I, Part III, Chapter IV.

3. John Braithwaite and David Biles, 'Women as Victims of Crime: Some Findings from the First Australian National Crime Victims Survey' (1980) 52 *The Australian Quarterly* 329.

4. Paul Wilson, *The Otherside of Rape*, 1978, University of Queensland Press, Brisbane.

5. Australian Women's Weekly Survey, *Women's Weekly*, 1980.

6. *Parliamentary Debates*, November 1976 (South Australia), at p. 2407.

7. Quoted *Festival of Light Newsletter*, South Australia, 1976.

8. Ibid.

9. N. Morris and G. Turner, 'Two Problems in the Law of Rape' (1956) 2 *University of Queensland Law Review* 247; see also *G.* v. *G.* [1924] P. 349, 357.

10. *Catholic Weekly*, Australia, 26.2.1953; cited Anne Summers, *Damned Whores and God's Police*, 1975, Penguin, Ringwood, Victoria, at p. 145.

11. Menachim Amir, *Patterns in Forcible Rape*, 1971, University of Chicago Press, Chicago.

12. Donald MacNamara and Edward Sagarin, *Sex, Crime and the Law*, 1977, The Free Press, New York, at p. 46.

13. Ibid., at p. 46.

14. This respondent was included in the category of 'rape — ceased' at 57 years, although there was a risk that the husband might recommence raping his wife at some time.

15. *Women's Weekly*, Letters Page, 23.7.1980, at p. 35.

16. Susan Brownmiller, *Against Our Will — Men, Women and Rape*, 1975, McGraw Hill, New York, at p. 291.

17. M. Schmindeberg, 'Criminals and their Victims', (1980) 24 (2) *International Journal of Offender Therapy and Comparative Criminology* 128, at p. 131. The sexist theme of this comment is evident also in the patronising tone: 'girls' marry *men* etc.

18. Royal Commission on Human Relationships, *Final Report*, Vol. 5, at p. 139 (emphasis added).

19. Carol O'Donnell and Heather Saville, 'Sex and Class Inequality and Domestic Violence', paper presented to the Women's Advisors Conference, 1978, Sydney; see also Carol O'Donnell and Heather Saville, 'Sex and Class Inequality and Domestic Violence' in *Violence in the Family*, Jocelynne A. Scutt, editor, 1980, Australian Institute of Criminology, Canberra, 79;

4

also published in *Family Violence in Australia*, Carol O'Donnell and Jan Craney, editors, 1982, Longman Cheshire, Melbourne, 52.

20. Susan Steinmetz, 'The Battered Husband Syndrome' (1977–1978) 2 *Victimology* 499; see also E. Pleck, J. H. Pleck, M. Grossman and P. B. Bart, 'The Battered Data Syndrome: A Comment on Steinmetz' Article' (1977–1978) 2 *Victimology* 680; S. K. Steinmetz, 'Reply to Pleck, Pleck, Grossman and Bart' (1977–1978) 2 *Victimology* 683.

21. *Festival of Light Newsletter*, South Australia, 1978, at p. 6.

22. Many of the rapes taking place in this study would not have been subject to prosecution under the law as conventionally read. In 1976 the law was amended in South Australia to provide some protection for women from rape by their husbands; however the law is unsatisfactory. (On South Australia, see Carol Treloar, 'The Politics of Rape — A Politician's Perspective' in *Rape Law Reform*, Jocelynne A. Scutt, editor, 1980, Australian Institute of Criminology, 191; also Jocelynne A. Scutt, *Monash Law Review*, op. cit., note 1 ante.) In 1977 the law was amended in Western Australia to provide that a husband living separately and apart from his wife could be prosecuted for raping her; in 1981 the law in Victoria was similarly amended. (For criticism of this type of provision, see Jocelynne A. Scutt, *Monash Law Review*, op. cit. and 'To Love, Honour and Rape with Impunity . . .', op. cit., note 1, ante; also Peter Sallmann, 'Rape in Marriage and the South Australian Law' in *Rape Law Reform*, op. cit.) The law in New South Wales was amended by the *Crimes (Sexual Assault) Amendment Act* 1981 to provide that there should be no presumption that a husband was incapable of raping his wife, so that the law now formally provides for protection of wives against rapist husbands as it protects unmarried women from rape.

23. South Australian Criminal Methods and Law Reform Committee, *Special Report — Rape and Other Sexual Offences*, 1976, Government Printer, Adelaide, at p. 14.

24. See John Willis (1976) 2 *Legal Service Bulletin* 31; Peter Sallman, 'Rape in Marriage' (1977) 3 *Legal Service Bulletin* 202.

25. Quoted John Willis (1976) op. cit. and Peter Sallmann, 'Rape in Marriage', op. cit., at note 24, ante.

26. See 'To Love, Honour and Rape with Impunity . . .', op. cit., note 1, ante, at p. 428.

27. William H. Masters and Virginia E. Johnson, *Human Sexual Inadequacy*, 1970, Little, Brown & Co, Boston; William H. Masters and Virginia E. Johnson, *Human Sexual Response*, 1966, Little, Brown & Co, Boston. See also Beatrix Campbell, 'A Feminist Sexual Politics: Now You See It, Now You Don't' in *The Woman Question — Readings on the Subordination of Women*, Mary Evans, editor, 1982, Fontana, London, at p. 125.

28. Larry Tifft and Dennis Sullivan, *The Struggle to be Human: Crime, Criminology and Anarchism*, 1980, Cienfueqos Press, London, pp. 114–115.

Chapter 7   Marital Murder

1. Tess Rod, 'Marital Murder' in *Violence in the Family*, Jocelynne A. Scutt, editor, 1980, Australian Institute of Criminology, Canberra, 95.
2. Ibid. See also Wendy Bacon and Robyn Lansdowne, 'Women Homicide Offenders and Police Interrogation' in *The Criminal Injustice System*, John Basten, Chris Ronalds, Mark Robinson and George Zdenkowski, editors, 1982, Australian Legal Workers Group/Legal Service Bulletin. 4; Wendy Bacon and Robyn Lansdowne, 'Women Who Kill Husbands: The Battered Wife on Trial' in *Family Violence in Australia*, Carol O'Donnell and Jan Craney, editors, 1982, Longman Cheshire, Melbourne, 67.
3. See Tess Rod, op. cit., note 1, ante; see also Judith Allen, 'The Invention of the Pathological Family: A Historical Study of Family Violence in N.S.W.' in *Family Violence in Australia*, op. cit., note 1, 1. (In Allen's historical study, it is found that during the early twentieth century 61 per cent of women killed by husbands had left the matrimonial home: 'In the majority of femicides, the woman's desertion or threat to desert because of violence precipitated the fatal attack. Even in the 1880s, these cases comprised 40 percent of the 35 femicides.' (At p. 5).
4. Reported *Daily Mirror*, 1 December, 1981, pp. 1–2.
5. Blackstone, *Commentaries on the Laws* of England, Vol. II.
6. Note, however, that in New South Wales following amendment to the *Crimes Act* 1900 in 1981, a judge now has a discretion to award a term of years for murder. This has been the case in the Australian Capital Territory since 1974 under the *Crimes Ordinance* (A.C.T.), s. 442 (1).
7. Taken from the judgment in the Court of Criminal Appeal, N.S.W., *R.* v. *Georgia Marie Hill*, No. 72 of 1981, Street, C.J.; Nagle, C.J. at Common Law, and Lee, J., Thursday 18 June 1981.
8. *R.* v. *R.* (1981) 28 S.A.S.R. 321.
9. *Johnson and Anor.* v. *The Queen* (1977) 51 A.L.J.R. 57.
10. *Johnson and Anor.* v. *The Queen* (1977) 51 A.L.J.R. 57, 58.
11. Ibid., 58.
12. Ibid., 59.
13. See Women Behind Bars, *Free Violet and Bruce Roberts*, pamphlet, 1979.
14. *Parker* v. *The Queen* (1964) 111 C.L.R. 665, 671.
15. *Parker* v. *The Queen* (1963) 111 C.L.R. 610, 619–620.
16. See, for example, *Moffa* v. *The Queen* (1977) 138 C.L.R. 601.

Chapter 8   Family, Friends and Others

1. Pizzey also found social workers to be unable to appreciate the anti-social nature of violence by husbands on wives, attributing it to the 'working class' way of a husband 'showing his affection for' his wife. See Erin Pizzey, *Scream Quietly or the Neighbours will Hear*, 1974, Penguin, Harmondsworth, England.

2. See also, for example, R. Langley and R. C. Levy, *Wife Beating: The Silent Crisis*, 1977, at p. 21: 'He asked me if I engaged in sexual relations with my husband. I told him no, that for some time we hadn't. The reason being that his repeated beatings made it impossible for me to be warm and loving toward him. That I feared I could never relax enough to have sex with him now . . . Gradually the tone of our conversation shifted. We had drifted away from the problem of my survival — of what I could do to try and maintain my sanity and my health while living with a man who . . . beat me — to what I was doing to cause all this trouble. When I realised what was happening, my heart plummeted. He didn't believe me, either. He implied that a woman who refuses to sleep with her husband should not only expect a beating or two but no doubt deserved it. He was a clergyman but nevertheless a man first. He had the same attitudes of the society at large, that I was here to serve my husband, and if I got slapped around some, I ought to search my soul and find out what I was doing wrong.'

3. One woman from a country refuge in New South Wales sought her doctor's help as a witness for the prosecution of the husband who had beaten her severely and left her lying exposed to the weather all night on their front door step. 'Don't you think you've punished him enough by leaving him and taking his children away from him?' asked the doctor, refusing to appear as a witness or give her a written statement of injuries received as a result of her husband's abuse.

4. S. K. Steinmetz, 'The Battered Husband Syndrome' (1977–1978) 2 *Victimology* 499.

Chapter 9   The Police

1. See Tess Rod, 'Marital Murder' in *Violence in the Family*, Jocelynne A. Scutt, editor, 1980, Australian Institute of Criminology, Canberra, 95; also Police Foundation, *Domestic Violence and the Police — Studies in Detroit and Kansas City*, 1977, Police Foundation, Washington, D.C.

2. See Western Region Women's Refuge, *Report: Police Involvement in Domestic Violence*, Western Region Women's Refuge, 1979, unpublished study, Melbourne.

Even in the Best of Homes

3. Erin Pizzey, *Scream Quietly or the Neighbours will Hear*, 1974, Penguin, Harmondsworth.

4. See generally Suzanne Steinmetz, 'The Battered Husband Syndrome' (1977-1978) 2 *Victimology* 499; see also *Sun Herald* 5.11.1982 report of a husband serving time for killing his wife, now claiming he should have been able to put forward as mitigation or a defence that she was a 'spouse beater', and that when he sought help from police after her 'beatings', this help was laughingly refused.

5. The Queensland police force has the highest percentage of women in any police force in Australia, mainly owing to the efforts of former Police Commissioner, Ray Whitrod. A submission to the *Lusher Enquiry into the New South Wales Police Force* in 1980-81 recommended that equal opportunity and affirmative action programs be extended to the force, to improve the numbers and position of women in the force. (See New South Wales Women's Advisory *Council Submission to the Lusher Enquiry*, 1980, Department of the N.S.W. Premier.) Similar recommendations were passed at the N.S.W. United Nations Mid-Decade for Women Conference in 1979 in Sydney and at the National United Nations Mid-Decade for Women Conference in Canberra in 1979. In the intake of women into the training program of the Australian Federal Police in November, 1982 it was reported that for the first time, women recruits outnumbered men (seven men and sixteen women). (See 'Women outnumber men in AFP training course' in the *Canberra Times* 1.12.1982, p. 3.)

6. See *Handcock* v. *Baker* (1800) 2 Bos. & P. 260, 126 E.R. 1270; *Smith* v. *Shirley* (1846) 3 C.B. 142, 136 E.R. 58; *R.* v. *Marsden* (1868) L.R. 1 C.C.R. 131; also generally Australian Law Reform Commission, *Report No. 2, Interim, Criminal Investigation*, 1975, A.G.P.S., Canberra.

7. The writer conducted interviews with individual police officers in the named states, as well as talking to police officers at many conferences on domestic violence and related issues (for example, at the Australian Institute of Criminology in 1979; La Trobe University in 1980; Newcastle Women's Electoral Lobby Conference in 1982; National Women's Advisors to State Premiers in Sydney in 1978). Additionally, a police officer from New South Wales telephoned the writer in 1982 and conducted a long conversation, giving his extensive views on the subject of domestic violence and police powers. See also article by K. Williamson, 'Battered Wives' in *The National Times* July 18 to 24, 1982 where limited views of police powers, as put forward by police, stand unquestioned.

8. C. Fogerty, *Interpersonal Violence — The Police Role*, unpublished paper delivered to the 11th International Conference on Health Education, Hobart, 15-20th August, 1982. p. 9.

9. The research of Penelope Stratmann of the South Australian Women's

Advisory Unit to the Premier confirms this. See P. Stratmann, 'Domestic Violence: The Legal Responses' in *Family Violence in Australia*, Carol O'Donnell and Jan Craney, eds, 1982, Longman Cheshire, Melbourne, 121.

10. Victorian Police Manual (emphasis added).

11. Tasmanian Police Manual (emphasis added).

12. On this issue, see Jocelynne A. Scutt, 'Land Rights for Women: Taking the Offensive Against the Patriarchy in the Fight for Equal Marital Property Rights' unpublished paper, 1982; Jocelynne A. Scutt, 'Equal Marital Property Rights' (1983) *Australian Journal of Social Issues* (March issue).

13. Victorian Police Manual (emphasis added).

14. Tasmanian Police Manual (emphasis added).

15. Ibid.

16. Victorian Police Manual (emphasis added).

17. Letter to the Editor, 1 (No. 3) *Reporter* (house journal of the Australian Institute of Criminology) (September, 1980), at pp. 1–2.

18. On this issue, see Jocelynne A. Scutt, 'Criminal Investigation and the Rights of Victims of Crime' (1979) 14 *University of Western Australia Law Review* 1.

Chapter 10   The Courts

1. This attitude is confirmed throughout the literature. See for example P. Stratmann, 'Domestic Violence: The Legal Responses' in *Violence in the Family*, Jocelynne A. Scutt, editor, 1980, Australian Institute of Criminology, Canberra; amended version in *Family Violence in Australia*, Carol O'Donnell and Jan Craney, editors, 1982, Longman Cheshire, Melbourne, 121; Western Women's Refuge Group, *Report on Police Responses to Domestic Violence*, 1978.

2. In its inquiry into the legal profession, the New South Wales Law Reform Commission has received numerous complaints about professional standards of solicitors and barristers. See N.S.W. Law Reform Commission, *Reports on Enquiry into the Legal Profession*, 1980, 1982.

3. On problems in the operation of the Family Court of Australia, see *Submissions to the Parliamentary Joint Select Committee on the Family Law Act, Official Hansard Report*, Canberra, A.C.T., 1979; *Family Law in Australia — A Report of the Joint Select Committee on the Family Law Act*, 1980, A.G.P.S., Canberra, A.C.T., Volume 1; the Sydney Women's Electoral Lobby has conducted extensive research into the operation of the *Family Law Act* and consumers complaints, and has published a number

of reports and submissions which are available from the W.E.L. office, 147a King Street, Sydney, N.S.W. 2000.

4. On this issue, see Jocelynne A. Scutt, 'Principle versus Practice: Determining Equal Rights to Marital Assets under the Family Law Act' (1983) 57 *Australian Law Journal* (March issue).

5. See Jocelynne A. Scutt, note 4, ante for a review of Family Court discretion; also Jocelynne A. Scutt, 'Land Rights for Women — Taking the Offensive Against the Patriarchy in the Fight for Equal Marital Property Rights', 1982, unpublished paper; Jocelynne, A. Scutt, 'Equal Marital Property Rights' (1983) *Australian Journal of Social Issues* (March issue). On the issue of discretion and judicial conditioning generally, see Stan Ross, *Politics of Law Reform*, 1982, Penguin, Ringwood; M. Sexton and L. W. Maher, *The Legal Mystique*, 1982, Angus and Robertson, Sydney.

6. *R. v. Jackson* [1891] 2 Q.B. 671.

7. Ibid.; and see Jocelynne A. Scutt, 'Violence in the Family: A Review of Social, Legal and Political Supports' in *Living Together*, 1979, ANU Continuing Education Department, Canberra.

8. This individual retired from the office some years ago.

9. Notably some jurisdictions, e.g. Western Australia, Victoria, have deemed it necessary to amend laws so as to protect (in theory) separated women from their husband's sexual attacks. See Chapter 6.

10. Numerous reports from the N.S.W. Anti-Discrimination Board, the Victorian Equal Opportunity Board and the South Australian Sex-Discrimination Board confirm, if evidence is required, that this is so.

11. See Di Graham and Jocelynne A. Scutt, *For Richer, For Poorer: Men, Women and Marriage* (work in progress).

Chapter 11 The Refuges

1. Melbourne Ladies' Welfare Society, *Report*, 1974, Melbourne; cited Women's Liberation Halfway House Collective, *Herstory of the Halfway House 1974–1976*, 1976, Melbourne, p. 4.

2. Further on the establishment of feminist-run women's refuges, see Vivienne Johnson and the Marrickville Women's Refuge Collective, *The Last Resort*, 1981, Penguin, Ringwood.

3. See for example, Howard James, *The Little Victims — How America Treats its Children*, 1975, David McKay and Co., Inc., New York; William John Munday and Monica Attard, *58 Years*, n.d., C. Murphy, Sydney.

4. On the rights of children generally, see Helen Gamble, *Law Relating to Parents and Children*, 1981, Law Book Company, Sydney.

5. Many newspaper items in 1980–1981 have extolled this view of spouse

assault; see also S. K. Steinmetz, 'The Battered Husband Syndrome' (1977–1978) 2 *Victimology* 499; E. Pleck, J. H. Pleck, M. Grossman and P. B. Bart, 'The Battered Data Syndrome: A Comment on Steinmetz' Article' (1977–1978) 2 *Victimology* 680; S. K. Steinmetz, 'Reply to Pleck, Pleck, Grossman and Bart' (1977–1978) 2 *Victimology* 683.

6. The writer does not endorse the 'welfare approach'. Obviously it is wrong that some men have to live by way of the soup kitchen and doss house. However the issue is that, relative to all men, women are inadequately provided for and have been since Australia was settled — a legacy from British treatment of women, and later, the treatment of women in every country from which immigrants have come to this country.

7. See generally Anne Edwards Hiller and Linda Hancock, 'The Processing of Juveniles in Victoria' in *Women and Crime*, S. K. Mukherjee and Jocelynne A. Scutt, editors, 1981, George Allen and Unwin, Sydney, 92.

8. In 1980, 33 women's refuges in New South Wales helped about 11 000 women and children, turning away over 3000 more for lack of space. N.S.W. Task Force on Domestic Violence, *Report*, 1981, Sydney. The Blacktown Women's Refuge sent the following telegram to the relevant minister: 'Crisis situation. At present our Refuge at full capacity with 26 women and children. Turn away figures for past six weeks 65 women and 102 children. Most women's refuges overflowing. Where do these people go? Please help them. Please contact us.'

9. Naomi Women's Shelter, *Naomi Report 1976–1977*, n.d., Adelaide, 'Introduction', p. 4.

10. Although the party politics of governments appear strongly to affect the question of refuge funding. For example, the Canberra women's refuge launched an appeal to the community for funds in 1982 when the federal Liberal government refused financial support: 'Appeal for funds for women's refuge' in *The Canberra Times*, October 1982, see A.C.T. *W.E.L. Newsletter* No. 97, November 1982, at p. 10. In Victoria, the new Labor government announced that it had 'a policy of supporting and strengthening the Women's Refuge program'. The Yarra Valley Women's Refuge Group was allocated $38 000 in the (Labor) State budget, after 'four years of battling for funds' under the previous (Liberal) government: 'Funds victory for Yarra Valley refuge' in *The Sun, Easterly Supplement*, 21 October 1982.

11. Australian Statement to the World Conference of the United Nations Decade for Women delivered by the leader of the Australian delegation, the Hon. R. J. Ellicott, Minister for Home Affairs on 16 July 1980, published as Appendix 4 to *Copenhagen and Beyond — Perspectives on the World Conference and Non-government Organisations Forum for the United Nations Decade for Women Copenhagen, Denmark, July 1980*, 1981, A.G.P.S., Canberra, 67, at p. 69.

12. *Spender Report*, 1981, unpublished but commented on in detail by a number of writers including Ruth Evatt, *Review of the Children's Services Programme*, June, 1981, Melbourne; Don Edgar and Gay Ochiltree, *Family Changes and Early Childhood Development, Institute of Family Studies Discussion Paper Number 6*, 1982, Melbourne.
13. See Jocelynne A. Scutt, 'Principle versus Practice: Defining "Equality" in Family Property Division on Divorce' (1983) 57 *Australian Law Journal* (March issue); Jocelynne A. Scutt, 'Land Rights for Women: Taking the Offensive Against the Patriarchy in the Fight for Equal Marital Property Rights' 1982, unpublished paper; Di Graham and Jocelynne A. Scutt, 'A Room of Their Own' (1982) 7 (No. 1) *Womanspeak* (May/June), at p. 8.
14. The Sydney Women's Electoral Lobby Family Law Action Group began the debate in Australia on the question of community of property or as it describes its own proposals for discussion, equal marital property rights. Di Graham of W.E.L. is the convenor of the group and major or joint author of the various submissions, discussion papers and other publications dealing with the question.
15. See various reports of the N.S.W. Anti-Discrimination Board; Kaye Hargreaves, *Women at Work*, 1982, Penguin, Ringwood.

Chapter 12   Ending Crime in the Family

1. See report, '"Emphasis on rehabilitating family" — Appeal over incest sentence dismissed', *Sydney Morning Herald*, 11.11.1982.
2. Donna Moore, editor, *Battered Women*, 1979, Sage Publications, Beverley Hills, California, at pp. 15, 16, 18.
3. Ibid., p. 19.
4. See Phil Raskall, 'Who's Got What in Australia: Distribution of Wealth' (1978) 2 *Journal of Political Economy* 3. I am grateful to Geoff Stafford of the Australian Bureau of Statistics, Canberra, for drawing this article to my attention. See also Frank Stillwell, 'Sharing the Economic Cake: Inequality in Income and Wealth in Australia' in *Who Gets What? The Distribution of Wealth and Power in Australia*, Theo van Dugteren, editor, 1976, Hodder and Stoughton, Sydney, 82; R.F. Henderson, 'Poverty in Britain and Australia: Reflections on *Poverty in the United Kingdom* by Peter Townsend' (1980) 52 (No. 2) *Australian Quarterly* 221; P. Saunders, 'What's Wrong with the Poverty Line?' (1980) 52 (No. 4) *Australian Quarterly* 388 and sources cited therein.
5. Work done at the Social Welfare Research Unit, University of New South Wales, confirms this. See for example Carole Keen and Bettina Cass, *Fiscal Welfare: Some Aspects of Australian Tax Policy — Class and Gender*

Considerations, 1982, U.N.S.W., Sydney; see also *The Politics of Taxation*, John Wilkes, editor, 1980, Hodder and Stoughton, Sydney, particularly Russell Mathews, 'The Structure of Taxation' in that volume, 82. On the issue of women as the poverty growth area, see U.S. National Advisory Council on Economic Opportunity, *Report*, 1982, Washington: 'All other things being equal, if the proportion of the poor in female household families were to continue to increase at the same rate as it did from 1967 to 1978, the poverty population would be composed solely of women and their children before the year 2000.' (Cited Irmtraut Lehrer, *Socialist International Women's Bulletin*, 1982.)

6. Christabel Pankhurst, 'The Government and White Slavery' pamphlet reprinted from *The Suffragette*, April 18, April 25, 1913, at p. 11; quoted Andrea Dworkin, *Pornography — Men Possessing Women*, 1981, The Women's Press, England, at p. 10.

Chapter 13 The Politics of Violence

1. Public Policy Research Centre, Social Research for Government and Business, *Domestic Violence Attitude Survey*, 1988, Office of the Status of Women, Department of Prime Minister and Cabinet, at p. 2.

2. For a discussion of this law and similar laws in other states and territories, see Susan E. Hatty, 'Policing and Male Violence in Australia' in *Women, Policing and Male Violence*, Jalna Hanmer, Jill Radford and Elizabeth A. Stanko, editors, 1989, Routledge, London, 70; Jocelynne A. Scutt, 'Going Backwards: Law "Reform" and Woman Bashing' (1986) 9 (1) *Women's Studies International Forum* 49; Jocelynne A. Scutt, 'Criminal Assault at Home: Policy Directions and Implications for the Future' in *Issues Facing Australian Families*, Wendy Weeks, John Wilson and Robyn Batten, editors, 1990 Longman Cheshire, Melbourne; and the following articles in *Papers from National Conference on Domestic Violence*, Suzanne E. Hatty, 1985, Australian Institute of Criminology, Canberra, A.C.T. — Noel Comley, 'The Police Role in Domestic Violence: Some Implications for Training', 533; Philip Cornish, 'The South Australian Police Department's Restraint Order System: "Three Years Later"', 92; Myf Christie, 'Family Violence — Perpetuation and Aftermath in the Family Court: A Lawyer's Perspective', 605; Suzanne Hatty and Jeanna Sutton, 'Policing Violence Against Women', 403; Vicki Jacobs, 'Domestic Violence: The South Australian Police Perspective', 503; Helen Long, 'Australian Domestic Violence Legislation: Proposals for Change', 465; Jude McCulloch, Police Response to Domestic Violence, Victoria', 523; Kay Moore, 'Family Violence — Perpetuation and Aftermath in the Family Court: An Introduction', 581; Nicholas Seddon, 'Legal Responses to Domestic Violence — What is Appropriate?', 387; Julie Stubbs, 'Domestic Violence

Reforms in New South Wales: Policy and Practice; Peter Waters, 'The Family
Court and Domestic Violence: More of the Rack and Less of the Rubric',
547. See also Women's Policy Co-ordination Unit, *Criminal Assault in the
Home: Social and Legal Responses to Domestic Violence*, 1985, Department
of Premier and Cabinet, Melbourne; Women's Unit, *Report of the Domestic
Violence Committee*, 1981, Premier's Department, Adelaide; South Australian
Committee on Domestic Violence, *Operations of Restraining Orders: Annual
Report, Police Statistics*, 1983, Premier's Department, Adelaide; Robyn
Lansdowne, 'Domestic Violence Legislation in New South Wales' (1985) 8
U.N.S.W. Law Journal 80; Tor Roxburgh, *Taking Control – Help for Women
and Children Escaping Domestic Violence*, 1989, Greenhouse, Sydney;
Queensland Domestic Violence Task Force *Beyond These Walls*, 1988,
Department of Family Services and Welfare Housing, Brisbane. Committees
in the various states publish reports on the operation of the laws and police
and court action as they review it. For a review of the position generally,
but with particular reference to developments in the United States, see
Rosemarie Tong, *Women, Sex and the Law*, 1984, Rowman and Allanheld,
N.J., chapter 5, 'Woman-Battering', p. 124ff.

3. See Julie Stubbs, note 2.

4. N.S.W. Department of the Premier, *Report of the New South Wales' Domestic
Violence Committee, April 1983 to June 1985*, 1985, Government Printer,
Sydney, at pp. 6, 7-12, 20-21, 25.

5. Information for Victoria obtained from *Seminar on Family Violence*, 4 April
1990, sponsored by Wangaratta Working Party on Family Violence in association with the Community Education Task Force, Victorian Government.
For the Northern Territory, see Gail Warman, *When a Man's Home is not
his Castle – New Laws on Domestic Violence*, unpublished paper, 9 November
1989.

6. See Philip Cornish, note 2 and Vicki Jacobs, note 2.

7. N.S.W. Bureau of Crime Statistics and Research, *Domestic Violence – Cases
Before Chamber Magistrates*, 1974, Department of the Attorney General and
of Justice, N.S.W., Sydney, also published in *Family Violence in Australia*,
Carol O'Donnell and Jan Craney, editors, 1982, Longman Cheshire, Melbourne, 28. See also N.S.W. Department of the Premier, note 4, at pp. 30-31.

8. Premier of New South Wales, N.S.W. *Legislative Assembly Parliamentary
Debates*, 9 November 1982.

9. See N.S.W. Department of the Premier, note 4, at p. 6.

10. Cited Philip Cornish, note 2, at p. 481.

11. The author is unaware of any civil action for damages having been taken
in Australia, at least in recent years, against a husband, by a wife, for trespass
to the person, despite numerous husbands who inflict violence upon wives
being executives, doctors, lawyers, accountants and other professionals with

not insubstantial incomes, or men in other trade or occupational categories with incomes and property of relatively substantial value. Discussions on the mode and the possibilities of this approach with (the late) Justice Lionel Murphy, and lawyer Patmalar Ambikapathy are appreciated. As for action under *Crimes Compensation Acts*, see Jocelynne A. Scutt, *Women and the Law — Cases, Materials and Commentary*, 1990, Law Book Company, Sydney.

12. In Victoria Melba Marginson, Malou Logan and others, and in Adelaide Eli Wilde and others have lobbied strongly on the problems surrounding women from the Philippines brought to Australia by unscrupulous Australian men. A proportionately large number of these women have been unlawfully killed by an Australian husband, de facto, or boy"friend". See 'Filipino Women Lured by Ruse', the *Age*, 6 April 1990, p. 18.

13. For example, in Victoria, Di Margetts and Marge Orpin, both with extensive experience in the Women's Movement and women's refuges, etc.

14. Australian Law Reform Commission, *Report No. 26 (Interim) Evidence*, 1985, Vol. 1, A.G.P.S., Canberra, A.C.T.. at p. 130. The immediately following quotation is from the same source, at p. 150. See also L. Hewitt, *Child Sexual Assault Discussion Paper*, 1986, Government Printer, Melbourne; M. Brennan and R. Brennan, *Strange Language — Child Victims under Cross Examination*, 1988, unpublished paper, Riverina Murray Institute of Higher Education, Wagga Wagga; Patmalar Ambikapathy, 'The Use of the Watching Brief as a Legal Tool for the Protection of Child Victims in the Criminal Justice Process' in *Proceedings on Children as Witnesses*, 1988, Australian Institute of Criminology, Canberra, A.C.T.; Ian Heath, *Incest — A Crime Against Children*, 1985, Government Printer, Melbourne.

15. Cited Polly Pattullo, *Judging Women*, 1983, N.C.C.L., London, at p. 18.

16. M.R. Brown, *Legal Psychology*, 1926, Bobbs-Merrill Co., Indianapolis, at p. 140. For a history of this approach see Gail S. Goodman, 'Children's Testimony in Historical Perspective' (1984) 40 (2) *Journal of Social Issues* 9; also Jocelynne A. Scutt, 'The Role of the Jury in Rape Trials' in *Rape Law Reform*, 1980, Australian Institute of Criminology, A.C.T.

17. Department of Attorney General, *An Inquiry into Sexual Offences Involving Children and Related Matters* ('The Sturgess Report'), at p. 106; see also Gail S. Goodman, note 16; Gail S. Goodman, Johnathan M. Golding, and Marshall M. Haith, 'Jurors' Reactions to Child Witnesses' (1984) 40 (2) *Journal of Social Issues* 139; Gail S. Goodman, Jonathan M. Golding, Vicki S. Helgeson, Marshall M. Haith and Joseph Michelli, 'When a Child Takes the Stand: Jurors' Perceptions of Children's Eyewitness Testimony' (in press) *Law and Human Behaviour*; Gail S. Goodman and Rebecca S. Reed, 'Age Differences in Eyewitness Testimony' (in press) *Law and Human Behaviour*; Kate Warner, *Child Witnesses in Sexual Assault Discussion Paper 1*, 1987, Law Reform Commission, Hobart.

18. *M. v. M.* (1988) 63 A.L.J.R. 108; *B. v. B.* (1988) 63 A.L.J.R. 112. See also Lynette Schiften quoted in 'County Court Judge Queries Family Court Judges' Views on Child Abuse' (1986) 21 (7) *Australian Law News* 10; Beatrix Campbell, *Unofficial Secrets — Child Sexual Abuse: The Cleveland Case*, 1988, Virago Press, London; Jocelynne A. Scutt, 'Confronting Precedent and Prejudice — Child Sexual Abuse in the Courts' in *Understanding and Managing Child Sexual Abuse*, Kim Oates, editor, 1990, Harcourt Brace Jovanovich, Sydney-New York, 312; Jocelynne A. Scutt, 'Law Reform and Child Sexual Abuse in Australia' in *Incest*, Penelope Heatherington, editor (in press).

19. The High Court also discussed the standard of proof to be applied, referring to Justice Dixon's statements in *Briginshaw v. Briginshaw* (1938) 60 C.L.R. 336, 362. For a critical analysis of the standard of proof and the High Court's reliance on *Briginshaw's case*, see Jocelynne A. Scutt, note 18.

20. *People v. Rincon-Pineda* 530 P. 2d 247 (1975), 14 Cal. 3d 864; see also Jocelynne A. Scutt, note 16.

21. For a more extensive review of this case, see Jocelynne A. Scutt, 'Judgments of Right Thinking Men: Marriage, Rape and Law Reform' (1986) 21 *Scarlet Woman* 23 (Autumn).

22. Judith A. Allen, *Sex and Secrets*, 1990, Oxford University Press, Melbourne, at p. 52.

23. It is notable that in marital murder cases where women are unjustly treated by the legal system (whether as accused or as victims), appeals are a consequence of action taken on the part of women and women's groups outraged at the outcome; if women were not to agitate, it is more likely than not that no appeal would be taken. On this, see also the cases referred to at chapter 7, 'Marital Murder', herein; see also Wendy Bacon and Robyn Lansdowne, 'Women Who Kill Husbands: The Battered Wife on Trial' in *Family Violence in Australia*, note 7; Wendy Bacon and Robyn Lansdowne, 'Women Homicide Offenders and Police Interrogation' in *The Criminal Injustice System*, John Basten, Chris Ronalds, Mark Robinson and George Zdenkowski, editors, 1982, Australian Legal Workers Group/Legal Service Bulletin, 4; Judith A. Allen, note 22.

24. A number of these cases were the subject of testimony at the Melbourne *Commemoration for Women and Children Who Lost Their Lives*, in 1989; for similarities in other countries, particularly the United States, see Ann Jones, *Women Who Kill*, 1981, Fawcett Columbine Books, New York, and the United Kingdom, see Susan S.M. Edwards, *Women on Trial*, 1984, Manchester University Press, London; Susan S.M. Edwards, 'Neither Bad Nor Mad: The Female Violent Offender Reassessed' (1986) 9 (1) *Women's Studies International Forum* 79.

25. Law Reform Commission, Victoria, *Discussion Paper No. 13 Homicide*, 1988, L.R.C.V., Melbourne, at p. 55.

26. *Zecevic v. Director of Public Prosecutions* (1987) 162 C.L.R. 645, 662. Justice Gaudron extends the criterion of 'death or grievous bodily harm' to include 'a threat of sexual violation, in circumstances in which reasonable apprehension stops short of death or serious bodily harm, capable of sustaining a reasonable belief in the necessity to inflict grievous bodily harm' on the attacker: at 683.

27. Bacon and Lansdowne, note 23.

28. *Zecevic v. Director of Public Prosecutions* (1987) 162 C.L.R. 645, 663. The immediately following quotation comes from the same source.

29. See Ann Jones, note 24.

30. Jocelynne A. Scutt, 'Spouse Assault – The Police Response' in *Family Violence in Australia*, note 7.

31. *Jayatilake v. Commissioner for Taxation* (unreported, 1990, Administrative Appeals Tribunal); on appeal to the Federal Court of Australia.

32. Robyn Holden, Royal Australian Nursing Federation, St Kilda Road, Melbourne, Victoria; see also Cross Talk, 'The Hostage Ward' (July 1985) *Psychology Today* 9; James Turner, *Violence in the Medical Care Setting: A Survival Guide*, 1984, Aspen Systems Corp., Co.

33. See Helen McGregor, 'Conceptualising Male Violence Against Female Partners' (June 1990) *A.N.Z. Journal of Family Therapy* (in press); Jocelynne A. Scutt, 'The Privatisation of Justice: Power Differentials, Inequality and the Palliative of Counselling and Mediation' (1988) 11 (5) *Women's Studies International Forum* 503.

34. See Jocelynne A. Scutt, *Growing Up Feminist – The New Generation of Australian Women*, 1985, Angus and Robertson, Sydney; Jocelynne A. Scutt *Women and the Law – Cases, Materials and Commentary*, 1990, Law Book Company, Sydney.

35. Elizabeth Janeway, *Powers of the Weak*, 1981, Morrow Quill Paperbacks, New York.

INDEX

Names of authorities cited and people named in law cases appear in SMALL CAPITALS throughout the index; reported cases appear in italics.

Jordan, Kitty, 125, 230
judiciary, 132, 184, 242, 256-9, 317
 and access, 303-5
 and custody, 15, 16, 22, 27-8, 32
 and discretion, 289-90
 and incest, 79, 303-5
 and murder, 175, 181, 184,
  189-90, 307-14 *passim*
 and property settlements, 29
 and rape, 148, 292-307 *passim*
 and training, 259, 315, 317
 women judges, 317
 see also courts, lawyers

Kennedy, Kate, 145
Kennedy, Marilyn, 82, 87, 89, 237-8
Kennedy, Sam, 101-2
King Rosemary, 125, 199, 217-18
KLECKNER, JAMES, 126-7
knives *see* weapons
KRAFT-EBBING, RICHARD VON, 122

Lane Linda, 151, 161
Langridge, Pam. 166
law reform, 196-7, 280-1, 286-7,
 288-98 *passim*, 299-303 *passim*,
 305, 306-7, 321
see also divorce laws
lawyers, 196, 221, 226, 231, 243,
 246-8, 249, 256-9
 and training, 259, 315
 see also courts; Crown
  Prosecutor's Office;
  judiciary; magistrates
leaving marriage, 92, 128-30, 170,
 181, 201, 203-4, 223, 225, 238,
 246-7, 249, 252, 253, 257
 abuse following, 102, 114-5, 127,
  130, 132, 157-8, 160, 180-1,
  238, 306, 309-10
 and finances, 57, 83, 92, 109,
  127, 128, 131-2, 133-4, 161,

163-4, 170, 204, 223
 and children, 115, 127, 131-33,
  161-2, 168
 and incest, 82, 83, 92, 253-4
 men, 267
 and police, 225, 235, 238, 246
 and rape, 156-8, 168, 306
 reasons for not, 127-8, 131-5, 139,
  160-2, 166, 173, 182, 185,
  203-4, 223, 235, 249, 257-8
 and returning, 182, 201, 220
 and spouse assault, 102, 108, 306
legal aid, 131, 132, 273
Lemmert, Sondra, 119, 255
LEVY, ANNE, 146
Loftus, Evelyn, 99, 200, 207, 218,
 221
Lomond, Sandy, 91
Longman, Ron, 105, 122
Longmore, Ellen, 68-9, 76-7, 265
Louisa Refuge, Queanbeyan, 272-5
LOVEJOY, FRANCES, 103
Ludgate, Julie, 82-3, 210

M. v. M., 303-5
MCCABE, SARAH, 61
MCCULLOCH, JUDE, 316
McDonald, Faith, 101, 117, 129, 177
McHale, Caroline, 248
McNair, Marion, 116, 164
MACKINNON, CATHARINE, 186
MACNAMARA, DONALD, 155, 156
Machin, Rosa, 202
magistrates, 13, 20, 30, 226, 229,
 245, 249, 252, 291-2, 296, 297,
 317
 and civil standard of proof vs.
  criminal standard, 293-7 *passim*
 training, 259, 315
 women as, 317
 see also courts; judiciary
Maguire, Dorry, 144, 149

unemployment 48, 70, 114-15, 155

valium, 52, 206, 207, 211
Vasseliu, Georgio, 180-1
victim compensation, 296

Wallace, Christine 168
Warne, Renate, 127, 249
Watkins, Doris, 57
weapons, 99, 104, 108, 114, 116, 117,
    132, 144, 157, 175, 181, 182, 185,
    188, 189, 218, 223, 226, 230,
    236, 244, 246, 249, 288, 292,
    296, 307-8, 309, 310, 312, 313
    see also cars as weapons
Weber, Daphne, 146, 149
welfare agencies, 199, 204, 209,
    226, 247, 263
West, Carmen, 218
Western Women's Refuge Group,
    Victoria, 232-3, 236-7
Weston, Shirley, 267
Wheeler, Christine, 219, 243-4
Williamson, Virginia, 243
Wilson, Megan, 145
WILSON, PAUL, 143
women
    Aboriginal, 11
    on courts and tribunals, 317
    and employment, 19-20, 27,
        29, 30-1, 54, 9102, 93, 111
        12, 134, 163-4, 212-3,
        234-5, 274-5, 282-3, 317
    non-anglo-Australian, 296
    and property, 11-13, 17, 19-20,
        28, 272-5, 284
    as property, 18, 26, 96, 141-2,
        144, 148, 159-69, 164, 181,
        249, 256
    socialisation of, 92-3, 131, 154,
        160-1, 185

speak out against violence,
    187, 319-20, 322
speak out against child sexual
    molestation, 298, 302,
    319-20, 322
status as persons, 320, 322
status in marriage, 10-11, 17-18,
    148, 149, 150, 152, 154, 159,
    172, 173
    see also leaving marriage
Women Against Rape, Western
    Australia, 68
Women's Electoral Lobby, 272, 317
Women's Legal Resource Group, 290
women's liberation movement, 2-3, 6,
    7, 25, 263-4, 269-70, 287, 310-11,
    314, 321
    Coalition Against Family
        Violence, 287
    Commemoration for Women
        and Children, 287,
Woodhouse, Shirley, 73-4

*Zecevic v. Director of Public
    Prosecutions*, 312-14